12 POINT METHOD PRODUCT CENTRIC MODEL

OPERATIONALIZATION GUIDE TO DIFFERENTIATE, ACCELERATE AND GROW BUSINESS

PORKKOVAN ELANGOVAN

ISBN
Paperback 979-8-89498-879-5
Hardcase 979-8-89544-808-3

Contents

*Thanks to all
my family members,
friends and colleagues*

Preface

Anand Murthy Raj, SPCT,
Asia's first SAFe Fellow, Gladwell India

As I got introduced to the concepts of agile, I was fascinated to internalize the science behind every aspect of it and I instantly fell in love with Agile. I started reading the book "From Projects to Products" by Mik Kersten, I realized the art of thriving in the digital world. For me this book is an extension to the concepts that helps one to thrive in the digital age with business agility.

This book is for every business leader, technology leader and to every professional who is in the business of developing solutions. It gives us the path to reset our mindset in living agility in solution building. It is a book for those who would like to adopt Agile as their primary development approach and realize that it is not enough to work for customers, one need to work with customers.

Strategies and business plans are all great unless we put them into action. The real action comes only when the rubber hits the road. This realization comes only when you are a part of the action. At times I always wondered how do we tell the organizations across all the departments that "Business agility can be achieved only when all the departments come together towards a common vision". This book for me is the answer to communicate a technique, an approach to get everyone together and achieve the unthinkable.

Many organizations are trying to declare themselves as "Business Agile" without even thinking about the agility in their portfolio. While it was not a good idea a couple of decades back, to make this statement, in today's world of AI, it is suicidal. Value flow across the whole enterprise is vital today. The more we accumulate the value the more we are killing its vitality. This book gives a path of how to establish "Flow" across the entire enterprise.

As I started reading the book, a story came to my mind. Long ago, many centuries back, there existed a Buddhist monk, a man with wisdom in a small place in India. All the people who lived there would come to him, share their problems and seek advice from him. A young man wanted to get the quickest and the simplest answer to his question "How can I be successful in life?". He approached the monk in a marketplace and questioned him expecting a quick answer. However, the monk realized that he was getting late to reach the monastery as it was getting dark. Hence, he asked the young man to accompany him to the monastery and both started to enjoy each other's conversation during their long walk to the monk's monastery. As they reached the monastery, the monk asked the young man to stay back that night and told him that he would teach him the technique to become successful the next morning. The next morning after they had their breakfast, the monk took the young man to a cave. The young man was very excited as it was the first time he was going into a cave and was a bit worried as it was a place he had never visited before. The monk took him inside and closed the entrance of the cave with a huge rock. The cave was completely dark, and the young man was very afraid. He shouted for help for hours and finally fell on the floor hungry, thirsty and tired. He cried for help and he even cursed himself for approaching the monk. As the day passed by, around 3 p.m. he suddenly could see a thin ray of light coming from a small hole up in the corner of the cave. He was delighted and cried for help, yet there was no response. He collected everything and anything he could find in the cave and started to make the hole bigger. As he tried again and again, the hole became bigger. He was delighted and encouraged. He struggled for a couple of hours and finally made a hole to push his body out of the cave. As he came out of the cave, he saw the monk sitting at the edge of the rock. The monk gave his hand and pulled the young man out completely.

The young man was furious and asked the monk the reason he had put him in such a peril. To this the monk asked the young man if he had realized or even experienced the answer to his question. The young man said that it was dark inside the cave, filled with a lot of waste and bones of dead animals. The monk said the path for success is the experience of how the young man in an unfamiliar place, when put into darkness was able to see a ray of light and created a path to come out successful.

For me this is the book that can help every business leader the path to become successful as we are all doomed to be out in darkness as disruption looms innovation every day.

James Carse in 1975 had written a book "The Finite and the Infinite games". Simon Sinek says that the leaders are not sure which game they are playing. Finite games are characterized by a game that has fixed duration, fixed players, and fixed rules. At the end of the game, there is a clear winner or a loser. Once the game is over, the platers go back and get ready for the next game. In an infinite game, there is no fixed duration, no fixed players and no fixed rules. The rules change constantly. There is a no winner or loser in the infinite game. We play not to win but to perpetuate the game. The business is an infinite game. There is no best company, best employer or even the best product. We need to change everything in an infinite game.

When you play the infinite game with a finite mindset, something bad happens and this results in lack of trust. The infinite game is not a sum of series of finite games either. Agile is not a series of small waterfall sprints. This book gives you an approach and thought to build products as an infinite game.

Remember "After a war, what is important is not what is right, it is what is left."

Porkkovan Elangovan has written a compelling guide to address some of these pressing issues that need a completely different mindset. May every reader who reads the book become more knowledgable and become successful professionals.

Building the Future: Digital Transformation and the Product-Centric Model

1.0 Introduction

1.1 Digital Transformation

The world has just emerged from the most disruptive event in recent history—the COVID-19 pandemic. Overnight, our lives were upended. Workplaces turned into ghost towns, bustling offices transformed into home setups, and in-person meetings became virtual interactions. Businesses faced an unprecedented challenge: adapt or perish.

For many companies, this was a wake-up call. The old ways of doing business were no longer sufficient. The pandemic forced companies to embrace new strategies, and at the heart of this shift was a concept that had long dominated the discourse: digital transformation. What once seemed like a distant goal suddenly became a pressing necessity. Companies had to pivot rapidly, finding new ways to connect with customers and manage business operations. The shift to online channels and remote work was the new norm. According to a McKinsey Global Survey, businesses accelerated the digitization of their customer and supply-chain interactions and internal operations by three to four years. Their portfolio of digital or digitally enabled products saw a jaw-dropping increase equivalent to seven years' growth.

Imagine this scene: A retail giant, its physical doors shuttered, makes a lightning-fast leap into the world of e-commerce. Across the globe, a manufacturing powerhouse, reeling from supply chain snarls, embraces cutting-edge digital tracking to steer its inventory and logistics. These aren't isolated stories—they represent a worldwide shift. Companies that once dabbled in digital initiatives now found them at the core of their business operations.

1.2 Traditional Approach for Digital Transformation

When it comes to digital transformation, companies are diving in but often flounder on the "how" part—how to effectively transform and remain competitive. Let's chat about the lay of the land in agile adoption. Despite the widespread shift from traditional waterfall methods to agile, the transition isn't always smooth or entirely agile. Organizations typically fall into one of three categories:

First, let us consider the example of an insurance giant eager to standardize its underwriting platform. They've lined up a massive plan: 50 Epics, 400 Features, and a whopping 6,000 user stories. Their strategy? To develop these incrementally, but here's the twist—they plan to go live with the full platform after a year. That's a marathon of patience and planning!

Next, we have the healthcare sector, where a company aims to enhance member experiences and boost revenue. They operate under what you might call 'agilefall.' It's a hybrid where they agilely sketch out epics and features, and sprint through user stories and unit tests. But then, they switch gears to a waterfall approach, integrating and releasing features either monthly or bimonthly. It's like meticulously laying bricks for a house but only painting it seasonally.

Lastly, enter a fintech player, a stark contrast to the first two. This dynamo optimizes business operations and boosts customer satisfaction by deploying user stories or microservices not just weekly, but sometimes several times a week! They're the sprinters in this transformation race.

Interestingly, companies like this fintech firm are rare birds, making up a tiny slice of the pie. A common thread among these varied approaches is a project-based agile mindset. This approach prioritizes flexibility and speed—think rapid project delivery. Yet, it often overlooks critical elements like true business value, customer focus, tangible outcomes, and employee engagement.

Organizations encounter numerous challenges with project workflows. The table below highlights some of the critical issues and their impacts: (next page)

what these industries are missing to ensure is whatever they deliver faster" is it really delivering right value to customer", "right business outcomes", is it enabling to "achieve organization business strategy", are these digital transformation initiatives enabling to "achieve competitive advantage" that they are looking for?.. all these questions are unanswered.

Organizations committed to the agile ethos must guarantee that their nimble processes significantly impact customer experiences and business viewpoints. Embracing a "product-centric model" in their ways of working propels them towards achieving these pivotal goals.

As the pandemic necessitated this rapid digital transformation, the shift from a project-based to a product-centric model became not just relevant but

Project Ways of working Challenges

Sr. No	Challenges	Impacts
1	Projects and programs are not aligned to Business objectives	Projects are not influencing business growth
2	Projects are more siloed, short term in nature and inward facing	Projects delivered are not addressing customer problems/needs
3	Projects based funding with multi cost center approval	Delay in funding approval and budget decisions are aligned to business value
4	Siloed Project identification, estimation and execution by various functions with in organization	Delay in funding approval and budget decisions not aligned to business values
5	It focuses on digital initiative specific to each Technology portfolio, not seeing its influence on business segments across organization	Projects not delivering full benefits and lead to adverse effects due to missing big picture
6	Project based approach does not enable early validation of project scope	Huge budget loss and delay in delivering projects
7	Projects are not aligned to Business operation value stream and business values	Multiple projects are delivered still no positive improvement in business process/operations
8	Project teams organized as siloed teams, dependencies are identified and managed properly	Delay in project completion, under utilization of project team capacity, blame game, impact on team motivation
9	It focuses on delivering full scope of project/very long lead time to deliver digital solutions	Leads to impact on market competitiveness
10	It focuses on measuring scope, schedule and cost/task completion. It does not enable measuring business outcomes	Its not providing true picture of cost spent Vs Business value delivered

imperative. The traditional project approach, with its temporary teams and limited scope, was no longer sufficient to meet the dynamic needs of the digital age. Instead, a new paradigm emerged: the product-centric model.

In product-focused world, teams don't just complete projects—they own products from concept to decommission. Imagine the difference in quality and employee engagement when teams own products instead of being treated like resources to be shuffled around. According to the Wall Street Journal in 2023, this approach transforms how teams operate, driving higher engagement and better outcomes.

Moving to a product-centric approach is essential for business success in the digital economy. This shift is supported by significant trends across major industries. A Gartner survey also reveals a striking trend: 85% of organizations are either planning to switch to or have already begun adopting a product-centric approach to application delivery. This model is particularly prevalent in organizations in the technology sector, where the need for rapid delivery and customer-centric development is high.

1.3 About This Book: A Guide to Operationalizing a Product-Centric Model

The journey toward digital transformation is proving to be a steeper climb than many organizations anticipated. Back in 2018, a Planview survey revealed a wave of optimism among executives, with 85% reporting they had either adopted or planned to embrace a product-centric model to navigate their digital overhaul. Fast forward to 2023, and the landscape looks markedly different. According to the latest findings by Planview, a mere 8% of organizations have successfully turned their project-focused operations into thriving product-centric systems. This stark reality leaves a whopping 92% struggling without the right foundation, their efforts to transform fizzling out before reaching the finish line.

This glaring gap between ambition and achievement underscores a critical demand for a roadmap that can bridge it. That's where this book comes into play. It's crafted to be your guide through the murky waters of digital transformation. Drawing on the robust principles and practices of SAFe and other leading industry practices, it introduces the "12 Point Method" framework—a blueprint designed to shepherd organizations from traditional project management to a dynamic, product-centric model.

This book unfolds in a narrative style, where an Enterprise Transformation Coach shares his firsthand account of steering one of the retail giants through a sea change in their business approach. He tells the story of how he convinced the senior leadership that their digital transformation hitches could be smoothed over by adopting a product-centric model. This isn't just a tale of strategy but a deep dive into the operationalization of this model across their retail stores division, spanning from the initial discussions in Chapter 2 right through to Chapter 16.

Imagine sitting down for a series of engaging conversations with a range of key players—from the C-suite heavyweights to the dynamic middle managers and the boots-on-the-ground team members. This book brings these discussions to life, making the complexities of a product-centric transformation approachable and relatable.

As our narrative unravels through the transformation saga, it pulls in compelling real-world examples from a spectrum of industries including Banking, Insurance, Healthcare, Life Sciences, Logistics, and Education. This book will enable both transformation coaching & practitioners (from CXOs to Product team members) community to operationalize product centric model across organization.

1.4 What's Product and Platform

1.4.1 What's Product

According to Scrum, "A product is a vehicle to deliver value. It has a clear boundary, known stakeholders, and well-defined users or customers. A product could be a service, a physical product, or something more abstract."

In the manufacturing industry, there are three main types of products. Here are some examples:

Type 1: Physical Products

These are tangible items that industries sell, like mobiles, cars, and laptops.

Type 2: Digital Products Integrated with Physical Products

These are digital components that enhance the value of physical products. For example, a car might have performance management gadgets or maintenance management systems.

Type 3: Standalone Digital Products

These are digital solutions that companies leverage to draw in, engage, and provide services to their customers. Take car manufacturers, for example. They use lead management systems as part of their internal platforms, which are utilized by employees in their retail showrooms (serving internal customers). Moreover, car manufacturing companies have begun to embrace selling cars exclusively through e-commerce websites, minimizing the need for physical retail showrooms, much like Tesla's approach. This shift means that digital products are now directly used by end-users who interact with the manufacturers for booking their vehicle, making payments, tracking orders, receiving deliveries, and accessing post-sale services, among other things.

"Understanding these product types helps us see how they fit into the bigger picture of delivering value,". "Each type of product plays a crucial role in the overall strategy of a business, whether it's enhancing a physical product, improving customer engagement, or streamlining operations."

Let's now dive into some examples of how products are defined in service industries.

Type 1: Core Services as Products

Imagine a renowned bank. For them, their core services are the products they offer to their customers. These include things like retail banking customer savings accounts, credit cards, fixed deposit, Mortgage loans and personal loans. Similarly, in an insurance company, the primary services offered include various insurance policies such as life, auto, home, and travel insurance. Other service industries, including healthcare, communications, media, retail, logistics, and travel & hospitality, also define their services as products. This approach of "productizing services" emphasizes customer centricity, outcomes, value, features, and benefits they offer, similar to tangible/physical products.

Type 2: Digital Products to Deliver Services

To deliver these core services effectively, these industries use a range of digital solutions. Picture the loan business line of the bank. They use digital products like digital marketing and campaign management tools to attract new customers, customer onboarding platforms to ensure a smooth start for new clients, document management systems to handle all the paperwork, customer applications

Product Definition and Hierarchy

Product: "A product is a vehicle to deliver value. It has a clear boundary, known stakeholders, well-defined users or customers. A product could be a service, a physical product, or something more abstract." – Scrum Guide

Number of products levels are decided based on its complexity and size. **Typical product Levels under specific business line:**

- Portfolio/Business Line (L1)
- Product Line (L2)
- Products (L3)
- Capabilities (L4)
- Functionalities (L5)

Illustrative Products Landscape Example based on Logistics Industry

Level 1	Shipping Business Line					
Level 2	Customer Operations Management					
Level 3	Lead Management			Customer Self-Service		
Level 4	Customer/Lead Profiling	Instant Shipper Quote	Smart Lead Management	Customer Account Mgmt	Customer Profile	Order Management
Level 5	Quote History	Carrier Dynamic Pricing	Sale Rep Profiling	User Role Definition & Views	Create Profile	Order creation & Management
	Win-Loss History	Shipper Dynamic Pricing	Lead Sales Rep Assignment	Self-account Creation	Edit, Save Profile	Order Status Updates
	Order History	Generate Instant Quote	Integrate with External source	Contact info Management	Contact & History	Order Modification
	Business Profile	View Instant Quote	Auto lead monitoring & Reassignment	Account upgrade	Personalize Needs	Service & Accessorial Request

management tools to keep track of applications, and repayment management systems to manage the loan repayments.

Very similar to the approach of "productizing services", these digital solutions, systems, and applications must be productized into "digital products" to highlight customer centricity, outcomes, value, features, and benefits they provide. This approach serves both internal users (business users and employees who use these digital products to interact with customers and deliver services) and external customers (who engage with organization through these digital products to access services independently).

Let's glimpse into the world of product hierarchy and explore some standout digital products from the logistics industry: (next page)

The structure of this product hierarchy is a snapshot. It could change with the industry context and the complexity of the product world. The more complex things get, the more layers you'll find in the product pecking order.

1.4.2 What's Platform

A platform is an orchestrating entity that facilitates interaction and communication among various products to deliver value. While it doesn't directly deliver value itself, it enables value delivery through its various products. A platform can be physical, virtual, or a service. It serves both internal users, like the developer community who reuse platform products and capabilities to build their digital products, and external users who interact with the organization to access their products or services. (next page)

1.5 About the Retail Industry

A Story of Need for Product Centric Model

To truly grasp the essence and effectiveness of the product-based model, let's dive into a real-world scenario that brings this concept to life.

Picture the heartbeat of a top e-commerce giant's development floor, alive with energy. Engineers, lost in a world of code, debugging, and teamwork, barely notice the world around them. Then, in a moment that feels like a scene from a movie, the doors burst open. The company's executive walks in, concern etched on his face, capturing everyone's attention.

"Does anyone here own this shopping cart?" he calls out, his voice laced with urgency. "There are critical issues that demand our immediate attention."

Illustrative Platform Landscape from Insurance Industry

Portfolio	**Level 1**			Platforms & Capabilities			
Platform	**Level 2**		Authentication				
Product Group	**Level 3**	KYC Onboarding			Login Management		
Products	**Level 4**	KYC Policy Management	One KYC	KYC Refresh	Enrollment	Web login	Access Management
Functionalities	**Level 5**	Manual KYC	Create Profile	Manual KYC Refresh	Standalone Enrollment	User Name & Password	Customer SSO
		Real-time Corporate KYC	Search Profile	Standard Due Diligence	Fast track	Customer Biometric	Federated SSO
		Corporate KYC Onboarding	Retrieve KYC	Refresh Outreach	Prospect	DIY Help Widget	API Driven Data Access
		KYC Updates	Policy Refresh	KYC monitoring	Admin Console	Passkey	Authentication Reporting

Silence engulfs the room. Engineers share nervous looks, the tension palpable. Then, breaking the silence, one voice emerges, "Well, the shopping cart was developed as part of a project. No one here actually owns it."

As an intriguing aside to our story, consider the curious aspect within this project-focused organization: the mysterious case of the ownerless shopping cart. Crafted and launched by a temporary project team, this digital cart was a fleeting triumph before the team dissolved into the ether. Now, when trouble brews or glitches emerge, they fall into the reluctant lap of the operations team who manages L1, L2 and L3 production support. These brave souls, armed with limited context and no real claim to the cart, navigate the murky waters of maintenance and troubleshooting.

Let's dive back into our story. The tension in the room escalates as the executive's frustration becomes palpable. "So, my request will just be added to a backlog, competing with other production incidents and enhancements?" he inquires, the annoyance clear in his voice.

The engineering lead leans in, a nod affirming the gravity of the situation. "Yes, if it's a minor enhancement, it'll be handed over to the production support team, who didn't originally build the product. They'll tackle it, juggling it alongside their other priorities. However, if the change is large and significant, we're talking about crafting a business case from scratch, pulling together a fresh team to dive deep into the existing work, devising a solution, rolling it out, and then disbanding the team once more. This isn't just a huge time sink; it's a massive undertaking, especially if you don't have the original team around."

The executive's voice, dripping with dissatisfaction, cuts through the air. "Aren't we meant to put our customers first? Are we not prioritizing outcomes over merely completing isolated tasks? Are we not achieving results through each business capability and functionality we implement? Do these business capabilities not impact business objectives? Shouldn't we be dedicated to continuously delivering value faster, with the team that created the product taking ownership to nurture and improve it continuously?" he demands, leaving the room with those pointed questions hanging heavily in the silence he leaves behind.

To understand why the situation we just described is so problematic and how it can be improved, let's explore the shift from a project-based model to a product-based model and what it means for modern businesses. Imagine if, instead of scrambling to find ownership and piecing together new teams for every incident or enhancement, there was a dedicated team that owned the shopping cart from Strategy to support. This team wouldn't merely solve problems as they emerge; it would consistently enhance the product to ensure it meets customer needs, continuously delivering value and operating smoothly at all times.

Shifting from projects to products transforms a company's heartbeat. It's no longer about rushing through a project to jump onto the next. Instead, it becomes all about playing the long game: creating products that genuinely connect with customers, solving their issues, achieving business targets, and constantly evolving to offer real value. This change ignites a sense of ownership and purpose across the organization, making every effort more meaningful.

This method completely changes the game for teams. Suddenly, everyone is more engaged in their work, aiming for top-notch results. They contribute to the company's business objectives of growth, customer experience, and operational efficiency while actually enjoying their jobs. When teams take ownership of products, they're not just in it for a project or a small scope of work; they're committed for the long haul, driven by a real desire to see their baby succeed.

Product teams focus on a business capabilities/functionalities scope that must be completed within a specific timeline. They are multi-skilled, seasoned, long-living, well-oiled feature machines that frequently deploy small units of functionality into production. If you involve them in enhancing the shopping cart, they will prioritize functionalities based on value versus implementation compared to other backlog items. They will then break down the work into valuable segments and start moving it into production as swiftly as possible. This approach reduces the time to realize value. – HBR, 2021

1.6 Empowering a Product-Centric Model: My Journey as an Enterprise Transformation Coach

Reading that HBR article sent me on a trip down memory lane, making me think about my own journey. Here, I am compelled to tell my own story about the power of product-focused teams in driving successful digital transformations, especially from my perspective as an Enterprise Transformation Coach.

I was hired as an enterprise transformation coach for Thiran, a leading retail company in North America that is located in airports worldwide. Thiran had shown consistent growth over the years and held an impressive 35% market share. But the winds of change were blowing. Competitors, hungry and cunning, began nibbling away at its territory, blending online and physical stores in a daring stroke of innovation. Meanwhile, nimble start-ups darted in, disrupting the scene with their slick online ordering and in-store pickup models, attracting customers with the promise of a superior experience at a fraction of the cost.

Thiran found itself at a crossroads. To maintain its position and continue growing, it needed to rethink its strategy. This is where my journey with Thiran began a couple of years ago. As I stepped into Thiran's bustling offices, I could sense the urgency. They needed a fresh perspective and a new way of working. The leadership team was eager but uncertain about how to handle this shift. My job was to show them the way, helping them understand the power of product-focused teams and how this approach could revolutionize their business operations.

A leading business consulting firm took Thiran under its wing, crafting a digital strategy and transformation plan that was nothing short of revolutionary. They shifted Thiran's focus from project-based to product-based, a move that's setting trends across industries. This approach meant rethinking everything from how they strategize and map out their digital products to how they envision customer experiences and pinpoint the value they deliver. It was about putting their money where their mouth is, investing in the design and swift delivery of products. This way, they could roll out improvements quickly, staying ahead of customer needs and nailing their business targets as shown in figure below.

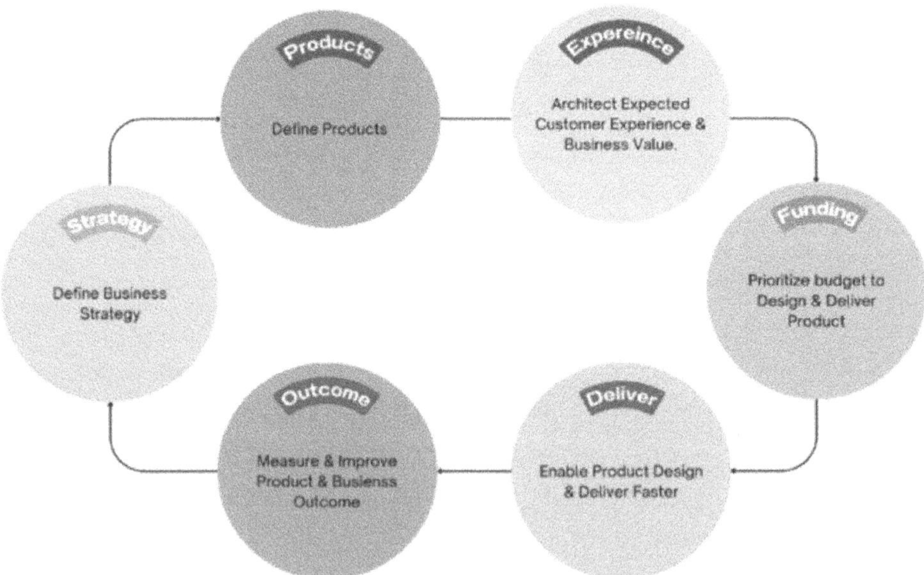

Figure: From Strategy definition to outcome

To implement the core of this product- centric model, we have established the 12 Point Method (see Chapter 3), which we leveraged for the retail industry. This book will guide you through the journey of implementing the 12 Point Method.

Confronting Reality

Despite having a well-defined roadmap, Thiran struggled to adopt the project-to-product transformation. Delays in rolling out digital transformations became the norm, and too often, these efforts fell short of their lofty goals. Guided by internal transformation coaches, freshly minted by a consulting firm, the team struggled. Their book smarts couldn't bridge the practical gaps in navigating this crucial transition. It became glaringly obvious that success would only be within reach if Thiran brought in external experts. These seasoned consultants could meld with the internal crew, bringing the sorely needed know-how and direction to steer this pivotal change.

This realization marked a significant turning point for Thiran. The stakes were high, and the need for a successful transition to a product-centric model was more urgent than ever. As an external consultant, I was there to bridge the gap, offering hands-on experience and a fresh perspective to drive the transformation forward.

1.7 Key Acronyms

Sr.No.	In SAFe	In this Book
1	Agile Release Train (ART)/Team of Teams	Product Group/Product Line
2	Release Train Engineer (RTE)	Product Group/Line Coach
3	Team Coach/Scrum Master	Product Team Coach/Product Coach
4	Portfolio Sync	Monthly Governance
5	Portfolio Strategic Review	Quarterly Business Review (QBR)
6	Epic	Business Capability
7	Feature	Functionality
8	PI Planning	Quarterly Product Release Planning (PRP)
9	LACE	Transformation Team
10	Operational Value Stream	Business Operation Value Stream

2

Redefining Horizons:
From Projects to Products

I was selected as an Enterprise Transformation Coach (ETC) to lead a project-centric transformation initiative for one of the business units: Retail Stores. Joining me in this effort was an internal agile coach, Mr. Agile, who had already been supporting the transformation. It was my ninth day in the organization, and with the help of teams on the ground, I gathered detailed insights into the digital transformation challenges that were heavily influenced by the project-oriented way of execution. However, I was eagerly waiting to hear directly from the top leaders about "what's the problem to solve."

2.1 First meeting with CXOs as an Enterprise Transformation Coach:

Mr. Agile, I, and a few next-level leaders were waiting for the CXO team to arrive. Since it was a CXO-level meeting, we made sure to arrive 20 minutes ahead of the scheduled time. The CXO team was expected to join us after their Quarterly Business Review (QBR) with one of their suppliers.

We had a clear agenda for the meeting:

Agenda 1: Discuss the challenges I had observed during my first week.

Agenda 2: Hear from the CXOs about the specific problems they needed to solve.

Agenda 3: Review the current business performance (business case for product centric model).

Agenda 4: Highlight the product centric model and how it addresses these challenges.

While we waited, the internal coach suggested we use the next 20 minutes to delve into the challenges I had identified. I agreed, seeing it as a perfect dry run for my upcoming presentation to the CXOs. So, I dove into the project-oriented work model I'd noticed during my first week at the organization, ready to peel back the layers of my initial impressions.

2.1.1 My Observation: Project-Based Pitfalls (Agenda 1)

Industries are striving to thrive in the market by consistently serving their customers with a focus on customer centricity. To stay competitive and grow their revenue and profits, they need to create a competitive advantage by:

Defining the right business strategy,

Designing innovative digital solutions, and

Delivering these solutions faster.

However, industries that rely on a project-based delivery model often struggle to achieve these goals. This model, with its temporary teams and fragmented efforts, does not support the sustained competitive advantage that businesses need.

Let's look at an example of how digital solutions are developed in a project-based model. Take Thiran's retail business. They serve their customers through various channels, including retail stores, online platforms, and wholesale operations.

To understand how their retail stores operate, let's break it down. First, they analyze customer spending patterns, market trends, and customer needs. Based on these insights, they identify target customers and attract them through marketing campaigns. They ensure that the right products are procured and available in stores. Customers have the option to order online and pick up their purchases in-store, have the products delivered to the boarding gate, or directly visit the stores, make their selections, pay at the cash counter, and leave with their items.

This is a straightforward overview of how Thiran's retail stores function. Thiran's retail store business line aimed to improve the efficiency of its end-to-end operations and enhance the customer experience for everyone involved. To achieve this, they planned to design, develop, and deliver digital solutions for key areas like Procurement, Vendor Management, Warehouse Management Systems (WMS), and customer engagement. These digital solutions were identified as initiatives and then broken down into programs and projects based on their complexity.

To understand the challenges of the project-based execution approach, let's focus on the digital solutions developed for the WMS space. These solutions were intended to increase efficiency, improve product shelf life, and optimize inventory. Thiran planned to implement these solutions in both the North American (NA) and China regions.

In North America, they already had existing digital solutions that needed modernization. In contrast, for China, they wanted to build entirely new digital solutions with new business capabilities.

Thiran started by launching a project to modernize the Warehouse Management System (WMS) in North America, introducing new business capabilities. This initiative was divided into multiple projects, each focusing on aspects of NA WMS modernization and managed by separate project teams. Once a project was completed, another would be initiated, either with the same team or a new one, depending on the budget approval and priority of the new project. Concurrently, Thiran began rolling out new WMS capabilities in China and other regions, utilizing separate project teams for each region.

However, this method presented significant challenges:

Siloed Scope: Each project was treated as an isolated effort, lacking a holistic view of the WMS business capabilities roadmap. There was no clear understanding of the expected value for each business capability, what customer problems or needs it would address, or how it aligned with the overall strategy.

Team Disbandment: Once a project was completed (which often didn't happen within the planned budget or timeline), the team would be dismantled. Starting a new project in the NA region required setting up a team from scratch, often delayed by budget approval or other business reasons.

Budget Overruns and Project Delays: When the first project in the North American region went over budget and missed its deadline, Thiran had to raise a budget change request and wait for approval. Because project budgets were cost-center-based (from retail stores, online business, wholesale business, etc.), this required approval from multiple leaders, which took additional time. Meanwhile, the project team couldn't just sit idle. They either had to be dismantled or take on a new project. They chose the latter, starting a new project to implement additional business capabilities for the NA region.

Internal Conflicts in Overcoming Challenges: This new project wasn't fully scoped or ready, but they had to proceed with their current understanding of the scope. Predictably, this led to scope creep, increasing both the budget and the timeline. While this project faced delays, the budget change request for the first NA region project was finally approved. However, concerns were raised about the initial project estimates and why the project had not been completed as planned. When concerns were raised, the blame game began. The Architecture team pointed fingers at the Product Owners, citing issues with interdependencies among legacy components that hadn't been properly identified. The Development team blamed the Design team for inadequate or delayed designs. The Testing team, in turn, blamed the Development team for late code deliveries. Amidst all this finger-pointing, the change request was approved, but with a clear directive: no additional budget would be allocated, and the team had to complete the project within the revised budget. The same project team now had to juggle both the first and second projects simultaneously. This led to conflicts in prioritization, constant starting and stopping, and significant time lost switching contexts.

Delays and Operational Issues: After several months of delays, the first North American project was finally completed. However, the business was dissatisfied with the unpredictable nature of project delivery. When the project went live, the Warehouse Management System (WMS) was plagued with production incidents. The delay in resolving these issues was substantial due to poor handover and knowledge transfer between the development and operations teams. Many defects made it into production because of a lack of best practices in development and inadequate regression testing, compounded by the pressures of tight schedules and limited budgets.

The Struggle in Demonstrating Business Value: After wrapping up their first project in North America, the project team hit a major snag: their work didn't clearly show any business value. Despite all their hard work, they couldn't prove that they'd made inventory management better or warehouses more efficient. The lack of concrete results made it tough to argue that the project was a success.

Lessons Lost Between Teams: Meanwhile, a new project team was formed to implement new business capabilities for the China region. This team, however, was entirely new and had little interaction with the North American project team. As a result, they couldn't leverage the experiences or lessons learned from the NA project. This disconnect led to repeated mistakes and inefficiencies, further delaying progress and impacting the overall effectiveness of the transformation.

Figure: How Projects selection were approved

The portrayal showcases the journey of how North American and Chinese projects were pinpointed, estimated, and brought to life through compelling business cases. It delves into the process where multiple vendors were scrutinized by a steering committee, leading to the selection of one standout vendor to whom the project was entrusted.

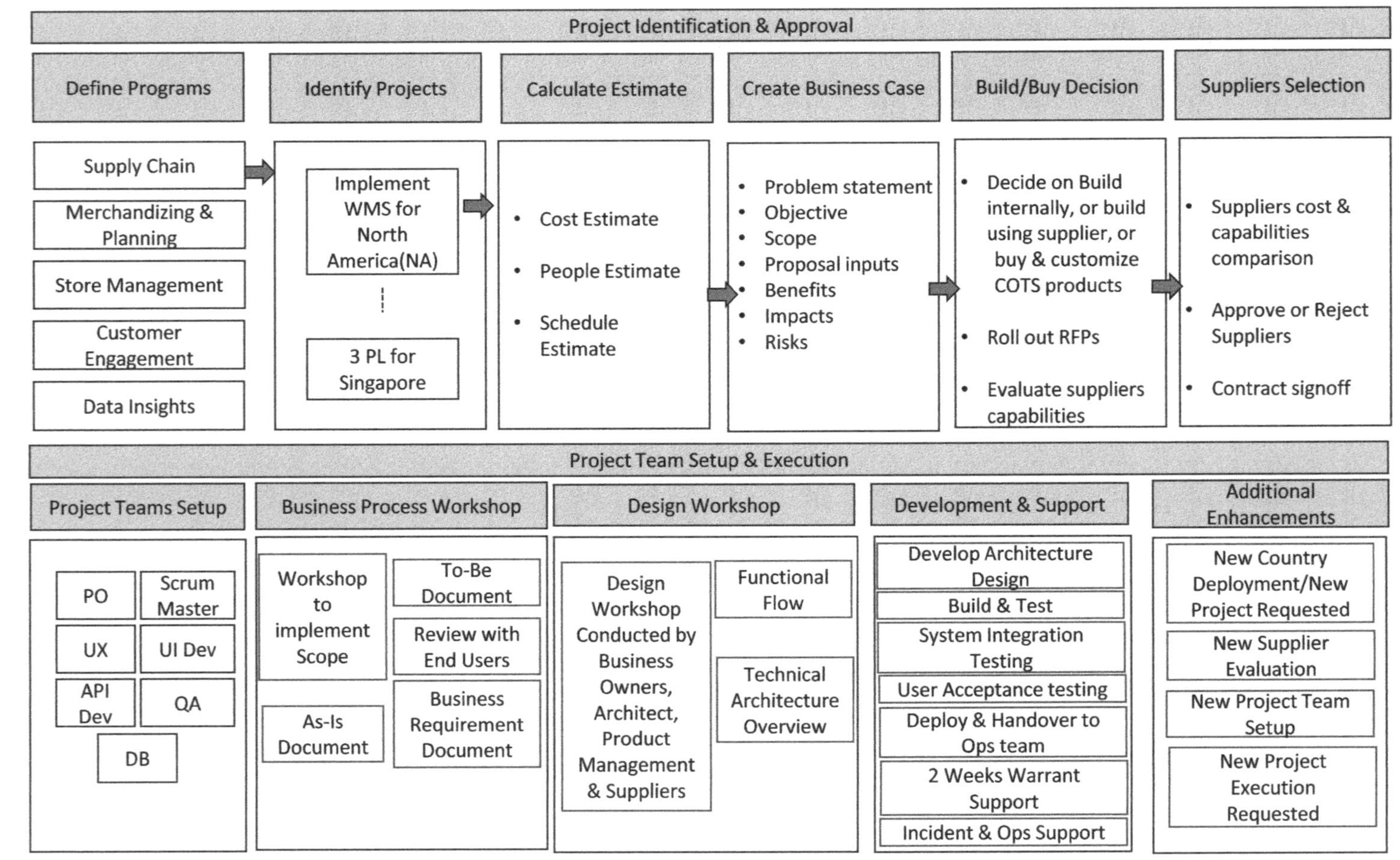

Project Identification & Approval
Define Programs
Identify Projects
Calculate Estimate
Create Business Case
Build/Buy Decision
Suppliers Selection
Supply Chain
Merchandizing & Planning
Store Management
Customer Engagement
Data Insights
Implement WMS for North America(NA)
3 PL for Singapore
Cost Estimate
People Estimate
Schedule Estimate
Problem statement
Objective
Scope
Proposal inputs
Benefits
Impacts
Risks
Decide on Build internally, or build using supplier, or buy & customize COTS products
Roll out RFPs
Evaluate suppliers capabilities
Suppliers cost & capabilities comparison
Approve or Reject Suppliers
Contract signoff
Project Team Setup & Execution
Project Teams Setup
Business Process Workshop
Design Workshop
Development & Support
Additional Enhancements
PO
Scrum Master
UX
UI Dev
API Dev
QA
DB
Workshop to implement Scope
To-Be Document
Review with End Users
As-Is Document
Business Requirement Document
Design Workshop Conducted by Business Owners, Architect, Product Management & Suppliers
Functional Flow
Technical Architecture Overview
Develop Architecture Design
Build & Test
System Integration Testing
User Acceptance testing
Deploy & Handover to Ops team
2 Weeks Warrant Support
Incident & Ops Support
New Country Deployment/New Project Requested
New Supplier Evaluation
New Project Team Setup
New Project Execution Requested

This overview details the process by which vendors establish POD teams, starting with conducting a business process workshop to grasp the business requirements. Following this, a design workshop is held, led by architecture and UX design experts, paving the way for the POD team to then develop, test, and deploy the solution into production. (next page)

After walking them through these detailed observations, I summed it up for the team.

"In summary," I began, "the project-based approach is failing to deliver value from both the business and customer perspectives. It isn't allowing us to deliver efficiently and effectively. We're not achieving zero defects, and the transitions from development to operations are far from smooth. This approach is preventing us from designing innovative digital solutions and delivering them quickly. As a result, the retail store business is struggling to sustain and gain a competitive advantage."

I paused, making sure everyone was with me. "To overcome these challenges, we need to shift to a product-centric model for delivering digital solutions. Here's how it would work and what it involves, which is part of our fourth agenda item today."

I outlined the key components of the product-centric approach:

- *Define the Business Strategy:* Start with a clear business strategy that aligns with our goals and customer needs.

- *Identify the Business Operational Value Stream and Current Product Landscape:* Understand our current operations and how our products fit into that landscape.

- *Identify Changes Needed in the Current Product Landscape:* Determine whether we need to modernize existing products, develop new ones, or a combination of both to achieve our business strategy.

- *Design and Deliver the Landscape Changes:* Implement the necessary changes efficiently and effectively, ensuring they deliver value continuously.

"This approach will help us move from fragmented efforts to cohesive, continuous improvement. It will enable us to be more agile, customer-focused, and capable of delivering innovative solutions faster," I concluded.

By the time I finished walking through all the challenges of project-based execution, Mr. Agile, the internal coach, received a call from the technology leader who was part of the Quarterly Business Review (QBR). From Mr. Agile's reaction, it was clear that we might need to reschedule our meeting.

After a minute, the call ended. Mr. Agile turned to me and said, "The QBR is taking longer than expected. The vendor's performance this quarter had a lot of issues, and they're challenging our ways of working. The discussions are taking more time than scheduled. The CIO has requested that we move our meeting to another day. We'll receive communication from one of their executive assistants soon. The CXOs have asked if you could send the presentation offline so they can review it and save time during our next meeting."

I agreed to send over the content, except for the business case part. Mr. Agile looked concerned and suggested, "Maybe you should include the business case as well."

I shook my head. "The business case is critical. I want to see their reactions and responses in real time."

He nodded, understanding my reasoning. "Fair enough. But since we have an hour, how about you give an overview of the product centric model?"

I considered this and agreed. "Alright, I'll provide an overview of what a product is and how it's defined. That's one part of agenda item 4."

With that, I prepared to dive into the explanation, ready to make the most of the unexpected extra time.

2.1.2 Diving into the Product Centric Model

"Let's break this down into two parts," I began. "Part 1 will cover the definition of products with examples (as discussed in chapter 1), and Part 2 will focus on the business operation value stream and the products aligned with it."

From part 1 perspective, Thiran's retail industry attempted to classify all their existing applications as products, which is not the correct way to define products. They rebranded each project as an epic, thinking this was enough to shift to a product-based model. However, they continued to execute these as traditional projects, which missed the mark entirely.They called it adopting a product model, but in reality, it was merely a rebranding of their current practices.

This misunderstanding highlighted a significant issue. Switching to a true product-based model isn't just about changing the words we use; it demands a whole new way of thinking. It's about defining products according to the best practices in the industry and completely rethinking how we work. The focus should be on continuous value delivery, not just renaming projects as products. This distinction is crucial for achieving real transformation.

Part 2:

Let's quickly dive into how products are defined and utilized in one of the service industries, taking the logistics industry as our example. This industry is crucial in bringing carriers and customers together, making it possible to move goods from one spot to another. In this context, Type 1 products, or core services, include options like full truckload and half truckload, among others. Meanwhile, Type 2 products focus on digital offerings, which we'll explore below.

Here is an Example of the Business Operation Value Stream and Its Digital Products, with Instances from the Logistics Industry (next page)

Products and Business capabilities:

During our discussion, the internal coach posed a challenging question. "What about the internally developed applications and commercial off-the-shelf (COTS) products, like Salesforce CRM? How do they fit into this product-based model?"

I nodded. "That's an excellent question. Most organizations define their internal applications and COTS products as 'products' but deliver them as projects. This is exactly what's happening with the WMS project implementation. As you know, this WMS has a mix of internal applications built in-house and external applications bought from the market. These are viewed from either an internal organizational perspective or an external market perspective. However, they're not defined from the customer's perspective, as per the product examples provided above for the service industry."

I paused to ensure everyone was following. "Products should always be defined based on the customers who will use them. These customers could be internal, like business users or managers, or external, like people who visit retail stores or shop on the e-commerce site. These customers can further be divided into personas."

I looked around the room, seeing the wheels turning in their minds. "So, we need to view and productize both our internal applications and COTS products from the customer's perspective. This shift in perspective is crucial. It's about understanding and delivering what the customer truly needs and values, rather than just completing a project.

Example of B2B Logistics Industry Business Operation Value Stream that manage and deliver freight from location to another location

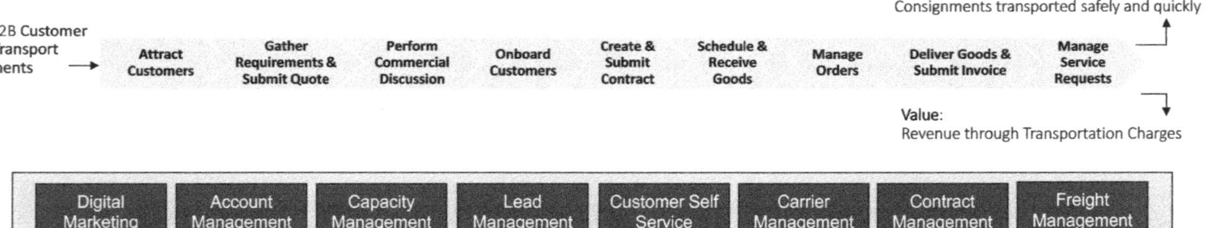

Note: The above example is illustrative only. It does not contain all the digital products to perform end to end business operations. Based on industry contexts these products may vary in type, complexity, number of products etc.

Example of B2B Logistics Industry Products & Business Capabilities

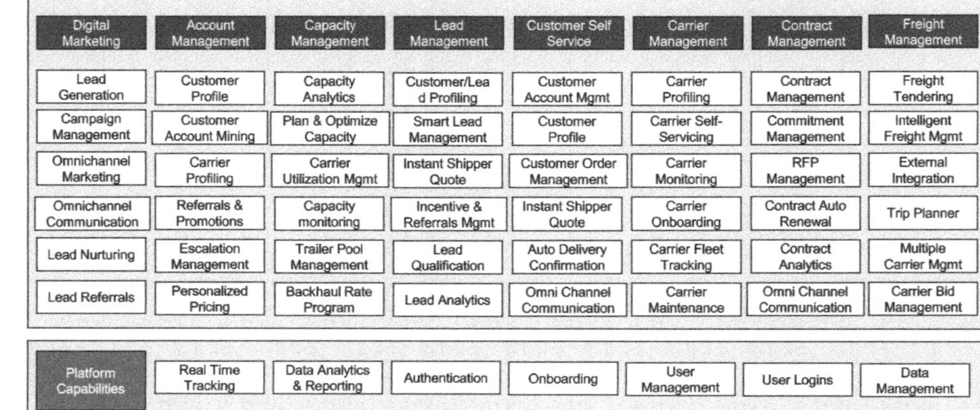

Digital Marketing	Account Management	Capacity Management	Lead Management	Customer Self Service	Carrier Management	Contract Management	Freight Management
Lead Generation	Customer Profile	Capacity Analytics	Customer/Lead Profiling	Customer Account Mgmt	Carrier Profiling	Contract Management	Freight Tendering
Campaign Management	Customer Account Mining	Plan & Optimize Capacity	Smart Lead Management	Customer Profile	Carrier Self-Servicing	Commitment Management	Intelligent Freight Mgmt
Omnichannel Marketing	Carrier Profiling	Carrier Utilization Mgmt	Instant Shipper Quote	Customer Order Management	Carrier Monitoring	RFP Management	External Integration
Omnichannel Communication	Referrals & Promotions	Capacity monitoring	Incentive & Referrals Mgmt	Instant Shipper Quote	Carrier Onboarding	Contract Auto Renewal	Trip Planner
Lead Nurturing	Escalation Management	Trailer Pool Management	Lead Qualification	Auto Delivery Confirmation	Carrier Fleet Tracking	Contract Analytics	Multiple Carrier Mgmt
Lead Referrals	Personalized Pricing	Backhaul Rate Program	Lead Analytics	Omni Channel Communication	Carrier Maintenance	Omni Channel Communication	Carrier Bid Management

Platform Capabilities	Real Time Tracking	Data Analytics & Reporting	Authentication	Onboarding	User Management	User Logins	Data Management

Note: its an illustrative view of digital products and business capabilities. Based on organization size and complexity, number of products and its business capabilities may vary. Platform capabilities are built and managed centrally that can be consumed by all business lines

"That's exactly what we discussed in the earlier examples," I explained. "Those are products from the customer's perspective."

The internal coach, eager to dive deeper, asked, "Can we define the products and capabilities for this WMS?"

"Absolutely," I replied. "In fact, that's one of the agenda items I wanted to cover in our next meeting with the CXOs. If you can arrange for a couple of Business Analysts (BAs) to help, we can create that view before the meeting."

The internal coach was visibly excited about the idea but wasn't sure about the availability of the BAs. He promised to try and get their assistance. Then he asked, "What's the approach to productize both internal and external COTS products?"

We had a detailed discussion on a bottom-up approach for internal applications. "First, we navigate all the functions in the application and document the functionalities at Level 5 (L5). Then, we logically group these functionalities to identify higher-level business capabilities at Level 4 (L4). Next, we group these capabilities to create products at Level 3 (L3). Based on the complexity and number of products, we can further group them into a product line at Level 2 (L2), all product lines are mapped to portfolio/business line Level 1 (L1)."

"For external COTS products, we need to follow a top-down approach," I continued. "We start with Level 1 (L1) and document down to Level 5 (L5). In a while, we will deep dive into product hierarchy as part of one of the steps in the 12 Point Method."

The internal coach agreed to make his best effort to capture these insights for the WMS. I was excited because this kind of view would provide clarity not only to the CXOs but also to the next level of leaders. Understanding products from this perspective is a critical first step towards successful product model transformation.

As we were wrapping up, I stopped for a beat and shared, " I would like to share something that really captures our journey here." Paraphrasing the words of fitness expert Jillian Michaels, I continued, *"It's not about perfect. It's about effort. And when you implement that effort every single day, that's where transformation happens."*

Summary of the Chapter

- *We've explored Thiran's journey as they transition from a project-based approach to a product-centric model within their retail business unit. This shift wasn't without its hurdles. Thiran faced significant challenges: isolated projects, tight budgets, and the complexity of managing multiple initiatives at once.*

- *Recognizing these obstacles, Thiran knew a significant change was necessary. The traditional project-based approach was no longer effective in meeting their strategic goals or delivering real value to their customers.*

- *During our discussions, we dove into the essence of what a product is, provided concrete examples, and explored the concept of the business operation value stream. We also identified the business capabilities needed to execute this value stream effectively.*

- *As the Enterprise Transformation Coach, my mission was to untangle the complexities of Thiran's current strategies. This chapter sets the stage, preparing us for the impactful CXO leadership workshop ahead.*

- *This upcoming workshop is crucial. It's where viewpoints will align, and the spark for transformation will be ignited. Collaboration here will be the driving force behind Thiran's success, unlocking the power of product-centric execution.*

3

Aligning on a Solution to Solve the Problem

Let's pause for a moment before we jump in. There's a sobering reality I want you to consider. The digital age has reshaped our world in unimaginable ways. Just look around. Think about the profound impact and countless benefits the digital revolution brings to organizations.

At its core, the digital era acts as a powerful catalyst. It's far more than just trimming expenses; it fundamentally transforms organizations into nimble, swift, and responsive powerhouses. Today's businesses focus on speed, rushing to get their products out there, and engaging in an endless loop of feedback and fine-tuning. This strategy keeps them perfectly in tune with the shifting desires and needs of their customers.

As you reflect on the transformative power of the digital era, let me take you back to the meeting I mentioned earlier. The air was thick with anticipation as we gathered around the table, ready to tackle the challenges ahead.

I started walking through the four agenda points we'd mapped out in earlier chats. Barely had I begun, when the CIO cut in. "We know the drill with the current challenges which is our first agenda," he said. "We've gone over them on our own, and, honestly, they hit close to home—both for us and our suppliers. Heck, one of our suppliers brought up pretty much the same points at the last Quarterly Business Review, turning it into quite the marathon session."

He stopped for a moment, then went on, "My only question is, by tackling these challenges, can we actually boost our overall business performance?"

"Absolutely, sir," I replied with conviction. "Actually, my third agenda item zeroes in on our business performance over the recent quarters and links it to the second item, which explores how our current practices impact that performance."

The CIO gave the nod, and I took that as my cue to dive deeper. "Next up, for our second agenda item, I'm really keen to hear about the hurdles you've been facing. And then, we'll roll into the fourth point: I'll share my take on how our product model can tackle these challenges head-on and boost our business performance. I'm hoping you all had a moment to check out the presentation

I sent over. It's packed with examples of how we can streamline our business operational value streams, products, and capabilities."

The CDO and CPO responded at the same time, "Yes, we did." The CPO continued, "I liked those product types and how products are defined from the customer's perspective. However, we need a deeper dive in our context. I have a question about the product definition view you shared in the presentation, especially regarding internal applications and external COTS products. Conceptually, I can connect the dots, but how is it done in real-time? Do you have any practical use cases?"

"Absolutely," I replied. "We will cover that. In fact, Mr. Agile has created a products view in Thiran's context with inputs from the BAs. We'll go through this as part of today's meeting."

The CIO chimed in, "I like the storyline. Let's start with the second agenda point and see the connection of the first and second agenda to the third."

The CTO and CMO also agreed with this approach, nodding in unison.

3.1 Hear from the CXOs about the specific problems they needed to solve (Agenda 2)

I suggested, "How about we grab some markers and hit the whiteboard? Let's write down the challenges we're facing right now."

Everyone was on board, so we huddled around the whiteboard. The room buzzed as we dove into a deep empathy discussion with all the CXOs. One by one, each executive scribbled their challenges on sticky notes, then thoughtfully placed them under the corresponding leadership roles. This wasn't just about airing out problems; it was an exercise in walking in each other's shoes, truly grasping the unique perspectives and pain points that each leader faced.

The room was alive with the buzz of activity and the hum of conversation.

At the end of 30 minutes, we had a clear view of the voices and insights aimed at dissecting the challenges in our digital transformation initiatives. Here are the key inputs from each participant:

3.1.1 CIO Inputs:

Approval Process Delays:

Delays in initial project approvals and change requests were identified as major culprits for prolonged lead times in delivering value.

Benefit Delivery & Measurement:

While some projects hit the mark, delivering tangible business benefits, others missed the boat. The real challenge lies in a lack of clear definitions and measurements, making it tough to truly gauge their impact on business.

Low Investments in Technology Modernization:

The lack of enough green lights for tech upgrade projects is really holding back the big wins we're all aiming for in the business.

Infrastructure Investment Prioritization:

The slow pace of green-lighting funds for infrastructure or tooling was putting the brakes on DevOps and automation efforts, slowing down the speed at which value was delivered.

Scope Changes:

Lack of clear planning and definition by tech teams meant projects kept changing mid-flight, throwing timelines and budgets out the window.

3.1.2 CDO Inputs:

Undefined Business Objectives:

Not having clear business goals and priorities made it really tough to figure out which digital projects should come first.

Decentralized Implementation:

Spreading out the execution of programs and projects across different business areas led to a messy overlap and efforts that were all over the place, not talking to each other.

Priority Conflicts:

Differing priorities across business units threw a wrench in the works, causing unexpected delays in rolling out projects tied to specific initiatives.

Legacy Technology Impediments:

Old-school tech and its clunky setups were like giant roadblocks, dragging down the fast lane to digital transformation.

Budget Approval Challenges:

Going through the maze of approval for digital project budgets, especially with the added complexity of multiple cost centers, turned into a major roadblock, causing frustrating delays in getting projects off the ground and across the finish line.

Resource Mobilization Hurdles:

Getting our team up to speed for the project took more time than we anticipated. Finding and bringing together the right people with the skills we needed turned out to be quite the challenge, mainly because everyone was spread out across different parts of the business.

Project Team Disbandment:

At the close of each project, we'd scatter the team to the winds, only to spend ages piecing together a similar skill puzzle for the next venture.

Inputs of Business Sponsors:

Cost and Time Estimate Fluctuations:

Wild swings in the cost and timelines of digital projects kept popping up, breeding a mix of uncertainty and frustration.

Execution Failures:

Some projects missed the mark, revealing holes in how things were carried out.

Integration Delays:

Struggles with meshing application modules and getting on the same page with other teams led to a double whammy: delivering features behind schedule and spotting bugs way too late in the game.

Production Impact:

When flaws from deployed projects sneak into the production environment, they throw a wrench into business operations, causing real headaches.

SLA Impact:

Freshly launched projects frequently threw business operations for a loop, straining SLAs and piling on more operational troubles.

ROI Misalignment:

Too often, projects delivered fell short of hitting the expected Return on Investment (ROI), sparking worries about the real value being delivered.

3.1.3 CPO Inputs

Business Value:

The projects we rolled out fell short of the mark, missing the mark on delivering the expected benefits and business value we were all hoping for.

Understanding Customer Needs:

Projects that are defined and delivered without addressing customer problems or enhancing their journey do not align with business objectives.

Data Security and Privacy:

Safeguarding customer data and ensuring privacy compliance is not achieved.

Optimizing User Experience:

Not prioritizing design for a better user experience means the team struggles to show improvements in the projects they undertake.

Measuring Success:

Lack of OKRs and KPIs fails to provide a true picture of the project's scope, its impact on the customer, the business, and employee engagement.

3.1.4 CMO Inputs:

Data Collection and Integration:

Gathering comprehensive data from various sources, such as sales, customer feedback, and online behavior, is always challenging. Integrating this data to form a cohesive understanding of customer behavior presents another challenge.

Customer Segmentation:

Segmenting customers effectively into meaningful groups based on demographics, behavior, and purchasing patterns is highly complex.

Predicting Spending Patterns:

Understanding and predicting spending patterns across different customer segments necessitates in-depth analysis of past behaviors, a task we are unable to accomplish due to limitations in our systems.

Personalization:

Customizing the shopping experience and marketing messages to fit each customer's unique likes and dislikes can be quite the challenge.

Adapting to Market Changes:

Staying in sync with rapid market changes, like new shopping trends or economic shifts, is crucial for keeping existing customers and boosting transactions.

Innovation:

Keeping ahead of our competitors through innovation in customer engagement and experience is a relentless pressure that we're struggling to manage.

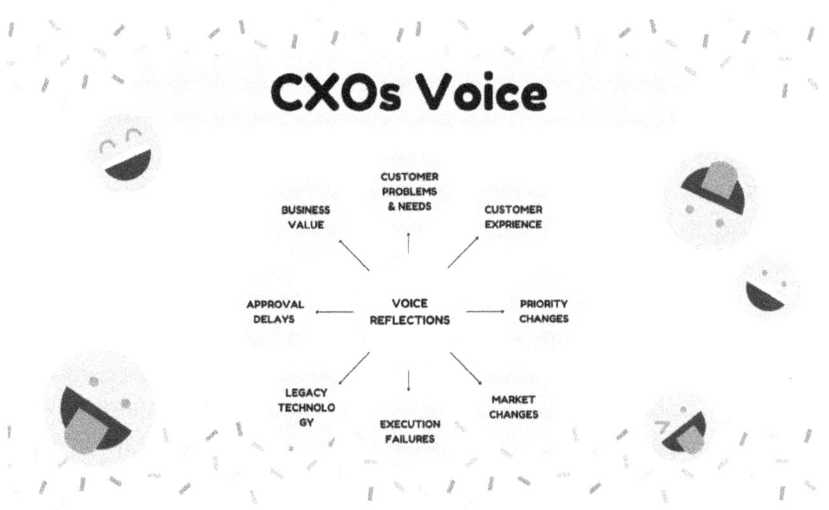

CIO		CPO		BUSINESS SPONSOR		CDO		CMO	
Approval process delays	Low investment for tech modernization	Understanding customer needs	Managing user experience	Cost & time estimate fluctuations	integration delays	Undefined business objective	Decentralized implementation	Customer Segmentation	Data colelction & integration
Benefit delviery & Measurement	Infra investment prioritization	Data security & privacy	Measuring succccss	ROI misalignement	Production & SLA Impact	Priority conflicts	Legacy technology impediments	Personalize customer needs	Adopting to market change

After digesting the inputs they shared, I took a moment to breathe and then dove back in.

3.2 Review the Current Business Performance (Agenda 3)

Next, I unveiled an overview of the retail industry's performance over the last four quarters, with respect to the retail stores' business lines.

This is a table that highlights the performance across four quarters, detailing revenue, profit, new customer traffic rate, existing customer retention rate, repeat customers percentage, revenue per customer, and operation cost per customer, among other metrics.

Retail Store Industry Business Performance Overview:

Quarter	Revenue (in millions)	Year-Over-Year Change	Gross Margin	Operating Expenses
Q2 2021	$5,000	-2%	35%	$1,700
Q3 2021	$4,800	-4%	34%	$1,750
Q4 2021	$4,500	-6%	33%	$1,800
Q1 2022	$4,200	-8%	32%	$1,850

Executive Summary

This report provides an analysis of the quarterly performance of our Global Retail Store for the fiscal year 2021-2022. Despite facing challenging market conditions, including increased competition and changing consumer behaviors, our efforts to streamline operations and enhance customer experience continue. However, the data indicates a declining trend in performance metrics across all quarters.

Key Performance Indicators

- **Customer Traffic**: Declined by 5% each quarter, reflecting reduced in-store visits.
- **Conversion Rate**: Decreased from 4.5% in Q1 to 3.8% in Q4, indicating lower sales efficiency.
- **Average Transaction Value**: Fell by 3% each quarter, suggesting a decrease in spending per customer.
- **Inventory Turnover**: Slowed down, with excess stock leading to increased clearance sales.

Market Analysis

- The retail industry has faced a downturn due to economic headwinds, with consumers prioritizing essential purchases over discretionary spending. The rise of e-commerce continues to impact brick-and-mortar stores, as reflected in our online sales outpacing physical store sales

I went on, "In your last two quarterly earnings reports, you pointed out how our competitors are nailing it with digital innovation—getting their solutions out there quicker than we can. This isn't just about speed; it's about how they're tuning into customer needs, pinpointing problems, dissecting spending habits, and keeping an eye on trends across various types of products and brands. They're steps ahead of us in so many ways."

I swept my gaze across the room, capturing everyone's gaze. "You've pointed out that although our organization dreams big with innovative visions,

Sr. No.	Challenges that Impacts Business Performance	Possible solutions
1	**Outdated Business Models** – Continue with traditional models without adopting Digital market trends	▪ **Digital Transformation** – invest in e-commerce and mobile platforms to expand digital footprints and sales channel
2	**Insufficient Supply Chain** – Delays in inventory management leading to stockout or overstocking	▪ **Supply Chain Optimization** – Implement advanced inventory management to improve stock levels and reduce costs.
3	**Poor Online Presence -** Lack of strong online order& pickup in store in an increasingly digital shopping environment	▪ **Enhanced Online Experience** – Re-design online shopping experience and deliver products at boarding gates to optimize shopping time and improve shopping experience
4	**Customer Experience** – Failure to provide a seamless experience both in store and online	▪ **Enhanced Customer Experience** – Re-design the in-store experience and improve online shopping interface to retain customers
5	**Marketing Strategies** – Ineffective marketing campaign that do not resonate with target audience	▪ **Targeted marketing** – Utilize data analytics to create personalized marketing campaigns that attract and retain customers
6	**Employee Training and Morale** – Insufficient training and low employee morale impacting customer service and sales	▪ **Employee Development** - Invest in employee training programs and create a positive work culture to boost morale and productivity
7	**Pricing Strategy** – prices not competitive with market leaders or failing to offer value for money	▪ **Competitive Pricing** – Analyze competitor pricing and adjust strategies to offer better value proposition
8	**Product Differentiation** – Lack of unique products or services that set the stores apart from competitors	▪ **Product Innovation** - Collaboration with suppliers and designers to introduce exclusive products that meet customer needs

we're stumbling when it comes to making these dreams a reality. We're grappling with crafting the right digital solutions and rushing them to market fast enough."

The CIO's nod was heavy with gravity. "Exactly. Our operating costs are on the rise, while our competitors are harnessing Gen AI to boost their business and ramp up engineering productivity. This is revolutionizing how quickly they can deliver new, innovative solutions."

I caught his drift immediately. "Just like you pointed out in your report, we've got a shot at bouncing back and outpacing our competitors. All we need to do is swiftly adapt to what the market and our customers demand."

So, if you link what we've been talking about with the project-based work challenges shared offline, and consider all the voices we heard from you, you'll start to see where I'm coming from. Here's the picture I'm painting: (previous page)

The CIO nodded, "Absolutely, Absolutely, you've pinpointed it perfectly. The link between what you picked out from our CEO's earning report statement and the challenges we're facing is unmistakable. Are you suggesting that tackling these issues could steer us back to peak performance?"

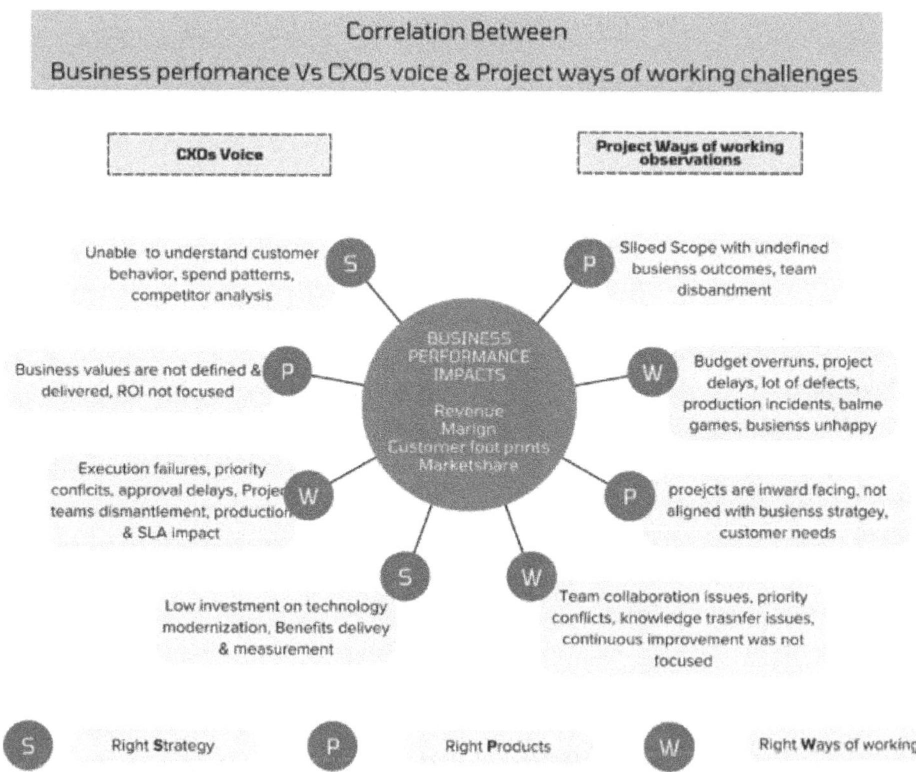

"No," I said, shaking my head. "What I've laid out are just the nuts and bolts, the execution stuff. We need your insights on the bigger picture, the strategic hurdles that we've pegged as our fourth agenda item."

"Connecting the dots between the challenges you've highlighted and what I've seen myself, it's crystal clear how these issues are directly impacting our business performance. It's just like the picture below shows": (previous page)

I scanned the room, ensuring I captured the gaze of every person present. "Addressing these challenges boils down to having the right strategy, the right products, and the right ways of working."

3.3 Highlight the product model and how it addresses these challenges (Agenda 4).

The room was silent as I began to elaborate.

Right Strategy

"The first step is really getting to the heart of what each business line hopes to accomplish in the next one to three years. It's a critical move, making sure our transformation efforts march in step with the unique goals and priorities of every business unit." I let that idea hang in the air for a moment, allowing it to really resonate before moving on.

Right Products

"The second layer peels back to reveal the heart of our mission: crafting technology-driven solutions that users will embrace to streamline their business workflows or enhance customer journeys. These products are the key players in bringing our strategic visions to life." As this was shared, nods of understanding and agreement rippled around the table.

Right Ways of Working

"The third key point is all about figuring out the best practices, tools, and teamwork needed to quickly design, develop, and deliver these chosen products. It's crucial that we make our processes smoother to guarantee we're working efficiently and can quickly adapt during our transformation journey." I noticed the CIO perking up, visibly captivated by the strategy.

"Successfully integrating these three components through the 12 Point Method (PM) Product Centric Model—inspired by the Scaled Agile Framework (SAFe) and enriched with other industry best practices—serves as a proven

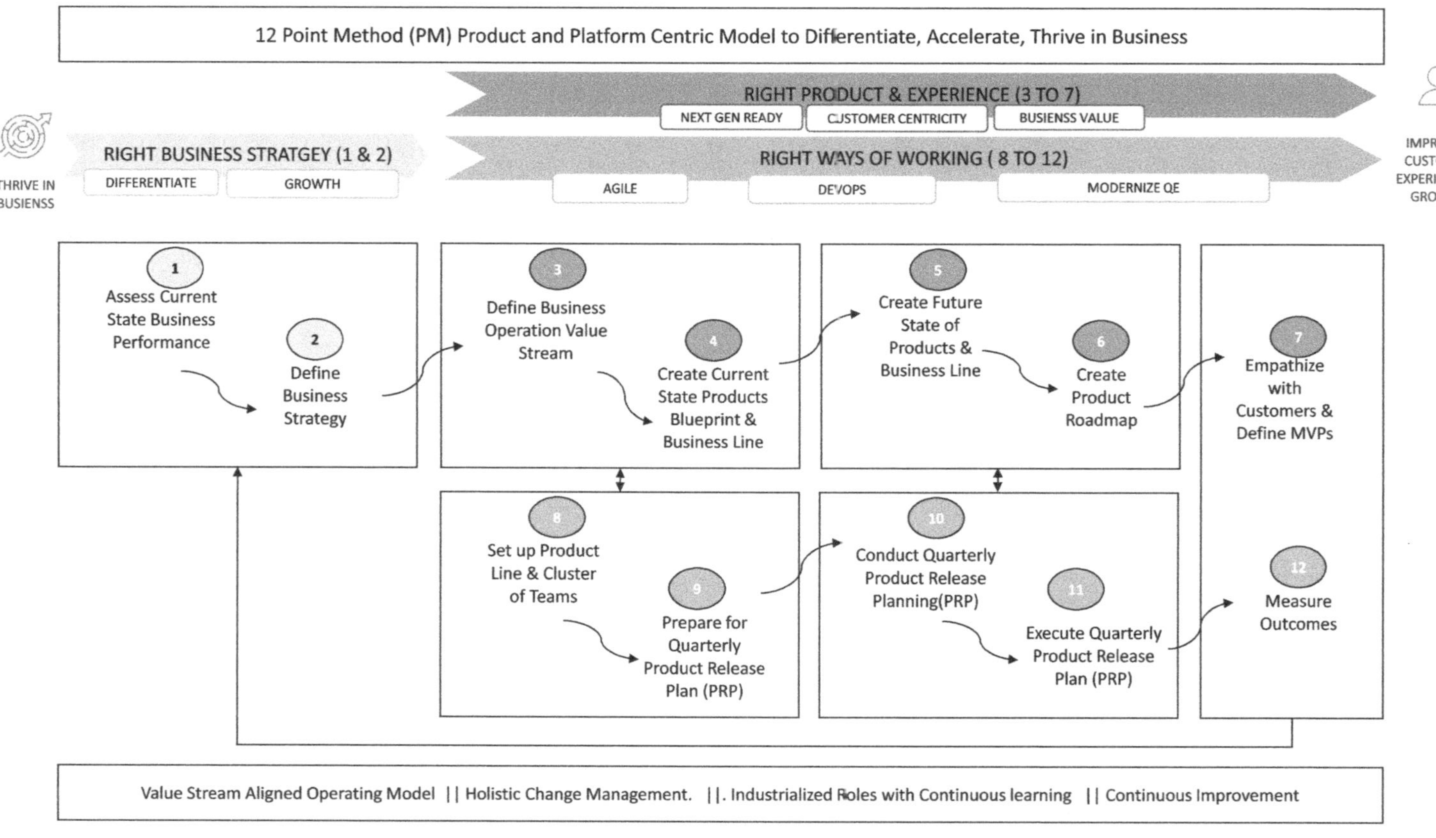

12 Point Method (PM) Product and Platform Centric Model to Differentiate, Accelerate, Thrive in Business
RIGHT PRODUCT & EXPERIENCE (3 TO 7)
NEXT GEN READY
CJSTOMER CENTRICITY
BUSIENSS VALUE
RIGHT BUSINESS STRATGEY (1 & 2)
DIFFERENTIATE
GROWTH
RIGHT WAYS OF WORKING (8 TO 12)
AGILE
DEVOPS
MODERNIZE QE
THRIVE IN BUSIENSS
IMPROVED CUSTOMER EXPERIENCE & GROWTH
1 Assess Current State Business Performance
2 Define Business Strategy
3 Define Business Operation Value Stream
4 Create Current State Products Blueprint & Business Line
5 Create Future State of Products & Business Line
6 Create Product Roadmap
7 Empathize with Customers & Define MVPs
8 Set up Product Line & Cluster of Teams
9 Prepare for Quarterly Product Release Plan (PRP)
10 Conduct Quarterly Product Release Planning(PRP)
11 Execute Quarterly Product Release Plan (PRP)
12 Measure Outcomes
Value Stream Aligned Operating Model || Holistic Change Management. ||. Industrialized Roles with Continuous learning || Continuous Improvement

blueprint for business transformation via digitization, producing measurable outcomes."

I paused, letting the room fall into a moment of quiet. I was keen on having everyone in high spirits and fully focused for our deep dive into the framework. So, with a smile, I suggested, "How about we take a 10-minute break? After that, we're diving headfirst into this framework, all in."

Right when we were gearing up to dive deeper into the discussion, it swerved into an unexpected direction. The Chief Information Officer (CIO) got this urgent call. You could see the tension wash over his face as he listened. Then, in a rush, he shared the news: significant production problems had popped up from projects they had just rolled out. He had to rush right then and there.

Feeling the pressure just as much, the Business Owner voiced the pressing need to tackle the unfolding situations head-on. The room was alive with a palpable mix of worry and haste. We all felt deeply the critical need to act swiftly on these matters.

"The CIO rose to his feet, urgency in his voice. "We've got to tackle these production issues head-on, and now," he said.

All the other CXOs were in agreement - it was obvious that the urgent production issues couldn't wait. We all agreed to put the meeting on hold for the moment. As everyone started to head out, the Chief Product Officer (CPO) hung back to talk to me. "I'd still like to dive into those product definitions, especially in the real-time context of WMS," he suggested.

I nodded. "Absolutely." With that, the room began to clear out. The internal agile coach, the CPO, and I agreed to meet after the break.

When we reconvened after the break, the internal agile coach unveiled an illustrative view of WMS product workflows:

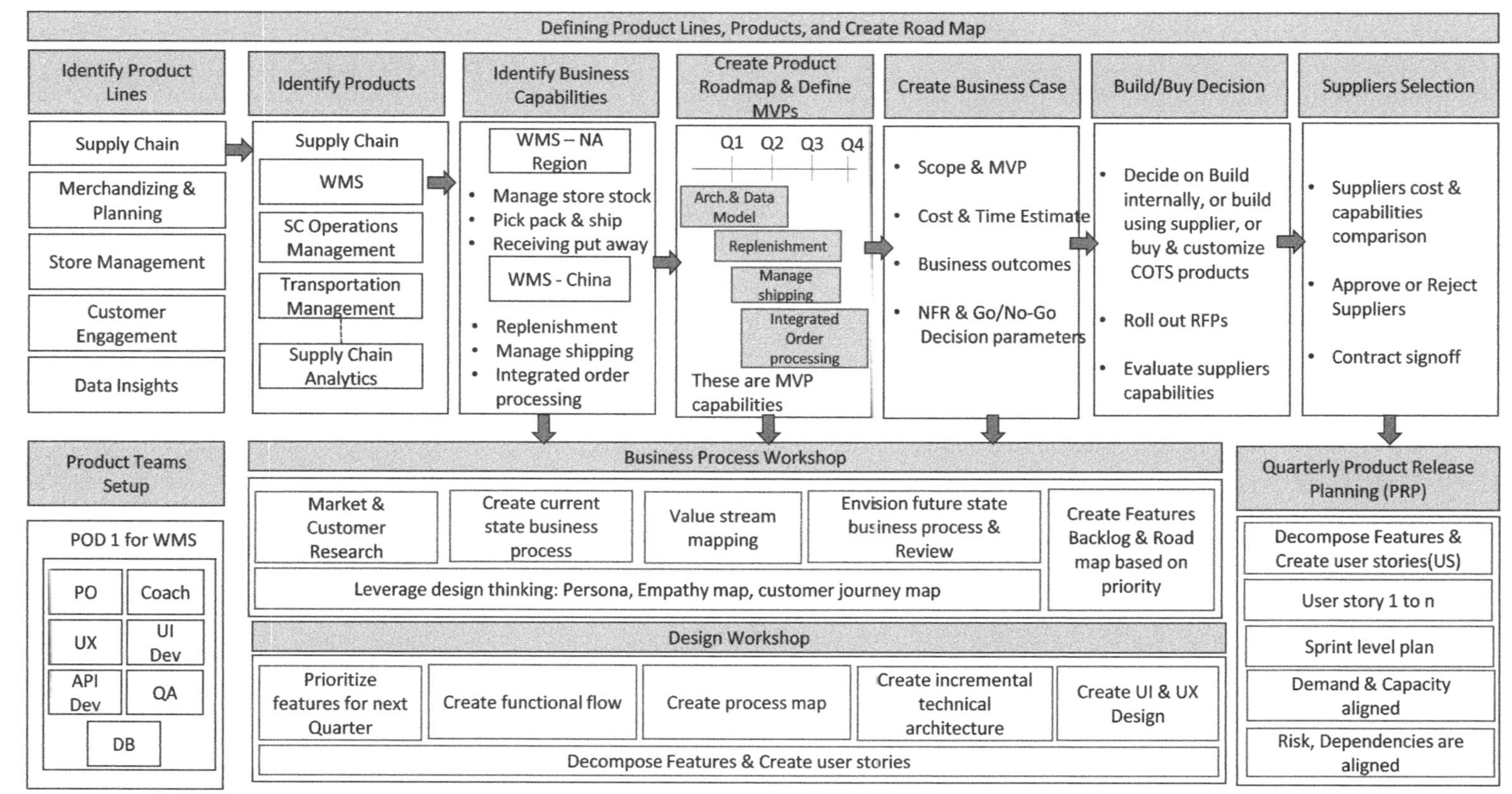

Defining Product Lines, Products, and Create Road Map
Identify Product Lines
Supply Chain
Merchandizing & Planning
Store Management
Customer Engagement
Data Insights
Identify Products
Supply Chain
WMS
SC Operations Management
Transportation Management
Supply Chain Analytics
Identify Business Capabilities
WMS – NA Region
Manage store stock
Pick pack & ship
Receiving put away
WMS - China
Replenishment
Manage shipping
Integrated order processing
Create Product Roadmap & Define MVPs
Q1 Q2 Q3 Q4
Arch.& Data Model
Replenishment
Manage shipping
Integrated Order processing
These are MVP capabilities
Create Business Case
Scope & MVP
Cost & Time Estimate
Business outcomes
NFR & Go/No-Go Decision parameters
Build/Buy Decision
Decide on Build internally, or build using supplier, or buy & customize COTS products
Roll out RFPs
Evaluate suppliers capabilities
Suppliers Selection
Suppliers cost & capabilities comparison
Approve or Reject Suppliers
Contract signoff
Product Teams Setup
POD 1 for WMS
PO
Coach
UX
UI Dev
API Dev
QA
DB
Business Process Workshop
Market & Customer Research
Create current state business process
Value stream mapping
Envision future state business process & Review
Create Features Backlog & Road map based on priority
Leverage design thinking: Persona, Empathy map, customer journey map
Design Workshop
Prioritize features for next Quarter
Create functional flow
Create process map
Create incremental technical architecture
Create UI & UX Design
Decompose Features & Create user stories
Quarterly Product Release Planning (PRP)
Decompose Features & Create user stories(US)
User story 1 to n
Sprint level plan
Demand & Capacity aligned
Risk, Dependencies are aligned

The figure above illustrates the productization of digital initiatives and the creation of quarterly product release plans.

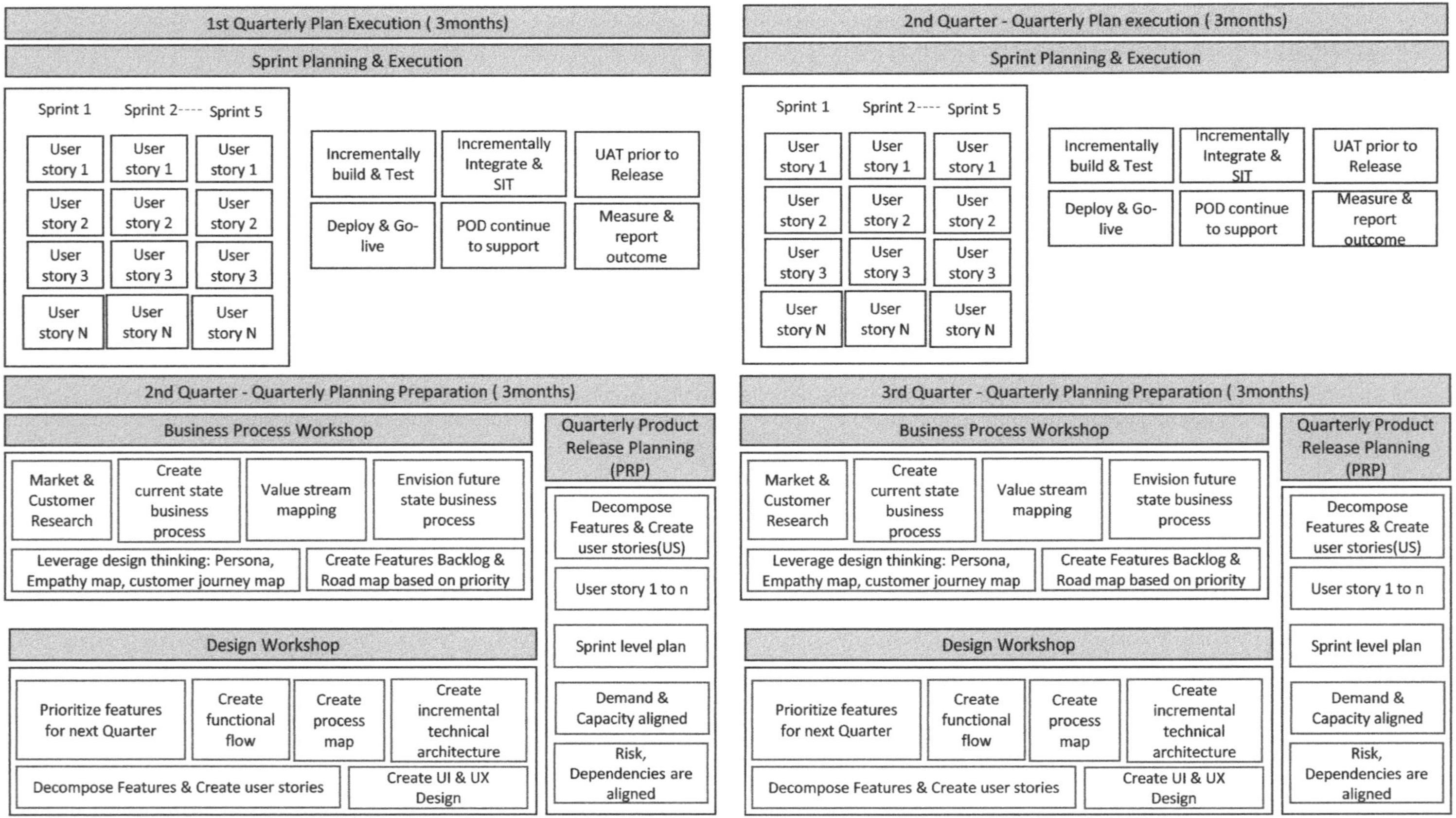

2nd Quarter - Quarterly Plan execution (3months)

Sprint Planning & Execution

- UAT prior to Release
- Measure & report outcome
- Incrementally Integrate & SIT
- POD continue to support
- Incrementally build & Test
- Deploy & Go-live

Sprint 1 | Sprint 2---- Sprint 5

- User story 1
- User story 2
- User story 3
- User story N

3rd Quarter - Quarterly Planning Preparation (3months)

Quarterly Product Release Planning (PRP)

- Decompose Features & Create user stories(US)
- User story 1 to n
- Sprint level plan
- Demand & Capacity aligned
- Risk, Dependencies are aligned

Business Process Workshop

- Market & Customer Research
- Create current state business process
- Value stream mapping
- Envision future state business process
- Leverage design thinking: Persona, Empathy map, customer journey map
- Create Features Backlog & Road map based on priority

Design Workshop

- Prioritize features for next Quarter
- Create functional flow
- Create process map
- Create incremental technical architecture
- Create UI & UX Design
- Decompose Features & Create user stories

1st Quarterly Plan Execution (3months)

Sprint Planning & Execution

- UAT prior to Release
- Measure & report outcome
- Incrementally Integrate & SIT
- POD continue to support
- Incrementally build & Test
- Deploy & Go-live

Sprint 1 | Sprint 2---- Sprint 5

- User story 1
- User story 2
- User story 3
- User story N

2nd Quarter - Quarterly Planning Preparation (3months)

Quarterly Product Release Planning (PRP)

- Decompose Features & Create user stories(US)
- User story 1 to n
- Sprint level plan
- Demand & Capacity aligned
- Risk, Dependencies are aligned

Business Process Workshop

- Market & Customer Research
- Create current state business process
- Value stream mapping
- Envision future state business process
- Leverage design thinking: Persona, Empathy map, customer journey map
- Create Features Backlog & Road map based on priority

Design Workshop

- Prioritize features for next Quarter
- Create functional flow
- Create process map
- Create incremental technical architecture
- Create UI & UX Design
- Decompose Features & Create user stories

The figure above showcases the execution of the PRP over the next three months, while also highlighting the preparatory activities carried out in tandem leading up to the next quarterly PRP.

The key value proposition of the above two illustrative views is as follows:

1. Product Line (PL) defined

2. WMS is one of the products under the supply chain PL.

3. Business capabilities (BC) for WMS are defined and assigned to a vendor for execution.

4. The vendor will maintain a full-stack, long-term team with all the necessary skills to deliver the BC from end to end.

5. Each Business Capability (BC) has a Minimum Viable Product (MVP), an envisioned future state business process view with optimized steps, which will improve the customer experience.

6. Develop an MVP by creating incremental architecture and UX design.

7. Implement incremental delivery of quarterly and bi-weekly releases, and evaluate the MVP

8. While the product team develops MVPs, the preparation work for the next set of functionalities for the same BC/new BC is prioritized, and its high-level design will begin.

9. Once one BC or two BCs in parallel are completed, the same product team will proceed with the next BC of WMS.

10. Every bi-weekly and quarterly product outcome is measured, the speed of value delivery is assessed, and improvements are made consistently.

We dove deep into discussions about why we need to shift our perspective towards productization in digital solutions, moving away from a project-centric view. I explained, "Let's talk about why we need this shift. My experience has shown that a product-focused view is more customer-centric and value-driven. It's crucial for us to be focused on customers and value when creating innovative solutions. Here, I present to you a table outlining the what and why." (next page)

The CPO looked at it, nodded, and prompted me to continue.

"We also need to understand what's different about the product model ways of working and what benefits it delivers," I said. "Our competitors have excelled

What and Why – Product Centric Model

Sr. No.	What	Why
1	Align Portfolio and product level OKRs	Enables to define expected product outcomes upfront
2	Define Digital Products from customer perspective	Our digital solution should solve customer problem and address their needs
3	Implement product based funding	Fund right product that will deliver more value with less cost
4	Align business and technology teams	Improved collaboration, trust between business and technology
5	Focus on designing innovative solution and faster delivery	Need to stay ahead of competitors to survive and thrive in the market
6	Focus on lean startup culture and MVP evaluation	Build products incrementally and validate with customer before building whole product
7	Focus on end to end ownership of product from design to support	Long living teams ownership enables efficient delivery and continuous evolution of the product
8	Setup cluster of product teams with all necessary skills around development value stream	It optimizes the time needed to deliver value and minimizes external dependencies
9	Incremental plan and execution – quarterly and bi-weekly	It helps to align demand Vs Capacity and what business objectives will be achieved
10	Measure and improve outcome – Process and product	It helps to validate if the product deliver outcomes, and are we able to deliver value predictable & faster

by adopting this model. They understand customer problems, needs, challenges, spending patterns, and behaviors more accurately with their innovative solutions. This is something the CEO highlighted in the earnings report – our competitors are ahead because they've embraced a product-centric approach."

I could see the CPO's interest piqued. "So, how do we get there?" he asked.

"First, we need to start viewing our internal applications and external COTS products from the customer's perspective," I explained. "This means understanding how these products fit into the customer journey and deliver value. It's the first step towards creating customer-centric innovative solutions."

The internal agile coach added, "It's about a fundamental shift in how we think about and approach our work. It's about ownership, continuous improvement, and always keeping the customer in mind."

The CPO leaned back in his chair, deep in thought about the discussion. "It requires a clear shift in mindset from project to product," he said. In other words, our team needs to start thinking from the perspective of the customer, focusing on outcomes and the business impact, which is currently missing. I replied, "You're spot on!" She nodded and added, "I see the value in this approach. I'm excited to hear more about the 12-Point Method and how we can implement it at our next meeting."

When the CPO braced himself to leave, I decided to leave her with a thought on what could be a significant source of support in our transformation journey: Gen AI.

The CPO inquired, "Could you elaborate?"

"Of course, Gen AI can play a huge role in all three phases of our transformation. For example, to define the right strategy, we can use Gen AI to gather insights on competitors' business performance and strategies through primary and secondary research."

"Once we have the research data," I continued, "Gen AI can help us define our business objectives based on these insights. By feeding this data into Gen AI, we can create a future state view of products and business capabilities to achieve these objectives. Gen AI can significantly support us in implementing the 12-Point Method of the product-centric model."

"This sounds promising," the CPO said, breaking the silence. "The potential of Gen AI in transforming our approach is becoming clear, but we still need to see the practical feasibility of applying Gen AI across these 12 points. I am sure you will deep dive into it in subsequent meetings," she added. "Of course," I replied. "I am looking forward to seeing you soon," she said, shaking my hand before leaving."

After the long hours of the meeting, the internal coach and I sat down for lunch. I couldn't hide my happiness. "I'm glad we got aligned with the CXOs on the problem to solve and with the CPO on product definitions," I said.

The internal coach nodded. "That's a big win, but getting the business owner's buy-in is crucial for defining the product view landscape. I had a lot of challenges just getting the BAs to create this view for WMS. We need to be ready for their questions and get their buy-in."

He paused, then added, "I also believe the business owner isn't fully on board with this productization need. One of the product managers told me she was asked to discuss it with me to see how it fits our organization, given my long tenure here."

"What was your response?" I asked.

"Of course, I supported this view wholeheartedly. I was hoping we'd get a chance to present this to all the CXOs and get their feedback. Unfortunately, we didn't complete it."

I thought for a moment. Let's present the product-focused perspective of WMS to the CXOs for them to review at their leisure. This will give them ample time to evaluate and contrast it against project views, encouraging them to come back with deeper questions about why we're taking this product-centric approach. We can address these questions they have in our next meeting. We should also plan individual walkthroughs with the business owner and a few business users before the next session to get their feedback. This approach allows us to confirm our grasp of the organizational context and tweak our strategy as necessary. It's crucial because it will boost their buy-in and support for this transformation."

The internal coach nodded, "That's a good idea. But until we validate this productization view and get the buy-in to create similar views for other products, let's keep our fingers crossed."

"You're right," I agreed. "Let's be practical and prepare for the next session rather than celebrating too early."

On the walk back from lunch, I took a moment for a quick mental recap. Here's what we covered:

We presented and discussed the last quarter's earnings, the related challenges, and how our competitors are performing. We analyzed their unique selling propositions (USPs) and what sets them apart.

We gathered insights from the CXOs about the current state challenges and how these issues have impacted our business performance.

We created a mind map that connected strategy-level and execution-level challenges, showing how these issues affect our overall business performance.

We discussed an illustrative view of what products and product ways of working look like in the WMS context. We identified the value that a product-centric approach provides compared to the traditional project-based approach.

We explored the unique value proposition of the product-centric model in Thiran's context and the general benefits of adopting this model.

Reflecting on all this, I felt a surge of excitement for what lay ahead.

12-Point Method for Product-Centric Transformation

Before we dive into the next big meeting, let's take a step back and look at the broader perspective. The shift from a project-centric to a product-centric operating model is a major transformation that many organizations are embracing to better align with business outcomes and customer needs.

To set the stage, let's consider the experience of GSK Tech in 2018. They said, "Over the past few years, we've invested heavily in transforming how we approach technology and fundamentally how we are structured as an organization to most effectively harness digital, data and analytics to drive better outcomes for our patients and customers. The challenge with 120,000 employees is transforming at scale. Core to this is to switch our organization from a project-centric operating model to a product-centric model. Our transformation journey encompasses organizational change as well as skills, cultural and technology changes, enough to fill a book, but what's most important is to understand what we're shifting to, where we were, and why these changes were essential to disrupt our previous operating model."

This statement from GSK Tech sums up the essence of what we're aiming for. It's about more than just changing the way we execute projects; it's about fundamentally altering how we think, operate, and deliver value. Understanding where we're headed, where we've been, and why these changes are necessary is crucial for driving meaningful transformation.

Now, I would like to take you through the much-anticipated third meeting that I was truly excited about. The room was buzzing with energy as the CXOs gathered, ready to dive into the details. We kicked things off with a quick recap of what we discussed in the last two meetings—understanding the problem we need to solve and a high-level overview of the product model.

Then, I reminded everyone of the 12-point method to implement the product-centric model, laying out the three crucial phases:

4.1 Introductions to 3 phases of 12 Point Method

Phase 1: Define and Align the Right Business Strategy

"This phase is about understanding our current state of business performance," I began. "We need to identify the services, products, and customer segments that our business should focus on. What growth opportunities are available in the market? What are our competitors doing?"

I paused to let this sink in. "Based on these inputs, we define our growth strategy—where we want to be in the market in the next two to three years. We'll refer to industry best practices, value chain analysis, and value proposition analysis to contextualize and implement this phase."

Phase 2: Define the Right Products and Experience

"This phase is about determining what digital products—technology-enabled solutions—need to be built or modernized to leverage digital opportunities in the market. It's crucial to define, prioritize, and fund these product strategies based on the expected values and business outcomes. These products are expected to play a vital role in enabling the organization to execute its business strategy effectively."

The room was silent, everyone listening intently. "We need to ensure that each product strategy is aligned with our overall business goals. Depending on whether we're a manufacturing or service organization, we'll define and implement the types of products needed, as discussed earlier. We'll leverage industry best practices like SAFe, product development principles, and the 'Project to Product' approach by Mik Kersten to guide us."

Phase 3: Define the Right Ways of Working

"This phase is crucial," I continued, making eye contact with each participant. "It's about the practices, tools, skills, and expertise needed to deliver these products to customers faster, cheaper, and with high quality. This is where we leverage industry-proven best practices from agile, DevOps, lean, and product development methodologies, as referred to in SAFe."

As I summed this up, I was prepared to thoroughly explore each of the three phases and delve into the twelve key points.

Phase 1: Define and Align Business Strategy

I began by asking some fundamental questions to set the stage. "Do we have a strategy defined for the Retail business line? What exactly is our strategy?"

The business owner responded, "We want to improve the operational efficiency of the stores."

"Can you elaborate on that?" I asked, inviting more detail.

The CDO stepped in, "We aim to optimize the business process from the moment an order is received to sending products to respective stores and requesting refill orders."

I leaned forward, "Have we measured the current business process as-is, end-to-end, in terms of lead time?"

The business owner admitted, "We didn't measure it precisely. But, based on our overall experience and insights, we aim for a 25% improvement from the current state."

"That's a good start," I acknowledged. "However, if we base our targets on a quantification of the current process and compare it to our competitors' performance, we can set more accurate targets. This will help us differentiate ourselves and gain a competitive advantage."

I continued, "Do we have any other objectives defined?"

The business owner nodded, "Yes, we have strategic objectives to retain our existing market share and expand in geographies like China. We aim for 15% revenue from China this year and 25% next year. We also plan to increase our North American market share by 10% year-on-year for the next three years."

"What are we doing to achieve these objectives? What differentiating strategies have we defined?" I asked.

The CDO responded, "We've identified a lot of digital initiatives, which are split into multiple projects. These projects are executed by various teams."

"Yes, I understand," I replied. "As we discussed, those two projects are examples. The WMS project is expected to improve store efficiency and support market growth. Similarly, the replenishment project aim to improve product availability for customers by replenishing stock faster based on consumption patterns."

The conversation was gaining momentum. "Great discussion," I said. "I hope we've defined business objectives and differentiating strategies based on our current business performance, competitor strategies, and our organization's vision and purpose."

The CDO replied, "Sort of."

The CIO added, "We did consider our current state performance, but we didn't do a formal deep-dive analysis, nor did we conduct a detailed market or competitor analysis."

Based on this conversation, we agreed to discuss in detail what industry best practices are in this space. This led us to the first two points of the 12-Point Method.

4.2 Point 1: Assess Current State Business Performance

"So, let's kick things off by taking a good look at where our business stands right now," I started. "We're going to check out four main areas: Are we focusing on being a cost leader, offering products and services at optimal costs, or are we differentiating ourselves in other ways? How quickly can we deliver new business capabilities or features? What does our revenue look like over the past few years, and what challenges have we faced? How much effort are we putting into digitizing our current business processes?"

"We need to collect data on these parameters," I continued, "and analyze it in the context of our existing competitors, upcoming startups, and our own strengths and weaknesses. The goal is to create a comprehensive current state business performance report."

"This report will show us how our current business is being executed, where we are excelling, where we need improvements, and where we need to focus immediately to stay competitive," I explained.

Illustrative view of the current system activity map of Wealth Management business line. This explains the steps of business value creation performed by an organization across its value chain.

Current System Activity Map for Wealth Management Business Value Chain

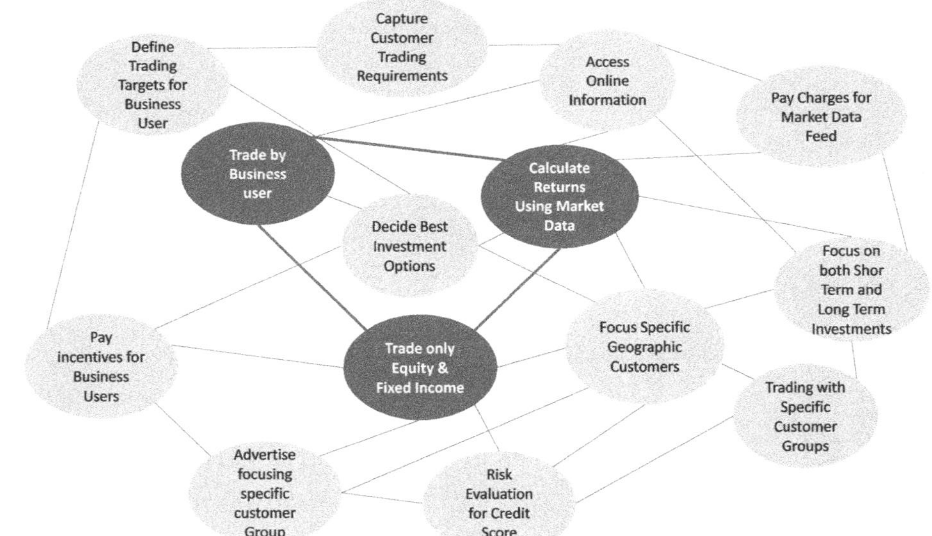

In line with the current system activity map, we have created a value stream for the current state of business operations as shown below:

Example of Current State Wealth Management Business Operation Value Stream that attract and provide Trading services

The room was engaged, understanding the importance of this thorough assessment. It was clear that this step was essential for setting a solid foundation for our transformation.

Below, you'll find a glimpse into the business performance of our Retail Lending Banking division:

Performance Parameters	Current State Performance	Inferences
Cost Leader Vs Differentiator	**Cost leader current state** • **Customer Acquisition Cost (CAC):** Average CAC is around $ 250 per customer. • **Operating cost** – Average loan servicing fee is around $50 per month • **Cost to Income ratio (CIR):** Cost to income ratio is increasing • **Cost to Serve (CTS):** Cost to Serve is increasing that impacts profits **Differentiator current state** • **Interest rate Vs Service Quality** – Customers are not interested to pay more interest as service quality is not on par with other banks • **Non- Sufficient Fund(NSF):** Customers are not willing to pay NSF • **Customer Loyalty Program:** Cost spent on loyalty program not increasing customer retention	• Increase in bank operations cost, CAC, CIR, CTS etc. are significant expense and its reduction is key profitability. Optimizing this will enable Bank to become cost leader • Increase in digital transformation cost, investment to increase experience etc. not increasing the customer's willingness to pay (WTP) • Bank implement strategies and governance measure to ensure increased cost spent by bank helps them to become cost leader (optimized operation cost CAC, etc.) and become differentiator (customer willing to pay high interest, NSF etc. as they receive best in class service)
Agility	• **Average lead time** to release new business functionality takes around18 to 20 weeks • **Employee Satisfaction:** only 55% of employee are happy and highly engaged and 35% employees considered a retention risk	• Average lead time to deliver new features seems to be very high in comparison competitors who started delivering in 3 to 5 weeks • Employee engagement and satisfaction needs attention to improve speed to deliver value and quality
Revenue Trajectory	• **Loan growth** is decreased by 10% (number of closed-end loan applications decreased by 30%) • **Personal Loan growth** is decreased by 5% • **Decrease** in unsecured personal loan year over year	• Overall loan growth is decreasing while loan interest is fluctuating • Customers retention and ability to provide unsecured loan getting difficult
Emerging Digital	• **Digital maturity** 5 in scale of 1 to 10, while competitive threats from fintechs are rising • **Average cycle time:** "time to yes" 1 day and "time to cash" to 3 weeks while benchmark in minutes and days respectively • **Pull through rate is decreased by 10%:** number of loans disbursed and number of loan applications submitted • **Customer Onboarding:** Customer onboarding time is increased by 20% • **Average % of customers** visiting bank monthly is 75%	• Overall digital maturity "medium" in comparison to competitor. Its very critical focus especially in the context of customer expectations for excellent digital experience continue to rise. • Average time it takes for most of the critical business operations seems to be high which result in increased bank operation cost. Immediate attention is needed to improve business digital maturity

4.3 Point 2: Define Business Strategy

"Now, let's move on to defining our business strategy," I said, setting the stage for the next critical step.

"Drawing from the insights of our latest business performance report, we're at a crossroads where we get to chart our future. What's our dream for where we'll stand as an organization in the next two to three years? This vision will be shaped based on our current successes, the moves our competitors are making, and the golden opportunities waiting for us out there in the market."

I looked around the room as I resumed. "Up next, we're diving into crafting a future state system activity map, which we'll explore shortly. This map serves as our blueprint to leapfrog the competition, enhance our efficiency, and protect us from newcomers attempting to disrupt our market. Based on this future state system map, we will create refined business operation value stream through which the organization will interact with customers and deliver value to them."

Here's a visual representation of what the future system activity map looks like for the wealth management business line:

Future System Activity Map for Wealth Management Business Value Chain

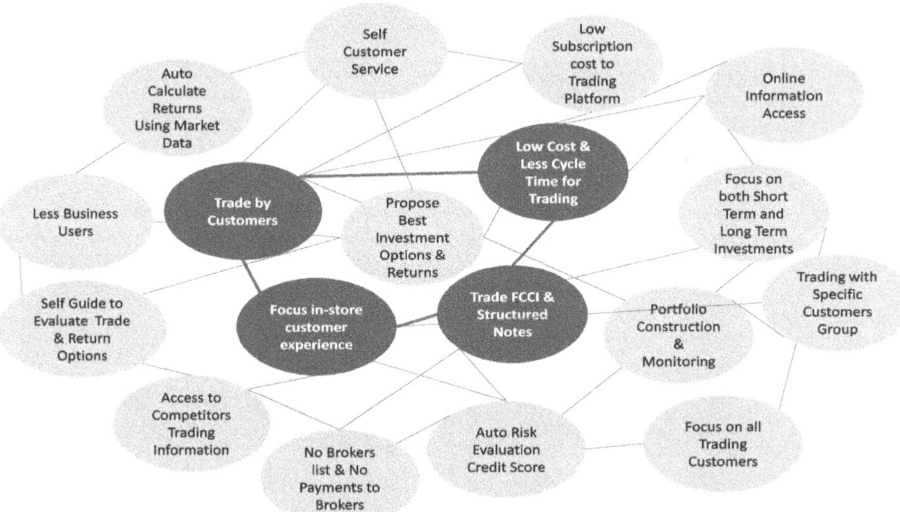

The room was all ears, eyes locked in anticipation. "With these system maps in hand, we'll refine future state business operation value stream, pinpoint the strategic drivers steering our course for the next two years. It's all about syncing our business goals with these key drivers, crafting digital initiatives to hit those targets, and setting up OKRs to track our triumphs."

Example of Future State Wealth Management Business Operation Value Stream that attract and provide Trading services

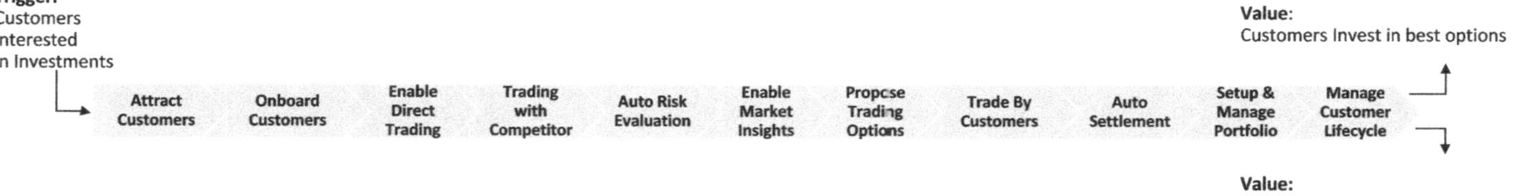

Here's an example of how the banking industry combines business strategy with digital initiatives:

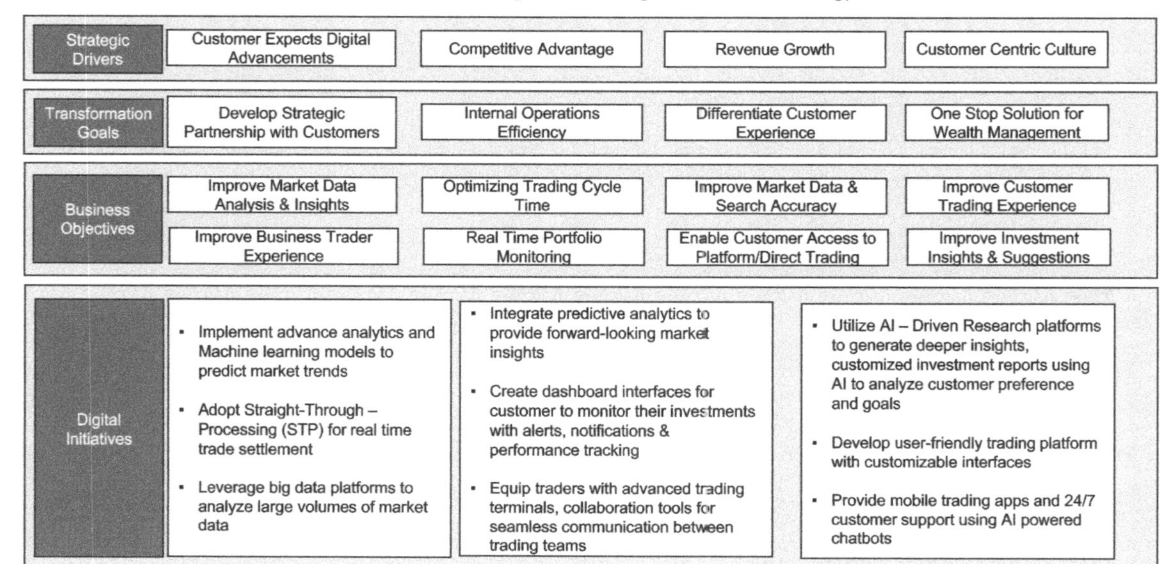

"Now that we have our business strategy defined," I continued, "let's talk about how we turn this strategy into actionable steps through digital initiatives."

"We need to prioritize these digital initiatives based on the type of business strategy we're adopting—whether it's to run, accelerate, or disrupt to differentiate. These prioritized initiatives will then be delivered through our digital strategy, which leads us into Phase 2."

I made sure everyone was following before proceeding. "Instead of converting these initiatives into traditional projects, we need to transform them into 'business capabilities' of existing products or new products. Essentially, we need to 'productize' these digital initiatives. Each product will offer a set of business capabilities that will help us achieve higher operational efficiency with optimized implementation costs, improve customer experience for retention and continued engagement, and enhance the effectiveness of customer spending patterns, forecasting, and procurement planning."

I saw nods of agreement around the room. "To achieve this productization, we follow the activities outlined in Phase 2 of the 12-Point Method. These activities include identifying the business operational value stream, existing products, and business capabilities, as well as new digital initiatives, new products and new business capabilities."

I paused to ensure everyone was still with me. "With this understanding, let's dive into Phase 2 of the 12-Point Method, where we will discuss points 3 to 7 in detail."

Phase 2: Right Products and Experience

In Phase 2, we dove deep into how we define our digital strategy that will realize our business strategy by transforming digital initiatives into robust products. We're particularly focused on points three through seven, starting with the business operation value stream.

Below, we present an illustrative overview of the definition of digital strategy.

The figure above gives you a sneak peek into the steps for crafting a digital strategy and turning initiatives into actual products.

4.4 Point 3: Define the Business Operation Value Stream

"Our first step in crafting our digital strategy," I explained, "is to clearly refine the business operation value stream. This is what we would be creating based on the inputs from the future state system activity map.

A value stream is the ecosystem that converts a trigger into value delivery through a series of value creation steps by leveraging people, process, tools, and information flow. For our retail business, this involves outlining the journey from a customer's initial desire to purchase a product, whether in-store or online, to fulfilling that desire through options like home delivery, delivery at a boarding gate, or in-store pickup. The need to purchase triggers our operations, and the delivery of the product represents the value we provide."

Seeing a mix of familiar nods and curious looks, I continued, "While this might seem like a well-known process to you, the key here is not just understanding it but documenting and aligning every team to this blueprint. It's about making sure that everyone in the organization not only knows but also supports this flow, optimizing our efforts towards a common goal of delivering business value faster to our customers."

The Business Owner raised an eyebrow, "We already know this, don't we? It exists."

"Yes, it does," I acknowledged with a smile. "But knowing isn't enough. In line with both the future system activity map and our defined business strategy, we have refined the business operation value stream. It will focus on enhancing efficiency, experience, and effectiveness. We're aligning and refining these processes to enhance efficiency and deliver more value. It's about reinforcing what works, fixing what doesn't, and discovering new opportunities to excel. Moreover, it's crucial to communicate these improvements to everyone across the organization, ensuring all are informed and engaged."

I continued, "Will our product managers and owners fully understand this value stream?"

The Business Owner shook his head, "No. They understand the value stream, but not necessarily in the context of the projects they're working on or how those projects influence the value stream."

I turned to the CIO, "What about our tech leads, developers, and testers? Do they grasp this concept?"

The CIO responded, "Probably not," and continued, "We need to create alignment between the business and tech teams on this refined business operation value stream." It's also crucial that our product managers deeply understand this value stream. This will enable them to lead the exercise of identifying the products and business capabilities leveraged by this business operation value stream."

Let's take a look at how business operation value streams function, using the healthcare industry as an example:

Example of Health Care Industry Business Operation Value Stream that attract and provide health care services

Note: The above example is illustrative only. It does not contain all the digital products to perform end to end business operations. Based on industry contexts these products may vary in type, complexity, number of products etc.

The Business Owner seemed to accept this perspective, nodding thoughtfully. Meanwhile, both the Chief Digital Officer (CDO) and Chief Information Officer (CIO) expressed a need to delve into subsequent steps to evaluate the overall necessity for the product-centric transformation in achieving our strategic objectives.

With that, we transitioned to point 4 of Phase 2.

4.5 Point 4: Create a Current State Blueprint of Products, Business Capabilities, and Applications

We moved to the next critical step: creating a current state blueprint of products, business capabilities, and applications. This step is essential and involves collaboration with business partners, product managers, business architects, solution architects, and tech leads.

"I kicked things off by stating that, in this exercise, our brilliant solution architects and tech leads will share details about all the applications our retail business uses, diving into the functionalities of each one.'"

I could see some nods around the room, so I continued, "Then, our business architects and product managers will group these functionalities into logical business capabilities that the business team uses during value-creation activities. Once we've identified these business capabilities, we'll logically group them as sets of products."

I went on to illustrate with the following example (next page), showcasing a set of products and the prowess of a business, all within the context of the business operation value stream I mentioned above.

"With the example provided," I explained, "we can clearly see the difference between applications and products. Applications are inward-facing, viewed from the organization's perspective. Products, on the other hand, are outward-facing, centered around the customer's perspective.

Building applications with a specific scope as a project tends to be more short-term, siloed, and lacks customer-centricity. But when we define products and focus on modernizing business capabilities, we bring in the customer's perspective, competitor analysis, and the need to achieve strategic objectives."

The CIO chimed in, "I agree with this view, but how are we going to address certain legacy applications that aren't compatible with modernized capabilities?"

Example of **Current** Healthcare Industry Products & Business Capabilities

Lead Sourcing & Optimization	Lead Nurturing	Leads Verification & Sales	Customer Onboarding	Customer Self Service	Care Management	Pharmacy Management	Claims Processor
Digital Lead Intake	Prospects Profile	Plan Comparison	Customer Profiling	Customer Profile	Care Coordination	Inventory Management	Claims Intake & Triage
Partner Lead Intake	Appointment Conversation	Physician Finder	Personalized Onboarding	Feedback & Support	Manage Health History	Prescription Processing	Automated Data Capture
Manual Lead Distribution	Eligibility Verification	Drug Cost Lookup	Omnichannel Communication	Bill Payment	Telehealth Services	Regulatory Compliance	Eligibility Verification
Call Routing	Share Marketing Materials	IVR SOA (Scope of Appointment)	Customer Referrals	Manage PHI	Treatment Planning	Customer Engagement	Claims Adjudication
Campaign Management	Guided Call Flow	Voice SOA	Customer Education	Medication Management	Remote Patient Monitoring	E-Prescribing Integration	Fraud Detection
Seminar Event Creation	Lead Auto Assignment	Electronic SOA	Onboarding Analytics	Omni Channel Communication	Outcome Tracking	Financial Management	Payment Processing

Application 1	Application 2	Application 3	Application 4	Application 5	Application 6	Application 7	Application 8	Application N

Platform Capabilities	Real Time Tracking	Data Analytics & Reporting	Authentication	Onboarding	Appointment Scheduling	User Logins	Data Management

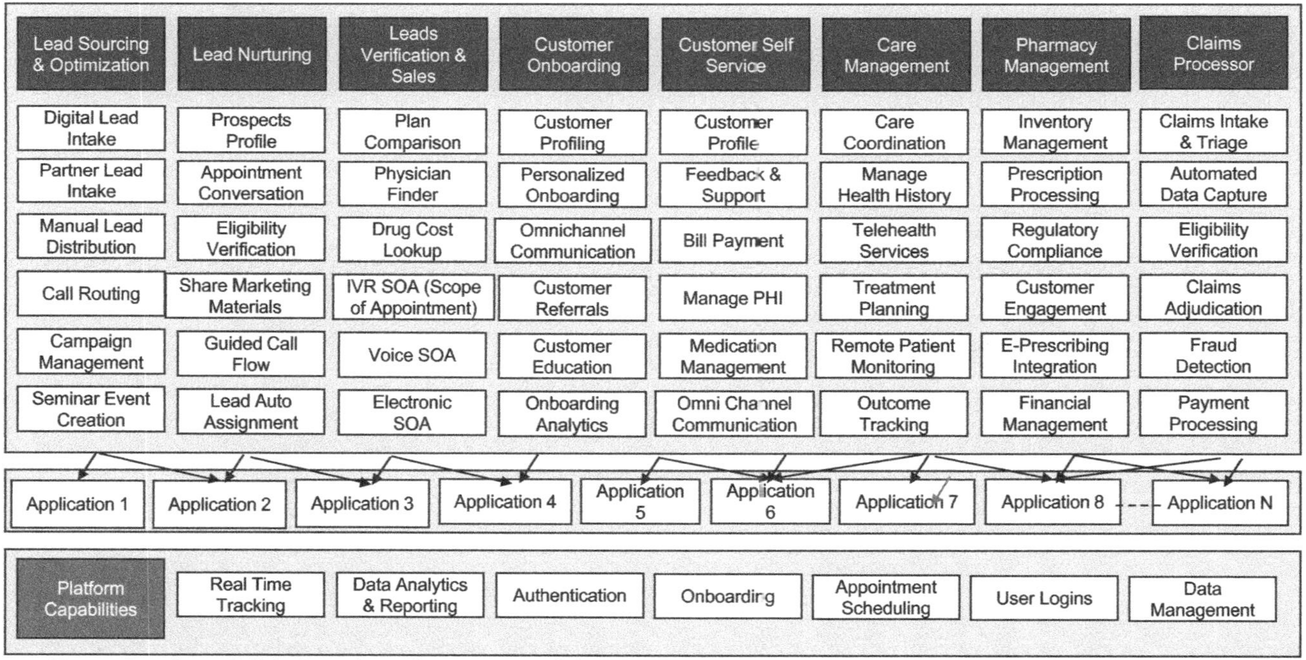

Note: its an illustrative view of digital products, business capabilities and applications. Based on organization size and complexity, number of products and its business capabilities may vary. Platform capabilities are built and managed centrally that can be consumed by all business lines

"Absolutely, you're spot on!" I responded. "That's why we need a detailed understanding of each product, including the underlying current applications, their architecture, and any constraints. We will deep dive into this as part of the current state blueprint creation workshop *(detailed in Chapter 8)*. This comprehensive view is crucial as we define new business capabilities to implement in existing products, which is the next step in our productization journey."

4.6 Point 5: Create Future State View of the Business Line

I continued, "Let's move on to creating a future state view of the retail business line. This step has two parts: analyzing and understanding the current state portfolio, and defining the future state that will enable us to achieve our business strategy."

"Part 1 involves analyzing and understanding the current state portfolio," I explained. "To do this, we will leverage the industry best practice of the business model canvas template. This approach helps document the current state and value proposition of the business line."

I highlighted the necessity of gathering additional details to fully understand our current state.

"As we've outlined in Points 3 and 4, we have already defined the value stream and products for the retail business line. Now, we need to gather more specifics, such as:

Current Programs and Projects: How many programs are currently delivering projects that align with specific business capabilities for the retail business line?

Team Composition: How many people are working on these projects? What are their skill sets and which departments do they belong to (Business, Architecture, Development, QA, Security, Operations, etc.)? Where are they located?

Budget: What is the budget for the various programs?

Customer Engagement: Who are our customers and through which channels do we engage with them?

Cost Structure: What are the costs (capex, opex, software licenses, infrastructure, etc.)?

Partners: Who are our partners?

Revenue Streams: What are our revenue streams?

KPIs/Outcomes: What are the KPIs and outcomes of this portfolio?

With these details, we will be able to understand and baseline the retail business line's performance in terms of current technology solutions, budget spending, and the outcomes we deliver."

As soon as I finished, the Business Owner, who had been listening intently, jumped in. "We have the P&L for our business line, which includes the budget spent and the revenues generated. What's new here?"

I replied calmly, "Of course, every organization has a P&L; it's fundamental to operations. But do we have these details broken down to the next level?"

The Business Owner looked puzzled, "What do you mean by that?"

I explained, "For example, can we see that these specific projects, delivered by these programs, had a budget of X million USD and contributed Y million in revenue? Can we trace this revenue back to the partners involved, the key activities performed, and the channels through which we engaged with the customer?"

Here is a snapshot that captures the essence of their business line's current state, bringing clarity and insight to their operations.

Current Portfolio Canvas — Portfolio Name Retail Sales — Date: 18.09.2022 — Version: 1.0

Value Proposition						
Value Streams	Products	Customers	Channels	Customer Relationship	Budget	KPIs/Revenue
Retail Sales Enablement	Prospects, Presales & Enrollment	Prospects, Agents, Members	Web Portal, Mobile, Email, Phone, IVR	Agent, Direct engagement, Pharmacy interaction, Providers	35 Mn USD	750mn USD Agents CX 70%
Producer/Agent Enablement	Agent Enablement & Support	Agents, Business users, Internal career	Web Portal, Mobile, Email, Phone, IVR	Direct engagement, Partners	18 Mn USD	Customer NPS 85
Producer/Agent Payments	Agent Payment & Book of Business (BO)s	Agents, Business users, Internal career	Web Portal, Mobile, Email, Phone, IVR	Direct engagement, Partners	10 Mn USD	Operation efficiency by 50%

Key Partners
- Sales Agents
- Direct Careers
- Community engagements

Key Activities:
- Define OKRs, Improve agent CX by 70%
- Define business capabilities & roadmap
- Prioritize epics, features and create quarterly plan
- Measure outcome, & continuous improvement

Key Resources:
- Epic owners, LPM, Product Managers, Enterprise and Solution architects,
- Transformation team, Value Management office
- Infrastructure

Cost Structure
- Capex cost – 45%
- Opex cost – 25%
- Licensing cost – 20%
- Infra cost – 10%

Revenue Streams:
- Health plan membership
- Healthcare services
- Pharmacy services

Both the Business Owner and the CDO replied in unison, "No, we don't have details at that level. But how is this going to help in our entire product-centric transformation journey?"

I nodded, appreciating their concern. "Good question. When we have these details, we can visualize which products are delivering valuable, impactful business outcomes and which are not. This allows us to redefine the prioritization of business capabilities that are impactful and allocate funds accordingly. Other products—whether its business capabilities or sets of business capabilities—can be pivoted or stopped from execution."

I continued, "This current state information will also be critical when we define the future state. Only when we understand our current state and have clearly defined business objectives can we effectively define the future state.

This will include identifying new business capabilities or products that we want to develop and their expected value or business outcomes. It will also help us visualize the current state regarding key partners, key activities, resources, cost structure, and revenue streams. These inputs are essential when we envision a future state that decomposes business strategy into business capabilities and products."

"In summary," I said, "it's about aligning the current state of our business line performance, defining the future state of our business line performance, and then reaching this future state to achieve strategic objectives."

The Business Owner, CDO, and CIO exchanged looks and nodded in agreement. "That makes sense," the CIO said.

"That's very clear," the CDO added. "I see the importance of having a detailed current state view to inform our future state planning."

The Business Owner nodded as well, "I agree. It's critical for us to have this clarity to move forward effectively."

Their agreement was very encouraging for Mr. Agile and me. We were ready to get started with the next step.

"As we start shaping our future," I continued, turning to the executives, "let's use the same inputs we talked about for where we are now. But, let's shift our focus to where we see this business line heading in the next 1 to 3 years."

I saw a few nods as I continued, "This means all our business canvas inputs will be futuristic. We'll consider questions like: What new products does this business line need to develop to achieve our strategic objective of revenue growth? Which new customer segments should we cater to? Through which new channels should we engage with our customers? What budget is required to develop new products or modernize existing ones with new business capabilities? How much revenue growth do we expect to achieve?"

"To create this future state view," I explained, "we need to perform the following activities:"

Leverage Current State Business Performance Report: Begin with a comprehensive review of the current state business performance report to establish a baseline for our strategic activities.

- SWOT Analysis: Understand the business line's strengths, weaknesses (internal perspective), and opportunities, threats (external perspective).

- TWOS Analysis: Convert these SWOT findings into actionable initiatives or sets of business capabilities or products.

- Business Case Creation: Develop business cases for all new or existing products at their business capabilities level.

- Prioritization: Prioritize business capabilities based on their outcome/value versus their investment.

- Approval: Secure approval for business capabilities and the overall budget required.

- Roadmap Creation: Establish a product-level roadmap highlighting which business capabilities will be implemented in which quarter of the year.

- Forecasting: Estimate expected revenue growth and efficiency gains.

- Partners and Suppliers: Identify new partners and suppliers needed to build these business capabilities and serve customers.

Figure shows illustrative view of SWOT for Health Care store business:

Internal

Strengths

What do you do well? What unique resources do you have? What do others compliment or praise?

* Strong marketing partnerships
* Strong community engagement
* Multiple Distribution Channels
* Best in-class agents

Weaknesses?

Where is there room for improvement? What resources do you lack?
What critiques do you receive?

* Limited lead funnel visibility
* Delayed assignment of leads
* Lack of connected marketing suite
* Lack of documented prospecting metrics & expectations
* Weak CRM Culture
* Business rules have created prospect silo

External

Opportunities

What opportunities do you have? What trends can you take advantage of?
How can your strengths be used?

* Consumers are becoming more digital savvy
* Cloud capabilities
* Enhance consumer journey with best-in-class agent injects
* Partner with sales leadership on 'CRM Culture'

Threats

What potential threats do you face? What changes in your industry are troublesome?
What threats do your weaknesses expose?

* New entrants/market players
* Competitors have more sophisticated CRM offerings
* 'Switching' is more common

The CDO interjected as soon as I finished, "Of course, we've done SWOT analyses before, and those inputs were considered for identifying digital projects."

I seized the moment to delve deeper, "Could you provide more details about that process? How did those insights shape our strategies?"

He responded, "Well, for example, one of the opportunities identified was to leverage an airlines partnership model"

"Absolutely, leveraging opportunities is the right approach," I agreed. "However, instead of directly converting opportunities into initiatives and projects, we need to compare the opportunities with our strengths and weaknesses. This allows us to leverage our strengths to capitalize on opportunities while being mindful of our weaknesses. This approach increases the probability of success and makes our initiatives highly competitive from a market and competitor perspective."

The CDO nodded thoughtfully, prompting me to continue. "For example, with the 'airline partnership' opportunity in our Retail industry, instead of jumping straight to identifying projects, we need to correlate this opportunity with our strengths, such as our huge existing customer base, and our weaknesses, like declining revenue due to competition. We then identify which new digital initiatives can help us capitalize on the opportunities. These initiatives are then decomposed into new products or business capabilities we need to build. These business capabilities are validated and finalized based on market research, including gemba walks, customer surveys, focus groups, and competitor analysis. The output of this exercise forms our product strategy. This method is known as TWOS."

Figure shows Illustrative view of TWOS analysis:

The Business Owner interjected, "That makes sense. So, how do we translate this into actionable steps?"

I replied, "These digital initiatives are converted into new business capabilities that need to be built or existing capabilities that need to be modernized."

"Once we have identified a set of business capabilities for new or existing products," I explained, "we interact with users—various personas—and empathize with them to create a product design. This design outlines how these business capabilities will be implemented. The output of this process is a user design with a set of functionalities that each business capability will offer. This entire exercise is implemented using a 'design thinking' approach. So, after the SWOT analysis, we continue with the design thinking approach to formalize the product strategy and user design. These defined capabilities are then created as a Business Capabilities/ epics Backlog."

Let's take a look at what the future holds for our business line:

Future Portfolio Canvas | Portfolio Name Retail Sales | Date: 18.10..2022 | Version: 1.0

Value Proposition						
Value Streams	Products	Customers	Channels	Customer Relationship	Budget	KPIs/Revenue
Retail Sales Enablement	Prospects, Presales & Enrollment	Prospects, Agents, Members	Web Portal, Mobile, Email, Phone, IVR	Agent, Direct engagement, Pharmacy interaction, Providers	45 Mn USD	1 bn USD Agents CX 90%
Producer/Agent Enablement	Agent Enablement & Support	Agents, Business users, Internal career	Web Portal, Mobile, Email, Phone, IVR	Direct engagement, Partners	25 Mn USD	Customer NPS 95
Producer/Agent Payments	Agent Payment & Book of Business (BO)s	Agents, Business users, Internal career	Web Portal, Mobile, Email, Phone, IVR	Direct engagement, Partners	18 Mn USD	Operation efficiency by 70%

Key Partners

- Sales Agents
- Direct Careers
- Community engagements

Key Activities:

- Define OKRs, Improve agent CX by 90%
- Define business capabilities & roadmap
- Prioritize epics, features and create quarterly plan
- Measure outcome, & continuous improvement

Key Resources:

- Epic owners, LPM, Product Managers, Enterprise and Solution architects,
- Transformation team, Value Management office
- Infrastructure

Cost Structure

- Capex cost – 45%
- Opex cost – 20%
- Licensing cost – 15%
- Infra cost – 10%

Revenue Streams:

- Health plan membership
- Healthcare services
- Pharmacy services

Here's a snapshot of one of the products where the product stands right now that needs to be modernized to achieve portfolio future state:

Then, as part of Point 6, we need to define the value of these capabilities and their products. We must prioritize these capabilities based on their value versus investment, then create a product roadmap. From this roadmap, we identify the Minimum Viable Product (MVP) and build and test its benefit hypothesis, focusing on desirability, feasibility, and viability.

Illustrative example of "Training Content Management " Product **Future** state View with Business Capabilities and its functionalities from Education Industry

Product OKRs: Increase Students Qualification % by 30% ; Improve Student experience by 50%; Improve Tutor Experience by 40%

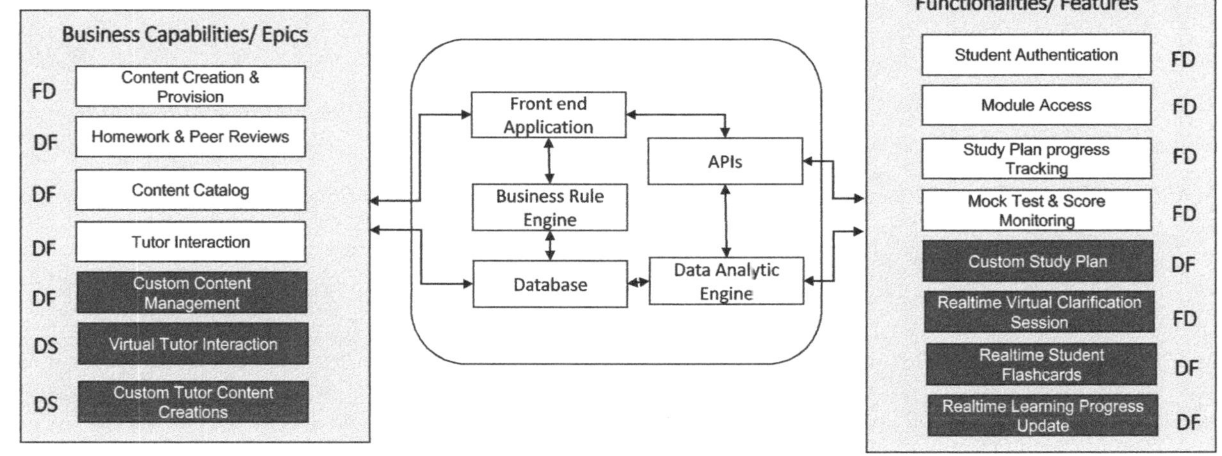

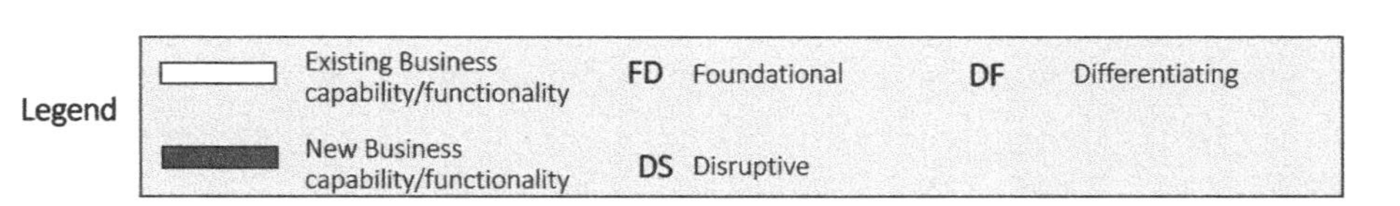

Note:: This illustrative view of Business capabilities and Functionalities does not include all that are needed for this kind of digital product. There are many more business capabilities and functionalities that are not shown here as it's an illustrative purpose

After laying out these steps, I turned to the Business Owner and asked, "Are we able to see the difference between our current approach and the expected approach, along with its benefits?"

The Business Owner nodded, "Yes, it makes perfect sense. But where do we find the time and resources to do this?"

"That's a challenge we need to manage as part of this transformation," I acknowledged. "We need to leverage the change management process. This involves defining new ways of working, clarifying roles, training, and upskilling our teams. It's also crucial to allocate the necessary time and effort to implement this approach effectively. We must communicate clearly on 'why' these new methods are essential and provide hands-on support to our practitioners as they adapt. By doing so, we ensure our success in delivering customer-centric products and achieving our business objectives."

4.7 Point 6: Create Product Roadmap

"Alright, let's dive into creating our product roadmap," I began, looking around the room at the attentive faces of the CXOs and other team members. "This process involves several key activities."

I listed them out:

- *Identify and assign value to each capability derived from digital initiatives, then prioritize them accordingly.*

- *Revisit prioritization after validation from the Solution Architect.*

- *Create a lean business case for each capability.*

- *Submit and approve the business case.*

- *Develop the product roadmap.*

"How exactly do we define the value for each capability?" the CDO asked, leaning forward with interest.

"Great question," I replied. "The product manager will drive this next step. They will start by interacting with business owners and business capability owners to understand the business value expected from each capability, which either improves efficiency, experience, effectiveness, or all three. This value is defined from three perspectives, collectively referred to as COD (Cost of Delay): the customer's perspective (user value and time criticality) and the organization's perspective (business value and opportunity enablement), along with risk reduction (optimizing the risk of future delivery).

"And then we prioritize these capabilities based on their values?" the CIO interjected.

"Exactly," I confirmed. "Each capability is prioritized based on the values we assign. But this isn't a one-time activity. The solution architects will validate this prioritization, especially considering the order of implementation. For example, some foundational capabilities might be necessary first, even if their immediate value seems lower."

"Can you give us an example?" the Business Owner asked, trying to visualize the process.

"Sure," I said. "Think about our WMS product from the last meeting. When we define it as a product with business capabilities such as integrated order processing, transportation management, and supply chain operation management, we expect to gain several benefits from CoD perspectives. Based on CoD for each capability and the effort needed to build these capabilities, it gets prioritized. We use SAFe best practice called WSJF (Weighted Shortest Job First)."

"That makes sense," the Business Owner nodded. "But how do we document this?"

"We'll use a lean business case for each capability," I explained. "The product manager will interact with business owners and business capability owners to detail this business case. It includes a description of the capability, a list of features, MVP features, overall and MVP business outcomes, and budgets."

"Let's dive into an example of a lean business case," I said, addressing the team with enthusiasm. "This will help us understand how we can structure and present our capabilities effectively."

I described an integrated order processing capability. "Imagine we streamline the order processing workflow to reduce lead times and improve accuracy. This would involve real-time order tracking, automated order verification, and integrated inventory management. For the MVP, we focus on just the real-time tracking and automated verification, aiming for an immediate increase in order accuracy by 15% and a reduction in lead times by 10%."

I continued, "The overall goal is to boost order accuracy by 30%, cut lead times by 20%, and enhance customer satisfaction scores. For the MVP, we propose a budget of $100,000 with 70 person-days of implementation effort out of a total of $0.5 million and 270 person-days to build the entire business capability."

"These business cases for each capability are then submitted to the Lean Portfolio Management Steering Committee for review and approval," I explained. "Based on their feedback, our roadmap might need adjustments to reflect changes in the order of business capabilities."

The CPO nodded thoughtfully. "So, the steering committee has the power to re-prioritize based on the overall value and implementation effort of these capabilities?"

"Exactly," I affirmed. "For instance, the committee might decide to delay the implementation of certain capabilities if they believe another capability offers more immediate value in the context of our overall strategy. In that case, we push that capability down the timeline, and our roadmap is updated accordingly."

Here's a look at our product roadmap(next page):

One of the business owners interrupted my explanation. "This all sounds perfect when you explain it, but I'm not sure how feasible it is to achieve this transformation without impacting our day-to-day operations. For example, our current product managers have more technical expertise. But clearly, from your explanation of step four, it's evident they need business domain skills as well."

"Absolutely," I agreed.

"So, how are we going to make this transition happen?" he continued. "How do we onboard new product managers with domain expertise, train them on new processes, and still sustain the delivery of our existing initiatives as planned?"

"All valid questions," I acknowledged. "These need clear plans and execution strategies, which we can manage through our Organizational Change Management."

I proposed a solution. "In this scenario, we can repurpose some roles. For example, we could elevate certain business analysts, senior product owners, and technically skilled product managers to become new product managers. These individuals would only need upskilling in new ways of working. Other product managers can be trained in both business domains and the new methodologies."

"Regarding the transition to new ways of working," I began, addressing the team's concerns, "yes, there will be an initial dip in overall productivity due to the learning curve. However, this dip will be temporary. We'll quickly reach our current

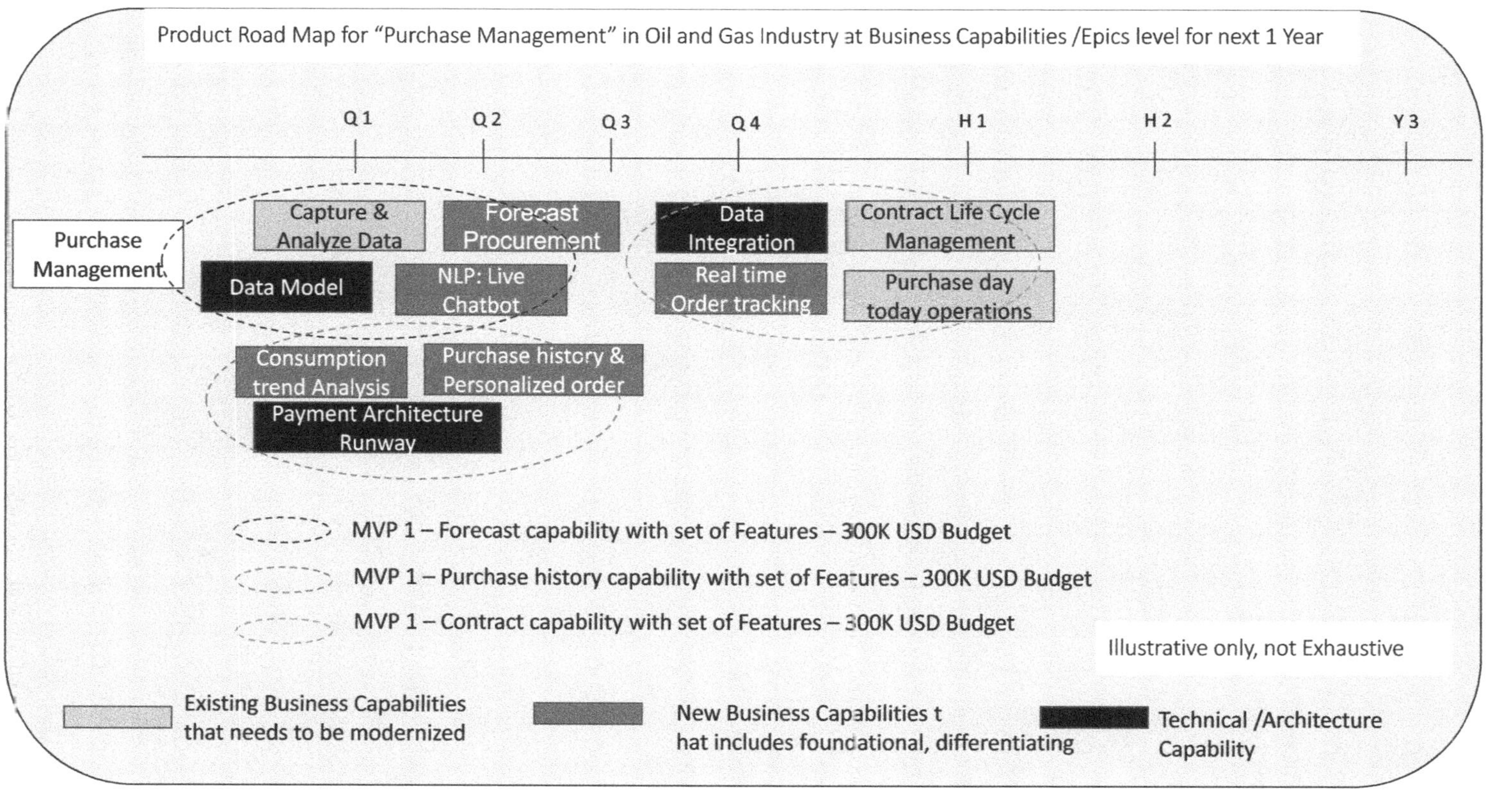

Product Road Map for "Purchase Management" in Oil and Gas Industry at Business Capabilities /Epics level for next 1 Year
Q 1
Q 2
Q 3
Q 4
H 1
H 2
Y 3
Purchase Management
Capture & Analyze Data
Data Model
Forecast Procurement
NLP: Live Chatbot
Data Integration
Real time Order tracking
Contract Life Cycle Management
Purchase day today operations
Consumption trend Analysis
Purchase history & Personalized order
Payment Architecture Runway
MVP 1 – Forecast capability with set of Features – 300K USD Budget
MVP 1 – Purchase history capability with set of Features – 300K USD Budget
MVP 1 – Contract capability with set of Features – 300K USD Budget
Illustrative only, not Exhaustive
Existing Business Capabilities that needs to be modernized
New Business Capabilities that includes foundational, differentiating
Technical /Architecture Capability

productivity levels, and as we fully transition to a product-centric approach, we'll see a significant increase."

4.8 Point 7: Empathize with customers and Define MVPs:

"Now, let's dive into Point 7," I said, pulling everyone back to what really matters. "Once we've got our products and capabilities all set, the next move is to really get into our customers' heads. We need to figure out how and why they use what we offer."

We broke it down into clear steps:

Define personas

Empathize with personas

Create journey maps

Identify new capabilities and features

"Personas are fictional characters based on real research," I explained. "They represent different types of people who might use our product in similar ways. We define personas based on various groups of internal business users and external end customers."

I continued, "Here are the steps to define personas:

Collect user information

Identify behavioral patterns

Create personas

Socialize personas

"For instance, we created a persona for an online pet food retail customer. Let's call her Emma. Emma has pets of different breeds and faces various challenges in finding the right food products. She has specific needs and preferences that we need to cater to."

Here's a snapshot of what the persona looks like for a 'digital student' who wants to take exams through an education industry provider that offers university qualification exams:

Design Digital Product from Persona perspective

Persona: Digital Student

Note: This persona represents. Student community who wants to prepare well, take exam and receive comprehensive feedback on their test score

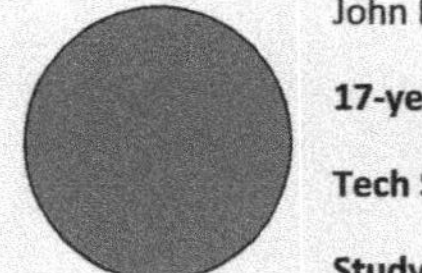

John Mike

17-year-old studying in USA

Tech Savviness Level: High

Study hours in a day 6-8 hrs

" It's important to receive feedback on my exam preparation, mock test score to align my study goals and learning plan accordingly

Key Pain Points

- Unable to create a comprehensive study plan based on past exam score

- Does not know how to identify focus areas and improve score based on practice test outcome

- Unable to view customized content as per my improvement areas

Goal and Motivation

- To successfully register for qualification exam

- To acquire necessary knowledge and skills
- To prepare well, take up mock tests and qualify for best universities

- Optimize/eliminate same errors that I committed in my previous exams

- Wants to receive real time update on my study plan progress and mock test score, area of improvements

Design Considerations

- Develop business capabilities with underlying applications that offers option to customize study plan based on test score

- Build business capabilities that provides chapter wise focus areas and day wise plan to learn

- Provide intuitive dashboard that provides insights on study progress against timeline, score improvement based on test etc.

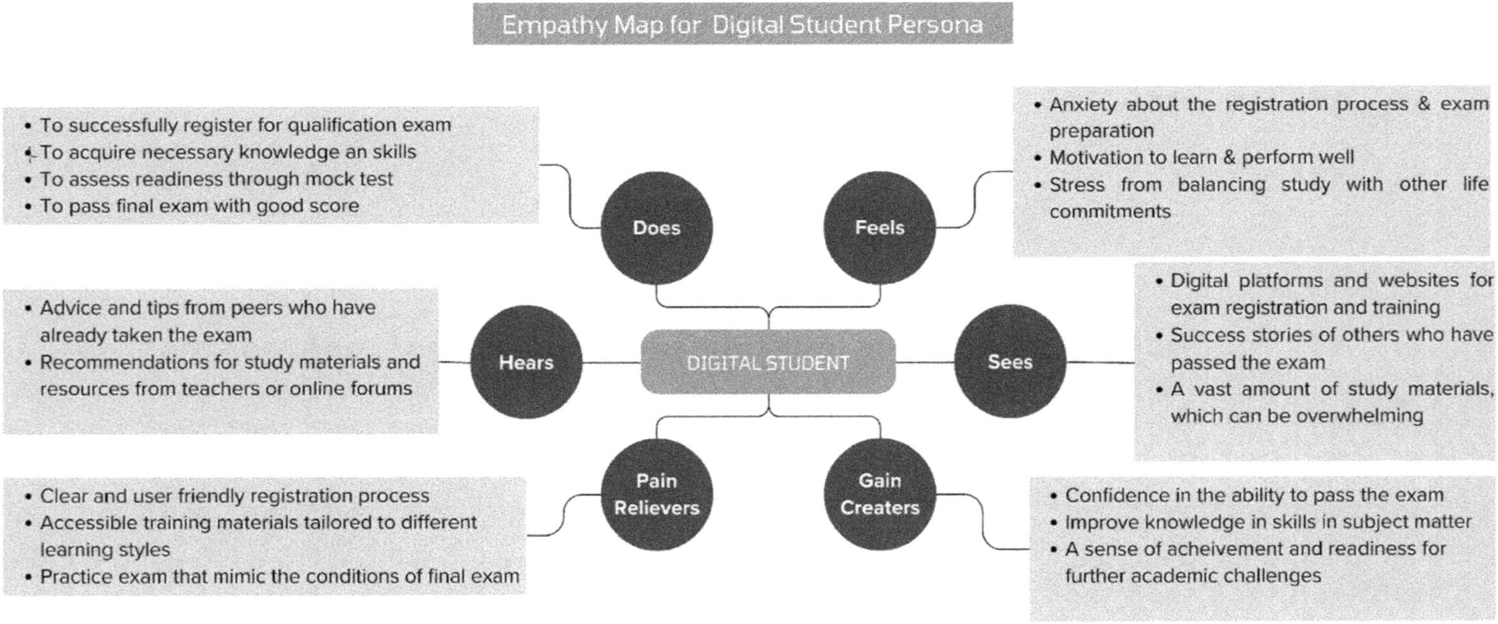

Empathy Map for Digital Student Persona

Does

Feels

Hears

DIGITAL STUDENT

Sees

Pain Relievers

Gain Creaters

To successfully register for qualification exam
To acquire necessary knowledge an skills
To assess readiness through mock test
To pass final exam with good score

Anxiety about the registration process & exam preparation
Motivation to learn & perform well
Stress from balancing study with other life commitments

Advice and tips from peers who have already taken the exam
Recommendations for study materials and resources from teachers or online forums

Digital platforms and websites for exam registration and training
Success stories of others who have passed the exam
A vast amount of study materials, which can be overwhelming

Clear and user friendly registration process
Accessible training materials tailored to different learning styles
Practice exam that mimic the conditions of final exam

Confidence in the ability to pass the exam
Improve knowledge in skills in subject matter
A sense of acheivement and readiness for further academic challenges

"The next step," I continued, "is to empathize with each persona to truly understand their problems, needs, and feelings. We select a sample group of people who fit the defined personas and conduct empathy interviews."

I paused, letting the importance of this sink in. "We empathized with one of our key persona of a digital student, and here's what we found." (refer previous page image)

I showed them an empathy map, highlighting the persona's thoughts and feelings. "This map helps us see things from the customer's perspective. It reveals what they need, the problems they're trying to solve when they interact with our organization or its products, what they feel, and what they hear from others. These insights are crucial for identifying new capabilities or features and for modernizing existing ones from 'how' and 'why' perspectives on their use."

Everyone keenly took in the information. "After empathizing with our personas, the next step is to create a customer journey map for each persona. This captures their experience as they interact with our organization through various roles and products. It's about understanding every touchpoint and ensuring we meet their needs at each stage."

Let's walk through a customer journey example of a digital student: (refer next page).

"In this approach," I explained, "we'll track every step a persona takes from logging in to logging out of our online retail app. We'll note all the challenges they encounter and the positive experiences they have with our products along the way. These insights are crucial for identifying where we need to make improvements."

"With this data," I resumed, "we can define new capabilities and features, or pinpoint exactly where existing ones need modernization. This guarantees that every product we offer is precisely tailored to meet our customers' needs and solve their problems."

Here's an example of what a product view, post persona, empathy map, and customer journey exercise looks like: (refer page number 75)

Student Journey Map that drives Product vision and Functionalities

Student Persona's Journey Map captured with integration touch points and journey experiences and improvement opportunities

1 Exploration	2 Registration	3 Training	4 Tests	5 Scoring & Feedback
"I am completing my high school next year, and I need to start preparing for college admission tests to beat the competition"	"I want to appear for entrance tests to qualify for the university admissions"	"I want to get Admitted to the best university to enhance my career"	"I will ensure that test anxiety does not hamper my performance"	"Accuracy is the key and will ensure college and career readiness"
Find Training Institute ▪ Website ▪ Social media ▪ Family ad friends ▪ Campus committees	**Register for Institute** ▪ Create my account ▪ Opt in for educational opportunity services(EOS) ▪ Select your test date ▪ Make use of your high school code	**Prepare for Test** ▪ Attend live online classes ▪ Prepare self paced course ▪ Tutoring ▪ Refer prep & Subject guide ▪ Refer free prep material	**Take Mock Tests** ▪ Refer Test day essentials ▪ Take mock tests ▪ Compare self scores ▪ Perform analysis	**Understand Scored** ▪ Compare within institute ▪ National ranks comparison ▪ Reporting Scores ▪ Verify your score ▪ Re-test policy
I FEEL CONFUSED	DECISSIVE	HOPEFUL	ANXIOUS	SATISFIED
I NEEED COUNSELOR	GUIDE	MENTOR	MOTIVATOR	ADVISER
Not able to find needed information quickly to analyze & decide about institute	Lot of documents to be uploaded manually, huge wait time for notification & confirmation	User interface for online classes is not very user friendly and number of navigations seems to huge	Test results and history tracking is not easy to access and interpret. Areas to improve not provided	Online exam page navigation to review unattended questions are not user friendly & consumes more time

Illustrative example of "Training Content Management " Product **Future** state View with Business Capabilities and its functionalities from Education Industry

Product OKRs: Increase Students Qualification % by 30% ; Improve Student experience by 50%; Improve Tutor Experience by 40%

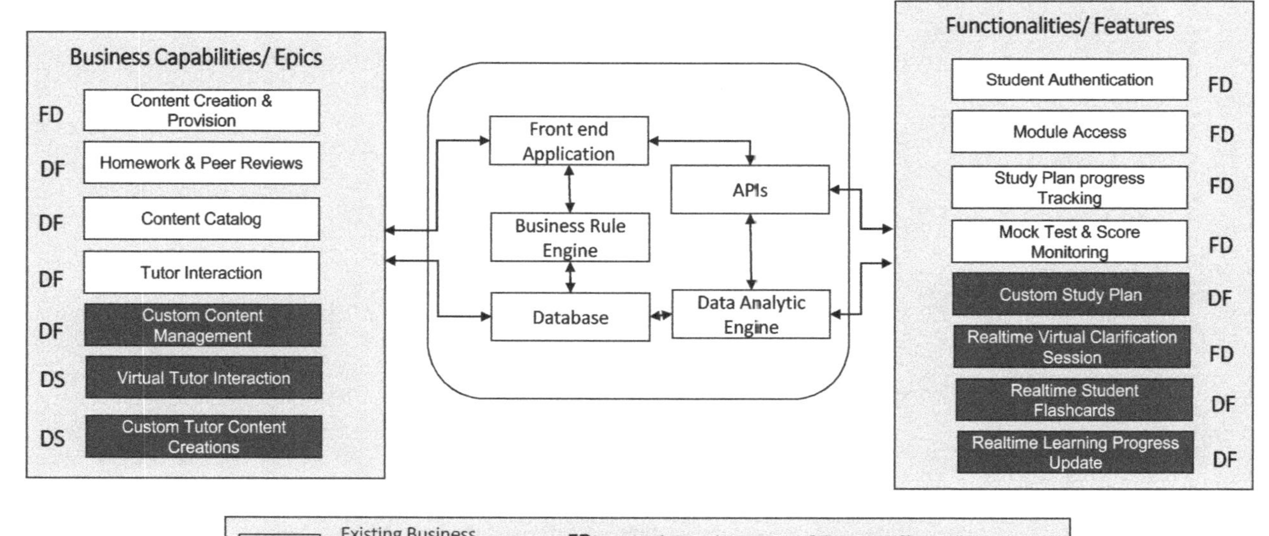

Note:: This illustrative view of Business capabilities and Functionalities does not include all that are needed for this kind of digital product. There are many more business capabilities and functionalities that are not shown here as it's an illustrative purpose

"Based on these newly identified capabilities and features and their priorities (Expected value versus implementation effort), we need to define the Minimum Viable Product (MVP) and create a feature-level roadmap."

Definition of MVP

I explained, "Once we decide on products, their business capabilities, and features, we don't design, develop, and deliver the entire product at once. Instead, we define an MVP that includes foundational business capabilities and features. We'll also outline the budget needed to build the MVP, the expected business value from its release, technical and architectural feasibility, and how we'll validate this MVP's value hypothesis at the end of its release."

Check out this roadmap that breaks down the business capabilities and big-picture goals, highlighting the MVP part for one of the oil and gas industry digital product 'Purchase Management'::

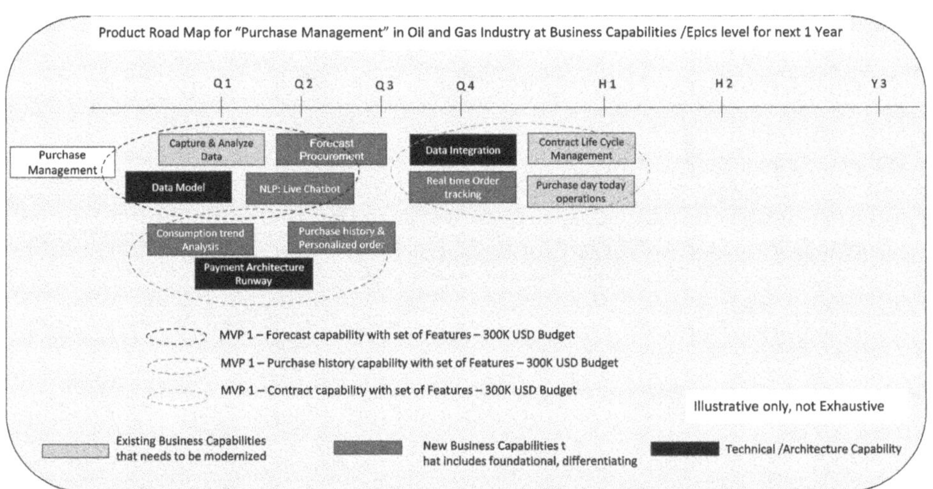

Here's a sneak peek at what's included in the feature roadmap, based on a logistics industry example: (next page)

After laying out the approach from persona identification to feature-level roadmap, the excitement in the room was palpable. The CXOs were clearly engaged and saw how it fit within their own context.

The CPO began, "In our case, merchants will be one of the key personas. Their journey involves identifying customer spending patterns, deciding which products to procure, forecasting, planning, and issuing purchase orders. These are the steps they'll follow."

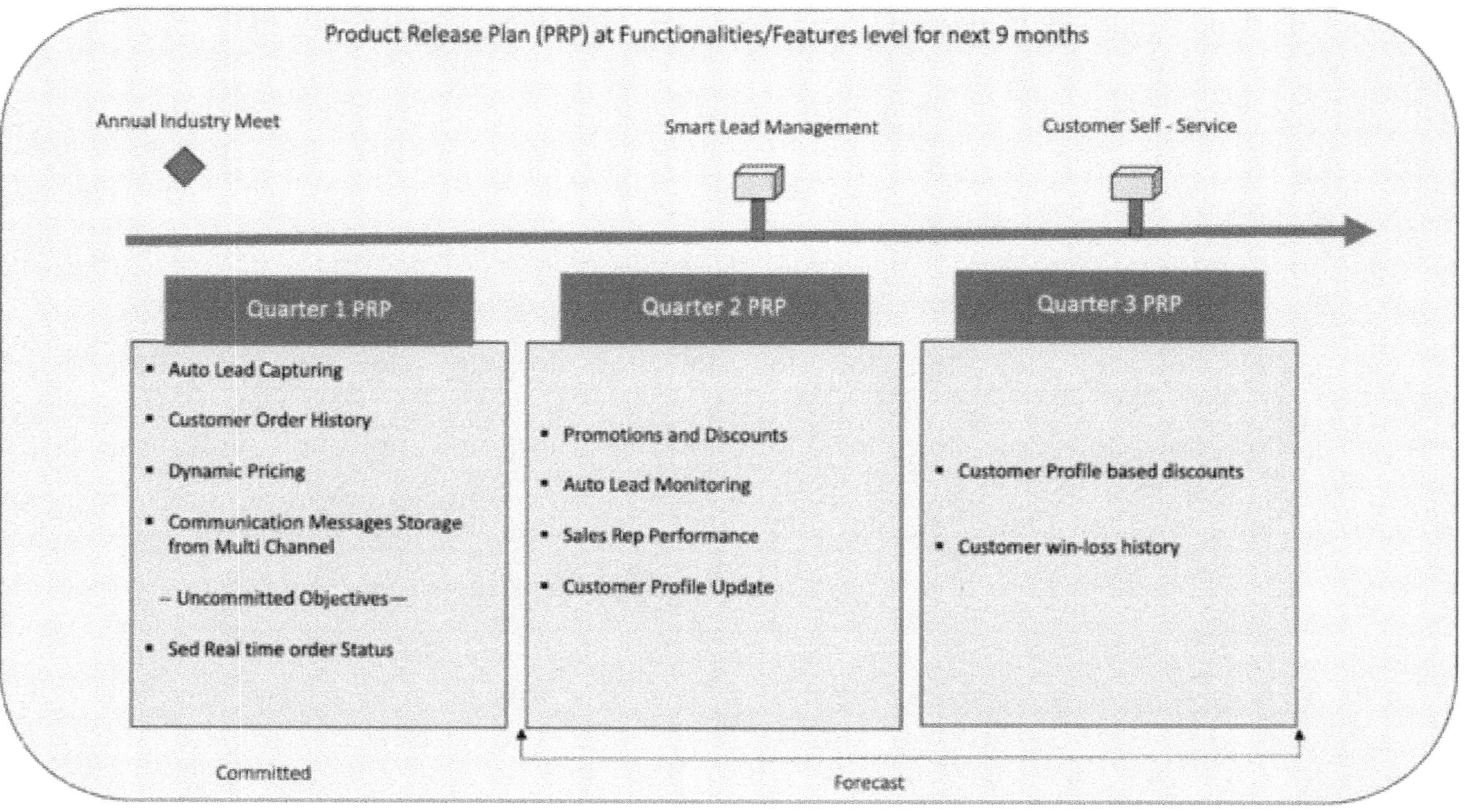

Product Release Plan (PRP) at Functionalities/Features level for next 9 months
Annual Industry Meet
Smart Lead Management
Customer Self - Service
Quarter 1 PRP
Auto Lead Capturing
Customer Order History
Dynamic Pricing
Communication Messages Storage from Multi Channel
— Uncommitted Objectives—
Sed Real time order Status
Quarter 2 PRP
Promotions and Discounts
Auto Lead Monitoring
Sales Rep Performance
Customer Profile Update
Quarter 3 PRP
Customer Profile based discounts
Customer win-loss history
Committed
Forecast

Through empathy and journey mapping, we can outline their current state experience. The Business Owner suddenly interjected, "Yes, exactly. Based on these experience inputs, product managers can identify new capabilities or features that need to be built or modernized to improve the merchants' experience and increase the efficiency of their process steps."

The CIO chimed in, "Of course, we also need to ensure these processes are performed effectively. For example, forecasting product sales efficiently is one thing, but it must also be accurate, considering customer spending patterns and past sales."

The internal coach and I shared a look, thrilled to see the whole team so well-connected and aligned. With this solid understanding, we were ready to move on to Phase 3.

Phase 3: Defining Full-Stack Teams and Planning

The focus of Phase 3 is to define the right set of full-stack teams to deliver these MVPs quickly, plan features and user stories for the quarter, evaluate MVP outcomes, and decide whether to pivot or persevere with additional business capabilities and features according to the roadmap.

The CIO interrupted, "Wait, are we planning features and user stories for three months? Isn't that just another form of waterfall?"

I responded, "That's a great point. The plan we create focuses on what business objectives will be achieved in those three months through these features. Priorities and timelines for features and user stories are decided and adjusted by the teams based on the progress they make during execution. At the end of the quarterly product release planning (PRP), teams will commit to the business objectives they will deliver and finalize user stories for the immediate sprint that begins after the PRP planning date. For subsequent sprints, high-level user stories are planned, and dependencies are committed to, but these are expected to change based on what we learn in each sprint."

4.9 Point 8: Setting Up the Product Line/Agile Release Train (ART) and Clusters of Teams

"Alright, let's move to the next point," I said, feeling the energy in the room shift. "Once we have defined the products and their MVPs, along with the necessary business capabilities or epics to test the product's benefit hypothesis, we need to set up multiple full-stack teams. These are our PODs—Product-Oriented

Development teams. They will independently handle everything from design to support, continuously evolving product capabilities and features."

I could see the CIO leaning in, clearly intrigued. "So, if we have defined the MVP," I continued, "we might need one POD for that, and a few more PODs for related products or business capabilities."

So, we're planning to set up Product Line or ART with multiple teams, like in the picture we're showing below. (next page)

Then the CIO raised his hand, "Does this mean all the people working from different functions—like business, architecture, design, agile, infrastructure, production support—need to move to a different organization and change their reporting managers?"

I smiled, knowing this question was coming. "No, that's not necessary," I replied. "This cluster of teams we set up is like a virtual organization, similar to a startup. It can include people from any function and any geography. They will continue to report to their existing functions or departments but will be dedicated to this Product Line or ART and work on delivering these products as long as they exist."

The CDO chimed in, "So, it's like creating a startup culture within our larger organization?"

"Exactly," I said, nodding. "The key objective is to ensure all necessary skills and personnel needed to deliver products and features end-to-end are organized around value. This organization enables them to deliver value independently and more quickly to market."

The CIO nodded thoughtfully, "That makes sense. It would allow us to be more agile and responsive."

The other CXOs were nodding as well, the concept clearly resonating with them. "This kind of startup culture setup, with dedicated multi-skilled teams, will help us deliver value faster," the CDO added.

4.10 Point 9: Prepare for Quarterly Product Release Planning (PRP) / PI Planning

The excitement was still crackling in the air as I geared us up for the next big leap. "Okay, team, let's dive into the heart of our Quarterly Product Release Planning, or PRP," I announced, all eyes snapping to me. "Starting from the MVPs we've

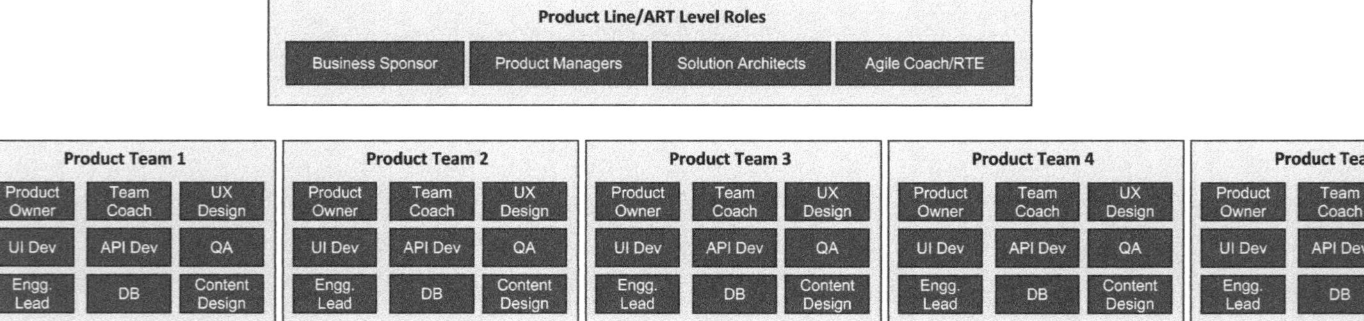

Team set up are done as multi skills teams in line with Team Topologies concept. Product Team delivers end to end features, while Platform provide services that can be consumed by all product teams, ad Enablement team deliver technology capabilities. Number of product teams varies based on product complexity, backlog size and timeline to deliver all of them

pinpointed for each product, we'll slice our epics into features, and those features into high-level user stories."

I could see the CDO nodding along, intrigued. "For instance," I continued, pointing to the illustrative product roadmap we had discussed earlier, "we have several epics planned. Out of those, only three are identified as MVPs at the epic level. Each of these epics contains multiple features. But, we're not going to implement all the features at once."

The CIO interjected, "So, we focus on the foundational features first?"

"Exactly," I responded. "We identify the foundational features necessary to evaluate each epic's value or benefit hypothesis—this is our MVP at the feature level. Each feature can have multiple user stories to implement. Instead of tackling all user stories at once, we identify the core ones. These are known as Minimum Marketable Features, or MMFs."

Check out the illustrative view below to get the scoop on MVPs at different levels and what MMF is all about: (next page)

The next step was all about ensuring we had everything ready for a successful execution. "Once we've identified the Minimum Marketable Features," I explained, "the product manager must ensure that incremental architecture—including technology stack selection, high-level microservices-oriented architecture, and UX design—is completed."

The CPO quirked an eyebrow in curiosity. "Why do we need enterprise architect involvement for product-level design?"

I smiled, expecting this question. "Good point. The enterprise architect ensures that the product's architecture aligns with the broader enterprise architecture guidelines. This alignment guarantees that our product works seamlessly with other upstream and downstream products. The EA team reviews and approves the architecture to maintain consistency and integration across the board."

"So, what's the output of this step?" asked the CIO.

"By the end of this step, we'll develop an incremental architecture and UX design based on all discovery inputs received from personas, journey maps, and empathy maps," I said. "Ideally, this design work should cover the entire scope for the next quarter. However, it's crucial to at least complete the design for the first couple of sprints' user stories. This way, the teams can start developing and delivering functionalities from the very first sprint after PRP."

Product MVP and MMF

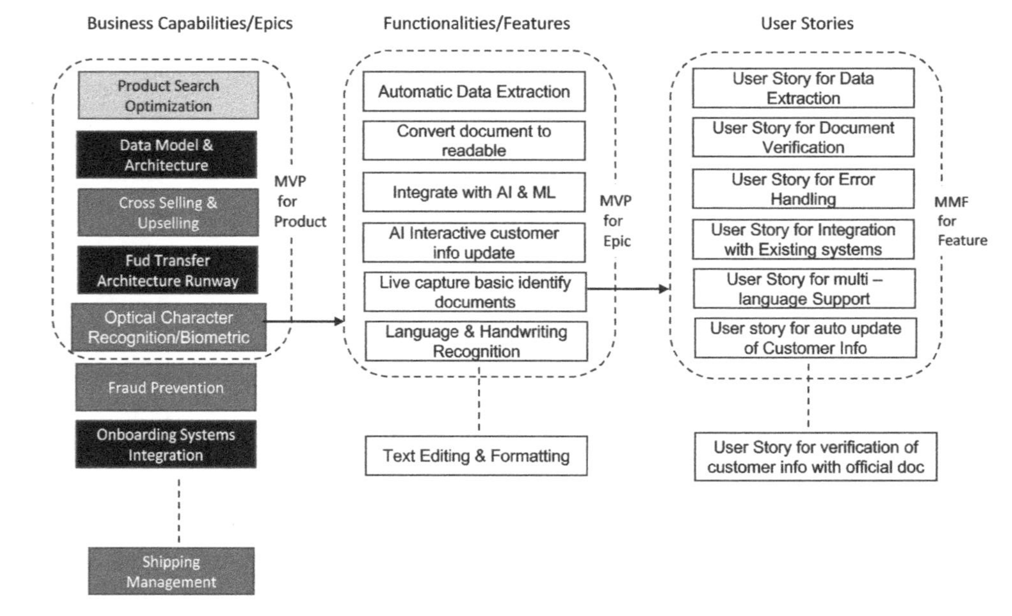

The room was filled with nods of understanding. "During this preparation," I continued, "the POD teams, part of this product line, decompose features into user stories that meet the Definition of Ready (DoR) criteria. They also identify dependencies and risks with other teams both within and outside of this product line."

"And what happens with these dependencies?" the Business Owner inquired.

"These dependencies are discussed, and additional ones might be identified during PRP," I answered. "We then align these dependencies with the relevant teams on a timeline, ensuring they are addressed promptly."

4.11 Point 10: Conduct Quarterly Product Release Planning (PRP) / PI Planning

We moved on to the crucial step of conducting the Quarterly Product Release Planning (PRP) or Planning Interval (PI). I emphasized the importance of this phase, highlighting that it is where all teams within the product line get aligned on the PI objectives for the next three months. "This is the time when we define the features and user stories that need to be designed and developed to achieve those objectives. We also determine when these objectives will be met within the quarter, what capacity we need to deliver those user stories, and align timelines for any dependencies with the respective teams."

Everyone was all ears as I went on, "So, the PRP event? It usually goes on for two to three days, depending on where the teams are from. And guess what? We've got five main goals we're shooting for with this planning gig."

I listed them out:

- Communicate business strategy/goals: Everyone needs to understand the overall direction we're heading.

- Communicate product vision: This helps in making progress towards the strategy.

- Prioritize features: Identifying the top priorities that will help achieve the product vision.

- Define user stories: Priorities, tentative timelines, dependencies, risks, and capacity requirements are all laid out.

Commitment from teams: All teams within the product line commit to the PI objectives that will be delivered in the upcoming quarter with high confidence.

The CIO leaned in, "So, what do we gain at the end of this event?"

I smiled, knowing this was a pivotal moment. "At the end of this event, the business will have great visibility into what objectives will be achieved in the upcoming quarter against the budget that will be spent. This upfront understanding is crucial for the business as they are the investors in these products, and they expect to achieve their strategic goals through these products."

Illustrative view of PRP/PI Plan:

ART PI Planning Board	Iteration 1	Iteration 2	Iteration 3	Iteration 4	Iteration 5	Iteration 6 (IP)
Milestones/ Events			Pharmacy Premium Predictor launch		Customer Care manager Bot Launch	
Trailblazers	FEA18 - Create new Static Header	FEA18 - Create new Static Header FEA23 - To correct Typographical Errors FEA25 - Disable Primary Reason Sold FEA1 - Complete/Submit IDV Dental Savings	FEA23 - To correct Typographical Errors FEA1 - Complete/Submit IDV Dental Savings FEA2 - Create Dental Savings Form 71120D	FEA2 - Create Dental Savings Form 71120D FEA3 - Create Dental Savings Form 71120D/72002V FEA5 - Save/Edit/Submit/Cancel/ Reuse for Dental Savings	FEA5 - Save/Edit/Submit/Cancel/ Reuse for Dental Savings	
Riders	FEA14 - Save and Submit MedSupp App FEA12 - Submit MedSupp App with Dsig	FEA14 - Save and Submit MedSupp App FEA12 - Submit MedSupp App with Dsig	FEA14 - Save and Submit MedSupp App FEA12 - Submit MedSupp App with Dsig FEA13 - Create & display SV and PV of a MedSupp App FEA15 - Ability to accommodate MedSupp Plans on EHub WB	FEA14 - Save and Submit MedSupp App FEA12 - Submit MedSupp App with Dsig FEA13 - Create & display SV and PV of a MedSupp App FEA15 - Ability to accommodate MedSupp Plans on EHub WB	FEA15 - Ability to accommodate MedSupp Plans on EHub WB	
Explorers	FEA18 - Building Cross-Sell capabilities for MedSupp & PDP App	FEA18 - Building Cross-Sell capabilities for MedSupp & PDP App	FEA18 - Building Cross-Sell capabilities for MedSupp & PDP App	FEA18 - Building Cross-Sell capabilities for MedSupp & PDP App	FEA18 - Building Cross-Sell capabilities for MedSupp & PDP App	
Snipers	FEA7 - Process eSignature MedSupp App FEA20 - Use Tsig as a Valid Signature for MedSupp App	FEA20 - Use Tsig as a Valid Signature for MedSupp App	FEA7 - Process eSignature MedSupp App FEA20 - Use Tsig as a Valid Signature for MedSupp App CR67 - Update Dev env for MedSupp MERE	FEA7 - Process eSignature MedSupp App		
Warriors	FEA19 - Create new Hamburger Menu	FEA19 - Create new Hamburger Menu	FEA19 - Create new Hamburger Menu 71120D/72024V	FEA19 - Create new Hamburger Menu FEA26 - View Pharmacy Calc, Phy Finder FEA4 - Create Dental + Vision	FEA4 - Create Dental + Vision 71120D/72024V	

4.12 Point 11: Execute Quarterly PRP/PI Planning

After the PRP event, the real work began. "So, the first sprint starts next working day, right?" the CPO asked, confirming the schedule.

"Exactly," I nodded. "Each sprint lasts two weeks, and we have six sprints in a quarter. The last sprint, however, is for innovation and planning (IP). There won't be any user stories planned for this period."

The CIO leaned forward, frowning slightly. "Wait, does that mean we're losing two weeks of productivity every quarter? That sounds costly."

I anticipated this concern. "It might seem that way, but it's actually an investment. These two weeks are crucial for continuous learning, innovation, and reflecting on our past performance. We also prepare for the next quarter during this time. It's essential for sustaining and scaling our delivery maturity across the portfolio."

"Alright," the CIO said, "but how do we ensure that we're not just wasting time?"

I replied, "saying it needs to be viewed as an opportunity to continuously learn, innovate new ideas, spend time to reflect on what we delivered in last quarter and leverage this learning next quarter so that we can improve continuously, spend time for preparation for next quarter planning and conduct next quarter planning event etc."

I explained further, "Though the plan is set for the entire quarter, only the first sprint plan is confirmed. Priorities and timelines for subsequent sprints can change based on what we learn. We deliver user stories at the end of each sprint that meet the Definition of Done (DoD). We also address dependencies, risks, and impediments through daily standups and Product line-level sync-ups."

The CPO seemed to understand better now. "So, we're adapting as we go?"

"Exactly," I said. "And after every sprint, we conduct a retrospective to identify and implement improvements. At the end of the quarter, there's a Product Line-level retrospective to gather insights from all teams."

The CXOs were nodding, seeing how this process fostered a culture of learning and continuous improvement. It wasn't just about delivering features; it was about enhancing our capabilities and aligning with our strategic goals.

The business owner interrupted, "Right now, our team delivers user stories once a month, and even then, not all stories committed during sprint planning get delivered. But you're saying we'll have consumable user stories every sprint. How is that possible?"

"It's a valid concern," I replied. "We need to perform value stream mapping for all activities we do from the moment a new feature or user story is requested to when it's delivered to the customer. By mapping out these steps, we can identify and eliminate non-value-adding activities and automate value-adding ones using DevOps and Gen AI. This will help us optimize lead time to deliver value. We'll start this exercise after executing a couple of sprints."

The CIO interjected, "That sounds like it will require a huge budget."

The business owner laughed, "We can spend the budget if it helps us achieve our goal of faster market response with new features critical for customer retention."

I nodded, "Absolutely. The value stream mapping will have clearly defined outcomes, and we'll measure our success after the exercise."

4.13 Point 12: Measure Outcomes

"Now we move on to measuring outcomes," I began, looking around the room to gauge their readiness. "This is where we evaluate our MVPs and decide whether to pivot or persevere."

"How do we make that decision?" asked the CPO.

"We evaluate from three perspectives: desirability, feasibility, and viability," I explained. "Desirability involves gathering feedback from customers on the delivered features. Did these foundational features address their problems? Fulfill their basic needs? If yes, we persevere and continue developing new features. If not, we pivot. This might mean repurposing the MVP for another use or scrapping it altogether to build a new one."

The CIO nodded thoughtfully, "What about feasibility?"

"Feasibility assesses if the product is technically scalable with additional features," I said. "Can we design, develop, and scale it effectively?"

"And viability?" the business owner asked.

"Viability checks if the product is helping us progress toward our business strategy," I continued. "Does it improve customer experience? Increase efficiency? If the product ticks these boxes, we move forward."

"Based on these evaluations, we decide whether to pivot or persevere," I concluded. "We measure business outcomes quantitatively, focusing on OKRs

(Objectives and Key Results) as lagging indicators and KPIs (Key Performance Indicators) as leading indicators."

Refer to the example below to see how current and future state product outcomes are measured, reported, and improved:

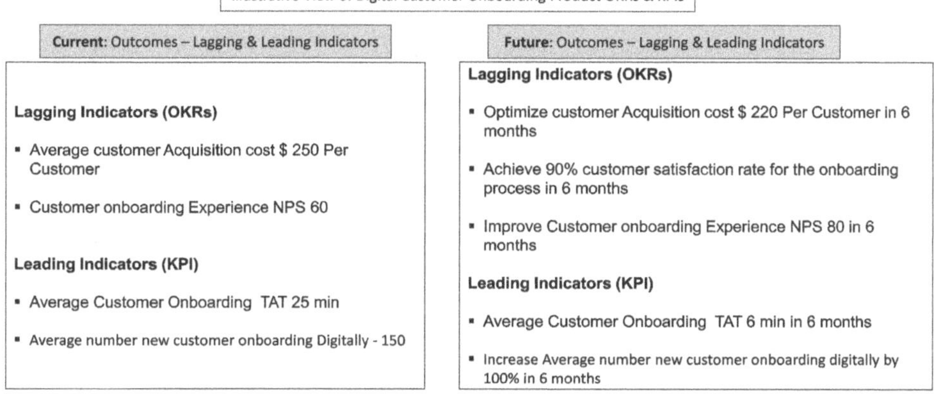

"We also measure the speed of value delivery at the end of each sprint and every quarter," I continued, trying to keep everyone on the same page. "We track metrics like velocity—story points delivered by each team—predictability—committed versus delivered story points—and sprint disruptions—number of user stories added or removed in a sprint —average lead time and cycle time for feature and user story —number of days it takes from start to complete."

Check out this illustrative dashboard showing how Product Line flow metrics work:

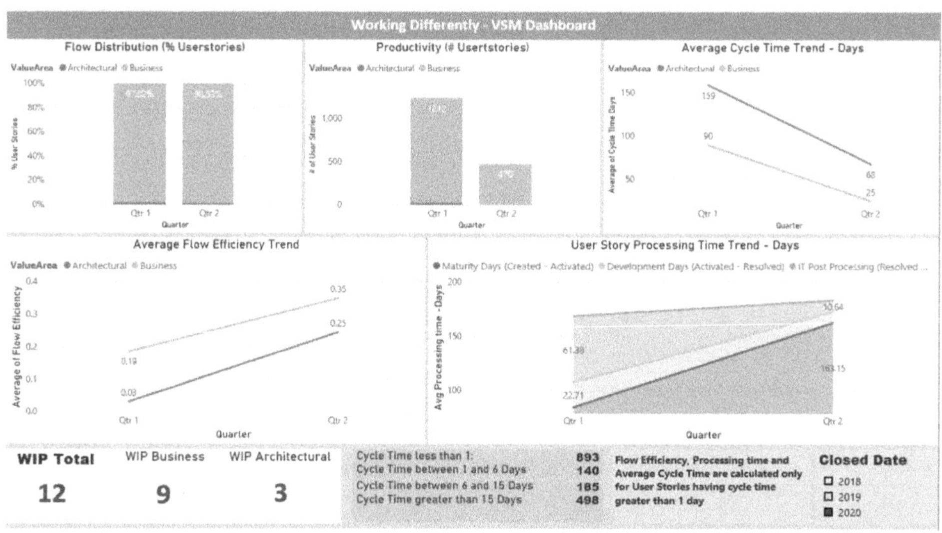

The room went silent for a bit as everyone let the information sink in. Then, the Business Owner leaned forward. "So, what's next?"

"Great question," I said, feeling the momentum build. "After explaining the 12 Points method of the product model, it's clear we need to pilot this in our retail stores business line. Here's what we agreed on for the next steps."

4.14 Get Started with Next Steps for Product Centric Model Transformation

I pulled up the slide outlining our plan. "First, we need to set up a transformation team. This team will have representation from all levels—CXOs, VPs, Directors, and middle management—and all skills, including Business, Engineering, Architecture/Design, Agile, Infrastructure, and Production Support."

The CPO nodded. "And then?"

"Next, we conduct SAFe Practice Consultant (SPC) training for all members of the transformation team," I continued. "This will ensure everyone is on the same page regarding our product model ways of working that we are going to transform to new processes."

I took a quick breather before going on, "Once that's sorted, we've got to get the word out about the need for change. Think podcasts, town halls, webinars – we've got to hit all the angles. We'll use all those channels to ensure everyone understands why we're making these changes. And finally, we'll implement the 8-step change management process from John Kotter and follow the SAFe implementation roadmap."

The moment I suggested SPC training, the CIO's eyebrow shot up in a mix of surprise and skepticism. "Do we really need to get our people trained in SAFe? Can't we create our own training content in line with these 12 points?"

I understood the concern. "I get where you're coming from," I said, "but as I mentioned earlier, these 12 points leverage all SAFe practices and other industry best practices. Training our people on SAFe will make it easier to adopt this model. Creating a custom product model framework for our industry context would require a tremendous amount of energy, effort, and extended timelines. We'd need a large workforce to define a contextualized framework and execute the transformation. Essentially, we'd have to operate as an internal consulting firm—defining processes, templates, guidelines, checklists, creating training materials, training and coaching people, and refining frameworks based on feedback. It's a massive organizational effort."

I shared an example. "In one of the organizations where I served as a transformation coach, they developed an excellent organization-specific product-centric model framework aligned with various industry best practices. They set up their own internal consulting team to define practices, tools, templates, and they built their own training curriculum for different roles. If we have the people, time, and money, we could follow that approach. However, leveraging SAFe, which already encompasses most of the practices related to our approach from points 3 to 12, is more practical. We can use other industry best practices for points 1 and 2."

After some deliberation, the executive leadership agreed. "Let's leverage the SAFe framework for implementing our product-centric model," the CIO concluded. "And we'll train all roles in line with the SAFe training curriculum and certification."

When the Business Owner expressed concerns about the upcoming transformation, I nodded, understanding the gravity of the situation. "We'll need to adjust roles, focus on upskilling, and manage this change with care," I said, meeting their eyes to emphasize our commitment. The Business Owner, after a moment's thought, nodded in agreement. "I see your point. Let's explore a potential pilot in one of our business lines."

The conversation shifted towards identifying which business line was under the most competitive pressure and evaluating the impact on current revenue performances. After a thoughtful discussion, the Senior leadership team and I arrived at a consensus. "Let's pilot this new way of working in our Retail Stores business line," we decided. This is one of the three business lines we're talking about:

Business Lines	Retail Stores	Wholesale	Online
Details	Thiran owned stores in both domestic & international airports globally	Supply goods to different retail partners who are authorized seller	E-commerce shop
Key Difference	Different Assortment model for different location	Different margin based on company & partner agreement	Differentiate by separate location and assortment planed for e-shop
Customers	Travelers, Conduct tours, Domestic customers	Partners/retailers holding license	Any online customers
Current Platform	AS/400, POS, SAP, WMS, Salesforce, PIM	Salesforce, SAP, WMS, AS/400, PIM	OMS, Co-mall, POS, PIM
Business Stakeholders			
Merchants	Yes	Yes	Yes
Planning	Yes	Yes	Yes
Wholesale	Yes	Yes	No
Logistics	Yes	Yes	No
Finance	Yes	Yes	Yes
Store Operations	Yes	Yes	Yes

4.15 illustrative example 8-step change Management process

I presented the 8-step change management process from John Kotter, which is leveraged by SAFe, using an example from a healthcare client to illustrate how we'll adopt product model ways of working.

"Let me walk you through an example of how this was applied in one of our healthcare customers," I began.

Step 1: Create a Sense of Urgency

In this healthcare organization, we saw a 30% reduction in the renewal of health insurance memberships at the end of each year. New member onboarding numbers were stagnating, and overall growth was declining.

We conducted a survey and discovered some troubling insights:

Members' experiences with enrollment, treatment, and claims processes were poor.

Medical expenses for members were increasing, meaning the selected premium plans during enrollment were not accurate, causing members to spend more money on top of their yearly premiums.

"This situation clearly calls for a change in the current way of working," I explained. "Transforming to a product model by adopting SAFe will help us get back on the growth path."

Step 2: Build a Guiding Coalition

After establishing a sense of urgency, the next critical step was forming a team to lead this transformation. We needed leaders from various portfolios—sales, clinical, providers, pharmacy, claims, and more. The selected leaders had the credibility and the decision-making power to drive this change. They became the guiding coalition that would champion this initiative.

Step 3: Form a Strategic Vision

The guiding coalition, along with the CXOs and next-level leadership, worked together to form a strategic vision. We translated this vision into measurable, differentiating business objectives:

Improve customer experience by 50%.

Increase customer retention by 40%.

Our mission was clear: to improve the health life of every serving member.

Step 4: Enlist a Volunteer Army

To achieve these ambitious goals, we needed to focus on the entire end-to-end journey of the member—from inquiring about the right health plan coverage to submitting claims and renewing memberships. This comprehensive approach meant touching upon all existing digital products.

We organized people from various portfolios and formed a network organization, a startup within the larger organization. We had to set up a couple of Agile Release Trains (ARTs) to deliver digital products across all product lines that would help us achieve the objectives defined in step 3.

"By forming these dedicated teams," I explained, "we ensured that everyone was aligned and working towards the same goals, driving the transformation with focus and agility."

Step 5: Enable Action by Removing Barriers

We launched two Agile Release Trains (ARTs) focused on enhancing the enrollment stage experience. One of the notable improvements was implementing a search and choose plan functionality, which significantly enhanced user satisfaction.

However, we faced initial barriers. Onboarding skilled personnel was a challenge, and the extensive architectural changes required coordination with various stakeholders. By working closely with these stakeholders, we successfully removed the obstacles and kept the momentum going.

Step 6: Generate Short-Term Wins

Our first ART's launch was a milestone. We implemented key business capabilities like the search and choose plan feature, which streamlined the healthcare plan enrollment process. Another significant achievement was the Pharmacy Predictor, which helped members select the most accurate premium plan during enrollment.

Step 7: Sustain Acceleration

To sustain this momentum, we continued implementing these changes over multiple Program Increments (PIs). We also launched a second ART to address the extensive set of Epics related to the end-to-end members' journey, ensuring continuous improvement and value delivery.

Step 8: Institute Change Acceleration

With the successful execution of two ARTs, we institutionalized the SAFe adoption across other portfolios, including Retail Sales and various segments like Medicare, Medicaid, and group business. Over three PIs, we implemented these key functionalities, cementing the change and ensuring sustained growth and efficiency.

"By systematically addressing each step," I concluded, "we not only improved our processes but also created a culture of continuous improvement and product centric model transformation."

After walking through these eight steps, the CXOs could clearly visualize the process we would follow to implement the 12 Point Method model. They also realized the level of their involvement in each step to make the transformation successful.

I wrapped up the session, saying, "Now that we've covered the framework, let's discuss our next steps in detail."

4.16 Create Transformation plan

The CIO leaned forward, "What's the first action we need to take?"

"We need to identify the right leaders and set up the transformation management office or Lean Agile Center of Excellence (LACE)," I replied. "These leaders will drive the change."

"Who should be part of this team?" the CDO asked, glancing around the room.

"We need people who understand both the business and technical aspects, who also have credibility with experience, able to make decisions and influence change," I explained. "Let's propose some names."

After a brief discussion, the senior leadership proposed several names. We evaluated their ability to fulfill the roles and secured their consensus to join the team.

They put together a transformation roadmap and clearly spelled out what they want to achieve at the end of each month.

Transformation Activities Milestones	Product Centric Model Transformation Activities	Month 1	Month 2	Month 3	Month 4	Month 5	Month 6	Month 7	Month 8	Month 9
Set up transformation office	Identify, onboard & train transformation team on SAFe	X								
	Communicate need for change/adopt product centric model ways of working	X								
Define Right Business Strategy	Perform current state business performance assessment	X	X							
	Define future state business strategy		X	X						
Create current state blueprint of products	Refine & communicate business operation value stream with customers, value delivered,		X							
	Identify current state digital products, business capabilities, Functionalities and applications		X	X						
	Identify technology, architecture constraints to achieve business strategy		X							
Envision future state of portfolio vision and future state product blueprint	Create portfolio current & Future state digital products, and customer experience			X						
	Define new products, business capabilities and create roadmap			X						
Select and setup product lines with product teams, and conduct trainings	Select product line/ART to pilot product model ways of working, setup product teams				X					
	Train all team members on SAFe aligned industry best practices				X	X				
	Define playbook, refine roles & responsibilities			X						

Transformation Activities Milestones	Product Centric Model Transformation Activities	Month 1	Month 2	Month 3	Month 4	Month 5	Month 6	Month 7	Month 8	Month 9
Prepare for Quarterly Product Release Planning (PRP)/Planning Interval (PI) Planning	Conduct product discovery with target customers/personas, create journey map				■					
	Conduct periodic workshops with PMs, Architects, UX design to ensure preparation for quarterly PRP				■	■				
Conduct quarterly PRP/PI	Conduct 2 to 3 days of breakout sessions with all the product teams						■			
	Create quarterly PRP/PI with Business objectives, Functionalities releases timeline						■			
Quarterly PRP/PI Execution	Quarterly PRP Execution – Sprint level plan & execution							■	■	■
	Conduct Demos, Measure outcome, Reflect on lessons learnt at the end of every sprint							■	■	■
	Implement Devops, built-in quality strategies, measure flow of value							■	■	
	Manage dependencies, risks and ensure improved predictability							■	■	■
	Incremental value delivery every sprint with integration of dependent functionalities							■		
	Prepare for next quarterly PRP/PI planning							■	■	
Measure outcomes & Continuous improvement	Measure ways of working and product outcome metrics at sprint and quarterly level							■	■	
	Quarterly reflect on lessons learnt and implement actions to demonstrate continuous improvement									■
Manage & Accelerate transformation	Handhold transformation journey for two quarters									■

As I stepped out with Mr. Agile for a quick breather, I let my mind wander over the extensive discussion we had just wrapped up.

"We've covered a lot of ground today," I remarked, taking a deep breath.

Mr. Agile nodded, "Absolutely. The product-centric model and those 12 points are really going to transform how Thiran operates."

I reflected on our detailed discussions, "Every point raised questions and concerns—whether about the necessity of these steps, challenges from the practitioners' perspective, or the difficulties of implementation. But we debated each issue thoroughly and reached a consensus."

"It was great to see how the senior leadership connected with the examples from different industries," Mr. Agile added. "It really helped them understand the 12 Point Method."

"Yes," I agreed. "The commitment to a deep dive assessment into two selected projects as samples is a big step. This will help us gather current state details on strategy, products, and ways of working."

Mr. Agile grinned, "And it sets the stage for communicating the identified problems with solid quantitative data."

"The leadership team is ready to pilot the 12 Point Method for our Retail stores business line," I continued. "If we can demonstrate success there, we'll extend this model to other business lines."

Mr. Agile chimed in, "Everyone—from the leadership team to the next level leaders and us as transformation coaches—is aligned on the next steps for implementing the 12 Point Method."

"We had a great discussion on how we'll leverage John Kotter's 8-step change management process," I added. "It's crucial for ensuring the success of this product-centric model transformation."

"Exactly," Mr. Agile said. "The leadership team is on board with communicating the sense of urgency for this change. It's essential for addressing Thiran's current challenges and ensuring our competitiveness and growth."

"And after this communication, we'll conduct in-depth assessments with full buy-in from program and team leaders," I noted. "That will lead us towards creating a future state blueprint."

Mr. Agile looked thoughtful, "It's going to be a lot of work, but with everyone aligned and committed, I think we're ready."

5

Creating a Winning Business Strategy

The last six weeks have been an absolute rollercoaster since we received the go-ahead from senior leadership for our product-centric overhaul. A real highlight was a 5-minute chat with our CEO, aptly named "Why Product centric Model." This interview caught fire within the company, with everyone glued to their screens watching it multiple times. As an enterprise transformation coach, the CEO shared insights on the importance of the shift and the positive impact it would have on us and our customers.

We also formed the Lean-Agile Center of Excellence (LACE) team. This team is made up of leaders who can make decisions and influence changes related to our organizational structure, role realignment, upskilling, tool and technology choices, infrastructure, and more. The LACE/transformation team completed their SAFe SPC training and then created a transformation roadmap. They began working in two-week sprints to plan, deliver, and reflect, all with the goal of achieving our transformation objectives.

Transformation team, in collaboration with business leaders, conducted extensive research on our current business performance and where we want to be in the next one to three years. Using these insights, we established a baseline of our current state and defined key objectives that will drive the growth and efficiency improvements of our retail business line.

In this chapter, we'll explore the journey of creating our business strategy. In today's digital disruption era, two significant factors stand out. First, customer needs and market demands are evolving rapidly as products and services become more accessible. Customers now have the convenience of fulfilling their needs at competitive prices. Second, technological advancements are enhancing industries' capabilities to meet these demands.

Industries are increasingly aware of these shifts and are attempting to turn disruption into opportunity. However, statistics reveal that only 20% of industries have successfully defined and executed a business strategy. The remaining 80% are either beginning to think about transformation or are still unsure where to start.

They face questions like, "How do we define a digital strategy? How do we execute it? What changes are needed in our business models, technology architecture, organizational structure, and culture?" These questions remain unanswered for many leaders.

As a CEO, some of the questions I frequently consider might include, "What is our organization's position in the market? Where do we want to be? How do we increase revenue by 50% while improving customer and employee experiences?"

If I were the CDO, I'd be thinking, "How can I support my CEO on this journey? Should I focus on implementing digital capabilities in small, manageable areas, or should I aim to build a comprehensive digital ecosystem by transforming technology solutions into products that enhance the customer experience?"

As a CPO, I would be thinking about what kind of new digital products or business capabilities introduced to the existing landscape will make us competitive in the market.

As the CIO, my questions would be, "How can I back up the CEO and CDO? How can I boost IT agility through smart strategies and a modernized technology landscape that delivers digital products and platforms within a product-centric, agile, and innovative culture?"

To answer all these questions and thrive in the digital disruption era, organizations must increase their pace of internal change to match the rapid market changes. They need to adopt a hybrid business strategy model that combines inside-out and outside-in perspectives.

The inside-out approach dives deep into the heart of the industry, weaving through the value chain, tapping into the true potential of supplier opportunities, and slicing down production costs. It's all about mastering the art of efficiency to lead the market in cost optimization . On the flip side, the outside-in perspective takes a walk in the customer's shoes, focusing on what truly matters to them. It's about crafting a value proposition so compelling that customers are happy to pay more, setting the industry apart.

As shown in the figure below, by focusing on reducing supplier costs while simultaneously increasing what customers are willing to pay, we're effectively widening the gap—the "wedge"—between them. This strategy is our secret to outperforming competitors, capturing more market share, and increasing profits.

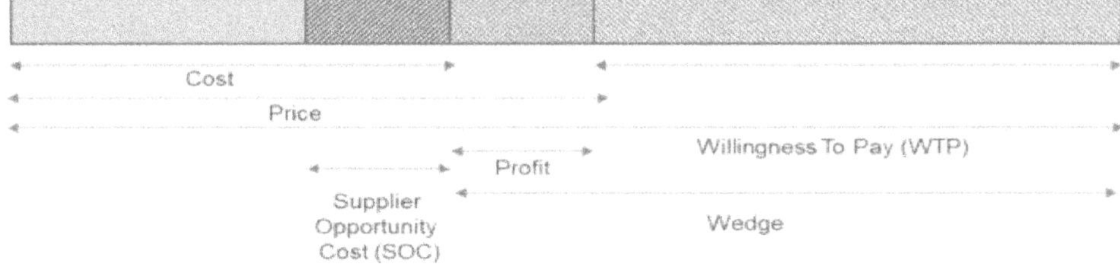

Hybrid Business Strategy's Value Proposition

In today's digital marketplace, people need banking services, but they don't need to visit a bank. They need groceries and everyday commodities, but they don't necessarily want to visit retail stores. They need healthcare services, but not exclusively at hospitals. They require prescription drugs, whether or not they visit a pharmacy. They need to purchase insurance policies, pay premiums, and process claims, but they don't want to meet insurance agents in person.

Customers expect these services to be digitally accessible and want them to be personalized and cover the entire service provision from start to finish. The hybrid business strategy focuses on meeting these expectations by delivering value through both optimized internal processes and enhanced customer experiences.

Example 1

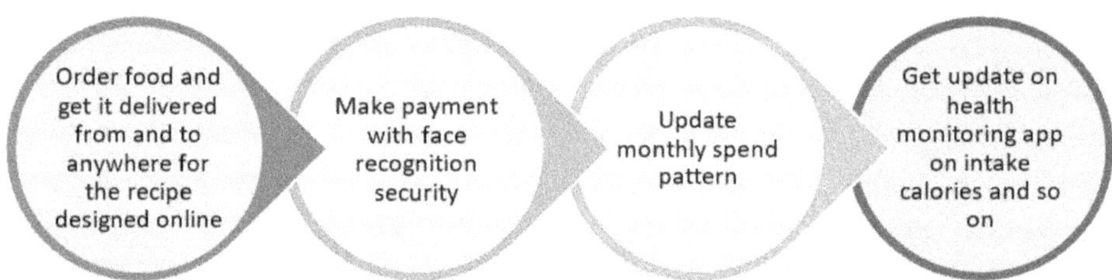

Example 2:

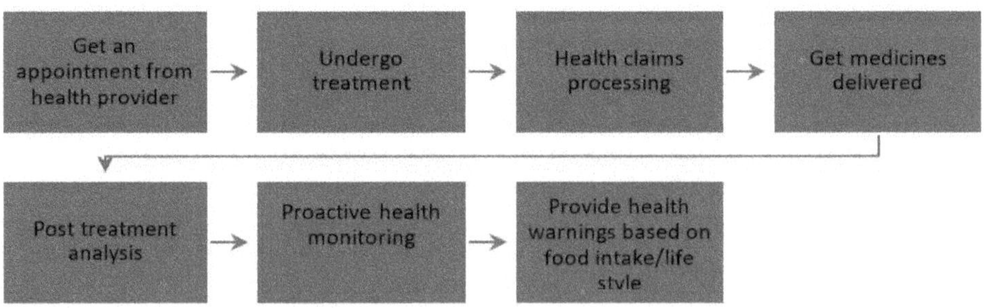

Don't these scenarios scream for a fresh take on business strategy? Aren't they nudging us toward the next wave of digital business models?

To map out this hybrid business strategy, we've got two major moves to make: first, take the pulse of our current business performance; then, use that insight to craft a forward-looking business strategy.

5.1 Diagnosis of Current Business Performance

To assess our current business performance, we implemented the CARE framework. This framework helps us understand the organization's current state by creating a report based on four key perspectives:

Cost Leader vs. Differentiator:

We performed a value chain analysis (comparing various costs against competitors) and a value proposition analysis (evaluating value proposition attributes against competitors). This helps us see if we're focusing on cost optimization through efficiency improvements or if we're standing out as a differentiator by emphasizing value through innovation.

Agility:

We assessed both business and IT agility, looking at technology, infrastructure, and people. This includes our ability to design innovative digital solutions and deliver them quickly and at scale, along with creating an environment that supports adaptability and a growth mindset.

Revenue Threat vs. Growth:

We evaluated our revenue health, identifying threats to existing revenue and opportunities for growth. This helps us understand where we stand and where we can improve.

Emerging Digital:

We examined our current digital capabilities to perform business operations and created a current state system activity map. This map shows our digital business maturity and how well we are leveraging digital opportunities for growth.

Based on the results from the CARE framework, we defined target state outcomes along with the expected timelines to achieve them. The current state of our organization's agility and emerging digital capabilities are key indicators. By improving these two areas, we can position ourselves as a market differentiator and become the first choice for our customers.

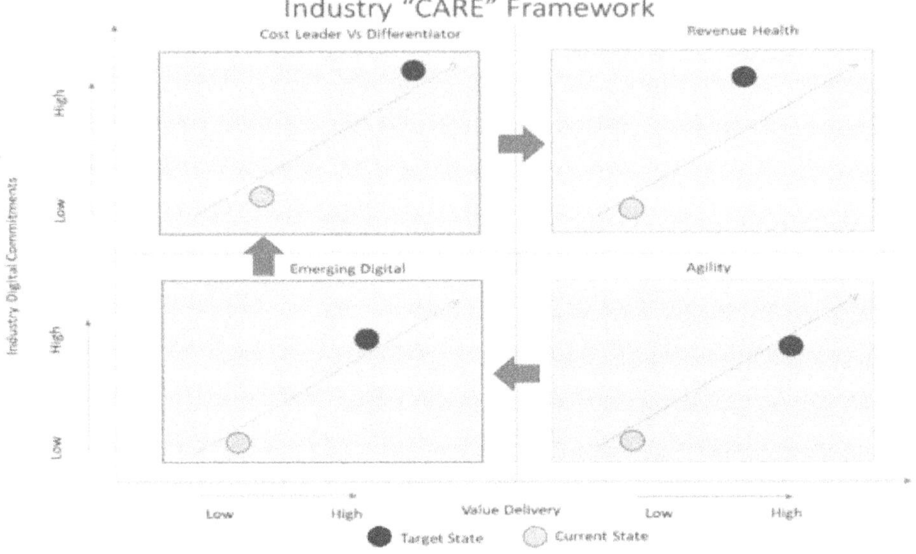

With this understanding of our current business performance, let's dive into the details of how we executed this using the CARE framework:

5.1.1 Gather Current State Data

5.1.2 Create current state activity map

5.1.3 SWOT and TWOS analysis

5.1.4 Analyze and create current state business performance report

5.1.1 Gather Current State Data

Part 1: Define Boundaries for Data Collection

First, we needed to define the boundaries and scope of the data collection process. This included:

1. Restate the Scope of Current Business:

Who are our customers? What are their needs? How are we currently fulfilling these needs?

2. Define Business Goals:

Goals include retaining existing customers, increasing new customer footprint, optimizing business costs, boosting customer satisfaction, and improving compliance and security.

3. Identify and Prioritize Competitors:

Identify the main competitors in our business area, the suppliers supporting product development or service provision, and profile the customers consuming our products or services.

Part 2: Define Parameters for Data Collection

We then defined the specific parameters for data collection, which included:

1. Financial Performance:

Assessing revenue, costs, and profitability.

2. Organizational Structure & Roles:

Understanding how our teams are organized and their roles.

3. Business Capabilities in Digital:

Evaluating our digital strengths and weaknesses.

4. Technology Capabilities:

Looking at our IT infrastructure and tech stack.

5. IT Agility:

Assessing how quickly we can adapt and implement new technologies.

6. Business Value Chain View & Cost:

Analyzing costs across the value chain.

7. Business Value Proposition View:

Understanding what sets us apart in the eyes of our customers.

Part 3: Collect Data

We collected data from two perspectives: Inside-Out and Outside-In.

Inside-Out View

This perspective focuses on our internal operations and capabilities. We evaluated the extent and maturity of our digital capabilities and how they serve our customers. We assessed the efficiency of our internal business processes in delivering products and services, and examined our technology capabilities to understand our ability to deliver quickly and adapt to changes. Additionally, we analyzed the key activities and costs involved in providing our products and services, creating a current state activity map. These parameters help us understand our strengths and weaknesses—our ability to supply and grow in the market.

Outside-In View

This perspective involves looking at our competitors and the market. From the competitor's perspective, we examined market share and key revenue-generating products and services. We also assessed their digital capabilities and maturity, the efficiency of their internal processes compared to ours, and their technology capabilities for faster delivery and agility. From the market perspective, we looked at the market share of all the competitors and identified emerging digital trends that could improve customer experience and business operation efficiency.

Additionally, we considered changing customer needs based on demographics, new technology trends that enhance efficiency and agility, and our value proposition compared to competitors. These parameters help us identify threats from competitors and opportunities in the market—our demand in the global market.

By collecting data from these two perspectives, we gained a comprehensive view of our current state. This includes understanding where we stand in terms of digital capabilities, internal process efficiency, and market competitiveness, as well as identifying areas for improvement to achieve our growth and market position.

For instance, an investment digital bank has the capability to onboard customers to its trading platform and enable direct trading. Similarly, a retail store might allow customers to pick up items in-store and check out using online payments via mobile. These examples illustrate how digital capabilities can enhance customer experience and operational efficiency.

Collecting data from these perspectives gives us a comprehensive view of where we stand and what we need to improve to achieve our growth and market position.

Here is the current state business data for our retail store's business line: (next page)

5.1.2 Create current state activity map

In the retail store industry, understanding the total cost associated with each step from product identification to the final sale and receipt of payment from the customer is crucial. This involves a comprehensive value chain cost analysis. Here's a high-level overview of the costs involved in each step:

- *Product Identification & Development:* Costs related to market research, product design, and development.

- *Sourcing & Procurement:* Expenses for finding suppliers, negotiating contracts, and purchasing raw materials.

Sr. No.	Business performance Parameters	Thiran Retail Store	Competitor
1	Finance performance	Revenue declines 10 to 17% QoQ with increasing debt	Revenue increases by 20% QoQ with 18% margin
2	organization structure & roles	Command & control functional oriented	Generative culture, Product centric
3	Business capabilities in digital	30% business capabilities digitalized	75% business capabilities are digitalized
4	Technology capabilities	40% applications are legacy and monolith architecture	90% of the applications are modernized with micro services architecture
5	IT Agility	Average time to deliver one project – 32 weeks	Average time to deliver one business capability – 18 weeks
6	Business value chain view & cost	75% of the total product cost	50% of the total product cost
7	Business value proposition view	5%	15 to 20%
8	Operations cost	Increasing by 10%	Decreased by 20%
9	Operations efficiency	Decreased efficiency by 15 to 20%	Improved efficiency by 30%
10	Employee Attrition	Increased by 15%	Decreased by 20%

- *Manufacturing & Production:* Costs for manufacturing, including labor, materials, and overhead.

- *Distribution & Logistics:* Expenses for warehousing, transportation, and handling.

- *Marketing & Customer Attraction:* Costs associated with advertising, promotions, and other marketing activities.

- *Sales & Operations:* Operational expenses for running stores, including staffing, utilities, and equipment.

- *Customer Service & Retention:* Costs for maintaining customer service teams and loyalty programs.

- *Payment:* Transaction fees and other costs associated with payment processing.

- *Returns & Refunds:* Costs for handling returns, exchanges, and refunds.

In the retail store industry, understanding value proposition by calculating the willingness to pay (WTP) for products is essential. WTP refers to the maximum price a customer is willing to pay for a product or service. This metric varies significantly among customers and is influenced by both extrinsic factors (like age, gender, and income) and intrinsic factors (such as personal preferences and values).

Here's a general formula to calculate WTP:

$$\text{WTP} = \square \ / \ \square$$

Where:

$\square$ is the value or utility that the individual derives from the product/service/resource.

$\square$ is the quantity of the product/service/resource.

For example, on Amazon, the average willingness to pay can be influenced by various factors such as the economy, product popularity, scarcity, and perceived quality. While specific figures for the average WTP on Amazon are not readily available, it's known that sale-related fees for sellers range from 8% to 45% of each product's selling price, with the average seller paying about 15%.

Understanding these costs and value propositions is vital for any retail business aiming to optimize their operations and better meet customer needs. By breaking down and analyzing each step of the value chain, retailers can identify areas for cost savings and efficiency improvements. Similarly, by understanding what drives customer willingness to pay, businesses can better position their products in the market, adjust pricing strategies, and enhance customer satisfaction.

This dual approach—analyzing both costs and customer value—helps retailers stay competitive and responsive in a rapidly changing market.

With an understanding of cost focus and value proposition focus, we aimed to gain a clear picture of our business strategy. To achieve this, we created a current state activity map by identifying key activities across the entire value chain. This map helps us understand our strengths and weaknesses. It shows whether our activities focus solely on operational efficiencies—doing the same things differently than our competitors—or if there are activities that provide a competitive advantage by offering unique value, which means doing different things altogether.

Take our retail stores at airports, for example. These stores gather customer insights, understand spending patterns, brand preferences, and shopping habits of specific segments. Based on this information, they curate an attractive product mix, allowing customers to buy in-store, pay with cash or cards, pick up products, and leave the store quickly. While these activities are similar to what other competitors do, the focus is on doing them differently to optimize costs. In this scenario, the airport retail stores position themselves as "cost leaders."

Below is an example of a current state activity map created for retail stores in airports:

Current System Activity Map for Retails Store Business Value Chain

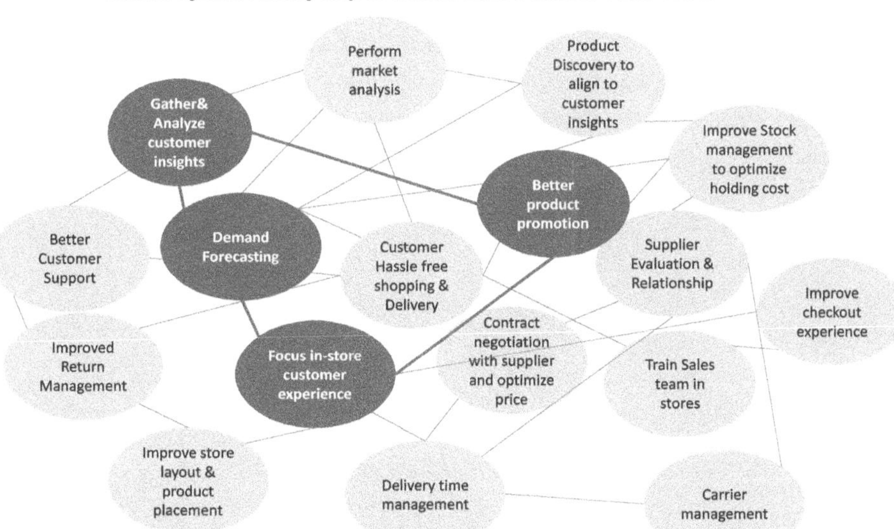

Based on the current state system activity map, we have created a high-level business operation value stream. This identifies customer needs and delivers value through a series of value creation steps, as illustrated below:

All these value creation steps in the current business operation value stream, which transforms triggers into value delivery, focus solely on optimizing costs by performing the same activities as competitors differently.

5.1.3 Conducting the SWOT & TWOS Analysis

With our current business performance data in hand, we gathered in the meeting room for a crucial workshop. The group included the Business Owner, Product Managers, the Business Architect, the Agile Coach, and myself. I had the agenda slide displayed on the LED TV screen, ready to dive into our discussion.

Just as I was about to start the briefing, the Business Architect interrupted, "Why didn't we call the Enterprise Architect? We need their input on the future state from a technical impact and feasibility perspective."

"Good point," I replied. "We definitely need their presence to complete the activities related to the future state business capabilities view. That's why we've planned to include them in the next meeting. Today, our focus is on discussing SWOT analysis, and considering different business strategies for defining our future state."

Most of the workshop participants had already completed their SAFe LPM and SAFe APM training. Some of the leaders were also trained as Certified Product Managers, well-versed in industry best practices. This background knowledge ensured everyone had a solid understanding of SWOT analysis, setting the stage for a productive session.

We kicked off the workshop by explaining each step of the SWOT analysis, then broke into smaller groups to gather everyone's input on our strengths. The breakout sessions were lively, with participants reviewing their preparation work and

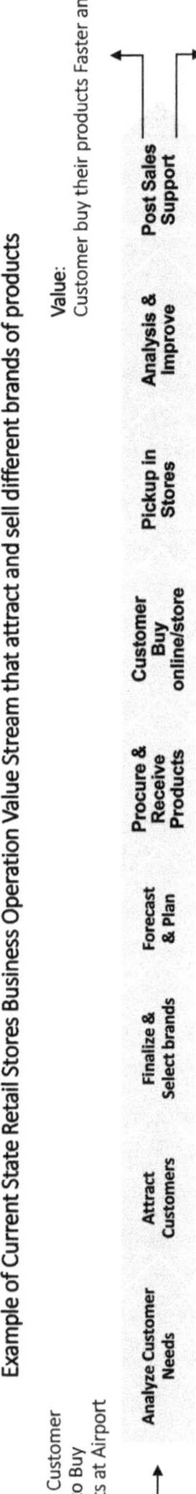

identifying key strengths. After 20 minutes, we regrouped to discuss the outcomes. We clarified some questions, then went back for another 10-minute breakout to finalize our strengths.

We repeated this process for weaknesses, opportunities, and threats. The room was buzzing with ideas, and after two hours, we had completed the SWOT analysis. The exercise was thorough and enlightening, yielding the following output:

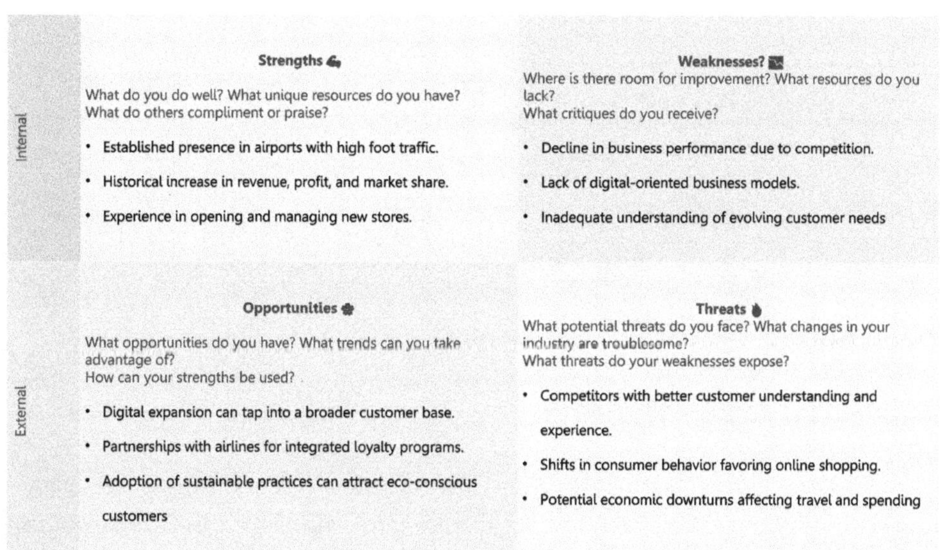

We broke for lunch, and I took the opportunity to casually check in with everyone about how they felt the workshop was going. Some of the product managers were excited, saying they felt more involved and that the structured approach was helping them consider all perspectives. The business leads shared that although they had done SWOT analyses before, they had never done it in such a comprehensive and structured way. They could see how this would be very useful for defining the future state of the portfolio and helping achieve our business OKRs.

After lunch, we dove into the TWOS analysis. This approach helps convert SWOT inputs into actionable steps. We needed to answer four powerful questions to guide our digital initiatives:

1. How can we use our strengths to exploit and maximize opportunities?

2. How can we apply our strengths to overcome present and potential threats?

3. How can we leverage our opportunities to overcome weaknesses?

4. How can we minimize our weaknesses and avoid threats?

We had breakout sessions for the next 1.5 hours to identify answers for each of the questions above, resulting in the following TOWS analysis:

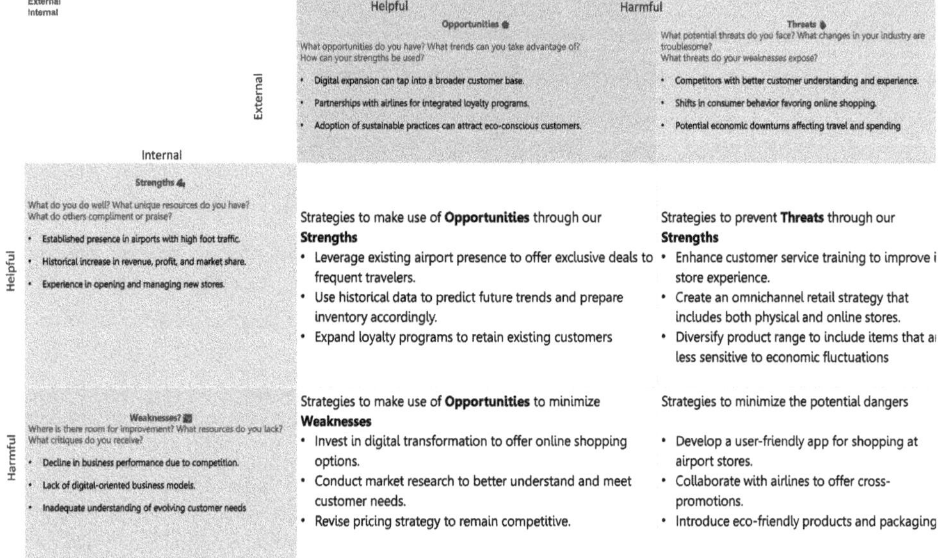

As part of diving into SWOT and TWOS analysis, we've pinpointed "digital initiatives" as the next big step our retail store must take. These initiatives will top our priority list and shape our vision for the future business strategy.

All the stakeholders in the meeting reviewed TWOS actions and we agreed to identify new business capabilities/ modernize existing business capabilities, or combination of both that will realize those TWOS actions/digital initiatives.

We then applied the logistics industry example discussed in Chapter 1 to understand the approach. According to this example, one of their strengths is "multiple distribution channels," and one of the opportunities is the customer being digitally savvy. They leveraged both to identify a digital initiative titled "Modernize Mobile App to Increase Customer Footprint," which falls into the first quadrant of the TWOS matrix (SO). To actualize this digital initiative, the team brainstormed and identified a set of new business capabilities and a set of existing capabilities that need to be built and modernized, as illustrated in the figure below:

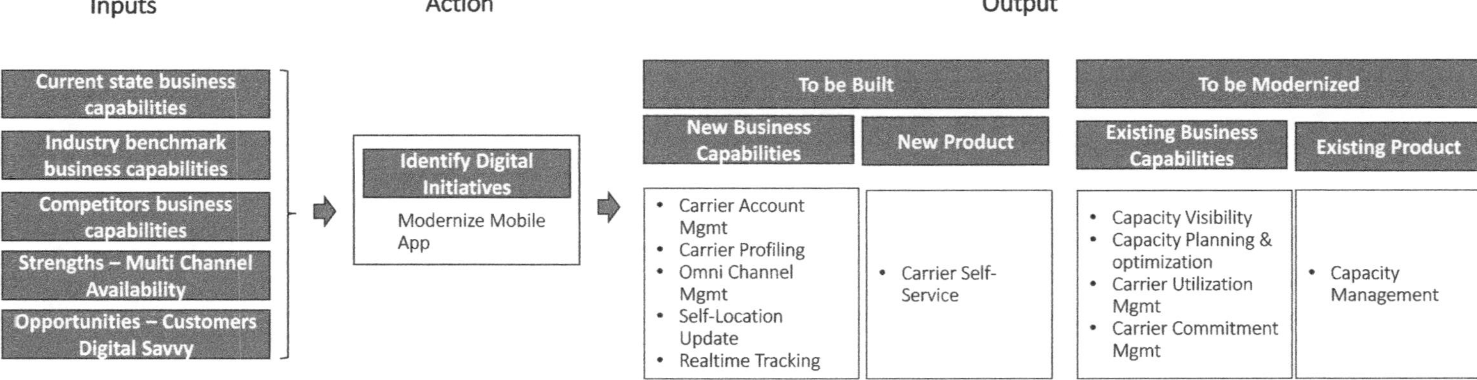

Inputs
Action
Output
Current state business capabilities
Industry benchmark business capabilities
Competitors business capabilities
Strengths – Multi Channel Availability
Opportunities – Customers Digital Savvy
Identify Digital Initiatives
Modernize Mobile App
To be Built
New Business Capabilities
New Product
Carrier Account Mgmt
Carrier Profiling
Omni Channel Mgmt
Self-Location Update
Realtime Tracking
Carrier Self-Service
To be Modernized
Existing Business Capabilities
Existing Product
Capacity Visibility
Capacity Planning & optimization
Carrier Utilization Mgmt
Carrier Commitment Mgmt
Capacity Management

Understanding how to transform TWOS actions/digital initiatives into new/modernized business capabilities, we divided into four groups. Each group committed to exploring one quadrant—SO, ST, OW, and WT actions—to identify new or modernized business capabilities. We agreed to reconvene after two hours of breakout sessions.

During these sessions, both the internal coach and I joined to clarify any questions that arose. We also gathered as a full group during the breakout to review progress and validate our approach.

At the end of the two-hour breakout sessions, we outlined the new business capabilities to be developed and listed the existing capabilities to be modernized to realize TWOS actions/digital initiatives. (next page)

5.1.4 Analyzing and Creating the Current State Business Performance Report

After gathering all the current state data, creating the activity map and SWOT/TWOS analysis, it was time to analyze the performance of the retail store from various perspectives.

First, we looked at revenue threats versus growth. We needed to understand the organization's current position in the S curve by comparing year-on-year growth to that of competitors. We evaluated digital investments and their impact on growth, such as the percentage of customers directly engaged with, the percentage receiving services via mobile, and the percentage of millennial customers. These metrics are crucial for assessing the strength of the current business strategy and for defining new digital business strategies to drive growth in the industry.

For example, consider an insurance company with a digital revenue of 20%, compared to competitors at 50%, and a potential market share growth of 30%. Their average product release cycle is six months, while competitors manage three months. Their Net Promoter Score (NPS) is 60, whereas competitors score 90..

Next, we analyzed the organization's current agility. This involved assessing how quickly they deliver value to the business and customers, their agility in identifying new digital products to solve customer problems, and their speed in leveraging digital opportunities to build new products.

Drawing from the latest business performance data, system activity insights, and a deep-dive SWOT analysis, here is a snapshot of how retail stores in airports are faring, all through the lens of the CARE framework: (page 112)

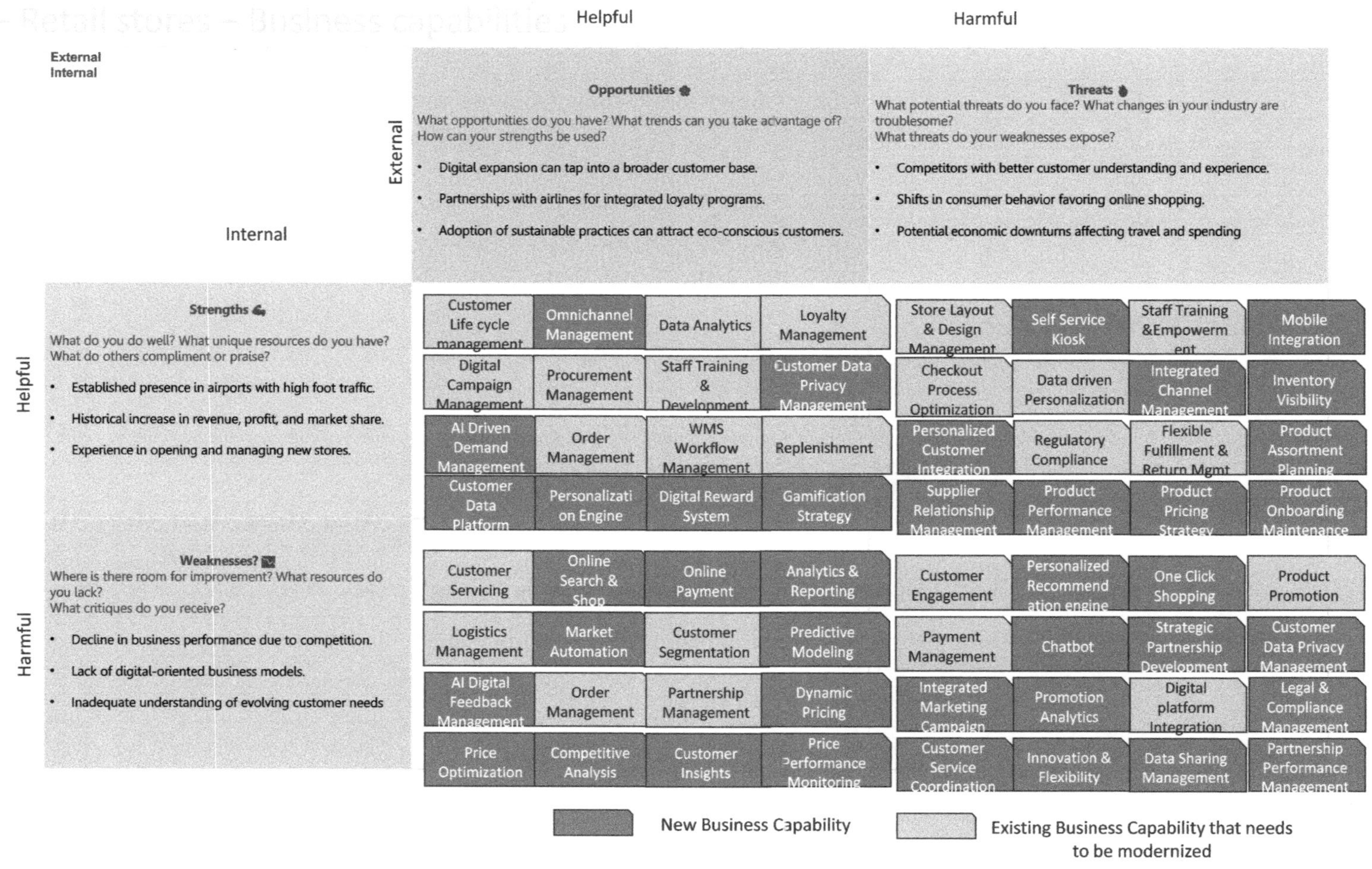

5 – Retail stores – Business capabilities

Helpful | Harmful

External
Internal

Opportunities

What opportunities do you have? What trends can you take advantage of?
How can your strengths be used?

- Digital expansion can tap into a broader customer base.
- Partnerships with airlines for integrated loyalty programs.
- Adoption of sustainable practices can attract eco-conscious customers.

Threats

What potential threats do you face? What changes in your industry are troublesome?
What threats do your weaknesses expose?

- Competitors with better customer understanding and experience.
- Shifts in consumer behavior favoring online shopping.
- Potential economic downturns affecting travel and spending

External

Internal

Helpful | Harmful

Strengths

What do you do well? What unique resources do you have?
What do others compliment or praise?

- Established presence in airports with high foot traffic.
- Historical increase in revenue, profit, and market share.
- Experience in opening and managing new stores.

Weaknesses?

Where is there room for improvement? What resources do you lack?
What critiques do you receive?

- Decline in business performance due to competition.
- Lack of digital-oriented business models.
- Inadequate understanding of evolving customer needs

Customer Life cycle management	Omnichannel Management	Data Analytics	Loyalty Management	Store Layout & Design Management	Self Service Kiosk	Staff Training &Empowerment	Mobile Integration
Digital Campaign Management	Procurement Management	Staff Training & Development	Customer Data Privacy Management	Checkout Process Optimization	Data driven Personalization	Integrated Channel Management	Inventory Visibility
AI Driven Demand Management	Order Management	WMS Workflow Management	Replenishment	Personalized Customer Integration	Regulatory Compliance	Flexible Fulfillment & Return Mgmt	Product Assortment Planning
Customer Data Platform	Personalization Engine	Digital Reward System	Gamification Strategy	Supplier Relationship Management	Product Performance Management	Product Pricing Strategy	Product Onboarding Maintenance
Customer Servicing	Online Search & Shop	Online Payment	Analytics & Reporting	Customer Engagement	Personalized Recommendation engine	One Click Shopping	Product Promotion
Logistics Management	Market Automation	Customer Segmentation	Predictive Modeling	Payment Management	Chatbot	Strategic Partnership Development	Customer Data Privacy Management
AI Digital Feedback Management	Order Management	Partnership Management	Dynamic Pricing	Integrated Marketing Campaign	Promotion Analytics	Digital platform Integration	Legal & Compliance Management
Price Optimization	Competitive Analysis	Customer Insights	Price Performance Monitoring	Customer Service Coordination	Innovation & Flexibility	Data Sharing Management	Partnership Performance Management

New Business Capability

Existing Business Capability that needs to be modernized

Performance Parameters	Current State Performance	Inferences
Cost Leader Vs Differentiator	**Cost leader current state** - **Customer Acquisition Cost (CAC):** Average new CAC is around $ 60 per customer. - **Sales per Square foot** – Average sales per Square foot and employee is very low - **Supply Chain cost:** Additional surcharge due to supply chain disruption increases to $ 3.5 per package - **Average Inventory cost:** For every dollar US retails make, they have $2.5 of inventory which is huge - **In Stock Percentage** – its very lower (70%) in comparison to competitors ((95%) **Differentiator current state** - **Price Vs Quality Effect** – Communication about value and the quality of products are not effective to justify pricing - **Expenditure Effect:** Customers spending capacity and their financial situation not analyzed properly to price products accordingly - **Fashion Effect:** trends and fashion analysis to decide type of products and brands are not effectively	- Increase in Retail store operations cost, CAC, Sales per employee, etc. are significant expense and its reduction is key profitability. Optimizing this will enable Retail stores to become cost leader - Increase investment in supply chain optimization, leads to increase operations cost etc. not increasing the customer's willingness to pay (WTP) - Focus on store ambiance, layout, analyze the trend and update product offerings, improve fairness pricing through extensive market research. It will enable organization to understand preferences, perceived value, and price sensitivity
Agility	- **Average lead time** to release new business functionality takes around 25 to 30 weeks - **Employee Satisfaction:** only 65% of employee are happy and highly engaged and 35% employees considered a retention risk	- Average lead time to deliver new features seems to be very high in comparison competitors who started delivering in 10 weeks - Employee engagement and satisfaction needs attention to improve speed to deliver value and quality
Revenue Trajectory	- **Average sale revenue** from in-store and online order is decreased by 10% - Average Transaction Value (ATV): last 1 year's ATV seems and sales per square foot to be consistent, not increasing - Gross Margin: quarter on quarter gross margin decreasing consistently by 2 to 5%	- Overall loan growth is decreasing while loan interest is fluctuating - Customers retention and ability to provide unsecured loan getting difficult
Emerging Digital	- **Digital maturity 6** in scale of 1 to 10, while competitive threats are rising - **Customer Onboarding:** Customer onboarding time is increased by 15% - **Number of customer visit stores and retail conversion rate are decreasing –** Digital maturity is significantly low in understanding customer behavior, spent pattern etc.	- Overall digital maturity "medium" in comparison to competitor. Its very critical area to focus especially on the context of number of customer visit, purchase value, number of transaction, customer behaviors etc. - Efficiency improvement initiatives from inventory management,

5.2 Defining the Target State Business Strategy

With a clear understanding of our current business performance, it's time to look ahead and define our future business strategy. This involves improving our ability to meet global demand and enhancing overall business performance. Here's how we envision this transformation:

5.2.1 Define the Future State System Activity Map

5.2.2 Create future Business Strategy

5.2.3 Define digital strategy

5.2.1 Define the Future State System Activity Map

We start by creating a future state activity system map. This map focuses on several key elements:

Key Activities: Identifying activities that set us apart from competitors.

Strategic Consistency: Ensuring that these activities align with our overall strategy.

Activity Reinforcement: Making sure these activities support each other to achieve our strategic goals.

Effort Optimization: Streamlining activities to maximize efficiency.

These activities are then logically grouped into critical clusters, known as strategic themes. Each strategic theme helps us define our business objectives.

Take a look at the image below, where "AI-driven customer insights" cluster together like stars in a constellation. This cluster includes activities such as optimizing the supply chain, tailoring promotions and product mixes with AI, and analyzing market trends through the same smart lens. We call this constellation a strategic theme, which guides us towards a specific business goal—like boosting sales revenue for the less affluent among us.

In our envisioned future, every action aligns with one overarching strategy: to elevate the customer experience by making shopping and delivery a breeze. Each activity, interlinked and supportive of the others, is dedicated to this mission, ensuring that every step we take enhances the customer journey.

This future state system activity map will serve as the foundation for redesigning the retail store's business operation value stream, as depicted below,

Future System Activity Map for Retails Store Business Value Chain

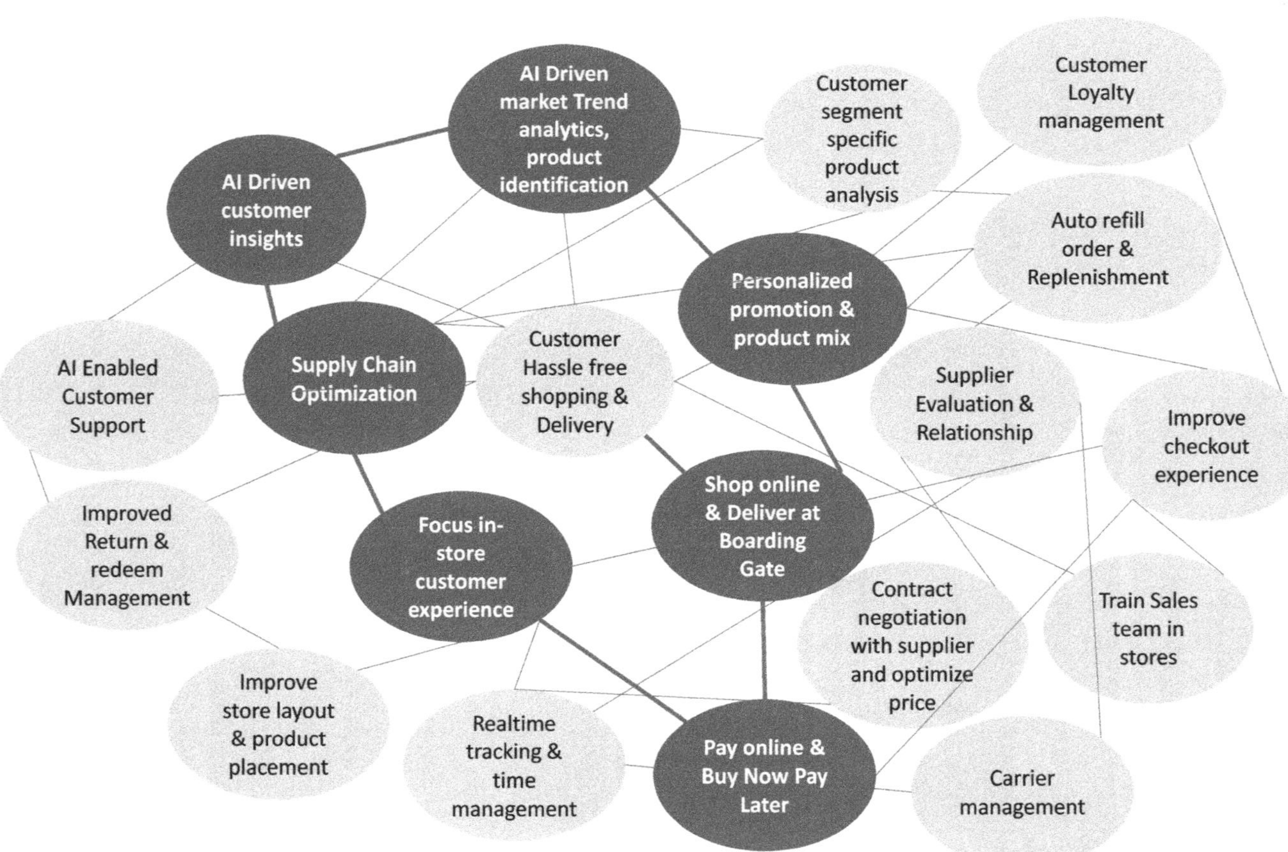

transforming customer needs into value delivery: (on right)

By diving into the heart of our business operation value stream, our retail store zeroes in on what customers truly want, delivering that value quicker than ever. Every step we take to transform a simple trigger into undeniable value is about cutting costs without cutting corners and standing out from the competitors.

5.2.2 Crafting Our Future Business Strategy

Our future business strategy revolves around strategic themes derived from our future state activity map and vision. Imagine this: we have distilled seven strategic themes down to four pivotal ones: leveraging AI for deeper customer insights and tailored product offerings, optimizing the supply chain, employing AI for market research and product discovery, and enhancing customer engagement through online shopping and payment solutions."

Each of these strategic themes aligns with transformation goals and specific business objectives. To achieve these objectives, we need to implement targeted digital initiatives. Think of these initiatives as the building blocks that will bring our strategy to life, each one feeding off the inputs from our future state system activity map.

Based on the outcomes of SWOT & TWOS analysis of initiatives, the current state of business performance according to the CARE framework, and future state system activity map outputs, the future state business strategy is shown: (next page)

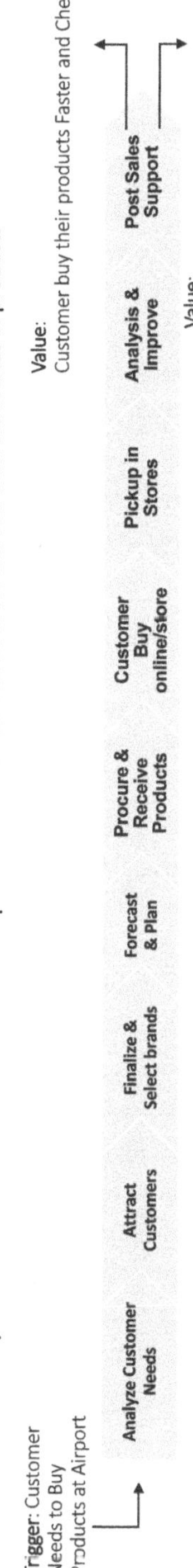

Retail Store Business line 'Vision'

"Our vision is to be the premier retail destination in airports worldwide, renowned for revolutionizing the travel retail experience".
- We aim to achieve a sustainable growth rate of 15% annually, elevate our profit margins by 2 to 5%, and foster customer loyalty by increasing repeat patronage and new customer engagement by 20%.
- We are committed to harnessing cutting-edge digital technologies and innovative business capabilities, such as advanced procurement and inventory management systems, to enhance operational efficiency, enrich customer experiences, and drive effectiveness across all touchpoints.
- We envision a future where every traveler's journey is enhanced by our exceptional service, curated selection, and seamless shopping experience.

Illustrative View of Retail Stores 'Business Strategy'

Strategic Drivers	AI Driven Personalized Promotion & Product mix	Supply Chain Optimization	AI Market research and identify products, brands for future travelers	Customer Engagement – Shop & pay online

Transformation Goals	Revenue Growth for new Customer Segments	Internal Operations Efficiency	Increase Product mix and brands	Differentiate Customer, Merchant Experience

Business Objectives	Expand market share through innovative service offerings	Boost revenue with enhanced customer purchasing options	Strengthen customer relationships and loyalty	Improve Customer and Merchant Experience
	Increase Sales Revenue for Less Affluent Customers	Optimize Operational cost by 25%	Improve Product Performance & Mix	Improve Investment Insights & Suggestions

Digital Initiatives

- Leverage existing airport presence to offer exclusive deals to frequent travelers.
- Use historical data to predict future trends and prepare inventory accordingly.
- Expand loyalty programs to retain existing customers & attract Less Affluent customers

- Invest in digital transformation to offer online shopping & pickup at Boarding gate options
- Conduct market research to better understand and meet customer needs, and revise pricing strategy to remain competitive
- Create an omnichannel retail strategy that includes both physical and online stores.

- Diversify product range to include items that are less sensitive to economic fluctuations
- Develop a user-friendly app for shopping at airport stores.
- Collaborate with airlines to offer cross-promotions.

Prioritizing Digital Initiatives

The digital initiatives we identify are crucial. They come from our TWOS analysis and our future state system activity map. Either we implement all these digital initiatives as they are or prioritize them based on the organization's overall vision. If we want to prioritize and implement only a few of them or decide on the order of implementation, we evaluate these initiatives based on three possible business strategy options.

Run to Optimize: This option focuses on sustaining our current business by optimizing operational efficiency. For instance, we could implement an IoT strategy to enhance inventory and supply chain management accuracy. Or, we could deploy AI for warehouse automation and intelligent process operations to reduce cycle times in customer service sectors like banking and insurance.

Accelerate to Grow (A): Dive into Digital Initiatives in Pockets (DIP) and tap into the latest industry trends to open up more ways to connect with customers. By ramping up customer engagement and enhancing their experience, you'll see a ripple effect: increased demand. And with that, your organization gets to boost its supply capabilities, all thanks to tech prowess. Consider an example from the banking industry where you are giving your customers the keys to a digital kingdom where they can "search & trade" on their own. They'll have access to the best trade options, prices, risks, and returns right at their fingertips. This draws more users to your platform and sparks improvements in your trading processes and platform performance, leveraging cloud and API strategies. It's a win-win: your customers get a top-notch trading experience, and your organization strides ahead in meeting demand with supply.

Disrupt to Differentiate (D): Launch a holistic digital ecosystem to roll out tailor-made services for specific customer groups and personas. Imagine an example of the healthcare industry where we are offering personalized healthcare right at the doorstep for seniors, transforming it into a proactive health management adventure. Think improved experiences with providers and pharmacies, powered by an IoT ecosystem with AI-driven automation—everything from medicine dispatch, monitoring consumption, refilling prescriptions, to updating health records, and tracking patient recovery, all seamlessly integrated. (next page)

Selecting our new business strategy depends on our current state readiness, appetite for growth, and the level of change we are willing to embrace. This could lead to various combinations of new business strategies:

RAD Business Strategies

	Run to Optimize	Accelerate to Grow	Disrupt to Differentiate
Objective	Enable core business to sustain and strengthen with existing customer base. Focus on value chain to improve efficiency	Extend core business with new products and service to cater to new customers & enhance customer experience. Focus on building digital capabilities in value chain	Build new product line & next gen model to generate new business opportunities for new customer segments. Focus on digital Eco-system for integrated personalized services
Digital Capabilities	• Robotic business process automation • IOT capabilities in business operations • ML AI strategy for business process decisions	• AI based business process automation • BoTs for business process execution	• Integrated digital platform/eco system • AI based automation for cyber security • Cloud strategy for SaaS/PaaS etc. • IOT strategy with AI for personalized service
Business Outcomes	• Improved productivity • Improved customer experience • Optimized ops cost/bottom line	• Increased Digital revenue share • AI based Business Automation	• New product lines /next gen digital eco systems • New Market penetration • Increased revenue/top line
Example Use Cases	• Improved visitors experience to Tate's museum through digital tourist guide, interactive sessions etc. • AI based market search & data for client to search best trading options	• Improved visitors experience to Tate's museum through digital tourist guide, interactive sessions etc. • AI based market search & data for client to search best trading options	• Air taxi services with flexible scheduling time & cost • Integrated healthcare services for improved provider & members experience

a. Only run to optimize (cost reduction/efficiency improvement), only accelerate to grow, or only disrupt to differentiate.

b. Run and Accelerate Together or Accelerate and Disrupt or Run and Disrupt

c. Or, the most ambitious, all three together: Run, Accelerate, and Disrupt.

From the simplest option (a) to the most complex (c), the level of change increases, requiring greater leadership commitment, extensive change management efforts, and higher investments.

For our Thiran retail store business, we've chosen the hybrid option—implementing digital initiatives that encompass all three strategies: Run, Accelerate, and Disrupt.

5.2.3 Defining Our Digital Strategy

Crafting a digital strategy for this hybrid business approach involves 4 critical elements:

- *Create Business Operation Value Stream:* We start by mapping out our value stream, understanding how each operation contributes to delivering value to our customers.

- *Decompose Digital Initiatives:* We break down these initiatives into current state products, business capabilities, and existing business processes.

- *Identify and Map Applications/Systems:* We then identify the applications and systems that will be refined or developed, mapping them to our capabilities and baselining current state performance.

- *Future State Products and Capabilities:* Next, we define future products, business capabilities, and processes that will be optimized, automated, or modernized using digital technologies like data integration, IoT, ML/AI, cloud strategy, and intelligent process automation.

The detailed development of our digital strategy will be explored in depth in Chapter 9.

To wrap up, this chapter has taken us on a journey through the essential steps of defining a business strategy. We began by exploring how to assess and create a current state business performance report, and then moved on to crafting a future business strategy.

We delved into the CARE framework, which helps organizations assess their current state. This involved gathering and analyzing data to create a comprehensive performance report. We discussed creating a 'current state system activity map,' which outlines the activities within the business value chain and highlights areas for improvement to stand out from competitors.

Next, we explored how to gather insights using a SWOT analysis and transform those insights into actionable initiatives through TWOS analysis. This process turns strategic analysis into practical digital initiatives.

We then moved on to the next crucial step: creating a future business strategy. This began with defining a 'future state system activity map,' which, along with the digital initiatives identified from the TWOS analysis, forms the basis of the business strategy.

We considered various business strategy options based on an organization's appetite for growth and risk. Ultimately, our retail organization chose to adopt a hybrid business strategy. Finally, we touched upon the components of a digital strategy necessary to achieve this business strategy.

By following these steps, organizations can align their operations with market demands and technological advancements, setting the stage for sustainable growth and competitive differentiation.

Aligning the Blueprint
with Business Strategy

Mr. Agile and I waited in the executive meeting room, which was adorned with inspiring quotes. It was one of the best executive ambiances I'd ever experienced. When I pulled back a curtain, a stunning sea view emerged, perfectly suited for discussing, debating, and deciding on strategies and visions.

Mr. CDO and CIO entered with great smiles, and we exchanged greetings. As I moved to close the curtain, CDO suggested we keep it open to inspire fresh thoughts, which made everyone laugh. The CIO then asked, "Hope you guys are prepared well for today's strategy alignment discussion?" as they settled into the most comfortable seats I had ever seen.

I began by welcoming everyone to this important meeting. "Thank you all for your active participation in defining our future business strategy," I said, appreciating the leadership team for their engagement.

"The objective of today's meeting," I continued, "is to align our business strategy with the execution activities we undertake, ensuring that all leaders speak the same language of strategy."

"To achieve this," I began, sharing my laptop screen on the LED TV, "we have a two-point agenda." The slide with the agenda appeared on the screen.

Agenda 1: Align business strategy with execution across all levels from digital products to user stories.

"Currently," I continued, "products, OKRs (outcomes), and KPIs (leading indicators) are not clearly defined. This lack of definition hinders our ability to measure the effectiveness of our strategy and monitor progress toward our goals. Additionally, there is a misalignment between our strategy and the work being done at the program, product line, and team levels."

Agenda 2: Align Business Strategy with Next-Level Leaders to Ensure Unified Communication

I added, "Right now, our next-level leaders don't have a clear understanding of our strategies. Without this alignment, it's challenging to expect middle management and teams to work effectively towards our goals. Moreover, we lack forums where these strategies are communicated consistently and repeatedly."

Mr. CDO responded, "Agenda 1 seems logical, but I'm not sure how to implement it practically." Before he could finish, Mr. CIO interrupted, "Before diving into strategy execution, I want to challenge agenda point 2. Our next-level leaders have always been aligned with previous strategies. We just need to communicate the new strategy, and we should be fine."

"Sure, let's validate that," I replied. "Mr. CIO, can we arrange a 30-minute call with all your next-level leaders?"

"Of course," he responded.

"Can I ask my manager to set it up in an hour?" "Sure," I replied. He quickly called his manager, asking to schedule the meeting here, and then hung up. I turned to everyone else, "While we wait for the leaders to join, let's dive into agenda item 1 and tackle the CDO's question." Everyone nodded with anticipation for the lively debate ahead.

6.1 Align Business Strategy with Execution

So, we kicked off with a whiteboarding session to get a clear picture of the CDO's question. Before we dove into that, I shared my thoughts on what enterprise strategy is, how it aligns with business line strategy, and I threw in some stuff about OKRs, KPIs, and other bits relevant to the Insurance industry. (next page)

After hearing the explanation, the CIO said, "Okay, I get the big picture and I'm all for it, from the top objectives right down to the digital stuff. But, here's my question: why do we need to loop in everyone at the execution level? I'm talking about the developers, testers, ops, and the architects. Shouldn't this be more of a leadership thing to own, lead, and push forward?"

I said "No," because it's super important that everyone across the whole portfolio or business line is clued in on the strategies and objectives. After all, everything we do is closely linked to achieving those goals. We also have to make sure that we've got clear OKRs and KPIs set for each goal and keep an eye on how they're doing."

Insurance Industry Enterprise 'Vision' and "objectives'

"Our vision is To revolutionize the insurance industry by providing innovative, customer-centric solutions that leverage technology for a seamless and secure experience".

- We aim to transform the insurance landscape by leveraging technology to create hassle – free insurance experience focusing on speed, transparency, and personalized offerings,
- We aim to improve customer retention by 30%, Optimize claim processing time by 50%, improve customer experience by 35%, increase Gen Z customer market share by 50%

Illustrative View of Auto Insurance Business line 'Business Strategy'

Strategic Drivers	Direct to Customers	Digital enabled Operations	Focus on whole product Solutions	Mobile channel engagement
Transformation Goals	Increase Segment wise Market share	Internal Operations Efficiency	Expand customer centric insurance products	Omnichannel Policy Management
Business Objectives	Increase Gen Z segment market share by 50%	Increase claims processing efficiency by 20%	Increase policy conversion rate to 80%	Increase mobility adoption by 100%
	Increase customer retention rate by	Optimize Operational cost by 25%	Increase whole insurance coverage customer percentage by 30%	Increase market share of first time insurance buyer by 30%

Digital Initiatives

- Implement partnership model to cross sell insurance coverage
- Enable telematics to offer usage-based insurance polices
- Implement Mobile app for policy management and claims filing

- Leverage big data analytics for customer insights and market trends
- Adopt blockchain for fraud prevention and secure transactions
- Utilize Ai and ML for personalized pricing and risk assessment

- AI driven real-time dynamic insurance premium calculation
- AI Driven marketing campaign and lead generation, management
- Develop Scalable platform for all customer segments.

Let me give you an example from our retail store's business strategy:

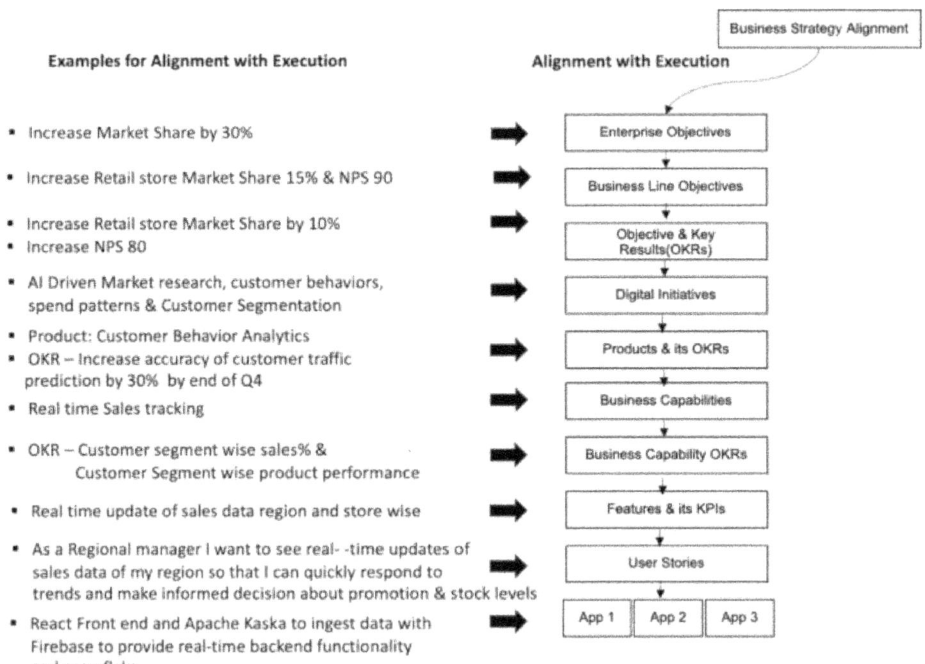

CDO agreed, saying, "I like this approach. Every piece of work, whether a large initiative or a small business capability development, needs to align with our business line objectives.Leaders and employees must understand the strategy and reflect it in their daily activities as part of their roles. This way, everyone will see the significance of their role and contribute effectively."

"Exactly," I replied. "A developer writing code will understand which customer problem or need the code addresses. Similarly, a tester won't just check if the code passes a test case; they'll see if it truly addresses the customer issue."

CPO chimed in, "When PMs write Features or User stories, they shouldn't just think of them as functionalities. They should also consider what customer problem this functionality will solve and what outcomes it will achieve for the business."

"Absolutely," I said. "That's how everyone in the product team, product line, or portfolio can demonstrate a 'product mindset' and an 'outcome-driven culture.'"

Mr. CIO interrupted, "I think I'm starting to understand. We need to ensure that each user story aligns with the overall business line and enterprise strategy."

Mr. CDO quickly added, "So, it also has to align with the features and applications in a parent-child relationship?"

"Exactly," I confirmed. "That's the kind of alignment we need. It's a minor shift from our current way of working but will make a significant impact."

"Instead of focusing on application to feature to user stories alignment, we need to emphasize the alignment from product to business capability to feature to user stories," I explained, pointing at the diagram on the screen. "It's delivered through one or many underlying applications."

CDO interrupted, "Oh yes, I get it. We need to show the underlying application with each product. That's how we maintain focus on all applications and their architecture requirements to implement features and user stories."

"Exactly," I replied.

Here's what you can expect to see:

Application Centric View

Digital Initiatives
↓
Decision to Build Various Applications
↓
Gather Business Requirements
↓
Design & Build Applications
↓
- Front end Application
- Business Rule Engine
- Database
- APIs
- Data Analytic Engine
↓
Applications Offers Functionalities
↓
Receive Feedback from Customers

Product Centric View

Digital Initiatives
↓
Digital Products
↓
Define Business Capabilities
↓
Defines Functionalities
↓
Design & Build Functionalities
↓
User Stories
↓
- Front end Application
- Business Rule Engine
- Database
- APIs
- Data Analytic Engine
↓
Receive Feedback from Customers
↓
Measure Outcomes

I continued, "In the product view, we ensure that each feature a product requires from a customer's perspective is implemented based on the value it delivers. While implementing those features, the impacted application will be modernized if it's a brownfield application, or developed from scratch if it's a greenfield application. Architecture requirements will be refined or defined accordingly."

"In both views, applications are involved in delivering a feature. The difference is that in the product view, business capabilities and features become the driving factors, not the application. Applications become underlying to business capabilities or products," I said, pointing again to the diagram.

"Now, let's talk about the second agenda item: how everyone's individual work contributes to achieving the strategy," I announced, turning to address the room. "This will also clarify CIO's question about how each person's work ties into the strategy."

6.2 Align Business Strategy with All Next-Level Leaders

"To achieve our OKRs and KPIs, we need clear strategies and action plans," I said, pointing at the example on the screen. "One strategy is building a new business capability. This capability is implemented through multiple features."

Each feature comes to life through a series of user stories, as illustrated in the following example:

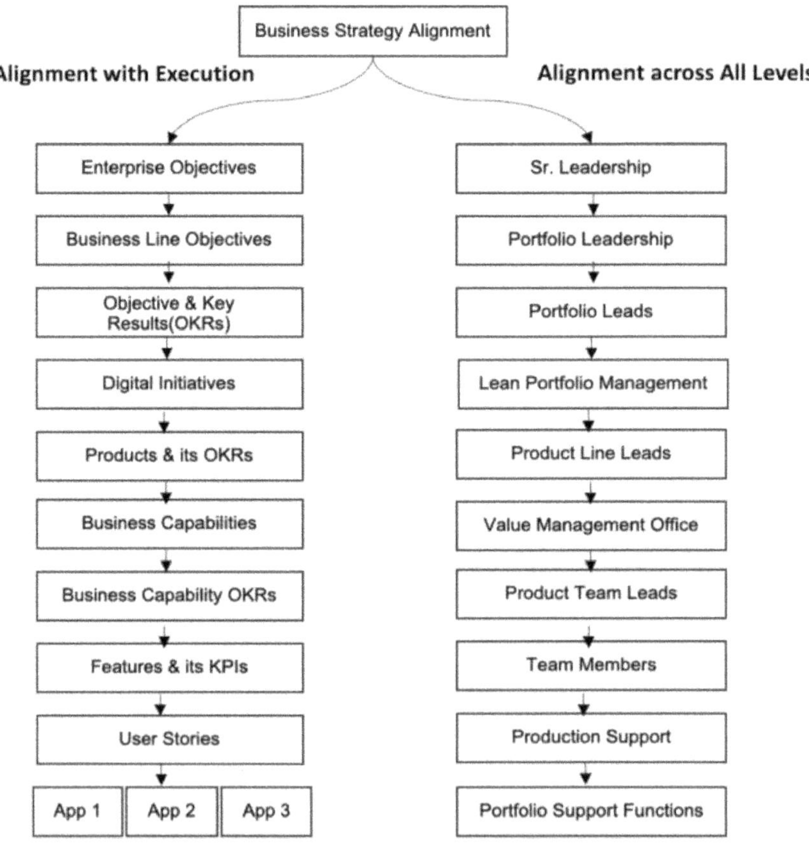

I continued, "Here's how it works: Business sponsors approve the overall budget. The product manager/Product line leads and the Lean portfolio management team prioritize it and allocate budget to products and their business capabilities. The product manager then breaks it down into features. Architects assess technical feasibility and build the architecture. Product owners decompose features into user stories. The CX team designs the customer experience. Developers build it, QE teams test it, and it's auto-deployed in production. Finally, the entire team manages it in case of any production support needs. Monitoring, reporting, and improving the portfolio-level work is done by the Value Management Office(VMO), with legal, sales, and finance teams involved in any financial or legal decisions. So, 'everyone in the portfolio across all levels contributes to achieving the strategy.'"

CDO and CIO nodded in agreement. "It makes sense," CDO said. "We need everyone in the organization, from top to bottom, aligned and aware of this strategy."

"Exactly," I replied. "If the UX designer, developer, or tester doesn't understand how their user story contributes to the overall strategy, they won't be motivated. Their work might not fulfill customer needs or achieve business outcomes."

As I finished explaining, the next level of leaders began arriving in the meeting room, while others joined virtually.

I set the context, explaining, "We're here to understand your level of exposure and alignment with our retail store business strategy." I handed out white paper to everyone in the room and asked those on the call to use a Word document. "Take 15 minutes to write down our retail store business line strategies," I instructed. "The goal is to evaluate how well everyone understands our strategy."

After 15 minutes, we collected the papers and received the inputs from online participants via Microsoft Teams. Out of the nine leaders, only three wrote strategies close to the actual one, but even those three were inconsistent, each missing different details. The other six had written entirely different strategies.

Mr. CIO acknowledged the need for alignment. "Let's have a strategy session with all of you next week," he suggested, referencing the whiteboard session we just had.

"Sounds perfect," I agreed. "It's a common issue in many organizations. We need to periodically align and validate our understanding of the strategy we're all working toward."

As Geoffrey A. Moore wisely said, "Most strategy dialogues end up with executives talking at cross-purposes because... nobody knows exactly what is meant by vision or strategy, and no two people ever quite agree on which topics belong where. That is why, when you ask members of an executive team to describe and explain the corporate strategy, you so frequently get wildly different answers. We just don't have good business discipline for converging on issues this abstract." This situation is common in many industries and requires leaders to rethink how they address this issue.

The CIO thanked his team, and they left the room. It was lunchtime. The CDO and CIO suggested continuing our workshop for 30 minutes after lunch to clarify a few points and plan the next steps.

Mr. CDO agreed with the recommendation, saying, "Next-level leaders need to be clearly communicated about the strategy and must be aware of the actions being implemented to achieve it. We need to define and communicate the strategy repeatedly across the organization through town halls, leadership meetings, and strategy review sessions. We should also plan to review progress in quarterly steering committee meetings, identify opportunities for improvement, and communicate those to everyone."

Both the CIO and I responded simultaneously, "It makes sense!" Everyone laughed. Then the CIO added, "After the first meeting with the next-level leadership, let's schedule a strategy alignment session with both top and middle-level leadership teams. We'll review objectives, OKRs, and KPIs, along with the related digital initiatives. This review will not only help gather their input on the strategy but also secure their buy-in for implementation at the team levels."

The CDO interrupted, "So, the strategies we've documented based on SWOT and TWOS analysis will guide us on which products we need to modernize or develop, and the related business capabilities we need to build, right?"

"Absolutely, madam!" I replied.

"Once we have complete strategy alignment, we'll hold a workshop with all leads from various capabilities—product, design, engineering, and agile—to document the current state of products and capabilities," I explained. "Then, we'll have another workshop to envision the future state, identifying new business capabilities we need to build or existing ones that need modernization."

The CIO added, "We should include the architect team as well, so they can provide insights on current constraints and the technical feasibility of implementing new business capabilities."

"Yes, architect involvement is critical," the CDO agreed. She then asked, "Will we be able to identify all products and business capabilities in one workshop, considering we have more than 50 applications?"

"Great point," I responded. "We can't do it all in one workshop. That's where we need both of your support to do some pre-work offline prior to the workshop, as part of the 'preparation for a two-day workshop.'"

Both the CDO and CIO nodded in agreement. "Yes, of course, we can do what we need to do," they said.

"Fantastic!" I said, requesting the involvement of a team of PMs, BAs, application architects, and engineering leads to review all applications and create a bottom-up view of functionalities, business capabilities, and products in their current state. "For this, we'll need considerable time from them."

Both the CDO and CIO agreed to free up some bandwidth from their current workload so that they could focus on this task. They asked Mr. Agile to coordinate with the leads and plan.

"Sounds good! Let's meet again for the strategy alignment meeting with our next-level leaders," I said. As everyone was getting ready to leave the executive conference room, the CDO received a call from business owners about a possible product available in the external market.

"Can we hold off on that discussion?" the CDO replied. "Let's first start with the strategy alignment meeting with all leaders, then create the current state of products and business capabilities view. After we make some progress on that, we'll have an external products evaluation meeting to see what products we can consider to deliver the digital initiatives. Please include ETC and Mr. Agile as well."

The CDO disconnected the phone and turned to me. "Hope you got it!"

I smiled and said, "Yes, madam! We'll discuss these external products and their business capabilities after our strategy alignment session. This way, we can ensure that whatever external product we select (if needed) aligns with our strategies and is feasible to implement and integrate with our technology stack."

Both the CDO and CIO gave a thumbs up and left the executive conference room.

Mr. Agile and I were having coffee after the meeting. Looking back at our meeting, we really dug into some important aspects. We discussed about how vital it is for us to see eye-to-eye on our business strategy. That means, first, getting all our leaders on the same page, and second, making sure everything we do, from big digital initiatives to the nitty-gritty user stories, lines up perfectly with our strategy.

In our discussion about breaking down work, we dove into how each activity helps the retail store hit its business goals and strategy. We looked at the way business objectives get split up and linked to OKRs, digital initiatives, products, what the business can do, functions, and user stories.

We pointed out the risks of not being on the same page—where everyone might be busy working, but their efforts don't really add up to support the big-picture business goals. In our mini-workshop, we showed how crucial it is for everyone, from the CEO to the engineers coding and testing every day, to be aligned with the business strategy.

At the end of our meeting, we unanimously concluded that leaders often aren't on the same page regarding strategy. We recognized the importance of holding several sessions to make sure the entire organization understands the strategy and knows how their work contributes to it.

We also talked about the importance of having enough bandwidth for leads to begin documenting the current state functionalities, business capabilities, and products. Both the CDO and CIO were on board, giving us the go-ahead to move forward. This groundwork is going to be immensely helpful for our upcoming workshop, where we'll be creating a current state blueprint of the products landscape. We'll dive deeper into this in the upcoming chapters.

Reflecting on these aspects, I couldn't help but smile. "The CDO will truly simplify our lives by establishing the context with the business owner. He's the toughest one to manage, and we need her buy-in for the product definition."

Agile took a sip of his coffee and said, "He wasn't too happy about the productization versus digital initiatives debate in the last meeting. I heard she might not fully cooperate with us."

"Are you saying he might hold back on identifying the current state products and capabilities?" I asked, feeling a sudden jolt of concern.

"Yes," he replied.

I was stunned. Just when I thought we were making progress, it seemed we had another major hurdle to overcome.

Prepare for a Two-Day Blueprint of Current State Products

The internal agile coach and I settled into the spacious 18-seater conference room. A few leaders joined us in person, while others logged in via Microsoft Teams. We waited a few minutes for everyone to get connected. Once all participants were present, I began the meeting.

"Alright, everyone," I started, "let's talk about why we're here today. Our goal is to prepare for the upcoming two-day workshop where we'll create a current state blueprint of our products. This is crucial for our transition to a product-centric model."

I paused to let that sink in before continuing. "Here's what we need to do before the workshop: First, we need to identify all the applications used in our retail stores business line. Then, we'll document all the functionalities these applications offer. After that, we'll logically group these functionalities to define our business capabilities. Finally, we'll cluster these capabilities into digital products."

I looked around the room, making eye contact with each person. "You, as application owners, product managers, solution architects, business architects, product owners, and business analysts, play a critical role in gathering this data. We have just four weeks to get this done."

I took a deep breath, scanning the room for any signs of confusion. "Any questions so far? Let's address them now before we dive into a sample view we created for the LifeScience industry's pharma products manufacturing & sales business Line."

As I was talking, I opened the PowerPoint and shared the sample view on the LED TV screen. Suddenly, one of the solution architects raised his hand.

"Why do we need to create this current state view?" he asked. "Why don't we just create the future state view of the products we need to deliver? Even if the current state is required, why don't we do it at a high level, focusing on business capabilities and products as understood by the business architect and product manager? Why go through all applications and start from documenting functionalities? It's going to be very exhaustive and time-consuming. Does it really add any value?"

I took a moment to collect my thoughts. I had explained this before, and our internal coach had communicated it to everyone, but it was clear we needed to revisit it. "First of all, that's a great question. Asking 'why' we need to do something is crucial for us to understand and be convinced before we dive into 'what'.

7.1 Objective for Creating a Blueprint of Current State Products, Business Capabilities, and Functionalities

I stopped sharing the PowerPoint and switched to the virtual whiteboard. "Alright, let me break this down," I began. "There are four main reasons why we need to create this current state view."

"First, to baseline our current state efficiency, experience, and effectiveness, we need to know exactly what our current state is in terms of functionalities, business capabilities, and products that deliver these 3 Es."

"Second, we need to identify the current state constraints with our applications and their architecture. Knowing where the bottlenecks and limitations are is crucial for any improvement."

"Third, this current state view is critical for converting existing projects into products. Without a clear understanding of what we have now, we can't effectively make that transition."

"And finally, unless we baseline our current state, it will be difficult to define and measure future state success. We need to know where we're starting from to track our progress accurately."

"Let's go through each of these points one by one."

7.1.1 Baseline current state Functionalities, Business Capabilities & Products

In the picture above, we see all the digital products, and its critical business capabilities needed from starting to R& D to managing the customers. Clinical Trials Management is one of the products with six key business capabilities: Protocol Management, Patients Monitoring, Regulatory Management, Drugs Delivery Management, Trials Site Management, and Communication Management. Let's focus on just one of these capabilities: Patients Monitoring.

Example of Life Science Business Operation Value Stream and its Digital products that attract and provide Pharma Products

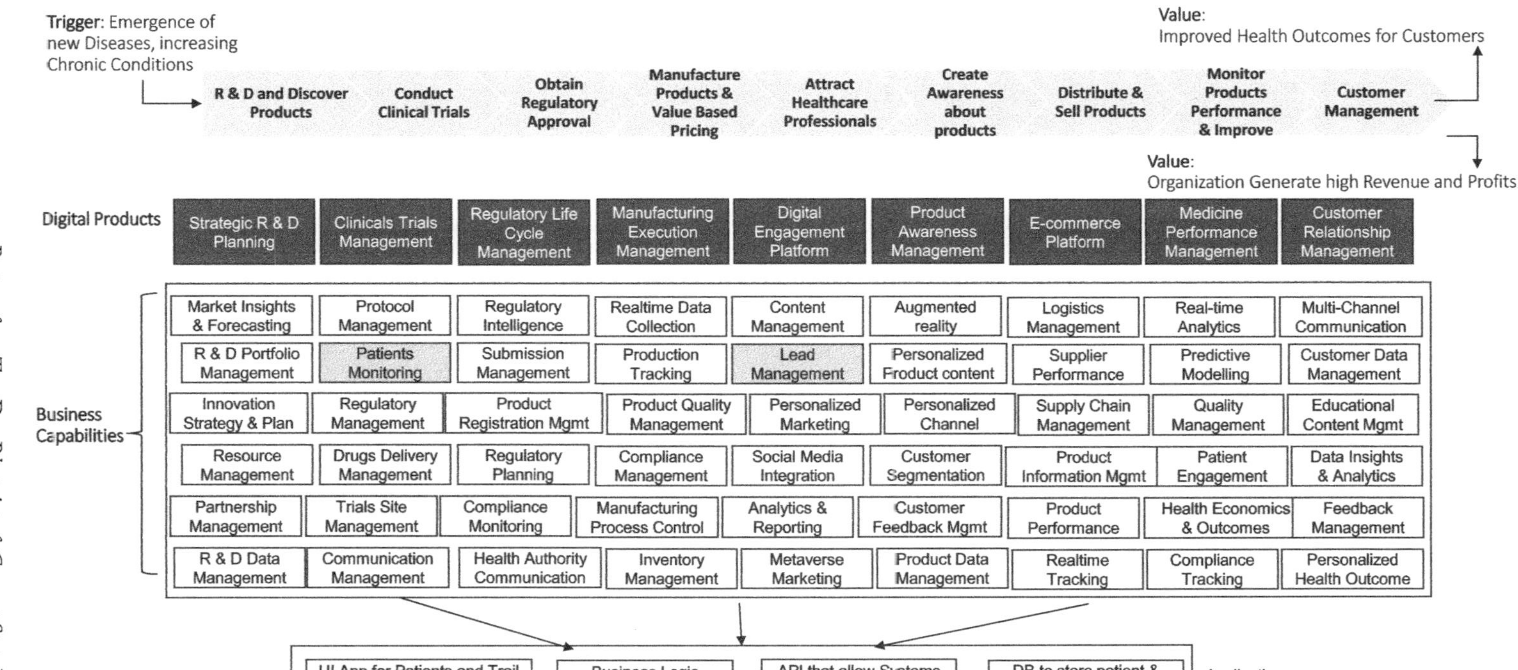

Note: These applications are either inhouse built or bought as COTS products to implement above business capabilities

Patient Monitoring encompasses nine functionalities, though there are many more; we are focusing on just nine for this discussion. These functionalities are spread across four different application layers. Below is a detailed look at that specific segment:

Let me demonstrate the double-click on that specific portion below:

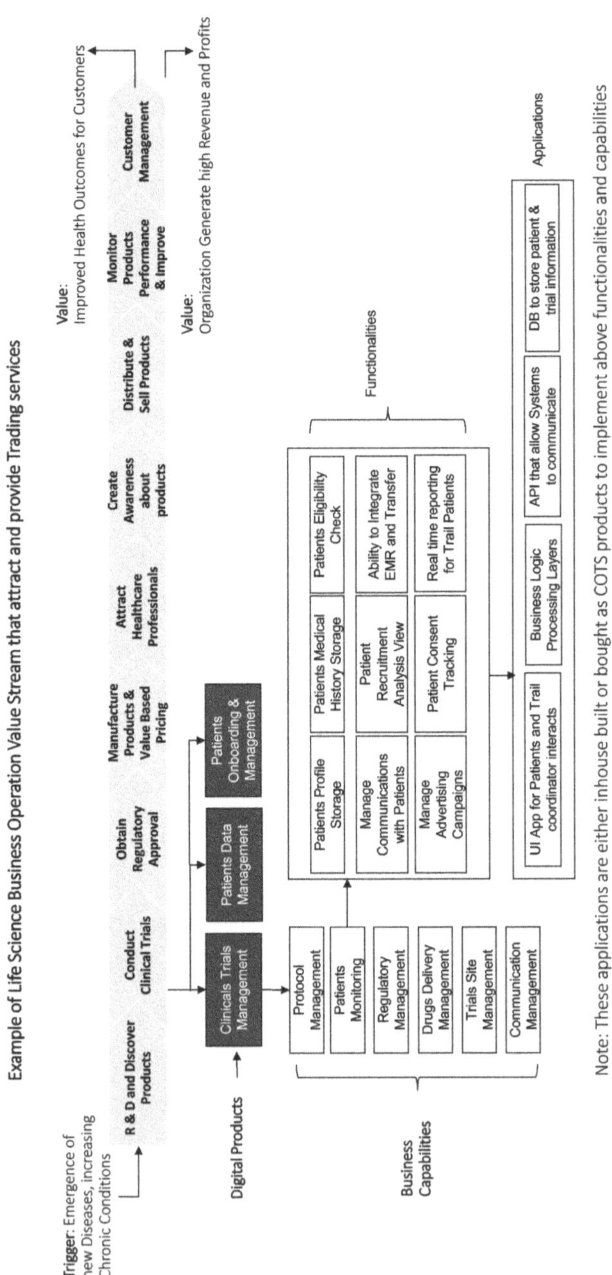

This is how we need to deep dive into all applications and identify the functionalities offered by them as a bottom-up approach. Then logically group those functionalities and define them as business capabilities. Then logically group a set of business capabilities and define them as a digital product.

After creating a current state blueprint of all digital products, we need to enhance the performance of each business capability by envisioning its future state (as per chapter 10). As an illustration, let's imagine trying to improve lead management for our Digital Engagement platform.To do that effectively, we need to dive deep into each functionality of the Led Management business capability, understand how it's currently being performed, and map out the business process flow. We need to measure and baseline the current lead time and efficiency.

To boost our lead management business capability performance, as part of the Digital Engagement platform, it's crucial to dive into how each function performs and understand the business process flow. Let's measure and establish a baseline for the current state's lead time and efficiency. This way, we're making informed improvements.

The product manager's design for lead management will resemble the following illustrative overview: (next page)

Using these insights, when we dive into the future vision of each business capability (as outlined in chapter 9), Product Managers will uncover opportunities to revamp and modernize these functions, streamlining business processes and catapulting efficiency to new heights.

One of the product managers suddenly interrupted, "How is it possible for a PM to do this alone?"

"Great question," I replied. "When I say the PM will do it, I mean the PM will lead the effort. This involves conducting a value stream mapping (VSM) exercise and a time study for each step. Of course, this will be performed with the support of the solution architect, business architect, business users, and the finance team to convert effort into cost."

7.1.2 Identifying Current State Application Constraints

"Now, let's talk about identifying current state application constraints," I continued. "Creating a detailed view of blueprint and performing an analysis will help us pinpoint the application-level constraints that hinder optimizing business process flow and efficient implementation of functionalities and business capabilities."

Illustrative view of Current State 'Lead Management Business' Capability with its Functionalities and Business Process Map

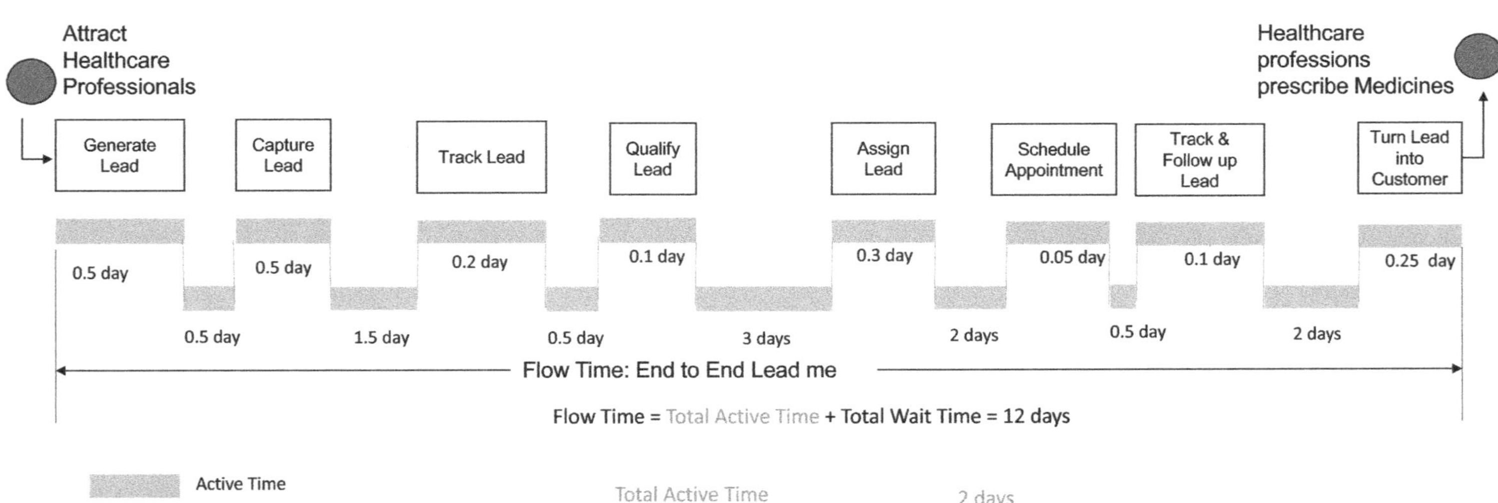

Here are some examples of these constraints: Legacy systems that aren't designed to integrate smoothly with modern technologies; interoperability issues between applications that lead to a fragmented customer experience; tech stacks that aren't scalable; complex applications with poor interfaces that make navigation difficult for customers; data silos that prevent a unified view of customer information, resulting in a disjointed customer experience; resistance to adopting new technology within organizations; and limited infrastructure that restricts deploying advanced technologies like cloud services, big data analytics, or Gen AI.

As soon as I finished explaining these tech constraints, the architect asked, "We have this view of constraints at the portfolio level. Do we need to have it at the product/business capabilities level too?"

"Absolutely," I replied. "We need those detailed views too. It helps us pinpoint constraints in applications, components, the middle layer, interfaces, databases, and more."

7.1.3 Converting Projects into Products

Next, let's talk about converting projects into products. We can only do this effectively when we have a documented current state view of all products and business capabilities. Here's how projects are typically created:

Option 1: Digital initiatives are broken down into multiple projects. Each project contains multiple epics. An epic, in agile terminology, is the largest requirement size according to industry frameworks and ALM tools. Sometimes, several projects are grouped into a single program. Each epic should be considered a business capability and mapped to the corresponding product, based on the new current state of productization as per sample shown in the above section 7.1.1. These epics and their features will continue to be delivered by the existing assigned teams. This is how each in-flight project will be transitioned into a business capability and linked to a product, as illustrated in the figure below: (next page)

When a new business capability needs to be designed and developed within an existing product, it's logged as an epic in our ALM tool. Each product will have a set of business capabilities owned by one product team. Each capability will have its own business case, MVP, outcomes, and budget. As we deliver this epic through multiple features, we measure the value of the epic/ business capability incrementally.

Option 1

Digital Initiatives
Project 1
Project 2
Epic 1
Epic 2
Epic 3
Epic 4
Epic 5
Epic 6
Epic 7
Business Capability 1
Business Capability 2
Business Capability 3
Business Capability 4
Business Capability 5
Business Capability 6
Business Capability 7
Mapped to
Mapped to
Mapped to
Mapped to
Mapped to
Mapped to
Mapped to
Product 1
Product 1
Product 1
Product 2
Product 2
Product 3
Product 3

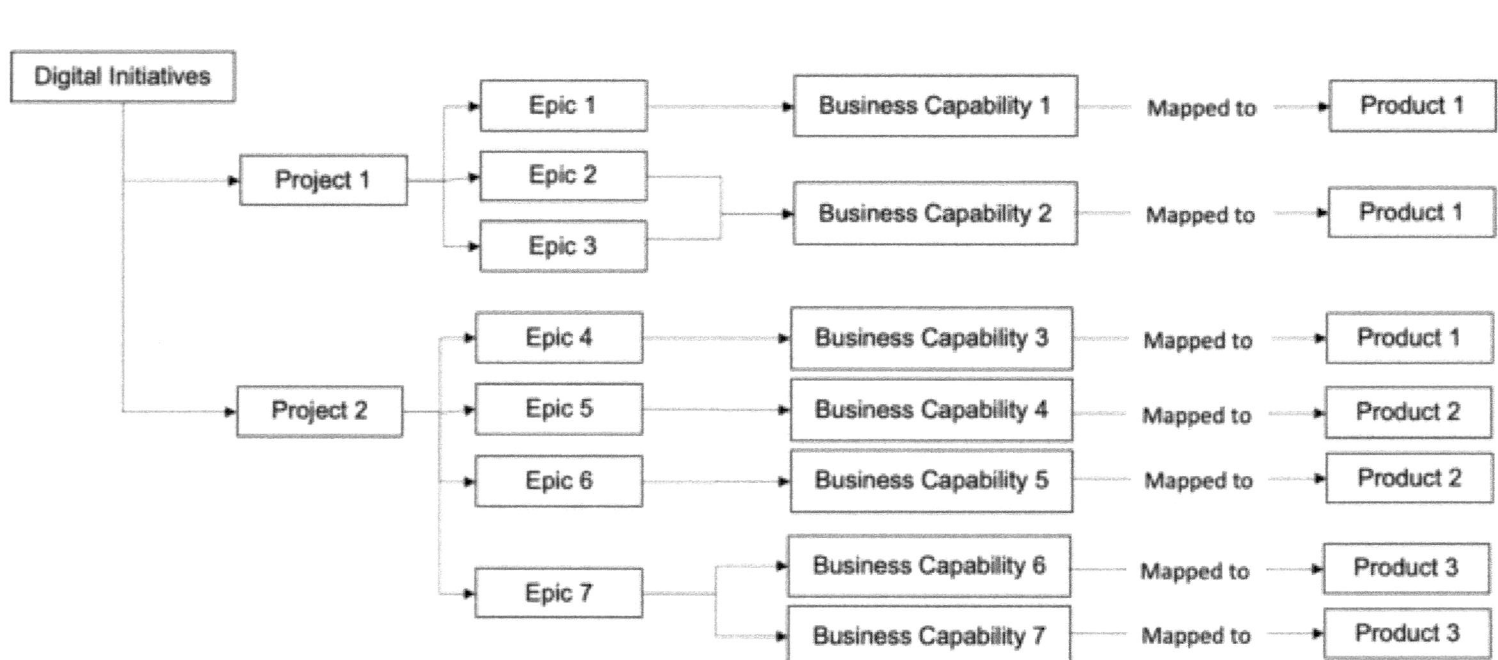

Option 2: Digital initiatives are broken down into multiple projects. Each project is considered an epic, logged, and tracked in ALM tools. Here, each epic is converted into a business capability (one-to-one) and mapped to the corresponding existing product, based on the new current state of productization as per the sample shown in the above section 7.1.1. (next page)

During our discussion, one of the product managers raised a question. "Why are we 'productizing' in the first place? What's the difference between our current agile approach and this new method of product identification?"

I nodded, anticipating this concern. "Great question. Let me explain."

Another team member chimed in, "Yeah, we've been following agile for a while now. How is this different?"

"Productizing our solutions," I began, "means starting with a clear understanding of our current state and then defining the future state, as we'll detail in Chapter 9. This approach is all about bringing customer centricity to our digital transformation."

A PM looked puzzled. "But we already focus on customers, right?"

"True," I replied, "but with our current project view, we can't define value from the customer's perspective effectively. We don't tend to identify their problems and needs prior to our solution definition. We're often too focused on the immediate project tasks rather than the overall product's impact on the customer experience."

"So, this shift," I continued, "is essential for any successful digital transformation. It helps us define and deliver value incrementally, ensuring we're always aligned with what the customer truly needs."

We tackled the second question by explaining that agile focuses on processes and practices to execute projects and products incrementally, faster, and with high quality. This is complemented by structured product management, which involves identifying products and business capabilities, creating business cases, defining MVPs, developing incremental architecture, and evaluating MVPs to ensure the benefit hypotheses are met. This structured approach helps us to identify and deliver digital initiatives that drive business growth, improve customer experience, and enhance operational efficiency.

7.1.4 When we don't measure and quantify current state performance, envisioning a future state quantitatively, measuring it, and demonstrating

Option 2

Digital Initiatives
Project 1
Epic 1
Business Capability 1
Mapped to
Product 1
Project 2
Epic 2
Business Capability 2
Mapped to
Product 1
Project 3
Epic 3
Business Capability 3
Mapped to
Product 1
Project 4
Epic 4
Business Capability 4
Mapped to
Product 2
Project 5
Epic 5
Business Capability 5
Mapped to
Product 2
Project 6
Epic 6
Business Capability 6
Mapped to
Product 3

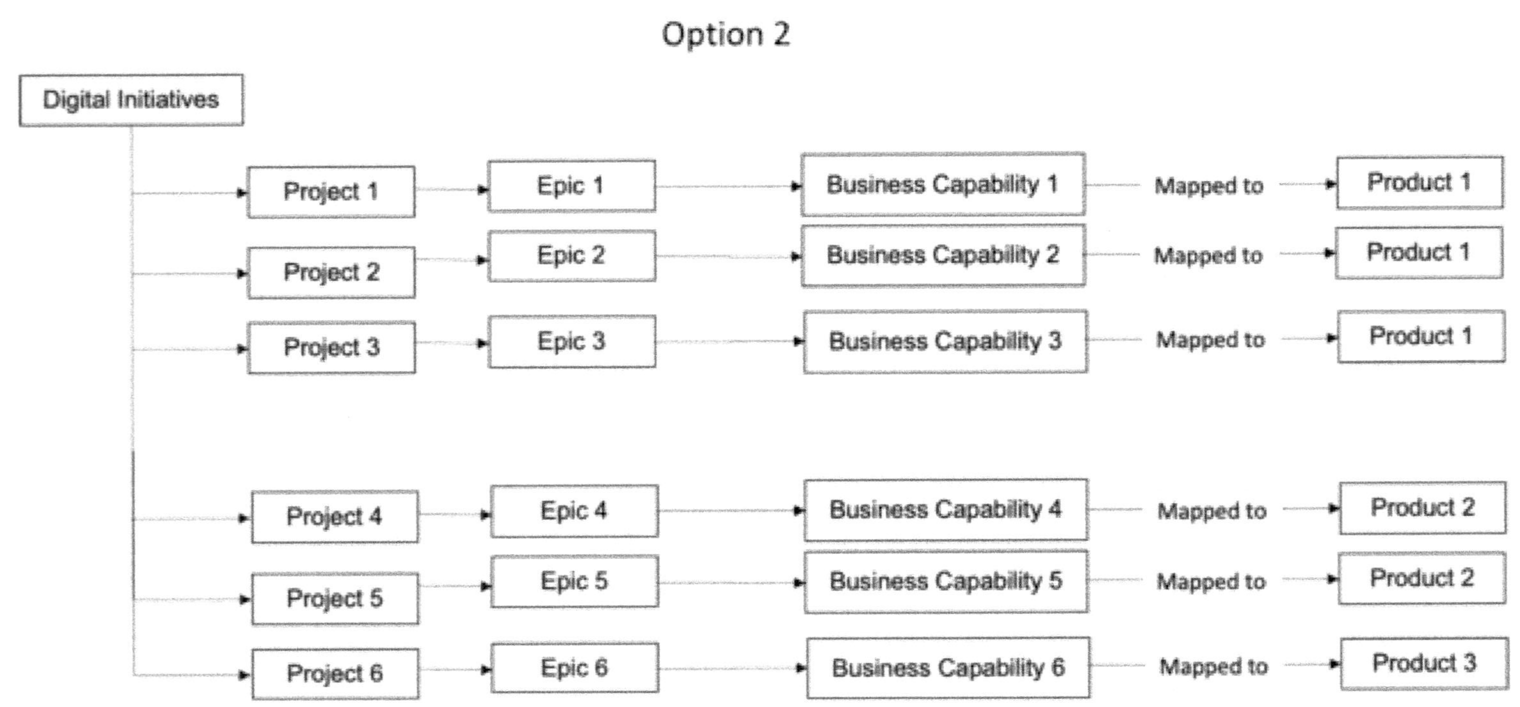

improvement becomes difficult. For example, to define the current efficiency, effectiveness, and experience for the "Lead Management product," we need detailed functionality level information and a value stream map (VSM).

7. 2 Identify and Document Functionalities, Business Capabilities, and Products:

With a solid understanding of why we need to identify existing products by productizing current applications, we moved on to discussing our approach. We focused on identifying one of the retail store products in the WMS space. As a group, we identified the following existing applications:

User Interface: React tech stack UI application.

Mobile App: iOS and Android apps.

App Server: Hosts the business logic and acts as a bridge between the front end and back end.

Integration Middleware: Facilitates communication between WMS and other platforms like ERP, CRM, or e-commerce platforms.

Database Server: Stores all data related to inventory, orders, and customers.

Data Analytics: Tools for analyzing warehouse operations and generating insights.

A visual representation of the application landscape would look something like this:

Illustrative view of Applications used in WMS product Line

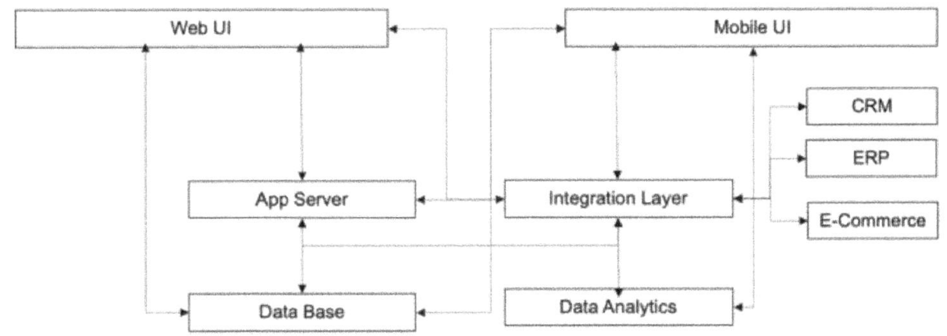

7.2.1 Breakout 1:

We proposed splitting into three breakout teams, each with eight participants, ensuring all roles were represented: business user, product manager, product owner, solution architect, application owner, and engineering lead.

"Alright, each group has 30 minutes to list all functionalities from these applications," I announced. "Open the applications, navigate through all the functional flows, and document everything. Use any existing documentation as a reference."

The teams got to work, diving into their applications and noting down functionalities. As they worked, the internal coaches and I rotated between the groups, answering questions and helping identify functionalities.

7.2.3 Breakout 2:

After the first session, it was clear that 30 minutes wasn't enough. There were too many questions and discussions.

"We need more time," one of the product managers said.

"Let's extend it to 60 minutes," I agreed.

With the extra time, each group managed to come up with a fairly comprehensive list of functionalities.

After our break, the entire team reconvened for another 30 minutes. Our goal was to consolidate our lists, removing duplicates, merging similar items, and adding any missing functionalities. By the end, we had our final list of functionalities.

Here's a snapshot of the functionalities identified and grouped under the Dashboard and Reporting business capability of the WMS product:

- *Inventory Levels and Status:* Track inventory quantities and conditions.

- *Order Tracking:* Monitor the status of orders throughout the fulfillment process.

- *Warehouse Location Management:* Visualize warehouse space utilization and location statuses.

- *Goods In and Out Processes:* Report on the efficiency of goods receipt and dispatch.

- *Shipping Management:* Gain insights into shipping schedules, carrier performance, and delivery statuses.

- *Order Picking and Packing Efficiency:* Measure the accuracy and speed of order picking and packing operations.

- *Returns Management:* Analyze return rates and processing times.

- *Labor Productivity:* Report on workforce efficiency and utilization.

- *Resource Allocation:* Monitor the use of equipment and human resources.

- *Performance Metrics:* Track key performance indicators (KPIs) for various warehouse operations.

- *Exception Reporting:* Identify and manage discrepancies or issues.

- *Forecasting and Trend Analysis:* Use predictive analytics for inventory and order management.

- *Custom Reporting:* Create tailored reports based on specific business needs.

7.2.3 Breakout 3:

In our next breakout session, we grouped all identified functionalities into the following business capabilities and mapped them to various roles based on which role uses which capability, including internal business users, store managers, and logistics managers. Here's how it breaks down:

Business Capabilities for Internal Business Users:

Dashboard and Reporting: Access to real-time data and analytics for decision-making.

Inventory Visibility: Real-time tracking of inventory levels and locations.

Order Management: Processing and fulfillment of customer orders.

Workflow Management: Automation and management of warehouse workflows.

For Store Managers:

Replenishment: Automated stock replenishment to maintain optimal inventory levels.

Performance Monitoring: Monitoring and managing staff performance and productivity.

Customer Service: Handling customer inquiries and issues related to inventory and orders.

Loss Prevention: Tools for monitoring and reducing shrinkage and theft.

For Logistics Managers:

Transportation Management: Planning and execution of inbound and outbound transportation.

Yard Management: Coordination of vehicles and trailers in the yard.

Cross-Docking: Efficient transfer of goods from receiving to shipping.

Compliance Management: Ensuring adherence to regulations and industry standards.

Resource Utilization: Maximizing the use of space, equipment, and labor to improve overall warehouse efficiency.

Labor Management: Optimizing workforce allocation and productivity within the warehouse.

Upon completing the exercise, the final overview of all functionalities, and business capabilities of the WMS product is presented as follows that are mapped to the applications mentioned above: (next page)

One of the PMs raised a hand. "This approach works for business projects, but what about technology projects?"

"What do you mean by technology projects?" I asked.

The architect chimed in, "Technology modernization projects."

"Portfolio rationalization projects," added an engineer.

"Cloud migration projects," the PM clarified.

"Great question," I responded. "All of those are excellent examples of technology projects. When these projects are implemented, end users and internal business users still interact with functionalities and business capabilities as part of their daily activities, right?"

7.3 Identify and Document Current State Products for Technology Initiative Projects

The room went silent, everyone considering the point.

"Let's take an example," I continued. "Imagine we're rationalizing 30 applications down to 20, 15, or even 10 because of redundancies from mergers and acquisitions. After this optimization, all current functionalities and business capabilities must still be available to customers, either as they are or improved, correct?"

Product, Business capabilities and functionalities

Product	Warehouse Management System (WMS)							
Business Capabilities	Dashboard & Reporting	Intelligence Order Routing	Labor Management	Shipping Management	Replenishment	Integrated Order Processing	Realtime Inventory Visibility	Picking & Packing Optimization
Functionalities	Inventory levels and status	Automated order allocation	Predict labor needs	Carrier integration	Ability to forecast future sales	View Orders in centralized view	Item level tracking	Intuitive warehouse layout
	Order tracking	Dynamic rules configuration	Automated staff scheduling	Automated shipping rules	Determine optimal stock	Orders Processing	Integrate POS and WMS	Picking method selection
	Warehouse location management	Multi location inventory sync	Training plan & execution	Automated Dispatch	Automated reordering	Realtime inventory sync	Automated data Capture	Products quality tracking
	Goods in ad out processes	Realtime order tracking from placement to delivery	Time & attendance tracking	Realtime tracking during transit	Order consolidation	Automated order creation	Real time reporting	Package material selection
	Shipping Management	Carrier rate shopping	Labor performance management	Generate and print shipping labels	Dynamic replenishment	Orders return management	Item level inventory prediction	Labeling accuracy verification
	Order Picking and Packing Efficiency	Customer proximity prioritization	Labor laws compliance tracking	Order bulk processing	Monitor replenishment strategy effectiveness	Realtime order reporting	Mobile view inventory updates	Monitor picking & packing performance
	Returns Management	Order splitting to expedite delivery	Labor cost analysis	Shipping documents management	Ability to monitor supplier lead time	Monitor order process metrics	Provide inventory update in different channels	Receive and analyze customer feedback
	Exception Reporting	Integration with various sales channel	Labor task management	Shipping data analytics	Supplier quality tracking	Shipping & delivery integration	Connect with supplier to monitor inventory	Metrics monitoring picking and packing quality
	Forecasting & Trend Trend analysis	Monitor order routing effectiveness	Employees self service functionalities	Automated notification to customers	Dynamic supplier selection	Order price update	Dynamic repricing	Select packing options
	Resource Allocation	Real time alerts order statuses	Realtime alerts on schedule conflict, absences	Manage international shipping requirements	Inventory tracking from all channels	Order Payment processing	Customer facing inventory data	Real time update on package conditions

Existing Functionalities

New Functionalities that includes foundational, differentiating

Multiple "yes" responses and thumbs-ups from online participants filled the room.

"Now, let's assume two applications offer the same functionalities to customers in different segments or geographies, a common scenario after acquiring smaller companies. The enterprise wants to decommission one and ensure all features are still available to customers. They'll decide which application to keep based on factors like the tech stack and modern architecture."

"For this technology initiative, instead of creating projects, we'll create products and business capabilities—or epics—in our ALM tool that need to be either migrated as is or modernized as per illustration shown below in scenario 1," I explained. (next page)

"In the case of migrating capabilities as is, we'll list each capability and then create features under them that need to be available to customers through Application 1. These features are currently offered by Application 2, which we plan to decommission. Each feature will have user stories detailing the configuration of these features for new segment or geography customers through Application 1."

"If the capabilities need to be modernized when moved, we'll document the functionalities that require updates. For example, if Application 1 is being retained and Application 2, which offers the same functionalities, is being decommissioned, each functionality will have user stories related to its modernization or enhancement. These modernized functionalities will be deployed for both existing and new customers. After deployment, we'll measure outcomes in terms of improved efficiency, experience, and effectiveness."

The room was quiet as everyone absorbed the details.

"Now, the same approach applies to scenario 2 as well. The only difference is that scenario 2 is implemented using an ERP, a COTS product."

"So, whether it's a business initiative or a technology initiative, productizing our digital solution is crucial. Documenting the current state product blueprint is critical for this process," I noted.

After a few hours of intense discussion, everyone seemed convinced of the need for this exercise. Then, one of the architects raised a concern. "Thirty percent effort for the next four weeks from around 25 FTEs seems like a huge commitment."

Illustrative view of Business Capabilities Implementation Scenarios during Applications Rationalization

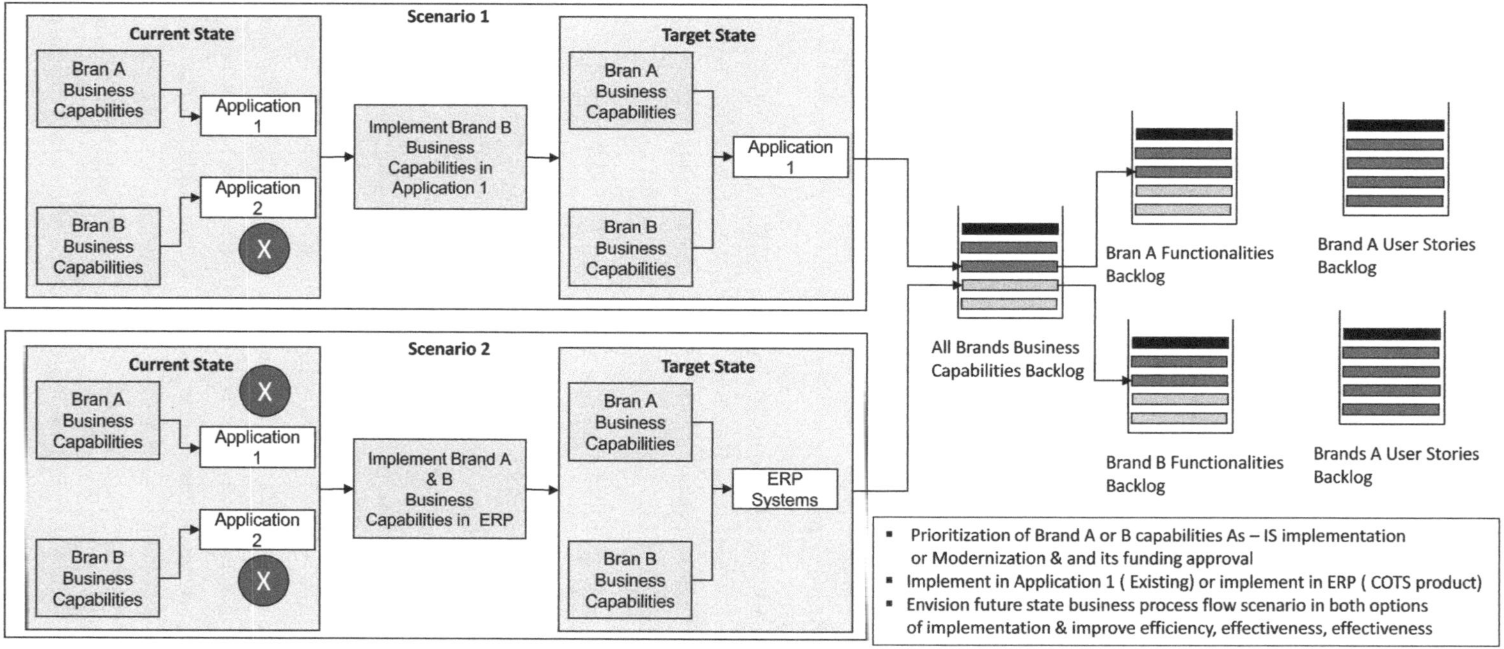

- Prioritization of Brand A or B capabilities As – IS implementation or Modernization & and its funding approval
- Implement in Application 1 (Existing) or implement in ERP (COTS product)
- Envision future state business process flow scenario in both options of implementation & improve efficiency, effectiveness, effectiveness

I nodded. "You're right, it is. But if we want to baseline our current state, define the future state, and achieve guaranteed outcomes at optimal cost, then this work is necessary."

"We can leverage Gen AI for this," I continued. "By providing the entire code repository of an application, Gen AI can create pseudocode. We can then convert that pseudocode into user stories, which can be further clustered or consolidated into functionalities. With a list of functionalities, we can manually group them into business capabilities and then into products. Using Gen AI for this current state products blueprinting can optimize manual effort by 50 to 60 percent."

The room buzzed with newfound energy as the middle management team from the retail stores business segment began to see the path forward. They understood how to identify functionalities from applications and logically group them into business capabilities. We agreed to tackle this exercise offline, working with a total of 45 applications in the portfolio. Each of the three groups would be assigned a cluster of applications.

We set a timeline of four weeks to complete the task, with weekly interim checkpoints to ensure we stayed on track.

With leadership already on board, we agreed to dedicate 30% of our group's time to this exercise over the next four weeks. This meant reducing their available capacity for team-level delivery to 70%. As the meeting wrapped up, everyone started logging off and those in the room began to leave.

One of the architects approached us. "I appreciate this exercise," he said. "I've been trying to get application owners and product managers to create a current state view for ages. They never saw the value in it. But thanks to your clear explanations, examples, and exercises, as well as addressing the 'why' and 'how,' you've managed to convince them."

His comments left me feeling energized and accomplished. As I waited for the Internal Coach to join me for lunch, I mentally recapped our progress: *We discussed why we need to productize our existing software applications, using examples from the Life Sciences industry. We covered products, business capabilities, functionalities, and applications. We also delved into the bottom-up approach: how we move from applications to functionalities, to business capabilities, and finally to products, illustrated with a WMS product example.*

We had a detailed discussion about the typical challenges we might face during this exercise and how to tackle them. Everyone—business users, PMs, architects, engineering leads, POs, and SMs—aligned on the approach and agreed on the timeline to complete this exercise.

As I sat down for lunch, feeling a bit more organized after my mental recap, the Internal Coach joined me. I was eager to hear his thoughts on the workshop. "So, how do you think the workshop went?" I asked.

That's when he dropped a bit of a bombshell. "The workshop went well, and everyone conceptually understands the approach and should be able to apply it to other applications," he said. But then he hesitated. "The real question is, will they actually have the time to do it?"

I was taken aback. "What do you mean? We've got leadership approval to allocate key people. Why would there still be a bandwidth challenge?"

He sighed, "It's all good on paper. But we've seen this before. When push comes to shove, reality often looks quite different. We have a critical release coming up in the next 45 days. Several projects are deep in the red, needing a lot of catch-up. How can they spare 30% of their effort for this productization exercise?"

I was silent for a few seconds, searching for a reply. He added, apologetically, "Sorry to disappoint you."

"No, no, not at all," I quickly responded, shaking off the initial shock. "I'll speak with the CIO's next level of leadership and see how we can make this work. We need to make it happen. Otherwise, the two days we spent in the workshop—and essentially the whole initiative—will be a failure."

8

Design Product-Centric Model Blueprint

It's exactly four weeks since our previous workshop where we discussed the preparation work needed for this two-day workshop. Today's the day! I logged into the virtual call, fully prepared to lead a two-day workshop on identifying business and development value streams—critical enablers for achieving "Business Agility." Participants started joining slowly, and soon all 36 expected attendees were present, including key leaders like business owners, product managers, product owners, IT leaders, solution architects, tech and QE leads, project and program managers, and scrum masters.

I kicked things off by presenting the agenda for the next two days and setting the context. "Welcome, everyone. Today, we're going to dive into why this workshop is essential and how it aligns with our overall product-centric transformation model. We'll tackle this agenda in three parts."

8.1 *Part 1: Defining Business Operation Value Streams (OVS)*

"We'll start by defining our business operation value streams. Who are our customers? What value do we deliver to them? What are their expectations?"

8. 2 *Part 2: Identifying Digital Products*

"Next, we will identify the digital products or technology-enabled solutions that our business value streams use to deliver value. We will examine the underlying applications that implement the product, business capabilities, functionalities, and the number of people working on these functionalities, along with their skill sets and locations."

8.3 *Part 3: Defining Development Value Streams (DVS)*

"Finally, we'll define the development value streams, which manage everything from feature intake to release and maintenance in production. We'll identify the Agile Release Train (ART) or Product Line that will carry out the development work. Additionally, we'll determine the team types and composition within the product line, enabling them to work independently and deliver value faster."

Below is an example of the current state blueprint we've designed for a client in the healthcare industry, focusing on their retail sales portfolio. It's depicted in three figures. By the end of our two-day workshop, we plan to create a similar view. (refer page 152, 153 and 154 images)

I noticed a heavy silence and a few shocked expressions on some leaders' faces. "Don't worry," I reassured them. "Our team has done extensive preparation to make this workshop as smooth as possible."

"Let me give you a quick overview of each figure."

"Figure 1 displays the business operation value stream. It shows all the products and business capabilities currently utilized to execute the value stream steps, along with the corresponding applications that deliver these capabilities and the platform capabilities supporting the value stream steps."

"Figure 2 provides additional details related to Figure 1. It includes information about the number of agile teams currently working to deliver these business capabilities, their locations, and the specific applications they need to work on to deliver each capability."

"Figure 3 offers a detailed view of a single business operation value stream step. It maps out the corresponding products, business capabilities, applications, and the number of agile teams involved. This figure also shows the impact on applications when building or modernizing each business capability, along with the various types of agile teams required and the complexity of work involved."

As soon as I wrapped up the agenda and walked through the sample figures, a few questions came up. "Don't we already know the business operation value streams we use to deliver value? Aren't we aware of the applications that serve our customers? And haven't we set up programs to build and deploy these applications? Why do we need this exercise?"

These questions echoed those from our senior leadership meetings, reflecting a mix of portfolio-level leaders and program and team-level leads.

I replied, "Yes, we do have these elements. Our business operation value stream has been redesigned to align with our new business strategy (Chapter 5). It hasn't been properly documented, communicated, or leveraged to drive business agility."

Figure 1: Business Operation Value Stream, corresponding Products, Business Capabilities, Applications and Platform Capabilities for Healthcare Retail Sales

Trigger: Prospects need of Retail Insurance Products

Value: Improved Health Coverage for Customers

Value: Customers enrolled for health insurance & Premium revenue

Lead Sourcing & Optimization	Lead Nurturing	Leads Verification & Sales	Members Onboarding	Sales Management	Sales Agents Onboarding	Book of Business Management	Business Intelligence
Digital Lead Intake	Prospects Profile	Plan Comparison	Customer Profiling	Multi Channels Sales Management	Onboarding Agents	Prospects Leads Management	Customer behavior Analytics
Partner Lead Intake	Appointment Conversation	Physician Finder	Personalized Onboarding	Sales Community Management	Agents Profiling	Members behavior driven Sales	Campaign Effectiveness Insight
Manual Lead Distribution	Eligibility Verification	Drug Cost Lookup	Omnichannel Communication	Sales Strategy Management	Members Plan Management	Members Retention Strategy	Sales Channel Wise Performance
Call Routing	Share Marketing Materials	IVR SOA (Scope of Appointment)	Customer Referrals	Sales Performance Management	Sales Team Training	Market Segmentation	Agents Analytics
Campaign Management	Guided Call Flow	Voice SOA	Customer Education	Sales Regulatory Compliance	Agents Performance Tracking	Product Knowledge Management	Healthcare Plan Analytics
Seminar Event Creation	Lead Auto Assignment	Electronic SOA	Onboarding Analytics	Members products Feedback	Efficient Inquiries Management	Omni Channel Communication	Retail Sales Analytics

Application 1 | Application 2 | Application 3 | Application 4 | Application 5 | Application 6 | Application 7 | Application 8 | ---- | Application N

Platform Capabilities	Real Time Tracking	Data Analytics & Reporting	Authentication	Onboarding	Appointment Scheduling	User Logins	Data Management

Figure 2: Business Operation Value Stream and corresponding Products, Applications and Agile Teams with its working locations

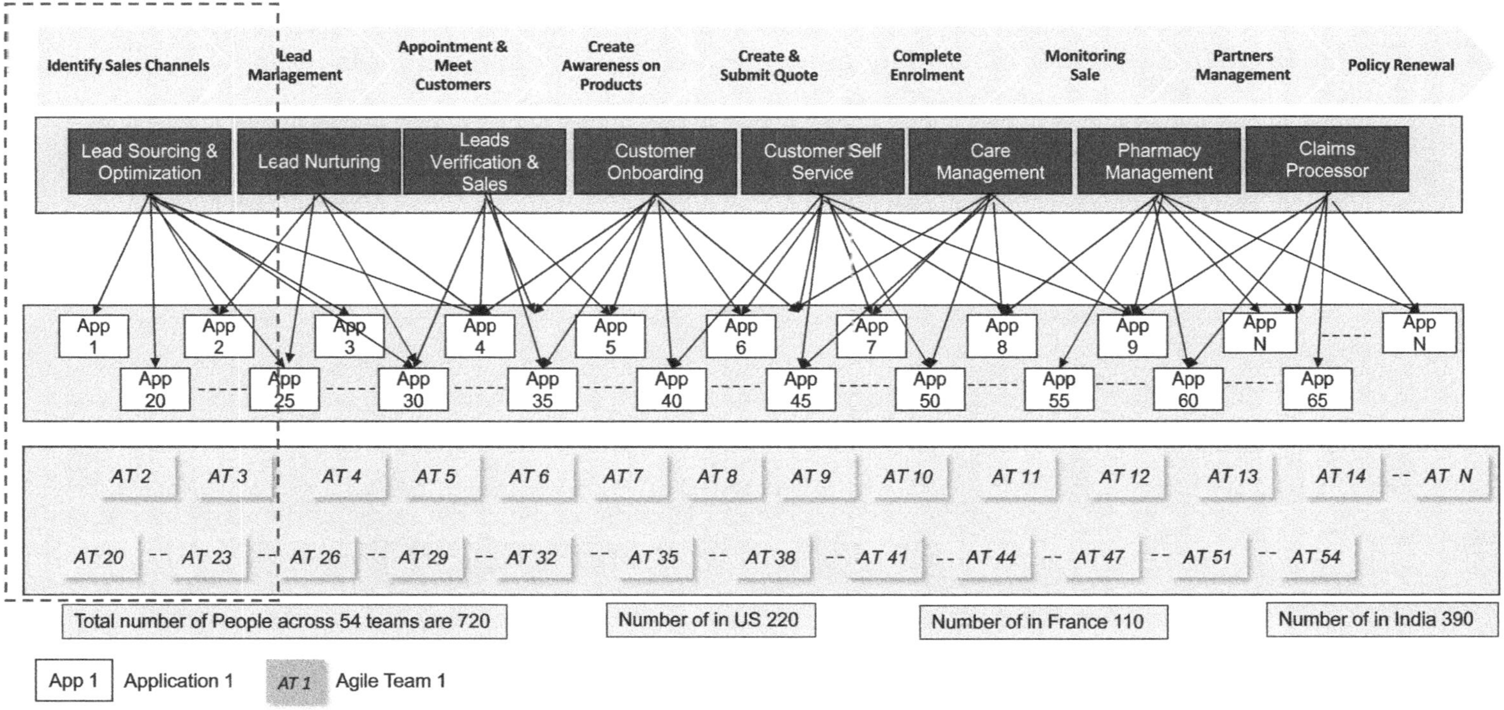

Figure 3: Double click view of one Value Stream Step and corresponding Products, Business Capabilities, Applications and Agile Teams

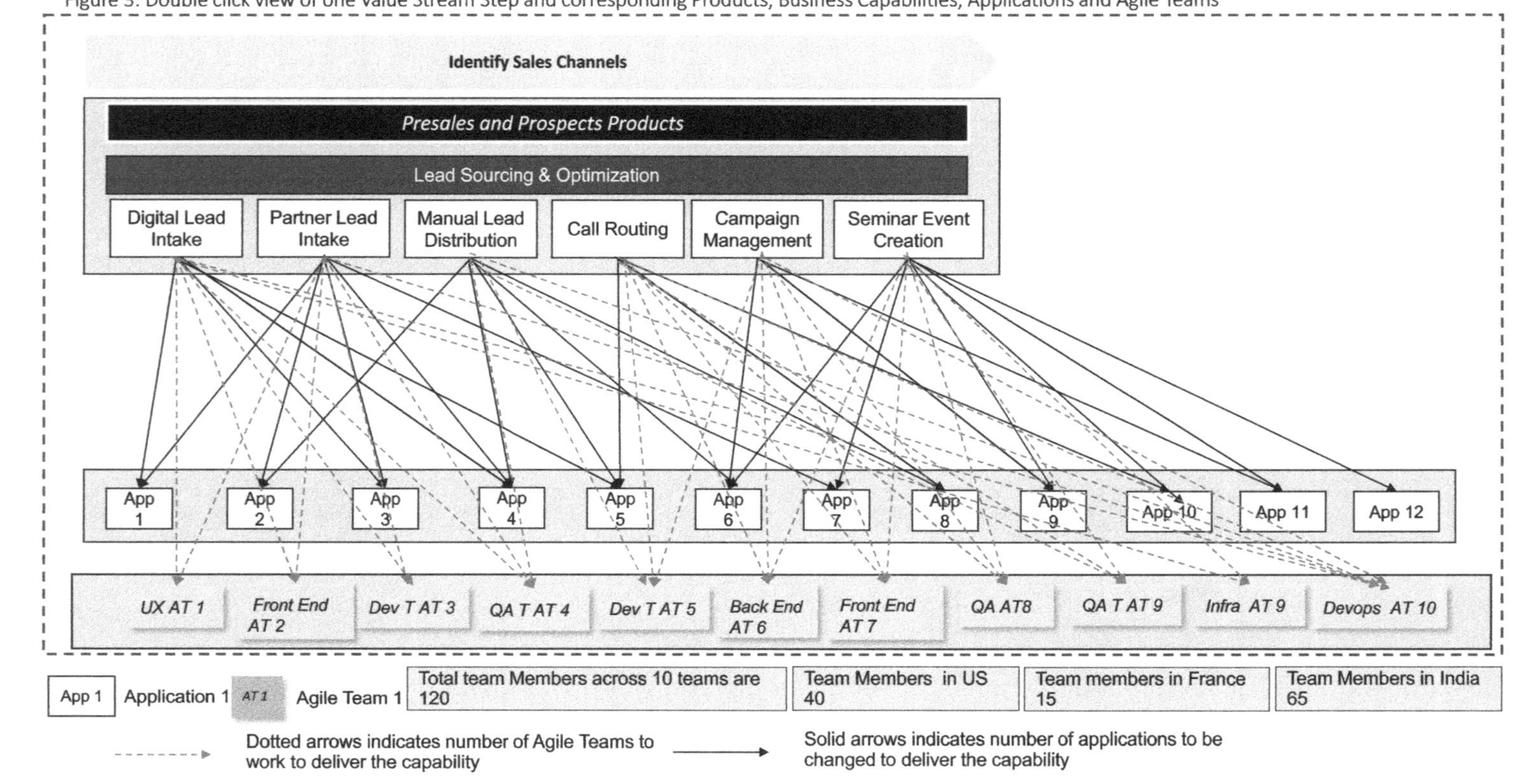

"For instance, not everyone on the team knows the business operation value stream our 'Retail Stores Business Line' uses to deliver value. Do we have a mapping of the business capabilities and functionalities we build versus the corresponding business value streams they improve? Are we aligned on what new business capabilities we need to build to achieve our objectives?"

I continued, "Take the healthcare industry as an example. Building an 'Auto Lead Assignment' capability optimizes agent allocation and improves the agent experience, which is critical for entering new market segments. Are we facing challenges in delivering value quickly to our business? According to our assessment report, it takes an average of 110 days to deliver a new feature request. One reason for this long lead time is how we've organized programs, with too many dependencies outside the program."

As the flurry of questions died down, I could see a mix of emotions across the room—curiosity, excitement, and a hint of anxiety about the mountain of tasks ahead.

I reassured everyone, "We've already done a significant amount of groundwork, and we're prepared to guide you through this process with plenty of examples and support. Together, we'll clarify this current state view."

I continued, emphasizing the need for strategic vision. "Understanding these three perspectives is crucial. Envisioning the future state of what new or modernized products and capabilities we need—as we'll discuss in Chapter 9 —is also vital for optimizing and enhancing the experience within our business operation value streams."

"And setting up PODs or product teams, and reorganizing programs into Product Lines or Agile Release Trains as detailed in Chapter 10, is foundational for enabling faster value delivery. With this setup for the future state portfolio, our organization can refine business operation value stream steps with the right business capabilities and innovative products. This will optimize our time to market and allow us to deliver these products faster than our competition."

Mr. Business Owner, who had been listening intently, added, "We've had extensive discussions about this at the leadership level and are aligned on the need for this kind of strategic view. It's critical for us to stay competitive. However, gathering all the application-level data, its functionalities, and corresponding business capabilities will indeed be a huge effort. That's why, with some of the leads and team members here, we have already started collecting those details."

I nodded in agreement, saying, "Exactly!"

I expressed my gratitude to all the team members for their outstanding preparatory work, which promised to make our two-day workshop flow seamlessly. "We've collaborated closely with business teams, architects, and tech leads to gather these details. We've logically grouped application functionalities and mapped them to business capabilities and products, as we discussed in Chapter 7."

The program leads and team members seemed encouraged. "This seems logical and sounds great!" they chimed in, and there was a collective nod of agreement. "Let's continue with Part 1 of our agenda and see how it evolves," the leads suggested.

Just then, a voice cut through the consensus. When I looked over, it was Mr. Tech Lead. "So once we identify the products and capabilities that we need to build, will they be executed as multiple projects?" he asked. It was a good question—although we had covered this in detail with senior leadership, it was clear that the same level of discussion was necessary for these leads and team members who are on the ground, executing every line of code and influencing every functionality they use.

"Let's discuss how projects are executed," I proposed, noting the importance of recapping for clarity. "Of course, most of us are familiar with this process as it's been done for decades. Still, let's have a quick recap, shall we? Typically, the business team starts by defining the scope of work based on business needs, then estimates the cost and schedule. Next, the business team details the requirements needed to deliver the scope, the design team creates the architecture, IT handles development and testing, and finally, it's deployed."

I resumed, "Now, let's dive deeper. Is the entire project scope defined upfront or incrementally?"

One of the business managers replied, "Of course, we define it upfront. We need to know the full scope to budget accordingly."

"Okay, got it. And how about the design? Is it done incrementally?" I asked.

The tech lead chimed in, "No, the design is also done upfront, along with building and testing the entire scope."

I continued, "What's the typical duration of a project?"

The test lead responded, "On average, around 6 to 9 months. Some projects may take a little less or more."

"So, customers receive value only every 6 to 9 months? Is the business fine with this timeline?"

Mr. Business Owner replied, "If we could deliver value earlier, it would be great too."

I then asked, "What percentage of projects are delivered on time, as per the plan?"

There was a brief silence. Mr. Business Owner said, "Around 20% of projects."

The tech lead added, "Maybe around 40%. Most projects are delayed because the design was late or the requirements weren't clearly defined."

The business team weighed in, "It's mostly due to delays from the system integration testing (SIT) team, which pushes back user acceptance testing (UAT)."

The test lead quickly responded, "We always receive the code from the development team very late, and there are a lot of defects we find during SIT that take time to fix."

"Exactly!" I said. "Projects are delayed for all these reasons, leading to a blame game. We need to fix these delays without pointing fingers. What do we do when a project is delayed?"

Mr. Business Owner began, "We get a change request (CR) from the tech team. It has to go through multiple cost center approvals, as we need to analyze the reasons and check for available funds."

"That takes additional time to get budget approval, which further delays delivering value," the IT lead added.

"That's true," I agreed. "The 'project way of execution' is the root cause of project delivery delays, blame games, and additional delays due to CRs."

"In the project way of execution, we fix the scope and let the schedule and cost vary. When the fixed scope isn't delivered as planned, we extend the schedule and cost. Instead, if we adopt a product-centric execution, we fund the product based on the 'value' it's expected to deliver. We define value for an increment, then design, build, and test that increment. If the scope isn't delivered within the defined increment period, we move the leftover work to the next increment. In this approach, the scope varies, while both the schedule (increment length) and cost (team size or capacity) remain fixed."

"When we adopt this approach, there's no schedule or cost delay, no CRs, and no blame game," I mentioned.

Suddenly, Mr. Test Lead interjected, "In this approach, if the scope isn't delivered within the increment period, we still end up spending additional time and effort in the next increment to deliver that work. What's the difference then?"

"That's a good point," I acknowledged. "Yes, there's still a possibility of scope creep, or the agreed scope not being delivered within the increment, which could lead to additional cost and time in the next increment. However, the chances of scope creep are minimized because we define scope only for a maximum of three months, taking all risks and unknowns into account. Even when scope creep occurs—it's not delivered fully—we hold a retrospective meeting at the ART or product line level at the end of every increment. As a team, we identify the reasons for not delivering the agreed scope and plan actions to implement in the next increment."

Mr. Tech Lead responded, "Even in the project execution approach, we analyze reasons and take actions."

"Yes, you are right," I said. "The differences here are significant, though. In the product-centric approach, we don't measure schedule and cost variances as strictly. This lack of metric reduces unnecessary pressure on the team, which in the project approach often leads to a blame game and can negatively impact team collaboration. Additionally, introducing the change request process in traditional methods leads to further delays and overhead. When teams are questioned about schedule variances, they rush to complete leftover work within the agreed additional time and cost, which often leads to quality issues. All these problems are largely eliminated in product-centric ways of working."

Mr. Business Owner nodded, "So, you're saying we address the same problems through a different approach without much harm to individuals or sacrificing quality or incurring additional overhead. You're spot on!"

"Let's quickly watch this video on project vs. product ways of working," I said, and played a YouTube video on the topic.

After the video, I announced, "It's time for our first break! When we come back, we'll dive into the first agenda item. I know we've spent a lot of time discussing the context and the need for this exercise, but it's been a good discussion. It's essential to align and agree on why we're doing this and what we're going to work on."

8.1 Part 1: Define Business Operational Value Stream

After the break, we started with the first agenda item: defining our business operation value stream. "Let's talk about who our customers are and what value we deliver to them. We'll outline the steps we take to create that value," I began. "We've already reimagined our business operation value stream in Chapter 5, but we need the buy-in and alignment from the middle management team for our product-centric transformation to succeed."

Customers: Our customers are the target audience who consume our products or services. This can include consumers of physical goods like cars, mobiles, laptops, or software like Microsoft OS and Intel processors.

"An enterprise might produce cars, mobiles, or laptops, which are consumed by end users—these are our customers," I explained. "Similarly, enterprises providing services like financial services (loans, credit cards), healthcare services, auto insurance, property insurance, and educational services have their target audiences."

"Our customers can be businesses (B2B) or individual consumers (B2C)," I continued. "Businesses consume our outputs as part of their products or services to sell or service their customers, while end users directly use our products and services."

I then started explaining the value we deliver to our customers. In the product industry, we sell physical goods like mobiles, cars, and laptops—that's the value we provide. In the service industry, the value comes from the services we offer, such as insurance, banking, and healthcare.

Next, I moved on to identifying a customer's trigger or need and the steps an enterprise takes to deliver value.

"A 'trigger or need' is when a customer decides to buy a product or use a service," I explained. "For example, a customer might decide to take out a mortgage, buy auto insurance, or purchase a laptop or mobile. It's the enterprise's job to identify these triggers through market analysis and customer spending patterns."

"Once we've identified customer needs, we then outline the value creation steps we perform to meet those needs. Our goal is to deliver products and services more efficiently and effectively, providing a better customer experience to gain a competitive advantage."

"Identifying customer needs and executing the sequence of value creation steps require people, processes, information flow, and technology to meet those needs and deliver value. This entire ecosystem is known as a 'value stream.' These value stream steps are typically at a macro or strategic level, with an average of 8 to 12 steps. They are always written from the enterprise perspective and start with verbs, such as 'Reach out to customers,' 'Attract customers,' 'Receive quotations,' and 'Review quotations.'"

Here is an example of a healthcare business operational value stream for retail sales: (refer next page top image)

What's laid out above zeroes in on the unique slices of the business world, like Individual, Group Business, Medicare, Medicaid, and the like. The digital products these sectors need fall neatly into three baskets. First up, we have the DIY digital marvels – those tailor-made solutions whipped up in-house to meet the specific demands of their niche markets (think custom-built platforms/products). Then there's the second basket – the ready-to-go digital gizmos that businesses can take off the shelf, tweak a bit, and put to work (CRM systems for managing leads and customer communications are prime examples).

And lastly, we've got those digital giants – the platform-level behemoths that provide foundational services across the enterprise, like logging in, authenticating users, and managing data. Each type plays a crucial role, ensuring that businesses are thriving in their respective domains.

The figure below illustrates the digital products utilized by the Group business line, encompassing all three categories of products. (next page image)

To deliver these three types of digital products for the entire business line, we might have multiple centralized Technology/IT portfolios and business line-specific portfolios.

"For instance," I explained, "we'll have a portfolio with teams owned by the respective business lines that deliver a particular type of products lets call these Basket-1 products."

The room nodded in understanding.

"Similarly, we'll have technology/IT portfolios that include areas like retail sales, payer, provider, and pharmacy portfolios that deliver products that might include Basket-1 and Basket-2," I continued.

One of the tech leads raised a hand, "And what about Basket-3 products?"

Trigger:
Prospects need for best Health Coverage

Healthcare Business Operation Value Stream

Value:
Improved Health Coverage for Customers

| Enroll & Shop | Send Welcome Kit to Members | Connect to Get Started | Follow up with Agent/Care Provider | Gets First Pill | Interact with Care manager | Visit Doctor /Provider | Receive & process Claims | Renew Policy Membership |

Value:
Customers enrolled for health insurance & Premium revenue

Figure 1: Business Operation Value Stream, corresponding Products, Business Capabilities, Applications and Platform Capabilities

Trigger: Prospects need for best Health Coverage

Value:
Improved Health Coverage for Customers

| Enroll & Shop | Send Welcome Kit to Members | Connect to Get Started | Follow up with Agent/Care Provider | Gets First Pill | Interact with Care manager | Visit Doctor /Provider | Receive & process Claims | Renew Policy Membership |

Value:
Customers enrolled for health insurance & Premium revenue

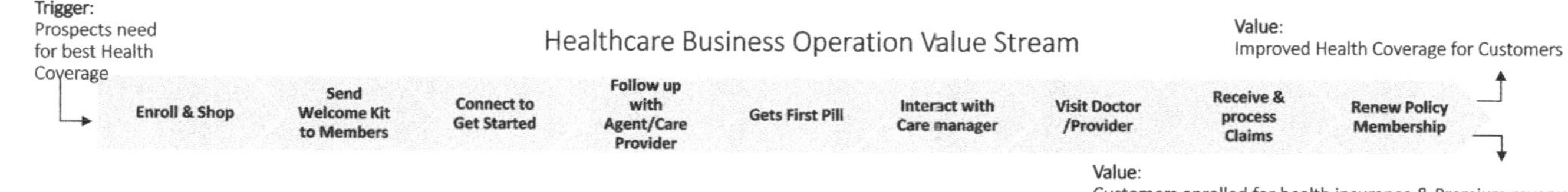

Lead Sourcing & Optimization	Lead Nurturing	Leads Verification & Sales	Customer Onboarding	Customer Self Service	Care Management	Pharmacy Management	Claims Processor
Digital Lead Intake	Prospects Profile	Plan Comparison	Customer Profiling	Customer Profile	Care Coordination	Inventory Management	Claims Intake & Triage
Partner Lead Intake	Appointment Conversation	Physician Finder	Personalized Onboarding	Feedback & Support	Manage Health History	Prescription Processing	Automated Data Capture
Manual Lead Distribution	Eligibility Verification	Drug Cost Lookup	Omnichannel Communication	Bill Payment	Telehealth Services	Regulatory Compliance	Eligibility Verification
Call Routing	Share Marketing Materials	IVR SOA (Scope of Appointment)	Customer Referrals	Manage PHI	Treatment Planning	Customer Engagement	Claims Adjudication
Campaign Management	Guided Call Flow	Voice SOA	Customer Education	Medication Management	Remote Patient Monitoring	E-Prescribing Integration	Fraud Detection
Seminar Event Creation	Lead Auto Assignment	Electronic SOA	Onboarding Analytics	Omni Channel Communication	Outcome Tracking	Financial Management	Payment Processing

Type 1

Type 2

| Application 1 | Application 2 | Application 3 | Application 4 | Application 5 | Application 6 | Application 7 | Application 8 | - - - - | Application N |

| Platform Capabilities | Real Time Tracking | Data Analytics & Reporting | Authentication | Onboarding | Appointment Scheduling | User Logins | Data Management |

Type 3

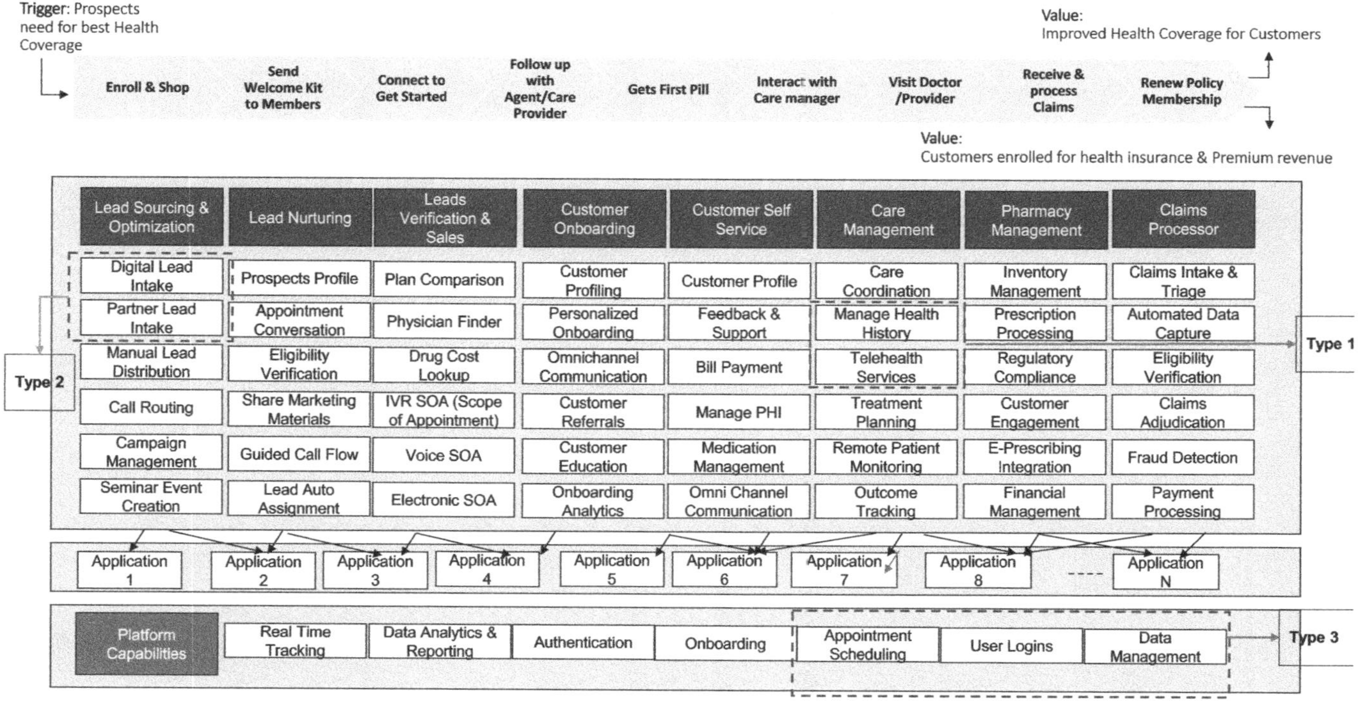

"Good question," I replied. "We'll have centralized 'platforms and capabilities portfolios' that deliver Basket-3 reusable and customizable platforms, products, and capabilities."

"That sounds ideal," said one of the business managers. "But how does it work in practice?"

"Typically, organizations have portfolios for Basket-1 and Basket-2 products," I explained. "However, Basket-3 products are often built by one of the first two portfolios. This leads to redundancies, increased development costs, longer lead times to market, and inconsistent customer experiences."

I saw some concerned faces. "We'll discuss more about platforms and capabilities portfolios in Chapter 17, where we'll talk about implementing a 'platform-centric model.'"

I took a breath and continued, "For now, let's focus on traditional Technology/IT portfolios. If we dive deeper into the business value stream steps, we'll uncover separate value streams for the respective technology portfolios."

The example view below is for a retail sales portfolio that encompasses all products within the business operation value stream of "Enroll & Shop": (next page)

"Similarly, we need to create product views for each portfolio—provider, payer, pharmacy, etc.—and modernize all related products to improve the end-to-end business operation value stream," I explained. "This means adopting a systems thinking approach to enhance efficiency, experience, and effectiveness across all value creation steps for a specific business line."

After our detailed discussion on identifying our customers, the value we deliver to them, and the value stream we use, we decided to focus on an exercise specific to the retail store business line.

"In this example," I continued, "we'll start with an assumption that all three baskets of digital products delivered by Technology/IT portfolios. Each portfolio will have a market/region-wise split or sub-portfolios. Eventually, we'll move towards adopting a third type of portfolio for 'platforms and capabilities.'"

We then split the entire team into four groups, each assigned to a separate virtual breakout room. Their task was to discuss these three aspects- trigger, value creation steps and value delivered and capture their insights. We planned a 45-minute session with quick sync-ups every 15 minutes to ensure they were on the right track.

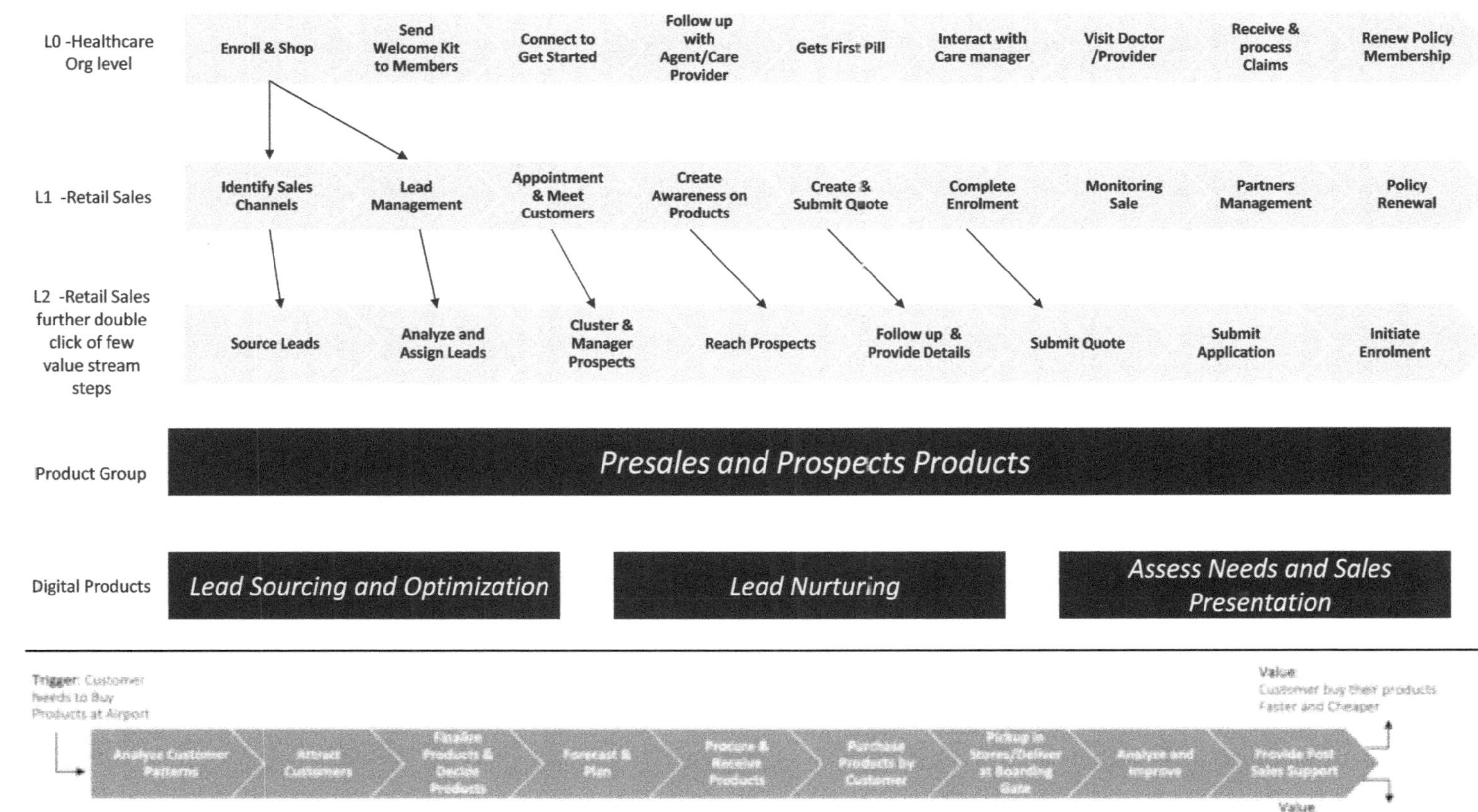

Healthcare Business Operation Value Stream

L0 -Healthcare Org level
Enroll & Shop
Send Welcome Kit to Members
Connect to Get Started
Follow up with Agent/Care Provider
Gets First Pill
Interact with Care manager
Visit Doctor /Provider
Receive & process Claims
Renew Policy Membership

L1 -Retail Sales
Identify Sales Channels
Lead Management
Appointment & Meet Customers
Create Awareness on Products
Create & Submit Quote
Complete Enrolment
Monitoring Sale
Partners Management
Policy Renewal

L2 -Retail Sales further double click of few value stream steps
Source Leads
Analyze and Assign Leads
Cluster & Manager Prospects
Reach Prospects
Follow up & Provide Details
Submit Quote
Submit Application
Initiate Enrolment

Product Group
Presales and Prospects Products

Digital Products
Lead Sourcing and Optimization
Lead Nurturing
Assess Needs and Sales Presentation

Trigger: Customer needs to Buy Products at Airport
Analyze Customer Patterns
Attract Customers
Finalize Products & Decide Products
Forecast & Plan
Procure & Receive Products
Purchase Products by Customer
Pickup in Stores/Deliver at Boarding Gate
Analyze and improve
Provide Post Sales Support
Value: Customer buy their products Faster and Cheaper
Value: Retails products Sales & Commission Revenue

As the teams settled into their breakout rooms, the energy was palpable. They had a lot of great questions and discussions, diving into the details. When they regrouped, they came back with comprehensive outputs on the operational value stream, clearly identifying our customers and the value we deliver to them.

Here are some of the great questions raised during the breakout discussions and their answers:

Why do we need to define the value stream with a maximum of 12 steps or at a macro level?

"The purpose of the value stream is to create a strategic-level overview," I explained. "Based on the need, we can zoom in on each step and detail them as part of analyzing improvement options. This deeper dive would be a level 2 value stream or process map, which is much more tactical."

What's the difference between a value stream and a customer journey?

"Value stream steps are always from the enterprise's perspective—what the enterprise does to realize value," I said. "In contrast, a customer journey is always from the customer's perspective, detailing what the customer does or how they interact with the enterprise to get value. If we zoom in on each step in the customer journey, we call those sub-journey steps."

Our whole team came together to review the outputs from all four breakout groups and we've put the finishing touches on part 1. Here's what the final version looks like: (previous page bottom image)

Based on my experience, our current value stream steps aren't much different from our competitors. We perform the same activities, just with a different focus on cost optimization and operational efficiency. To gain a competitive advantage, we need to redesign our business operation value stream as discussed in Chapter 5.

"It's time for lunch," I announced. "Let's take a 45-minute break and then come back to discuss Part 2."

Just then, Mr. Business Owner raised a question. "You mentioned two types of customers initially, but we've only discussed end-user customers. What's the other type?"

"Great point, thanks for the reminder," I replied. "After lunch, we'll dive into the second type—internal customers. These are the users who leverage our technology-enabled solutions to provide value to our end-users. We'll start with that after lunch."

During the lunch break, I checked in with Mr. Agile Coach for general feedback. He shared what he heard from Mr. Tech Lead, who seemed quite nervous. "He's worried about the alignment on products that we might not get from the business partners."

"Alright," I said, "that's the next part we'll tackle. Let's deal with it head-on after lunch."

I asked for feedback on Part 1 that we just completed. Mr. Business Owner mentioned that he had spoken to the CIO, who thought our work looked good academically but couldn't see how it would impact the strategy and execution of product-centric transformation.

"That's a fair point," I replied patiently. "Part 2 of this workshop should provide more clarity toward our end goal, and we'll cover the rest in Part 3."

Mr. Agile Coach chimed in, "Let's hope for the best," and we both laughed. Despite feeling a bit nervous about the feedback, I kept my composure to maintain the positive energy.

After lunch, we started with an icebreaker game where everyone shared their weekend plans. It was great to see so many similarities and like-minded people. Some even planned to meet up after the discussion. It was a good warm-up, especially post-lunch.

We then began discussing products and our second type of customers—internal customers.

8.2 Part 2: Define Digital Products (Technology-Enabled Solutions)

"Let's do a quick recap on what a product is and who its users are," I began.

"As we discussed in Chapter 7 and earlier in this chapter, we have products and technology-enabled solutions used by end-users or external customers to interact with our organization. These allow them to access services, purchase products, manage orders, and request customer service. We've already talked about how end-users receive value as a product or service."

Similarly, internal customers (business users) also use these products for internal operations or to interact with end users.

"For example," I explained, "in the online retail industry, once a product is purchased by an end user, the fleet manager (an internal customer) needs to organize the shipping. They manage fleets, assign products to specific areas, and so on."

"So, both internal and external customers use products (technology-enabled solutions) to perform activities. To help them do this faster (efficiently), more accurately (effectively), and with less hassle (better experience), we need to focus on modernizing these products or developing new ones from both perspectives. The first step toward this goal is identifying existing products and business capabilities."

One of the solution architects, who hadn't been in the initial discussion, asked, "We have existing applications, so each one of these is a product, right?"

"That's a good question," I said. "Let's clarify this, as many of you might have the same question. Remember the difference between applications and products from Chapters 2 and 3? It's essential to understand why we need to 'productize' our technology solutions."

Everyone agreed on the need to identify products, so I began explaining the bottom-up approach to doing so.

"In specific areas of the operation value stream, certain applications are leveraged to perform various functionalities," I said. "Let's take the supply chain area as an example. Applications like AS400 and DMS are used here. Each of these applications, whether on their own or integrated with others, offers functionalities that are used by end users or internal users."

"For instance," I continued, "some of the functionalities provided include receiving, invoicing, and updating inventory. These functions are essential for both our end users and internal customers."

The following picture provides a detailed view of the same: (next page)

Suddenly, Mr. Dev Lead chimed in, "This is already known to everyone. What difference are we talking about?"

"Yes, you're right," I responded. "It's known, but has it been documented? Maybe not. Why do we need to document it? That's the purpose of this workshop, and I'll explain the 'why' in a few minutes. For now, let me explain what else we need to do."

"Once we've mapped functionalities to applications, we need to logically group those functionalities into business capabilities that the business team will use. Then, we group those business capabilities into logical products from

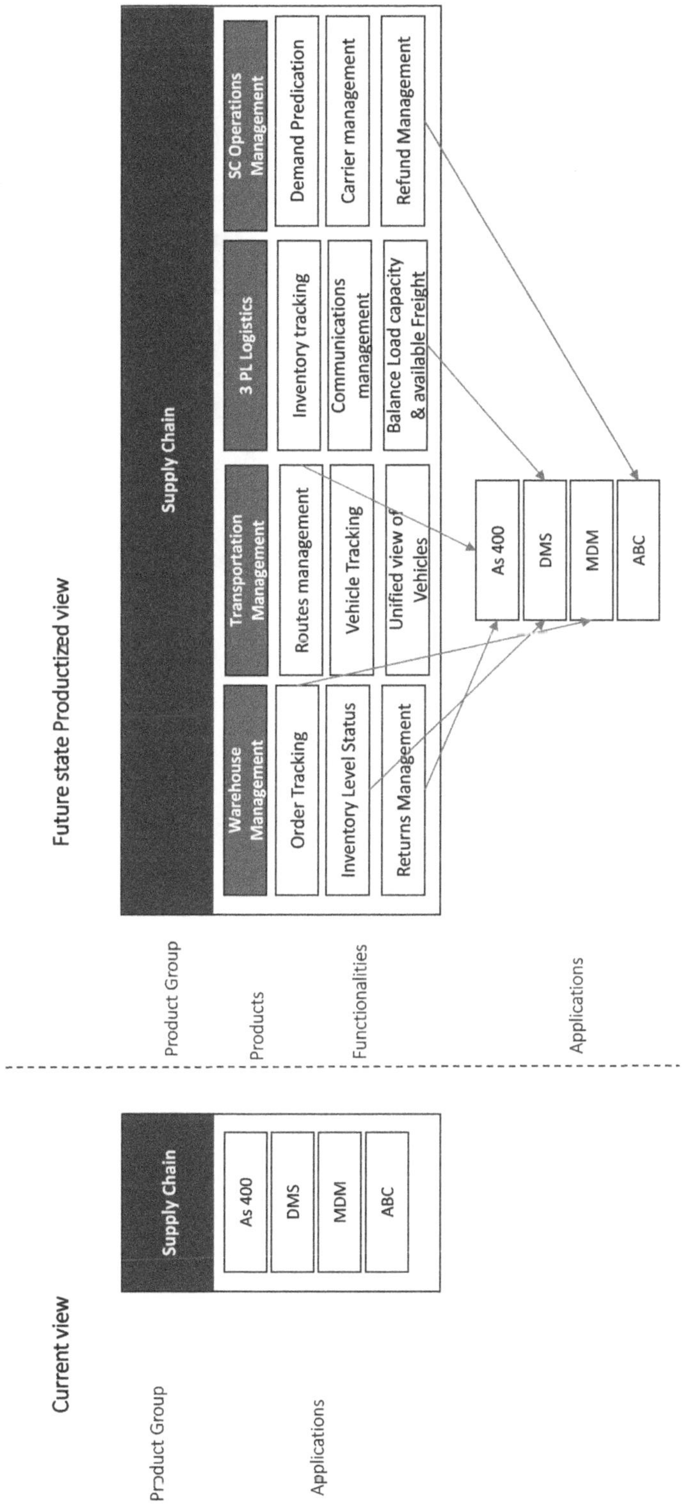

Current view

Future state Productized view

Product Group

Supply Chain

As 400
DMS
MDM
ABC

Applications

Product Group

Products

Functionalities

Applications

Supply Chain

Warehouse Management
Order Tracking
Inventory Level Status
Returns Management

Transportation Management
Routes management
Vehicle Tracking
Unified view of Vehicles

3 PL Logistics
Inventory tracking
Communications management
Balance Load capacity & available Freight

SC Operations Management
Demand Predication
Carrier management
Refund Management

As 400
DMS
MDM
ABC

both internal and external customer perspectives, as shown in our future state productized view."

Mr. Business Owner interjected, "I believe we do have details on business capabilities."

"Do we have them documented with these relationships?" I asked. The answer was "no." "Have we mapped them to product teams to own and deliver?" Again, the answer was "no." Currently, PODs/agile teams are mapped to projects.

"Let me explain the need for mapping functionalities to business capabilities and then to products. As we discussed earlier, only when we have the products and their current business capabilities defined, we can compare with the market and competitors. This helps us create a product strategy that enables us to achieve several things:

- *Define the product's value and business benefits from the customer's perspective.*

- *Align product strategy and vision with competitors and customer needs.*

- *Identify new business capabilities and functionalities (innovative/disruptive capabilities).*

- *Create a product roadmap.*

- *Refine application architecture.*

- *Deliver according to the roadmap and measure value and business benefits.*

The six steps we just discussed are detailed in Chapter 9. They are essential for achieving business agility. Without a current state view of our products and business capabilities, we can't accomplish these steps or deliver business value. So, defining products and business capabilities is a critical foundational step in our journey to business agility.

The business owner responded, "That makes perfect sense. Let's do this. But can we complete it in this workshop? Gathering and mapping all this information is a huge task."

"As I mentioned earlier, we've done the pre-work with support from all business users, PMs, POs, and tech leads. We've gathered all the applications, functionalities, and business capabilities. Now, we just need to review it with the entire team and define the products."

"Wow, that's great! I'm happy to see everyone's involvement and progress. Let's start reviewing and finalizing the products."

It was encouraging to receive such positive feedback from the business sponsor, a critical stakeholder in the Retail business line. Getting his buy-in was a great starting point for achieving the workshop's outcomes.

We had detailed breakout discussions while reviewing the grouping of functionalities into business capabilities, made minor updates, and logically named the products.

After three hours of discussion, including two breaks and multiple breakout sessions, we reached a final view at the end of day 1. We successfully completed the definition of the business operation value stream, finalized the products, and outlined the business capabilities and functionalities, mapping them all to the underlying applications. (on the right image, page 170 and 171 images)

As shown in the figure, agile teams are organized as "component teams" and "application-specific teams." This structure leads to several key challenges:

- Teams are organized by function and aligned to applications, which impacts overall efficiency and productivity.

- Product owners and scrum masters need to collaborate with multiple teams to implement a single functionality.

- This collaboration and coordination among multiple teams often lead to miscommunication and delays.

- Functionalities are defined across frontend, API, and backend, reflecting the teams' structure.

- When multiple teams work on one functionality, the overhead of tracking increases, leading to priority conflicts as each team has its own priorities.

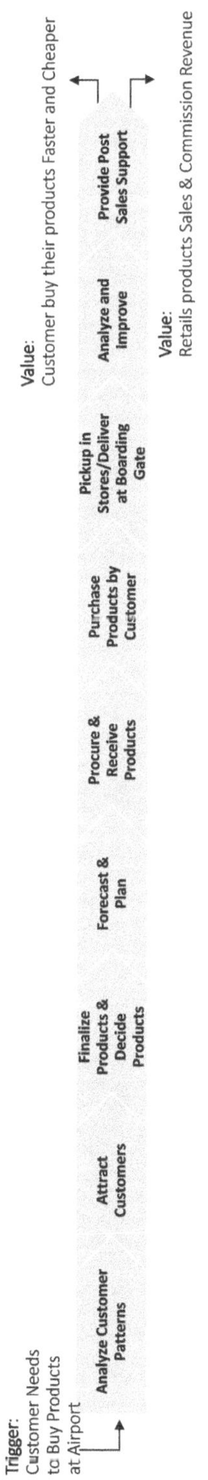

Figure 1: Retail Store Business Operation Value Stream

Figure 2: Current State Products Group, Products, Business Capabilities for Retail Stores

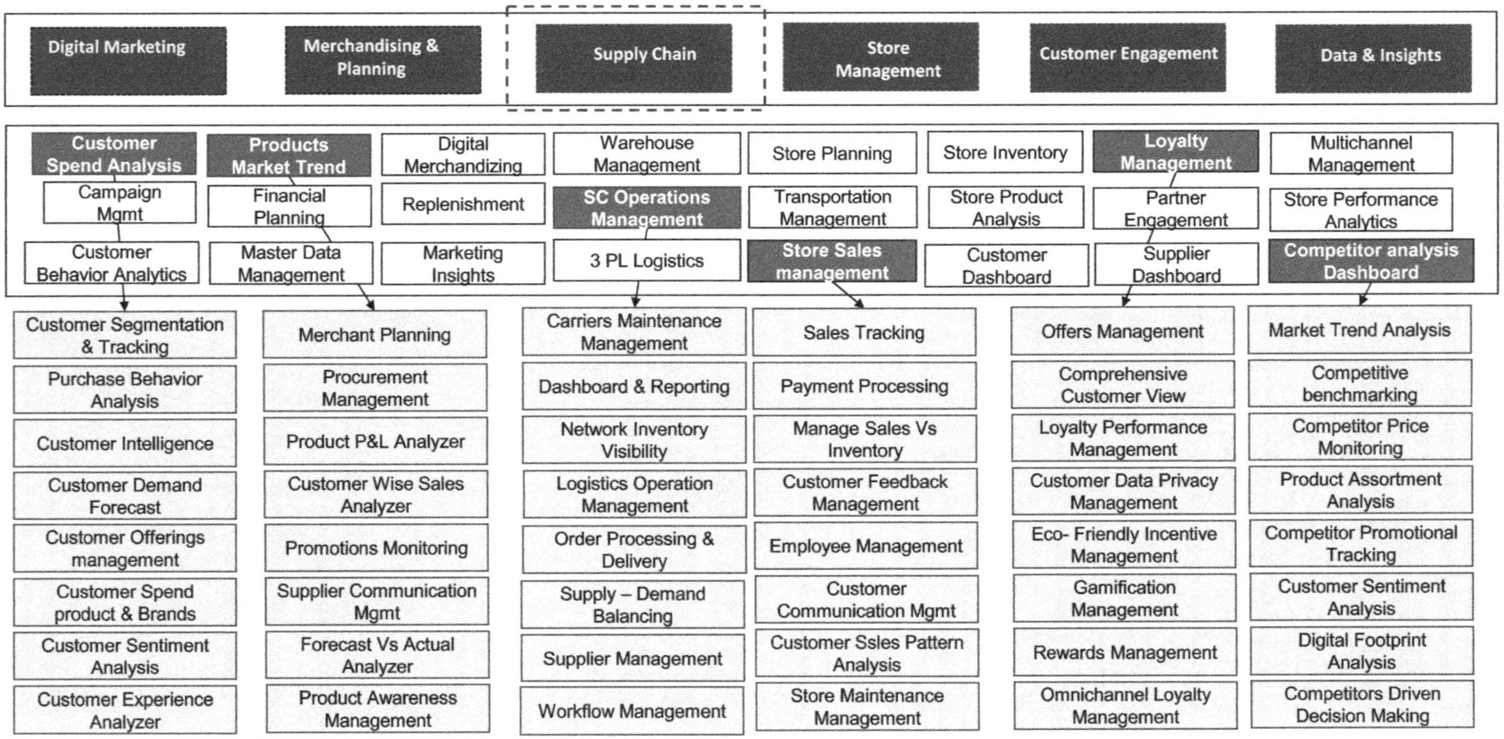

Figure 3: Double Click view of Supply Chain Product Group, Product, Business capabilities

Product Group: Supply Chain (SC)

Products	WMS	Transportation Management	3 PL Management	Supply Chain Analytics	SC Operations Management	Inventory management
Business Capabilities	Dashboard & Reporting	Carriers Maintenance Management	Order Processing & Delivery	Network Inventory Visibility	Order tracking	Workflow Management
	Labor Management	Goods in ad out processes	Logistics Operation Management	Supply & Career Connectivity	Supply – Demand Balancing	Inventory Tracking
	Replenishment	Returns Management	Demand Forecasting	Risk Management & Mitigation	Unified Demand Forecasting	Product Wise Inventory Monitoring
	Integrated Order Processing	Carriers Utilization Management	Logistics Performance Management	Suppliers Product Lead time Analyzer	Supply Chain performance Trends	Storage Quality Management
Functionalities	Order Processing	Carriers Allocation	Logistics Approval tracking	Suppliers order tracking	Supply Chain data Ingestion	Inventory Quality condition monitoring
	Order return Management	Carriers Drivers Allocations	Logistics onboarding	Suppliers order lead time benchmarking	Different Perspectives of Data Presentation	Storage Environment conditions Tracking
	Order price update	Carriers Maintenance status	Logistics Performance Evaluation	Supplier Order cancellation management	Supply Chain Risk Reporting	Automated identification quality inspection
	Order Analysis	Carriers Performance monitoring	Logistics performance benchmarking	Suppliers Order wise Cost analysis	Real-time time Supply Chain Performance	Storage tracking with compliance Requirements

Existing Business Capabilities that needs to be modernized

Figure 4: Double click view of one Value Stream Step and corresponding Products, Business Capabilities, Applications and Agile Teams

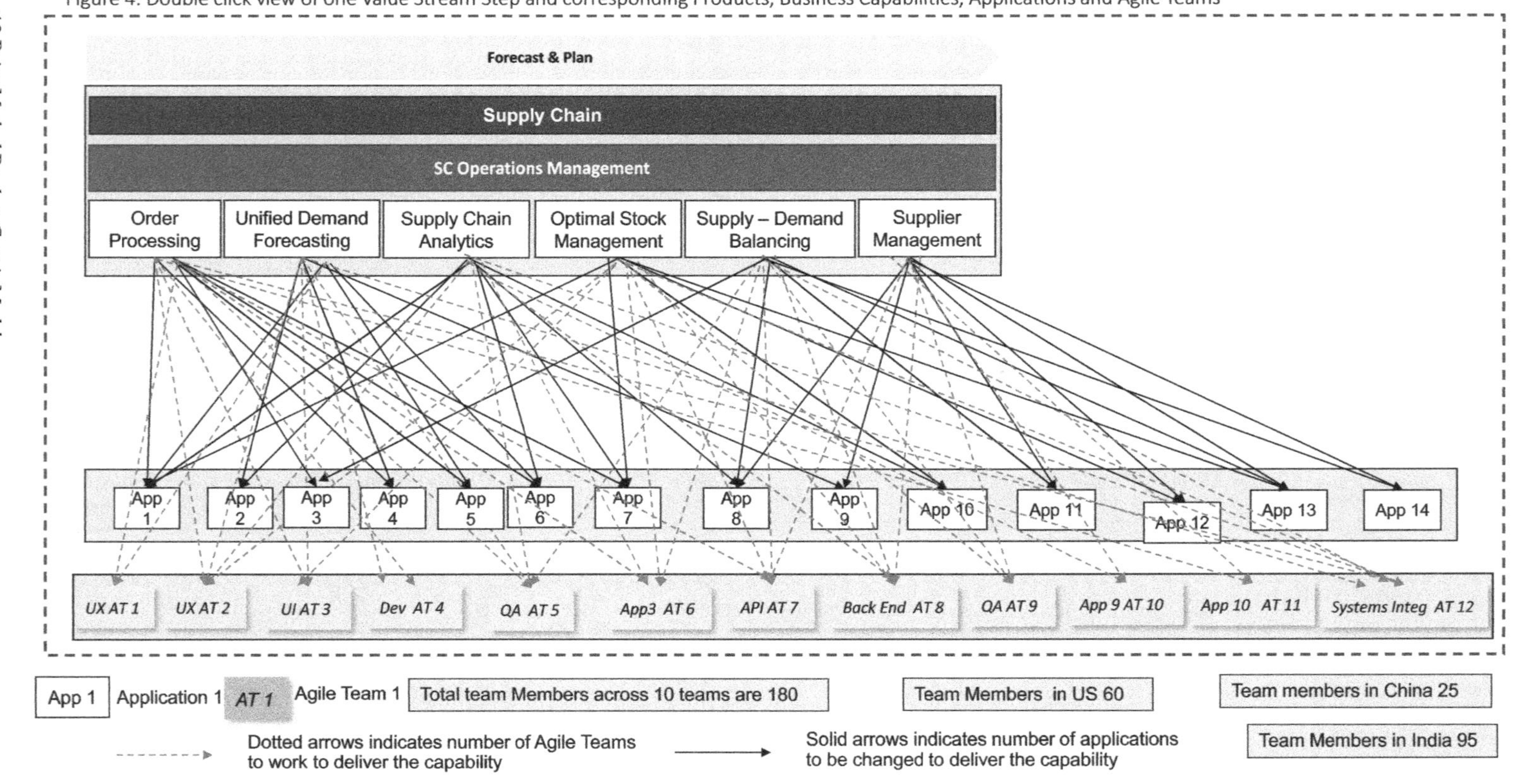

- This current state of creating functionalities and function-aligned team structures makes it difficult to focus on delivering end-user value and deliver them faster.

- Team members often feel disconnected and disempowered from the customer value perspective.

- "We need to organize teams that have all the necessary skills and work towards the common goal of delivering end-user value," I explained. "Organizing teams according to team topologies will help address these issues, improve collaboration, minimize dependencies, and boost efficiency and productivity. We'll discuss more about future state teams in Chapter 10."

We concluded Day 1 on the note that we had completed the "current state view of business operation value stream and products." This will be leveraged as we envision future state products in Chapter 9. These products will align with our future state business operation value stream defined as part of our business strategy in Chapter 5.

The tech lead asked, "What's different in the future state business operation value stream?"

I responded, "The current state value stream focuses on cost optimization by doing the same activities as our competitors but in a different way. This won't help us thrive in the business. So, we've created a future state value stream, as detailed in Chapter 5, that focuses on both 'performing the same competitor activities differently' and 'doing different activities than our competitors.' This approach will help us create a competitive advantage."

After a very tiring but satisfying day, Mr. Agile Coach and I met for dinner. We had a great conversation about the day's outcomes, having completed Part 1 (defining the operational value stream) and Part 2 (applications to product view). While Mr. Agile Coach was happy with the progress, he mentioned the challenge we would face tomorrow. Though I was prepared for the next day's challenges, I suggested we enjoy today's accomplishments for a bit before discussing the strategy.

As we talked, we saw someone familiar approaching us. It was Mr. Tech Lead. We greeted him and invited him to join us. He hesitated at first, not wanting to disturb us, but then agreed since he was alone and had come for a quick drink before bed. He had traveled all the way from Chicago for this two-day workshop.

The tech lead said, "I understand the importance of capturing the current state view. But achieving improvement is a challenge. With our legacy tech stack and mainframe applications, it's tough to modernize products."

"Your point is valid," I replied. "We're discussing with senior leadership how to leverage Gen AI to modernize some of our mainframe codes to be interoperable with modern systems. We're proposing a Gen AI Center of Excellence model to pilot a few use cases. In fact, one of the pilot teams converted COBOL code to Java, saving 55% of the effort as part of the legacy modernization program. The next step is to convert this monolith program to microservices. In the Gen AI era, legacy modernization has become a much easier journey."

The tech lead responded, "I've gone through some Gen AI overview training. I have my own views, but let's see how it develops. As long as we achieve our goal, we're fine."

Day 2 Meeting:

As I stood before the team on Day 2, I could feel the anticipation in the room. "Good morning, everyone," I began, making eye contact with each participant. "Today, we're moving into part 3 of our agenda. We're going to identify the development value stream that delivers new functionalities and features."

I walked over to the whiteboard, marker in hand. "First, we'll map out the entire process," I said, drawing a timeline. "This includes everything from receiving a new feature request to its release to the customer."

I paused to ensure everyone was following along. "We'll dive into the various skills needed at each stage," I continued, jotting down roles such as developers, testers, product owners, and scrum masters. "We'll discuss how each person contributes to managing the end-to-end delivery."

I glanced around the room, gauging reactions. "It's crucial we understand not just the steps involved, but the collaboration required to make this process seamless and efficient. This holistic view will help us pinpoint areas for improvement and ensure we deliver high-quality features quickly."

"Let's dive in," I said with a smile, ready to lead the team through this critical analysis.

8.3 Part 3: Defining Development Value Streams and Product Teams

As participants started joining, both virtually and in person, I prepared my agenda slide for Day 2. Within the next five minutes, everyone had logged in.

"Welcome to Day 2," I began, smiling warmly. "Before we dive into today's agenda, let's quickly recap our working agreements for the workshop: no emails or phone calls during the session, and please keep your video on for better interaction." I noticed a few people opening laptops and checking emails. "Let's stay focused on this session," I gently reminded them.

We kicked off with a fun icebreaker. "Share your favorite cuisine," I prompted. Participants eagerly shared their preferences, and we found many common tastes. We created an affinity diagram to highlight our diversity and similarities. This exercise reinforced that, despite our differences, we are united in working towards a common goal.

After some hearty laughs, I transitioned to the main content. "Let's look at an example from the healthcare industry's retail sales portfolio," I said, displaying a slide. "Here, we see the number of Development Value Streams (DVS) identified and the agile teams needed to deliver value through each DVS. Our goal today is to create a similar view for our organization."

"Our task," I continued, "is to determine the number of DVS and agile teams needed for each one. Based on this, we'll decide how many Agile Release Trains (ARTs)/Product Line we require." (next page image)

The figure above shows the retail sales portfolio of the healthcare industry, featuring four product groups and their corresponding applications. Each product group's business capabilities and functionalities are organized into different development value streams, based on the clustering of applications and their dependencies. They had four product groups or ARTs to design, develop, and deliver the functionalities and business capabilities related to each group. All agile teams within each product group were organized under one ART.

"Let's start with a list of activities we do in the project-based execution method," I said, sharing a screen that displayed the WMS project scope, timeline, and overall objectives. I paused for a few minutes to allow everyone to read and recall. This project, executed for the supply chain area within the retail business line (as discussed in Chapter 2), was familiar to almost everyone, given its many challenges during and after execution.

Figure 1: Business Operation Value Stream, Product Groups, DVS, ARTs, and Agile teams

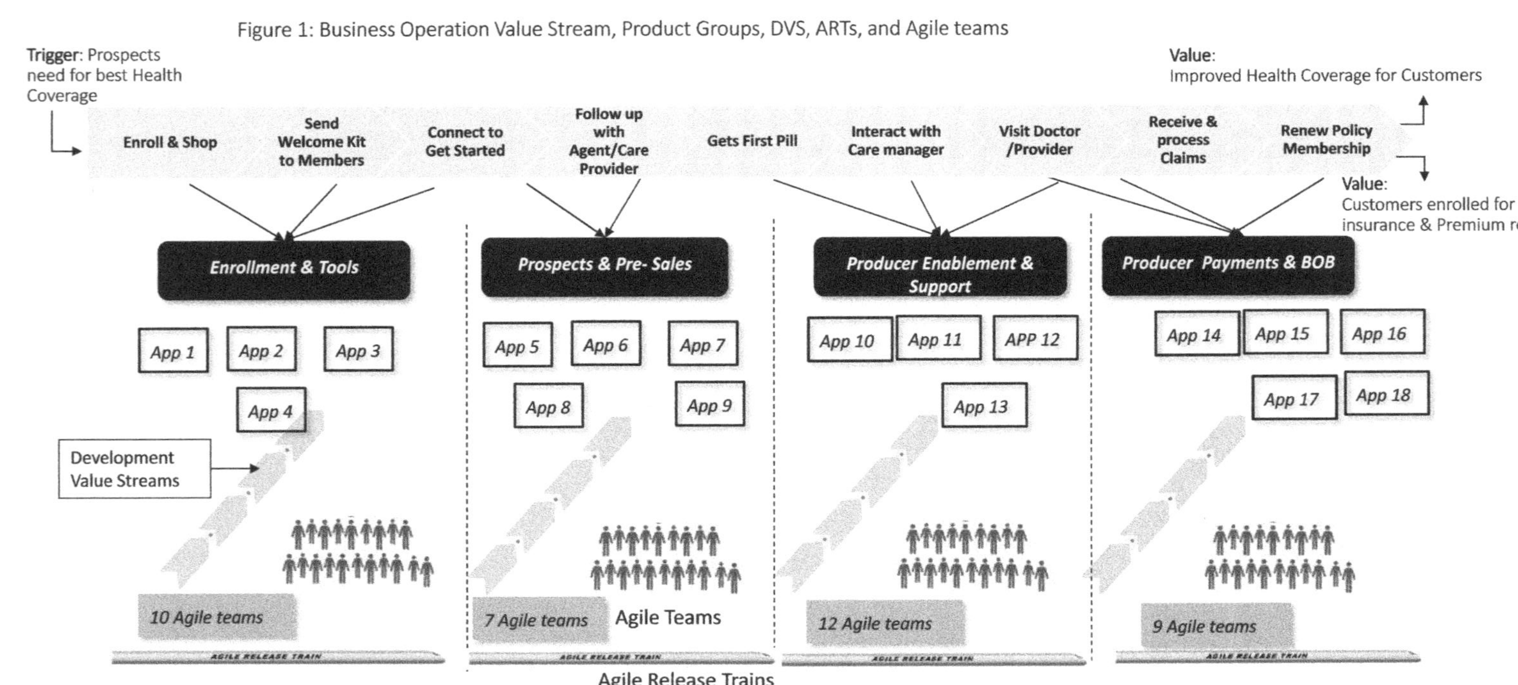

After everyone had read about the project, I asked the team to share their inputs on the challenges faced during its execution. While we had captured challenges earlier from an external and leadership perspective, we now needed to hear from the team on the ground who executed each activity. These insights would likely be different and crucial for addressing the transition to a product-centric way of working. Only with their buy-in could we successfully implement the new approach.

We used the Miro online virtual tool to capture everyone's inputs. Participants started adding their challenges on sticky notes. After refining, removing duplicates, merging, and consolidating, here's the final list of challenges:

- ***Extended Lead Time:*** The overall lead time to deliver the project was set at six months but exceeded by 30%. The business highlighted this as a significant delay in time to market.

- ***Team Setup and Disbandment:*** It took two months to set up the project team, which was disbanded after the project's completion. Now, for the WMS project in China, we are working with a completely new team.

- ***Development Delays:*** Development was delayed by a month due to scope changes.

- ***Change Request Overheads:*** The change request process for additional budget approval caused a 15-day delay and added overhead. Some team members left as their allocation ended.

- ***Testing Delays:*** Testing started a week late because testing members were delayed due to their prior project's release running late.

- ***Lack of Operations Involvement:*** The operations team was not involved or informed about the scope, development, and testing activities, leading to a conflict-ridden transition from development to operations. There were many conflicts during the two-week post-go-live support overlap.

- ***Quality Issues:*** Despite following the quality gate process at the end of each phase (requirements, design, and development), the timeline was still delayed, costs exceeded, and many quality issues leaked into production. The operations team is currently resolving many incidents.

- ***Manual Processes:*** While DevOps practices and tools for continuous build, integration, deployment, and testing were used, many manual activities injected defects and delayed delivery.

- **Rework Due to Late Integration:** Late integration of features with other systems caused significant rework and further delayed the go-live date.

The challenges listed above clearly show that a major issue is the lack of collaboration between multiple teams. This has led to delays, dependencies, and quality problems. Additionally, there are issues like the lack of an agile way of working and insufficient automation in CI/CD and testing.

Our first priority is to address the lack of collaboration and communication delays. We need to reorganize the project team members into a single stream-aligned team focused on the development value stream—taking new feature requests and deploying them as functionalities in the production environment.

As I explained this, I noticed some confusion among the team. It was clear they didn't fully grasp the concept yet.

Then, I drew the picture below. Let's recall all the activities that were performed during project execution (as discussed above): (next page top image)

The typical project took a whopping 54 weeks from start to finish. But, by redefining our approach with a set of new value creation activities aligned with scaled agile methodologies, we're reshaping every activity to be more efficient and impactful as shown below: (next page bottom image)

"This is called the Development Value Stream (DVS)," I began, drawing attention to the screen. "It's the process that takes new feature requests and translates them into value through a series of value-creation steps, supported by people, processes, and tools."

I saw some puzzled faces in the room, so I continued, "Think of it as a streamlined assembly line. Each person and tool plays a crucial role in transforming an idea into a working feature."

I paused to let that sink in, then added, "On average, it takes about 18 to 24 weeks to execute end-to-end business capabilities or epics."

One of the team members raised a hand. "But how do we avoid the execution challenges we've faced in the past?"

"Great question," I responded. "To prevent those challenges and optimize our delivery time, we need to identify and organize all the necessary skills required for these DVS steps. We'll form a dedicated virtual network of teams. This

Figure 2: Retail Store Development Value Stream – Project Based Ways of Working

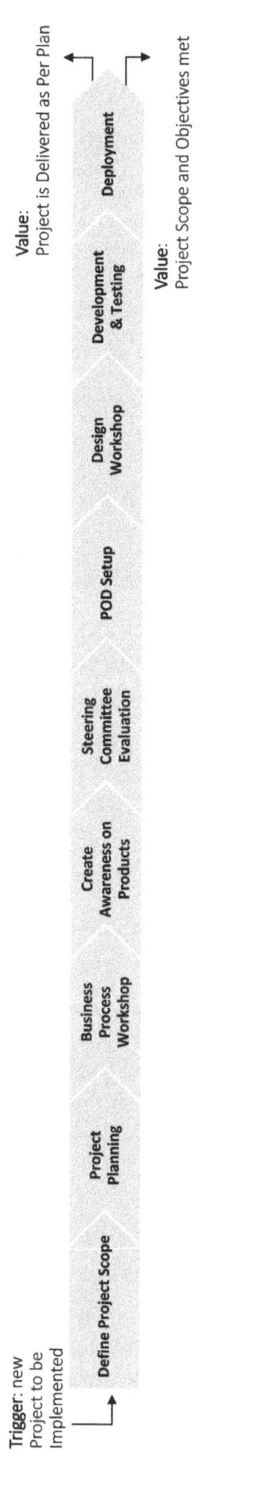

Figure 3: Retail Store Development Value Stream – Product Based Ways of Working

network will stick with the DVS as long as the products and business capabilities it delivers exist."

I noticed nods of understanding and continued, "Now that we understand what the DVS is and how we'll reorganize team members with various skills, let's revisit the Business Operation Value Stream (OVS), the products, and the applications view for the retail business line we defined in Part 2 of this workshop."

I switched the slide to show the diagram from section 8.2. "Here's our OVS, products, and applications view. Next, we'll define the DVS and determine the number of cross-skilled PODs or product teams we need."

Before moving on, I looked around the room. "We've also gathered details of everyone currently working on delivering various product line backlogs, such as Supply Chain, Plan & Procure. This information will help us in forming our new teams."

With guidelines such as the number of people per team, and each team should be multi-skilled, etc., we identified the total number of teams as shown below. There are a total of 48 agile teams working for this Retail sales portfolio that deliver features and user stories related to various epics/projects (business capabilities and products): (next page image)

Looking at the picture above, it seems like we have one DVS to deliver all products and epics. However, that might not be practical. We can't organize all these teams under one DVS.

Let's discuss how many DVS we need to deliver all the product epics and features for the entire retail stores business line. The number of DVS required depends on the number of applications impacted to implement a new feature.

"For example," I explained, "if nearly all applications are impacted by a new feature, then we need one DVS under which all the product teams or PODs will be set up. This is because we can't logically group a set of applications to deliver features and align them under one DVS."

"However," I continued, "if only some applications are impacted by new features, we can logically group those applications and their related products under one DVS."

I pointed to the next slide. "This picture illustrates the guidelines we can use to decide the number of DVS needed for any portfolio or business line."

Figure 4: Retail Store Development Value Stream – Product Based Ways of Working

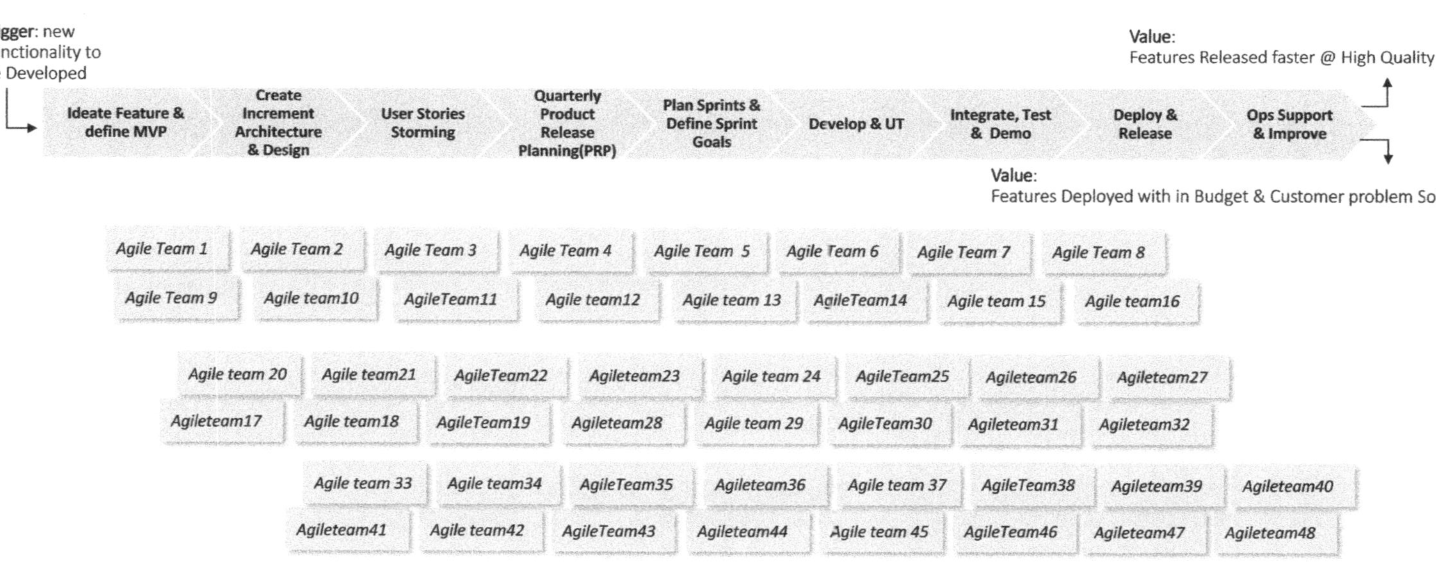

Figure 5: How to Decide on Number of Development Value Streams Needed

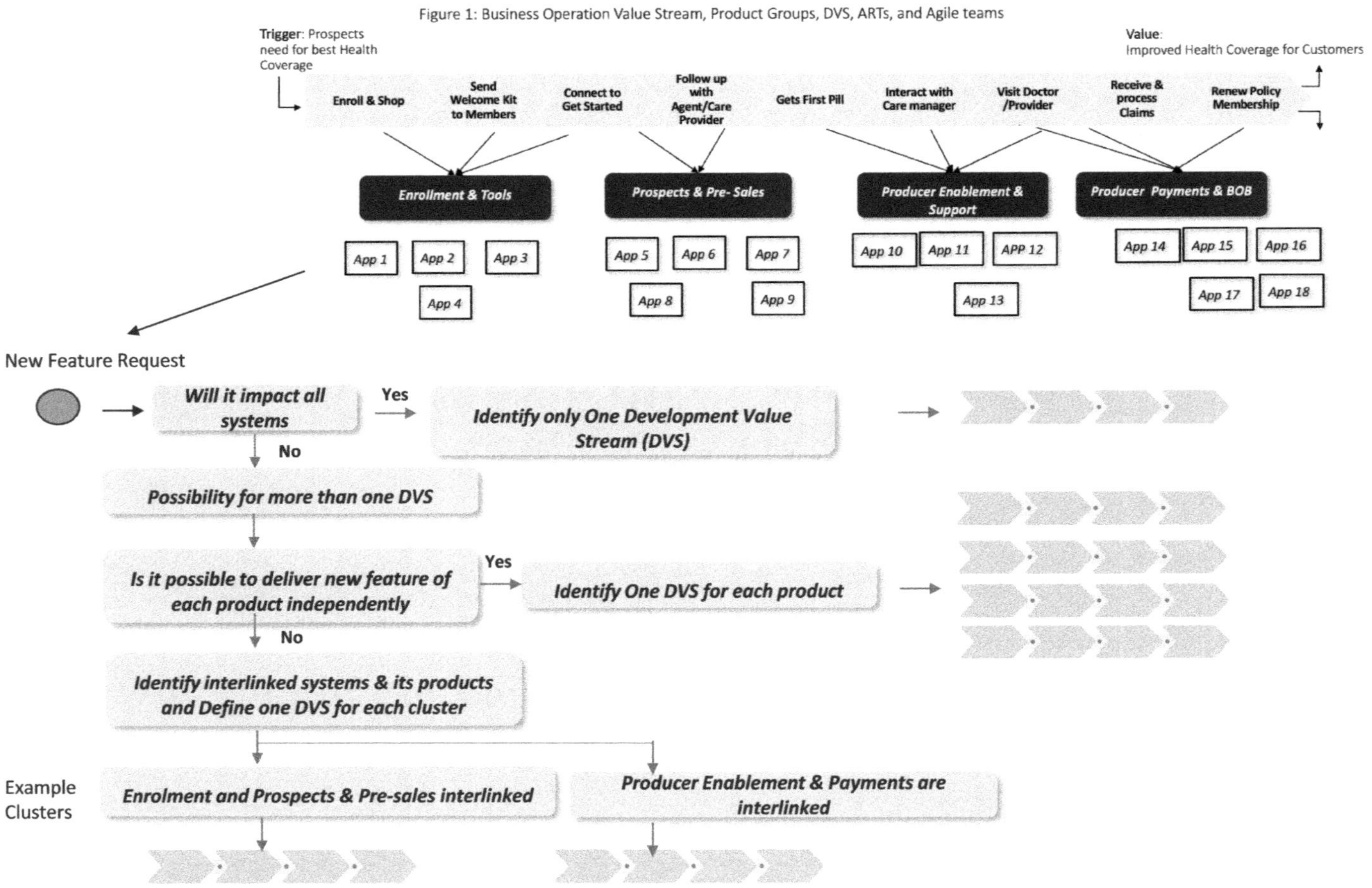

Figure 1: Business Operation Value Stream, Product Groups, DVS, ARTs, and Agile teams

Let's understand this guideline with the example of a retail sales portfolio from the healthcare industry, as shown: (previous page image)

The figure below offers guidelines for determining the number of product groups/ARTs required per DVS: (next page image)

"Let's take an example from our retail industry," I began. "We have a feature called 'implement goods receiving and recording functionality.' How many applications will be impacted to implement this feature? Let's look at the picture above."

As I moved to the Miro board where we had the Part 2 picture with all the impacted application names, Mr. Tech Lead started responding, "DMS, PIM, and OMS."

Then Mr. Architect added, "Web Rekey, Salsa, and E-Shop applications."

By the time I opened the Miro board and shared it with the entire team, it was exactly as mentioned by Mr. Tech Lead and Mr. Architect.

"So, it seems we can group these applications logically and form a DVS for them," I noted. "Now, let's take a few more examples of features and discuss which applications will be impacted."

All the team members enthusiastically participated, providing inputs on the impacted applications and validating the existing picture where we had all applications marked.

Finally, as a team, we concluded that we will have three DVSs:

- One for Merchandising & Planning, and Supply Chain.

- One for Store Management and Customer Engagement.

- One for Digital Marketing and Data & Insights.

These three DVSs will be set up to deliver the underlying products and applications effectively.

The picture appeared as follows (Picture for Retail Business Line DVSs): (page 185 image)

We've decided to design a canvas for the Development Value Stream (DVS) to clearly outline its value proposition. For the Retail Store DVS, we plan to develop this view offline. Here's an example of a DVS from the Healthcare Industry: (refer page 186 image)

"Now, let's break into three groups to identify all the team members and skills needed to deliver features related to the products and applications of each

Figure 5 a: How to Decide on Number of Agile Release Trains/Product Groups Value Streams Needed

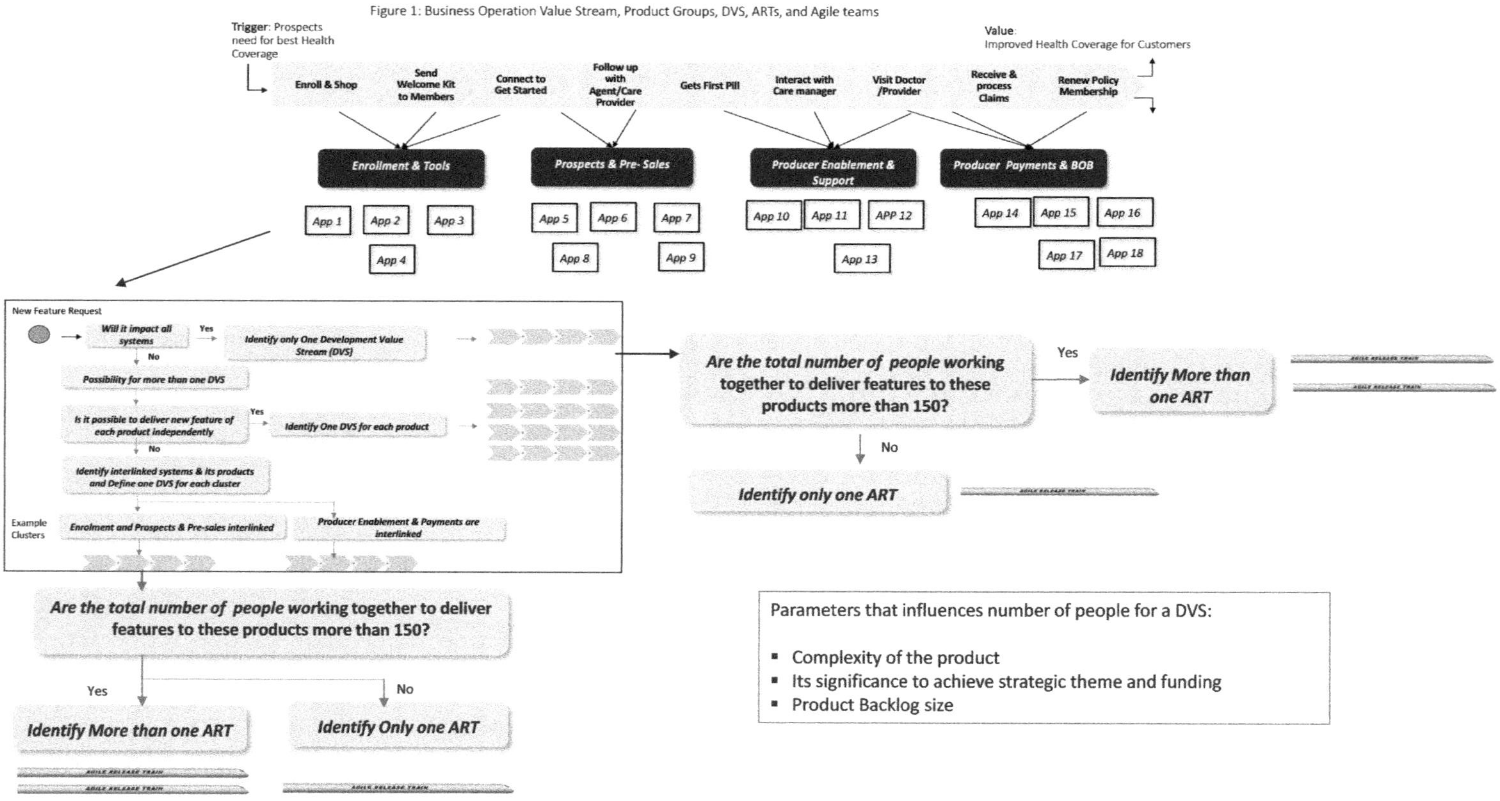

Figure 1: Business Operation Value Stream, Product Groups, DVS, ARTs, and Agile teams

Figure 7: Current State Products Group, Products, Business Capabilities for Retail Stores with Development Value Streams

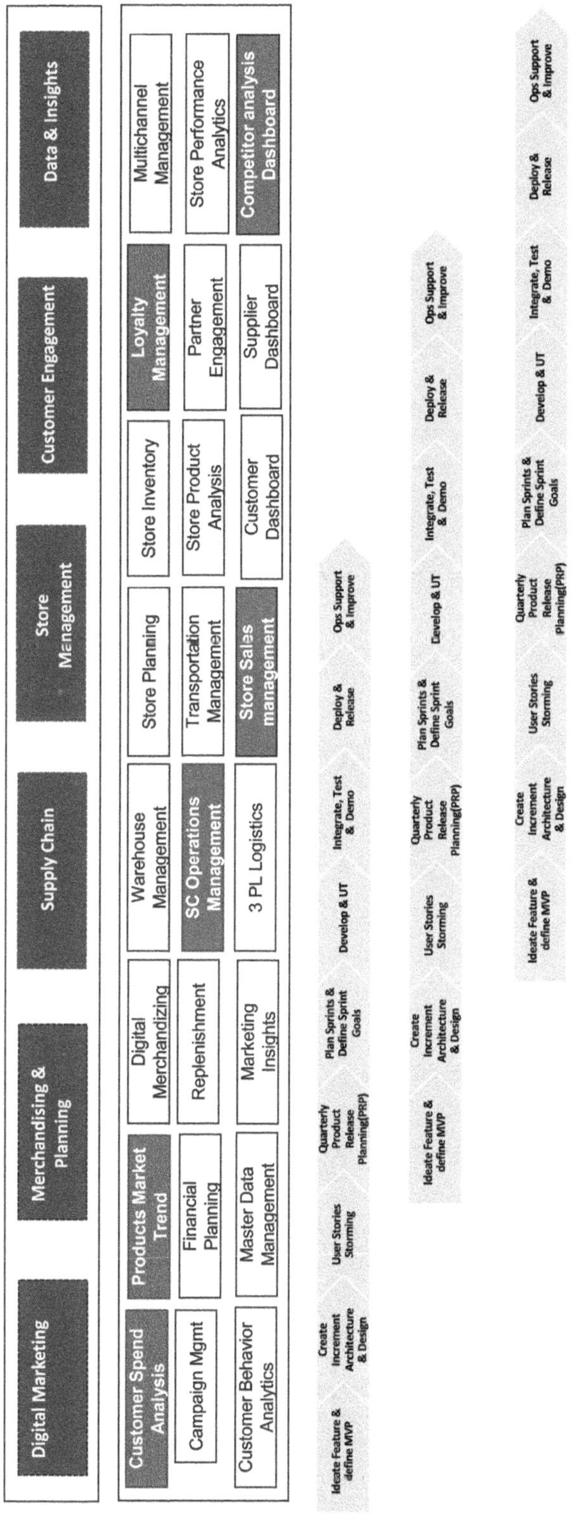

Development Value Stream Canvas: [Enrolment Hub]

Business Operation Value Stream supported

Shop & Enroll → Review Welcome Pack → Connect to get started → Follow up with Agent/Care provider → Gets first Pill → Interact with Care Manager → Visit Doctor → Process Claims

Value proposition

FOR Medicare, Medicaid customers

WHO want to purchase best health plan
THE Enrolment services product
IS AN enable to search and shop health plan

THAT provides all insights for customer to choose competitive plan

UNLIKE current product requires more interactions with agents, client for clarifications

OUR SOLUTION. Improve experience of shopping and very competitive price, efficient enrolment process and easy transition from previous client

Solutions

Enrolment Services (for all channels)

Customer Segments

Customer segments served: Medicare, Medicaid across NA regions

Budget

Onshore FTE: 2 mn $, Onshore FTE: 3 mn $, Licensing & infrastructure: 2 mn $

Solution Context

Customer access solution through agents, direct login and search, shop health plan, predict pharmacy expense

Channels

Direct, External Agent, Internal Humana careers

KPIs / Revenue

% of increase in members retained YoY
% of increase in new members

People and Locations

Estimated number of people, 54 FTE (US 15; IND 39)

Customer Relationships

Customer relationships are managed through agents, direct engagement (support, IVR), pharmacy interaction, providers,

Economic Framework

- MVP hypothesis to be proven for full budget allocation
- Each should have leading and lagging indicator to measure outcome
- Review , allocate rolling budgeting plan

One ART Identified

ARTs Name

Enrolment ART (to support all system that gets impacted by this enrolment solution)

Identify RTE, Product management team and train as new roles to ensure successful launch of ART
Ensure all required skills related FTEs are onboard: Java, micro service architecture, UX/UI. DB development, Native cloud development, Python, AI/ML, Test automation, Devops

DVS," I said. "When we discuss forming cross-skilled teams based on the scope of work each team does, we can consider four team topologies to decide each team type: Stream-aligned teams, Complicated subsystem teams, Platform teams, and Enablement teams."

"Let's understand each of them in detail," I continued, explaining each team topology leveraged from "Team Topologies" by Matthew Skelton and Manuel Pais.

Stream-aligned team – Organized around the flow of work and has the ability to deliver value directly to the Customer or end user

Complicated subsystem team – Organized around specific subsystems that require deep specialty skills and expertise

Platform team – Organized around the development and support of platforms that provide services to other teams

Enabling team – Organized to assist other teams with specialized capabilities and help them become proficient in new technologies

With a clear understanding of the team topologies, I instructed, "Let's start the breakout sessions and perform these two steps:

- Identify team members and skills needed to deliver products and applications for DVS 1, 2, & 3.

- Split the total number of team members from each DVS into different types of teams as needed."

"We'll spend 60 minutes on this with an interim check at the end of every 20 minutes to clarify any questions and ensure we're making progress in the right direction."

I moved around to join each breakout session, and Mr. Agile Coach joined a few in parallel. We both clarified doubts and helped the teams stay on track.

After a 60-minute breakout session, each team presented their results, including the number of teams and the size of each team aligned with DVS 1, 2, and 3. Every team was defined by the multi-skills required and was aligned with a specific product. The outcome of one of the breakout sessions looked like this: (refer next page image)

Note: Details about the number of people needed for each skill, their locations, the ratio of onshore to offshore resources, and the scope of L1 and L2 support are discussed in Chapter 10 as part of the future state product line/ART.

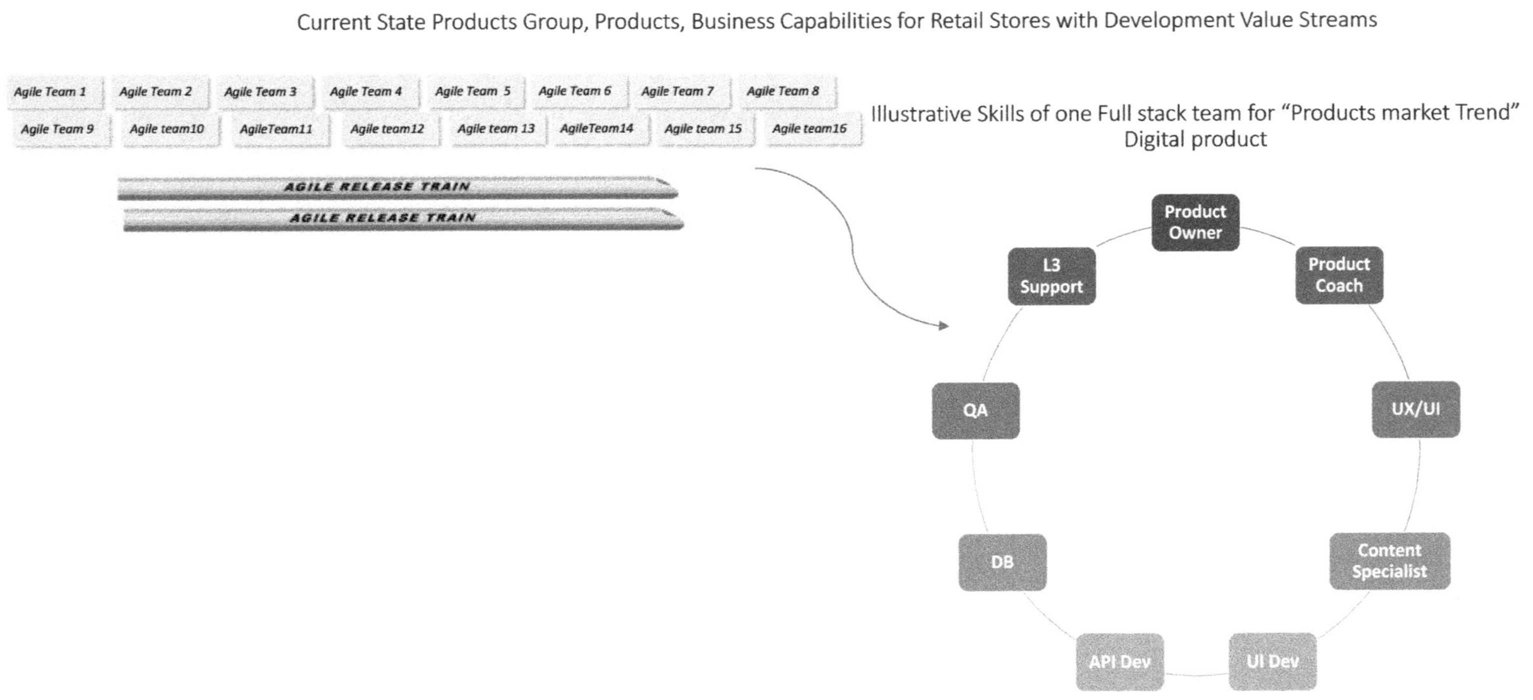

Current State Products Group, Products, Business Capabilities for Retail Stores with Development Value Streams
Agile Team 1
Agile Team 2
Agile Team 3
Agile Team 4
Agile Team 5
Agile Team 6
Agile Team 7
Agile Team 8
Agile Team 9
Agile team10
AgileTeam11
Agile team12
Agile team 13
AgileTeam14
Agile team 15
Agile team16
AGILE RELEASE TRAIN
AGILE RELEASE TRAIN
Illustrative Skills of one Full stack team for "Products market Trend" Digital product
Product Owner
Product Coach
UX/UI
Content Specialist
UI Dev
API Dev
DB
QA
L3 Support

Figure 8: Current State Products Group, Products, Business Capabilities for Retail Stores with Development Value Streams & ARTS, Agile Teams

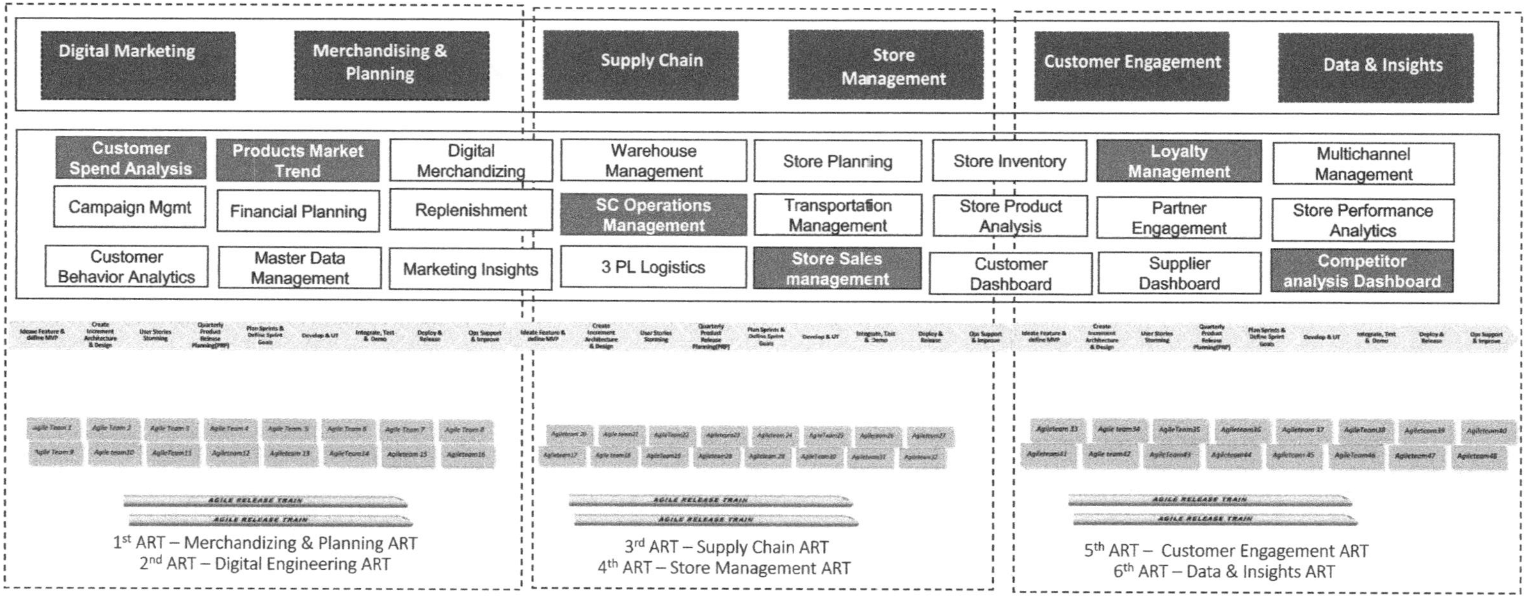

We continued our exercise to define the number of ARTs/Product lines needed to deliver value through the three DVSs. Using the ART definition guidelines provided in SAFe, we organized three breakout sessions, each lasting 60 minutes with checkpoints every 20 minutes.

During these sessions, each group identified the necessary teams and people for their DVS. We then reviewed and finalized the number of teams and ARTs/Product lines for each DVS based on the outputs from each breakout team.

This collaborative approach ensured we were thorough and aligned in our planning, setting us up for success in implementing our product lines. The illustration below provides a visual representation: (refer previous page image)

If we consolidate the outputs of the above three sections, we will have the final output of the two-day workshop. Here, we have identified product groups, products, business capabilities, functionalities, number of DVS, number of full stack Agile/product teams, and the number of Product groups/ART needed. This is what the final figure will look like: (refer next page, page 192 image)

"The final output shows the business operation value stream we use to perform retail store operations," I said, pointing to the detailed diagram on the screen. "To execute all these value creation steps, we have product groups like Digital Marketing, Merchandising & Planning, and Supply Chain."

Mr. Tech Lead leaned in, "And these product groups include digital products like Customer Spend Analytics and Warehouse Management (WMS), right?"

"Exactly," I confirmed. "We also have products like Product Market Trend Analytics. Each of these products supports our business capabilities. For instance," I said, highlighting a section on the diagram, "Customer Spend Analytics has specific business capabilities."

Ms. Architect interrupted, "And what about the Supply Chain product group?"

"I'm glad you asked," I replied, zooming in on the section for Supply Chain. "Here's a detailed view of the Supply Chain product group with its set of business capabilities and functionalities."

I moved to the next part of the diagram. "You can see we've also mapped out all three DVSs, along with their full-stack agile/product teams. This includes the number of product groups or ARTs needed to deliver all digital products for the entire business operation value stream."

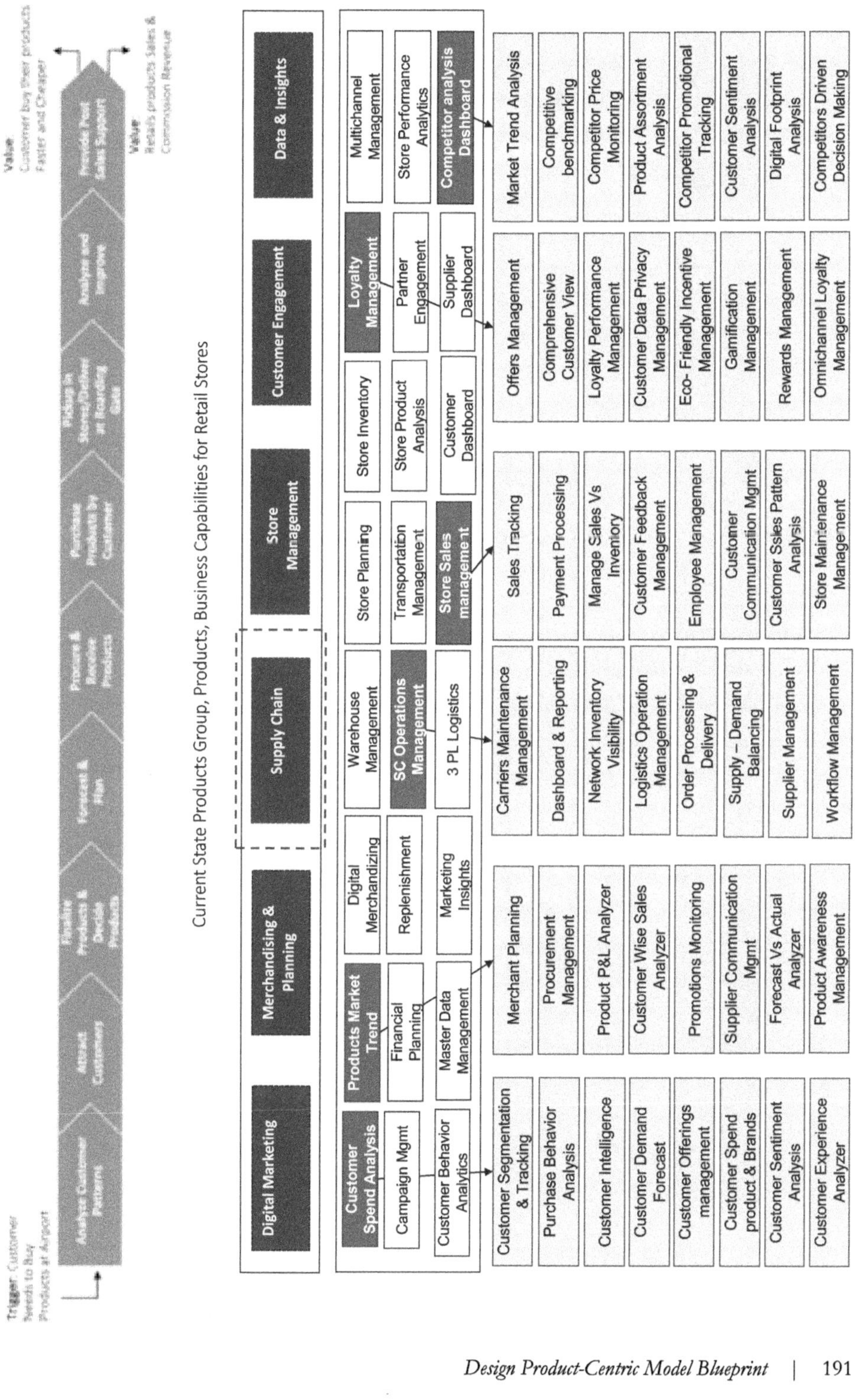

Current State Products Group, Products, Business Capabilities for Retail Stores

Double Click view of Supply Chain Product Group, Product, Business capabilities, and 3 DVS and ARTs/Product Groups for Retail Store Business Line

Product Group	Supply Chain (SC)					
Products	**WMS**	**Transportation Management**	**3 PL Management**	**Supply Chain Analytics**	**SC Operations Management**	**Inventory management**
Business Capabilities	Dashboard & Reporting	Carriers Maintenance Management	Order Processing & Delivery	Network Inventory Visibility	Order tracking	Workflow Management
	Labor Management	Goods in ad out processes	Logistics Operation Management	Supply & Career Connectivity	Supply – Demand Balancing	Inventory Tracking
	Replenishment	Returns Management	Demand Forecasting	Risk Management & Mitigation	Unified Demand Forecasting	Product Wise Inventory Monitoring
Functionalities	Integrated Order Processing	Carriers Utilization Management	Logistics Performance Management	Suppliers Product Lead time Analyzer	Supply Chain performance Trends	Storage Quality Management
	Order Processing	Carriers Allocation	Logistics Approval tracking	Suppliers order tracking	Supply Chain data Ingestion	Inventory Quality condition monitoring
	Order return Management	Carriers Drivers Allocations	Logistics onboarding	Suppliers order lead time benchmarking	Different Perspectives of Data Presentation	Storage Environment conditions Tracking
	Order price update	Carriers Maintenance status	Logistics Performance Evaluation	Supplier Order cancellation management	Supply Chain Risk Reporting	Automated identification quality inspection
	Order Analysis	Carriers Performance monitoring	Logistics performance benchmarking	Suppliers Order wise Cost analysis	Real-time time Supply Chain Performance	Storage tracking with compliance Requirements

1st ART – Merchandizing & Planning ART
2nd ART – Digital Engineering ART

3rd ART – Supply Chain ART
4th ART – Store Management ART

5th ART – Customer Engagement ART
6th ART – Data & Insights ART

Mr. Agile Coach nodded, "So, for each ART, we created a canvas to propose the value proposition that each ART will deliver?"

"Exactly," I said, feeling the room's energy shift towards understanding. "This canvas helps us outline the specific value each ART brings to the table."

Here is an illustrative view of one of the ARTs: (refer next page image)

We agreed to regroup for another workshop (which we'll cover in Chapter 10) to decide which ART to launch and what changes are needed in those ARTs. Typical changes include introducing new roles, defining roles and responsibilities, and moving team members between teams. We'll also set a launch date for the new product line/ART and define the future state of products and business capabilities that will be delivered by this product line (as discussed in Chapter 9).

At the end of the second day, after everyone had left and I was alone in the empty room, I took a moment to reflect on our journey. We had tackled three key points: identifying the current state business operation value stream, identifying products, business capabilities, and applications, and identifying the current state development value stream and its teams.

Before diving into these, we discussed the current state challenges at both the program and team levels and how these challenges could be addressed through a product-centric approach.

We delved into documenting the current state business operation value stream (OVS), covering its key elements. We also explored the differences between the current and future state value streams, as defined in Chapter 5, and why leveraging the future state value stream is crucial when defining new products and capabilities (as per Chapter 9).

Next, we identified products, business capabilities, and corresponding applications, leveraging inputs from Chapter 7. As a result, we mapped all products, business capabilities, and applications to the business operation value stream.

Our final agenda item was understanding the development value stream (DVS): how to identify DVS, determine the number of DVS needed for each business operation value stream (OVS) based on SAFe guidelines.

We then discussed identifying the necessary skills, the number of people, their locations, and the teams currently working on each DVS-related application, business capability, and product.

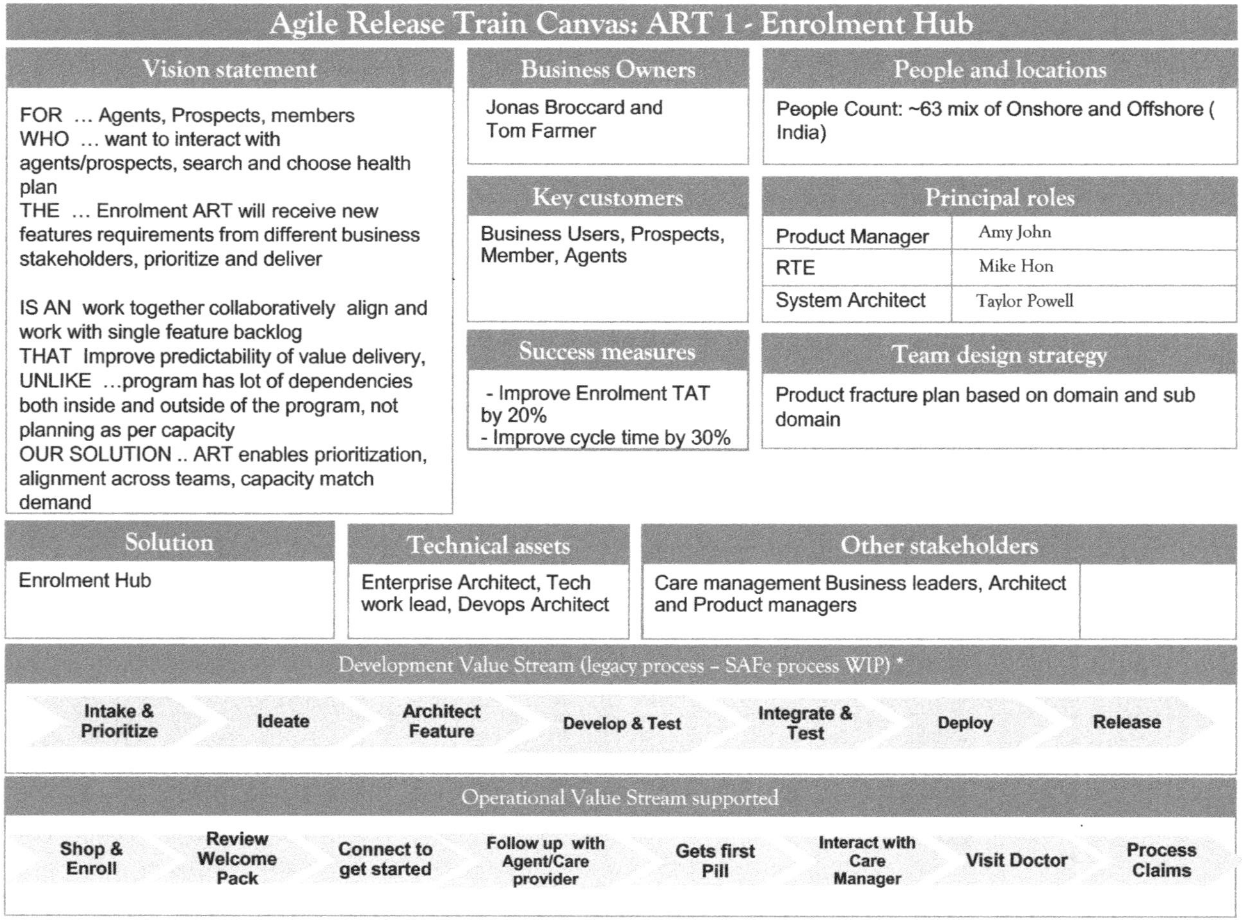

Agile Release Train Canvas: ART 1 - Enrolment Hub

Vision statement

FOR … Agents, Prospects, members
WHO … want to interact with agents/prospects, search and choose health plan
THE … Enrolment ART will receive new features requirements from different business stakeholders, prioritize and deliver

IS AN work together collaboratively align and work with single feature backlog
THAT Improve predictability of value delivery,
UNLIKE …program has lot of dependencies both inside and outside of the program, not planning as per capacity
OUR SOLUTION .. ART enables prioritization, alignment across teams, capacity match demand

Business Owners

Jonas Broccard and Tom Farmer

People and locations

People Count: ~63 mix of Onshore and Offshore (India)

Key customers

Business Users, Prospects, Member, Agents

Principal roles

Product Manager	Amy John
RTE	Mike Hon
System Architect	Taylor Powell

Success measures

- Improve Enrolment TAT by 20%
- Improve cycle time by 30%

Team design strategy

Product fracture plan based on domain and sub domain

Solution

Enrolment Hub

Technical assets

Enterprise Architect, Tech work lead, Devops Architect

Other stakeholders

Care management Business leaders, Architect and Product managers

Development Value Stream (legacy process – SAFe process WIP) *

Intake & Prioritize	Ideate	Architect Feature	Develop & Test	Integrate & Test	Deploy	Release

Operational Value Stream supported

Shop & Enroll	Review Welcome Pack	Connect to get started	Follow up with Agent/Care provider	Gets first Pill	Interact with Care Manager	Visit Doctor	Process Claims

We talked about forming full-stack teams according to team topologies to minimize dependencies and boost efficiency and productivity. We also identified the typical skills needed in these full-stack teams.

We recapped the full output of the two-day workshop, from the business operation value stream to the number of agile/product teams and ARTs/product groups.

We also discussed creating a DVS canvas outlining its value proposition: its purpose, the products/solutions it will deliver, the OVS it connects to, the customers, KPIs, budget, and the product lines/ARTs needed to deliver these products.

Additionally, we covered the Product Line/ART canvas, detailing its purpose, stakeholders, involved roles, success measures, and its connections to OVS and DVS.

Creating these DVS and Product Line/ART canvases is crucial for aligning on the why, who, what, and how of these efforts. This alignment across stakeholders and roles is critical to achieving the expected outcomes and ensuring better governance.

After my mental recap, I felt energized and joined the Agile Coach for evening coffee in the cafeteria. We were celebrating the accomplishments our business line had achieved. I was excitedly explaining how thrilled I was to envision the future portfolio view and select product lines to launch an ART.

The Agile Coach looked serious. "I have some bad news to share."

"Come on, Coach! No shocking news now," I said, half-jokingly.

"You need to know this," he insisted. "We have to address it because it's critical to move forward with the next steps of our transformation."

"Oh, so it's a bottleneck for the transformation?" I asked, growing concerned. "Go ahead and talk about it. Are they doubtful about achieving benefits from this model?"

"That's part of it," he replied. "But they don't even believe that project-related problems will be solved through this method. They also have concerns about the practical implementation of this model."

"Who are 'they'?" I asked.

"Middle management and practitioners/team members," he said.

"Interesting," I mused. "Have you gathered more details about why they feel this way?"

"Yes, I have," Coach confirmed.

"Great," I said, feeling more determined. "Let's go through their concerns tomorrow and figure out how to get senior leadership support to address them with convincing answers. As you rightly said, they are critical to taking this transformation to the next level."

I continued, "Let's try project Vs product centric model individual roles behavior simulation workshop that will help them to experience positive differences of product centric model behaviors."

We clinked our coffee cups, knowing that the real work was just beginning.

Visualize Future State Portfolio View

As we prepared for the next crucial phase of our transformation, we embarked on defining the future state of the Retail stores business line. This journey involved two workshops and several preparatory exercises before and after the workshops.

9.1 First Workshop Agenda

"Let's start with the agenda for our first workshop," I announced to the team.

Review Inputs from Previous Workshops: We revisited the current state portfolio view of the Retail stores business line and the current state product blueprint created, as discussed in Chapter 8.

Analyze SWOT and TWOS Output: We analyzed the digital initiatives based on SWOT and TWOS outputs from Chapter 5.

Perform Product Discovery: We identified new products and business capabilities/ epics that needed development or modernization, based on competitor and market analysis.

Recap Business Objectives and Strategy: We mapped the identified products and business capabilities to the selected business strategy.

9.2 Second Workshop Agenda

"For the second workshop," I continued, "here's what we focused on:"

Review Existing Products and Business Capabilities: We reviewed the list of products and business capabilities created in Chapter 7.

Review New Products and Business Capabilities: We examined the new list of products and business capabilities generated from the first workshop.

Create Future Retail Business Line Portfolio View: We developed a comprehensive future portfolio view.

Create Product Roadmap: We discussed the approach and necessary inputs for creating a product roadmap.

Based on these two workshops, we held weekly meetings to progress the creation of business cases for each business capability. We also engaged in Lean Portfolio Management (LPM) processes to review, approve, or reject these capabilities, create product roadmaps, prioritize tasks, and discuss and decide on product funding.

"While preparing and conducting the workshop for project-to-product model behaviors to demonstrate various roles behavior differences in project environment Vs product centric model environment," I explained, "we simultaneously conducted our 'first workshop'. Let's quickly recap what we did there."

9.1 Review Inputs, Conduct Product Discovery, and Map Business Capabilities to Business Strategy

9.1.1 Review Inputs from Previous Workshops

"Let's start with the first agenda item," I began, addressing the team. "Our business leads, product managers, and business architects have been hard at work preparing for this workshop. Here's what they've done:"

Research and Gather Details: They collected a wealth of information, including the last three years of business performance reports, competitor business performance, and details about their products and business capabilities.

They also looked into operational expenses, market share, customer segments we serve, total market and available market, digital opportunities, and new competitors entering the market.

Review Current State Product Blueprints: We revisited the current state product blueprints to ensure we have a solid understanding of where we stand.

Review SWOT and TWOS Analyses: We identified digital initiatives based on these analyses to inform our strategy.

9.1.2 Product Discovery 1

"Next, let's move on to Product Discovery," I said, feeling the energy in the room as everyone prepared for the deep dive.

The agenda slide was displayed on the LED TV screen. As I was about to start, the Business Architect interrupted, "Why didn't we call the Enterprise Architect? We need their inputs on future state technical impact and feasibility."

"Great point," I replied. "We definitely need their presence to complete our activities related to the future state business capabilities view. We've planned to include them from the next meeting onward. Today, our focus is on reviewing the inputs of digital initiatives and performing a detailed discovery to identify what products and business capabilities we need to build and for whom."

The methodology for this would resemble the following:

Figure 1: High level Approach for Product Strategy & Road map creation

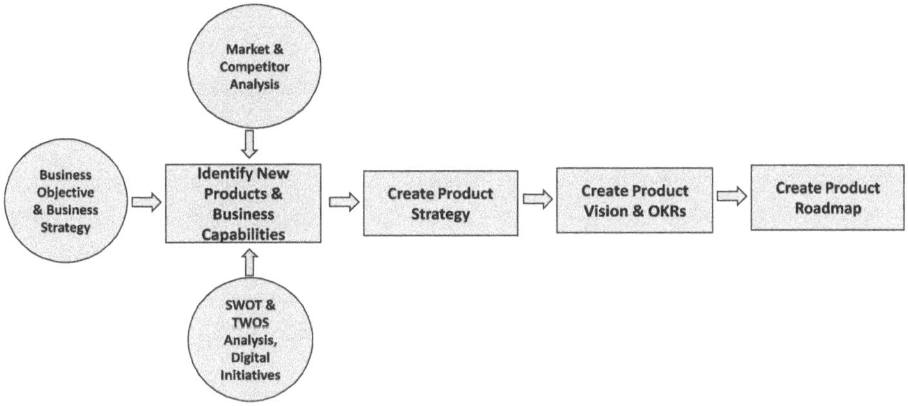

We began with a quick recap of our business strategy, objectives, OKRs, SWOT, TWOS, and digital initiatives for the retail business line, as detailed in Chapter 5. We also reviewed the current state portfolio view from Chapter 8. Then, we dove into discussing how to perform market research, using the following structured approach from the book "Innovation Games" by Luke Hohmann:

Figure 2: Market Research Approach

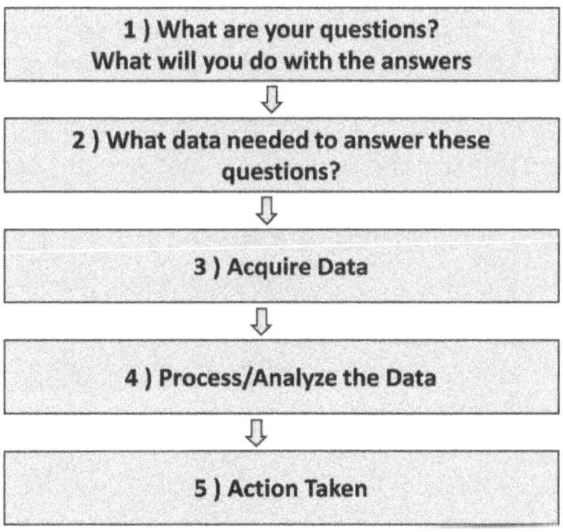

This is an illustrative the output of market research conducted leveraging few of the "innovations games" book suggested approaches: (next page image)

Above table summarizes the market research findings using the "Innovation Games" methodology. It identifies key customer needs, aligns them with potential digital features, and shows the game results that helped prioritize these features. The final column suggests the product concept derived from the research and the target customer profile for whom the product will be built. This structured approach helps in making informed decisions about product development based on direct customer input.

This is another illustrative example of market research output: (next page)

This illustrative example demonstrates how the "Innovation Games" approach can be utilized to conduct market research for airport retail stores. By engaging directly with the customers and understanding their challenges, retailers can develop digital products that are closely aligned with the needs and expectations of their target audience. The insights gained from such exercises can significantly inform the development process, ensuring that the final product truly resonates with the customers it's designed for.

Before lunch, we took a moment to check in with the team. During casual conversations, I asked, "How's everyone finding the process so far?"

One of the product managers responded enthusiastically, "I'm really excited! Being able to contribute and consider all perspectives, especially with the detailed market and competitor research, is helping us define the future state of our products more comprehensively."

Another product manager nodded in agreement. "Yes, it's a refreshing change. We're not just guessing; we have solid data to back our decisions."

A business lead chimed in, "We used to do market research, but never in such a structured way. This approach is making us realize how useful it will be to define the future state of our products and achieve our business OKRs."

After lunch, we returned with renewed energy. Using the inputs from product discovery, TWOS analysis, and our business strategy, we began productizing our digital initiatives. "Alright, let's identify the business capabilities we need to build or modernize," I said, getting everyone back into the flow.

Figure 2: Market Research Output

Customer Need	Feature	Game Result	Product Concept	Target Customer
Efficient shopping experience	Virtual queuing system	High priority in "Buy a Feature" game	A mobile app with virtual queuing to reduce wait times	Business travelers and frequent flyers
Easy navigation in stores	Interactive store maps	Top voted in "Prune the Product Tree" game	An app feature for real-time navigation inside airport retail stores	Tech-savvy tourists and transit passengers
Personalized shopping	AI-driven product recommendations	Strong positive feedback in "Speed Boat" game	Personalization engine in the app for tailored product suggestions	Young professionals and luxury shoppers

Market Research Objective: To explore opportunities for a digital product that enhances the shopping experience in airport retail stores.

Innovation Game Selected: "Speed Boat" - This game involves customers identifying what might hold back the 'boat' (in this case, the shopping experience) and how to move forward faster.

Execution:
Customer Selection: Frequent travelers who shop at airport retail stores.
Identifying Anchors: Participants list factors that negatively impact their shopping experience at airport retail stores.
Proposing Solutions: Participants suggest digital solutions that could address these pain points.

Outcome: The most common 'anchors' identified are:
Long checkout lines
Difficulty finding specific products
Lack of personalized shopping experiences

Analysis: The feedback indicates a need for a digital solution that streamlines the purchasing process, aids in product location, and offers personalized services.

Digital Product Concept: A mobile app that provides:
Virtual queuing to reduce wait times at checkout.
Interactive store maps for easy navigation and product finding.
Personalized shopping assistant using AI to recommend products based on user preferences and purchase history.

Target Customer Profile:
Business travelers who value time efficiency and convenience.
Tech-savvy tourists looking for a personalized shopping experience.
Frequent flyers interested in discovering new products quickly.

We then logically grouped these capabilities, mapping them to existing products or forming new products, or a combination of both. The output of this section appears as follows: (refer next page image)

"What we see above is just a snapshot," I explained, pointing to the screen. "This isn't an exhaustive list of all products and business capabilities for the Supply Chain product group. There are many more product groups, products and capabilities in this portfolio."

I paused to let that sink in, then continued, "Based on the complexity of the business line, its size, and its presence across different geographies, we might have even more product groups, products, and corresponding business capabilities. For instance, in one healthcare organization, their 'Group Business Insurance' portfolio had about 15 product groups, 50 products, and over 300 business capabilities."

9.1.3 Recap of Business Objective, Strategy, and Mapping Business Capabilities

"Alright, let's move on to our next agenda item," I said, directing everyone's attention to the next slide. "We need to quickly discuss our business objectives and strategies to ensure we're all aligned."

The team quickly dove into the discussion. "So, we're following a hybrid business strategy, combining all three options as mentioned in Chapter 5," someone summarized.

"Exactly," I confirmed. "This means we need to focus on digital initiatives, building new digital products and business capabilities, and modernizing existing ones. Our goal is to achieve all three business strategy objectives."

Another team member added, "This approach allows us to be more flexible and responsive to market demands while ensuring we stay ahead of the competition."

"Precisely," I agreed. "By aligning our digital initiatives with our business objectives, we can drive growth, enhance customer experience, and improve operational efficiency."

A quick recap of the same is provided below:

Business objectives:

Product Group, Product, Business capabilities

Product Group	Supply Chain (SC)							
Products	WMS	Transportation Management	3 PL Management	Supply Chain Analytics	Digital Twins	SC Operations Management	Inventory management	IOT
Business Capabilities	Dashboard & Reporting	Automated Scheduling & Routing	Customized Logistic Services	End to End Analytics	Supply Chain Optimization	Customer Data Privacy & Management	Real Time Inventory Tracking	Integrated Supplier and Carrier Connectivity
	Intelligence Order Routing	Carriers Maintenance Management	Cloud Logistics Service	Network Inventory Visibility	Store Layout planning	Order Processing	Workflow Management	Automated Replenishment
	Labor Management	Carriers Utilization Management	Order Processing & Delivery	Integrated Demand Forecasting	Product Flow Optimization	Warehouse location management	Automated Reordering	Integrated Returns Management
	Shipping Management	Goods in ad out processes	Real Time Logistics Monitoring	Supply & Career Connectivity	SC Performance Management	Supply – Demand Balancing	Cloud Based Data Storage	Omnichannel Fulfillment
	Replenishment	Shipping Management	Digital Document Storage & Management	Advanced Reporting & Dashboard	Asset Management	Segmented Supply Strategy	Integrated Sales Channel stock Management	Smart Shelves
	Integrated Order Processing	Order Picking and Packing Efficiency	Comprehensive Inventory Oversight	Risk Management & Mitigation	Sustainability Tracking	Real Time SC Intelligence	Multi Device Access	Wireless Shipment Tracking
	Real- Time Inventory Visibility	Returns Management	Logistics Operation Management	Cost -to –Serve Analytics	3D Virtual Walkthrough	Unified Demand Forecasting	Supplier Management	Products Condition Monitoring
	Picking & Packing Optimization	Staff Training & Development	Demand Forecasting	Sustainability Metrics	Inventory Stocks Management	Collaborative Network Management	AI based Customer Demand Forecasting	Energy Management

Existing Business Capabilities that needs to be modernized

New Business Capabilities that includes foundational, differentiating

Sr. No.	Business Objective	OKRs
1	Expand market share through innovative service offerings	• Launch 'buy now pay later' options in 50% of stores by Q3 • Achieve a 20% increase in market share in targeted demographics by the end of the year.
2	Boost revenue with enhanced customer purchasing options	• Increase overall revenue by 30% through the 'order online and get delivered at the boarding gate' service by Q4 • Grow average transaction value by 15% with the introduction of new payment options by Q2
3	Strengthen customer relationships and loyalty	• Improve repeat customer rate by 25% within six months • Enhance customer satisfaction scores by 20% by implementing convenient shopping models by year-end

Business strategies:

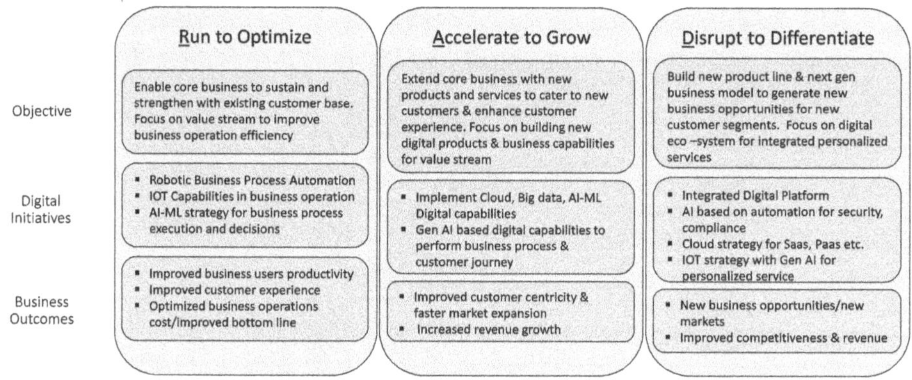

The product management team agreed to review the master list of all product groups, their products, and business capabilities identified in the previous section. Their task was to create a sub-list needed to achieve our hybrid business strategy.

We concluded Workshop 1 with a plan to reconvene for Workshop 2 in a week to review the outcomes of these offline exercises.

After the first workshop, it took the product management team and other SMEs two weeks to review all the deliverables, including market research outputs, and the identified products and business capabilities. They then mapped these to our selected hybrid business strategy. For instance, this is what it might look like for the "Supply Chain Product Group": (next page)

"As shown in the figure," I explained, pointing to the slide, "our business strategy directly influences our product strategy. This helps us determine what products and business capabilities to build and for whom."

"For example," I continued, "if we decide to follow a 'Run to Optimize' business strategy to achieve our objectives, we'll focus on products like Supply Chain Operation Management and corresponding business capabilities such as

Potential products and business capabilities to be focused to build/modernize based different Business Strategies Options

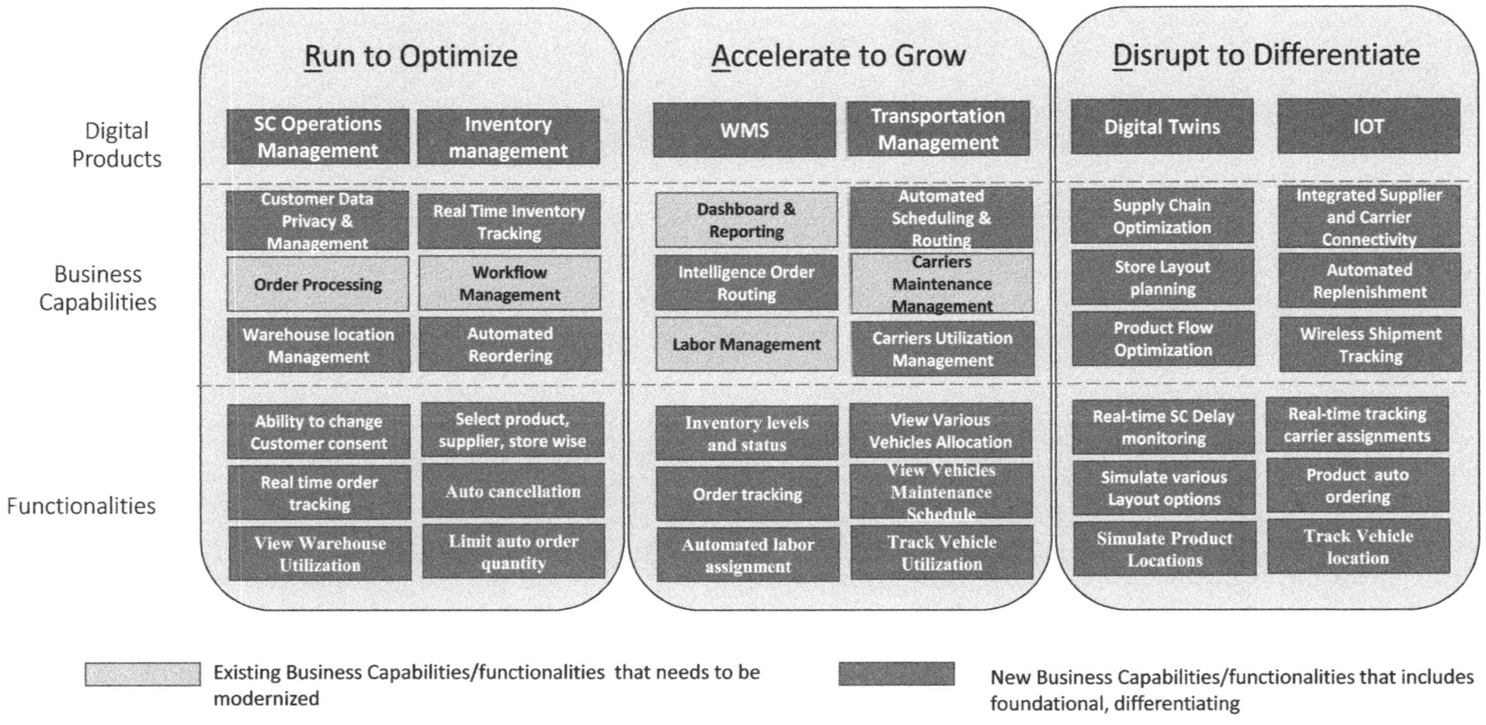

Digital Products
Business Capabilities
Functionalities

Run to Optimize

SC Operations Management
Inventory management

Customer Data Privacy & Management
Real Time Inventory Tracking
Order Processing
Workflow Management
Warehouse location Management
Automated Reordering

Ability to change Customer consent
Select product, supplier, store wise
Real time order tracking
Auto cancellation
View Warehouse Utilization
Limit auto order quantity

Accelerate to Grow

WMS
Transportation Management

Dashboard & Reporting
Automated Scheduling & Routing
Intelligence Order Routing
Carriers Maintenance Management
Labor Management
Carriers Utilization Management

Inventory levels and status
View Various Vehicles Allocation
Order tracking
View Vehicles Maintenance Schedule
Automated labor assignment
Track Vehicle Utilization

Disrupt to Differentiate

Digital Twins
IOT

Supply Chain Optimization
Integrated Supplier and Carrier Connectivity
Store Layout planning
Automated Replenishment
Product Flow Optimization
Wireless Shipment Tracking

Real-time SC Delay monitoring
Real-time tracking carrier assignments
Simulate various Layout options
Product auto ordering
Simulate Product Locations
Track Vehicle location

Existing Business Capabilities/functionalities that needs to be modernized

New Business Capabilities/functionalities that includes foundational, differentiating

Customer Data Privacy & Management, and Order Processing. These capabilities are essential for users like warehouse managers and store managers."

"Implementing these capabilities," I emphasized, "will improve operational efficiency and help us achieve our related business objectives."

"Similarly," I continued, "if the organization decides to implement a business strategy of 'Accelerate to Grow,' they will select different products and business capabilities. And if the strategy is 'Disrupt to Differentiate,' we'll look at the same products from 'Accelerate to Grow' along with new Gen AI or digital-enabled capabilities that will disrupt our current business model and create a new competitive advantage in the market."

"Based on the chosen business strategy," I explained, "we decide the product strategy—what products to build and for whom. This, in turn, helps us define the product vision and OKRs."

"As we mentioned earlier, Thiran Retail Store wants to focus on all three strategies. This means we'll implement all products and business capabilities that influence these three types of strategies. Here's a detailed view of how this looks."

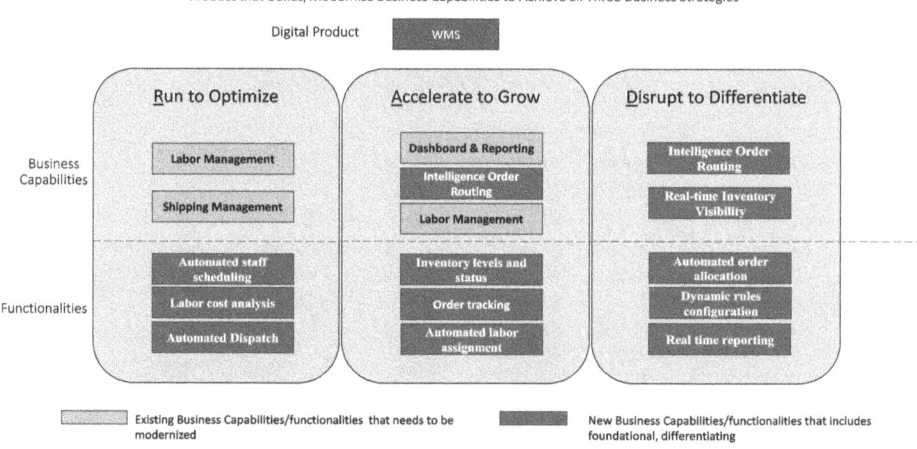

"For the WMS product, our **product strategy** would be as follows," I began, addressing the team.

Innovate: "We'll integrate cutting-edge technologies such as AI and IoT to forecast demand, automate replenishment, and minimize stockouts."

Collaborate: "We'll develop partnerships with leading logistics and supply chain experts to refine our offering."

Expand: "Our goal is to grow our market presence by targeting small to medium-sized retail businesses with a scalable solution."

Educate: "We'll offer comprehensive training and support to ensure all users can leverage the full capabilities of our WMS."

I paused for a moment to let everyone absorb the information before continuing with the vision.

WMS Product Vision

"Our vision for the WMS product is to revolutionize the retail industry by providing a state-of-the-art digital WMS that optimizes inventory management, enhances operational efficiency, and delivers an unparalleled user experience for all stakeholders."

I could see the team's interest piqued, so I elaborated, "Imagine this: Warehouse managers and shipping personnel can easily identify products, transport and load them into vehicles using robots, monitor products in real-time, and automate communications about shipments. The system will automatically update inventory and store records once products are received and inspected for quality."

"As a result," I added, "we're not only enjoying a seamless operational experience, but our customers are delighted because they get their products on time. This leads to increased customer foot traffic and revenue."

WMS Product OKRs:

Sr. No.	Product Objective	OKRs
1	Streamline warehouse operations to improve efficiency	• Increase inventory picking speed by 25% within six months • Reduce order fulfillment errors by 50% by the end of the year.
2	Enhance real-time visibility of inventory and operations	• Achieve 100% accuracy in real-time inventory tracking within the next quarter • Implement a dashboard for live monitoring of warehouse activities by Q3
3	Optimize warehouse space utilization	• Increase storage capacity by reorganizing layout to reduce unused space by 20% within four months • Deploy an automated storage and retrieval system (ASRS) in one of the airport retail stores by Q2 that optimizes WMS operations effort by 30%
4	Drive Innovation in WMS Capabilities	• Introduce 2 new AI-driven features for inventory forecasting by Q2. • Develop and deploy an IoT-based real-time tracking system for inventory by Q3 that optimizes tracking manual effort by 50% and achieve NPS 80 • Publish 4 success stories showcasing the benefits of our WMS by Q4

We completed the exercise of creating product strategies, visions, and OKR definitions for all the products we plan to build over the next year to achieve our hybrid business strategy.

9.2 Review Existing Digital Products & Create Portfolio Future State View

We then moved on to our second workshop, bringing together the same stakeholders. This workshop was a one-day session where we covered four key agendas, as mentioned earlier in this chapter.

Agenda 1: Review Existing Products and Business Capabilities

We started by reviewing the existing list of products and business capabilities that were created in Chapter 8.

Agenda 2: Review New Products and Business Capabilities

Next, we reviewed the new list of products and business capabilities identified in the previous workshop. During these discussions, we clarified any questions and aligned our understanding.

9.2.1 Create Portfolio Future State View

Agenda 3: Create Portfolio Future State View

Moving on to the third agenda, we focused on creating the portfolio's future state view. We aimed to show how the portfolio will look when these new products and business capabilities are developed and leveraged to execute the retail stores portfolio business.

"We'll use the business model canvas template for this purpose," I explained, "with a few customizations. It has three major components:"

Value Proposition: "What unique value will we deliver to our customers?"

Key Partners, Resources, and Activities: "Who are our essential partners? What key resources and activities do we need?"

Cost Structure and Revenue Streams: "How much will it cost to deliver these solutions, and what revenue streams will we generate through the value we provide?"

All the leaders began providing inputs using our template. We captured everything except for "what development value streams (DVS) are needed" to deliver the solutions/products as we've already identified, as discussed in Chapter 8. We also debated whether any changes were needed in the DVS, considering the new products and business capabilities. We concluded that the three DVS identified in Chapter 8 were sufficient, and all new products and capabilities could fit under one of these DVS.

Portfolio Canvas

| Portfolio Name Retail Store | Date: 18.09.2021 | Version: 1.0 |

Value Proposition						
Value Streams	Products	Customers	Channels	Customer Relationship	Budget	KPIs/Revenue
Supply Chain Management	Merchandizing & Supply Chain	Merchants, Suppliers, Partners	Web Portal, Mobile, Email, Phone, IVR	Personalized assistant, Partners	18 Mn USD	Operation Efficiency by 30% Merchants NPS 80
Customer & Store Operations	Customer engagement & Store Management	Travelers, Sales Agents, Airport staff, Store managers	Web Portal, Mobile, Email, Phone, IVR	Direct engagement, Partners	36 Mn USD	3 bn USD Customer NPS 85
Marketing & Insights	Digital Marketing & Data Insights	Business leaders, Sales Representatives, Market Managers	Web Portal, Mobile, Email, Phone, IVR	Direct engagement, Partners	27 Mn USD	1 bn USD

Key Partners

- Social Media Partners
- Brand Partners
- Airlines
- Logistics companies

Key Activities:

- Define and align Retail store OKRs with Enterprise
- Identify digital products to be developed and modernized, define product OKRs, road map, and MVPs
- Plan quarterly features, objectives, execute & measure outcomes

Key Resources:

- Epic owners, LPM, Product Managers, Enterprise and Solution architects,
- Transformation team, Value Management office
- Infrastructure, POS

Cost Structure

- Capex cost – 50%
- Opex cost – 20%
- Licensing cost – 25%
- Infra cost – 5%

Revenue Streams:

- Sales of goods
- Online sales through store's website or app
- Rental income from brands for in-store concessions

We then discussed the number of product lines/ARTs needed to build these products and capabilities. "For now," I said, "let's stick with the existing product lines/ARTs identified in Chapter 8. They should be enough to deliver these products."

This is an illustrative view of the future state portfolio: (previous page image)

9.2.2 Identify Digital Products to Achieve Envisioned Portfolio Future State View

"To achieve this future state," I explained, "we need to develop and deliver these digital products through their respective business capabilities. Here's how we'll proceed to create the roadmap, leading us to our next agenda item."

First Level Prioritization of Business Capabilities: "We need to prioritize the business capabilities first."

Value Stream Mapping (VSM): "We'll then map out the value streams."

Business Case Creation: "Next, we'll create business cases for these capabilities."

Prioritization and Approval through LPM: "These business capabilities will then be prioritized and approved through Lean Portfolio Management (LPM)."

Product Roadmap: "Finally, we'll create the product roadmap."

With these steps clearly laid out, we ensured everyone was ready to move forward. The discussions were lively and focused, as we aligned on the path to achieving our envisioned future state.

9.2.2.1 Initial Prioritization

During the second workshop, the LPM team provided initial prioritization scores for each business capability using WSJF. Based on these scores, we selected a set of business capabilities expected to be delivered in the next 3 to 6 months for the next activity: value stream mapping.

9.2.2.2 Value Stream Mapping

We then discussed the approach for value stream mapping (VSM) and business case creation by using an example. The team agreed to conduct this exercise offline for all business capabilities and to meet weekly for the next two weeks to perform LPM activities and create the product roadmap.

"Let's start with value stream mapping," I said, setting the stage. "First, we need to analyze the current state of the business process, focusing on existing business capabilities, and create the current state VSM. Then, we'll envision the future state business process, either through new or modernized business capabilities, and create the future state VSM."

For the next hour, we worked on creating a value stream map. I used the example of the existing business capability of "integrated order processing," which is part of the WMS product. We analyzed the current state business process performed with this capability and created the current state VSM. This exercise was done by the team in a breakout session, ensuring everyone was actively involved.

The illustrative view of the current state process is shown below:

Illustrative view of Current State 'Integrated Order Processing' Capability with its functionalities and business process map

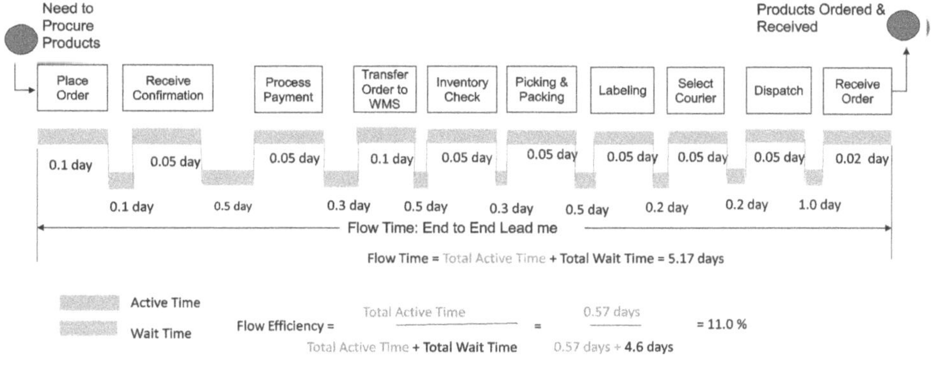

Average end-to-end lead time: 4.6 days

Manual effort involved throughout this process was: 0.57 days per order

Accuracy of ordering process: 80%

Next, the team dove into discussing the future state VSM for the "integrated ordering process" business capability, envisioning its transformation through modernization.

"We need to leverage our research inputs," I said, pointing to the board, "including competitor analysis, digital opportunities in the market, and industry best practices."

For the next 45 minutes, we analyzed potential optimizations, improvements in effectiveness, and enhancements in user experience. As a result, we created the following future state VSM:

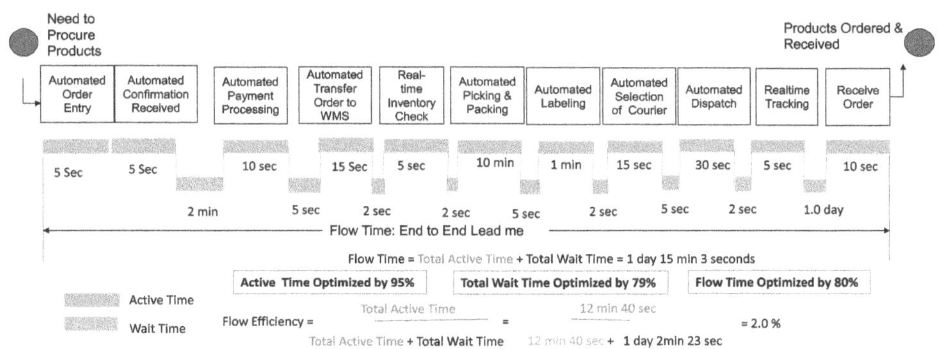

Illustrative view of Future State 'Integrated Order Processing' Capability with its functionalities and business process map

Average end-to-end lead time: 1 day, 2 minutes, and 23 seconds

Fully automated process with minimal manual effort: 12 minutes and 40 seconds per order

Accuracy of the ordering process: 98%

"This future view includes more automated process steps," I explained. "We've leveraged Gen AI to make logical decisions, optimizing the end-to-end lead time and reducing manual effort from order placement to delivery."

Since this future state VSM was created with inputs from business users, PMs, architects, UX designers, and other functional SMEs, we had already evaluated the feasibility of implementing this business process as part of the "modernized order management business capability."

"Based on all these inputs," I concluded, "the PM will create a business case for modernizing this business capability."

9.2.2.3 Business Case Preparation

"Let's get into the business case preparation," I said, gathering everyone's attention. "Each business case needs to include a description of the epic, all functionalities/ features required to complete the epic, the MVP scope of features, expected business outcomes in terms of leading and lagging indicators, and the cost needed for both the MVP and all features."

I shared an illustrative business case on the screen for everyone to see.

Business Capability Business Case

Integrated Order Processing Business capab lity/Epic Business Case		
Funnel Entry Date: 09.09.2021	Epic owner: Ms. Sarah Mike	Stakeholders: Product manager, Solution architect, Business Architect, UX Design Lead

Epic Description:

Integrated order processing from placement and delivery improve efficiency and customer experience through intelligence automation

For Warehouse Manager

who manages all orders from receipt to delivery.

the Smart Order Processor

is a solution that leverages store, supplier, partner, warehouse data to place new order.

that optimizes manual effort, improve accuracy and speed of order processing.

unlike order management that requires lot of manual effort and refers data from multiple systems
our solution process orders automatically from centralized system with improved accuracy order placement, real time tracking, dynamic repricing, delivery to warehouse.

Business Outcome Hypothesis:

- Improve customer satisfaction scores by 20% within the first year post-implementation.
- Achieve a 15% reduction in order fulfillment times within six months.
- Increase order processing capacity by 30% without additional headcount

Leading Indicators:

- Order accuracy rate
- Average order fulfillment time
- Customer satisfaction index
- Cost per order processed

In Scope:

- Centralized order management across all sales channels
- Real-time inventory updates and synchronization
- Automated order routing based on location and inventory

Out of Scope:

- Development of new CRM or ERP systems
- Creation of new production lines or services
- Overhaul of existing supply chain infrastructure

Nonfunctional Requirements:

- Performance: system should handle peak load during sales seasons
- Reliability: Order processing system uptime of 99.9%
- Usability: Intuitive user interface for employee and CX

Minimum Viable Product:

- Real time inventory sync
- Automated order creation
- Realtime order reporting
- View order in centralized view

Additional potential features:

- Track orders
- Order return management
- Monitor order process metrics
- Shipping & Delivery integration

Analysis prior to implementation

- Evaluate technical, financial, and operational feasibility
- Identify potential risks and develop mitigation strategies
- Understand needs and concerns of all affected stakeholders

Go/No-Go Decision parameters

- Alignment with business objectives
- ROI- Cost benefit analysis
- Customer NPS
- Acceptable level of risk and mitigation plan in place

"With this, we wrap up our second workshop," I announced. "We'll meet weekly to cover the remaining parts of the fourth agenda. Before our next meeting, please repeat this exercise for all business capabilities. Define their values, implementation costs, and add them to the portfolio-level epics backlog with prioritization scores. Remember, epics with higher value vs. lower implementation costs will be prioritized."

The team agreed to complete this in the next two weeks.

9.2.2.4 Prioritization of Business Capabilities Based on VSM and Business Case Inputs

Two weeks later, we reconvened. The team had completed the VSM and business case exercises for all high-priority business capabilities for the next six months, based on the initial prioritization from the entire LPM team.

"Let's revisit our initial priority scores," I suggested. We reviewed the scores based on the VSM and business case inputs.

"This is the updated list of prioritized business capabilities/epics with revised WSJF prioritization scores as per SAFe," I said, displaying the list for everyone to see.

List of Prioritized Business Capabilities

Business Capabilities	Business Value Score	Implementation Effort Score
Integrated Order Processing	20	05
Automated Scheduling & Routing	20	08
Carriers Maintenance Management	13	05
End to End Analytics	20	13
Dashboard & Reporting	13	08
Intelligence Order Routing	08	05
Real Time Inventory Tracking	08	08
Shipping Management	05	01
Replenishment	01	05
Automated Reordering	03	02
Integrated Returns Management	08	05

We then discussed the process of submitting these epics to the Lean Portfolio Management (LPM) team and how they manage them:

Epic Submission: The epics are submitted to the LPM team, which includes business sponsors, business leads, lead product managers, enterprise architects, and SMEs. The team reviews these epics and considers them for the participatory budget process.

Budgeting Meeting: During this meeting, each business capability will either be fully funded, partially funded, or rejected if the business case isn't compelling enough. These epics are logged in the ALM tool and visualized through the Portfolio Kanban view.

I displayed an illustrative view of how all epics are managed through the Epics Kanban, showing their progression from intake to approval, adding to the roadmap timeline as per priority, and finally implementation. (refer next page)

"This Portfolio Kanban board," I explained, "is created in SharePoint to manage business capabilities from intake to 'Done.' When we click the 'New Idea' tab, LPM or the business capability owner can enter a new business capability that will go to the reviewing stage. Each stage has exit criteria defined, and only when those criteria are met will it move to the next stage. Each stage also has a Work In Progress (WIP) limit."

I pointed to the drop-down menu at the top middle of the screen. "This allows us to select a product group, showing business capabilities/epics at different stages in the Portfolio Kanban. For example, here we see the 'Supply Chain' product group epics at various stages."

9.2.2.5 Participatory Budgeting Process for Product Funding

We've embraced a product funding approach that really shakes things up, tapping into a participatory budget process as outlined in SAFe. This means the whole budget gets allocated at the development value stream level.

Here's what we need to get this going:

The total budget allocated to each value stream.

A list of prioritized and approved business capabilities.

Budget details for both MVP and full rollout of these capabilities.

Business cases for each, detailing why they're worth the investment.

Portfolio Kanban Board

| Retail Stores Portfolio | Add New Idea | Supply Chain | Intake Funnel | Done : 9 |

Reviewing	Analyzing	Backlog	Implementing - MVP	Implementing – Full Epic
Supply Chain	Supply Chain	Supply Chain	Supply Chain	Supply Chain
Dashboard & Reporting	End to End Analytics	Integrated Returns Management	Picking & Packing Optimization	Omnichannel Fulfillment
Carriers Utilization Management	Supply Chain Optimization	Automated Reordering	Staff Training & Development	Workflow Management
Order Picking and Packing Efficiency	Product Flow Optimization	Real Time SC Intelligence	Demand Forecasting	Wireless Shipment Tracking
Order Processing & Delivery	Unified Demand Forecasting	3D Virtual Walkthrough	Cost -to –Serve Analytics	Order Processing
Digital Document Storage & Management	Warehouse location Management	Returns Management		
Risk Management & Mitigation		Logistics Operation Management		

All this information is sent out a week before the big budgeting showdown, ensuring every leader involved arrives well-prepared, with a solid grasp of the business capabilities, the associated products, the funds needed, the expected outcomes, and the nitty-gritty of the business cases.

On the day of the budget event, the VMO lead takes the helm. She lays out all the details: the total budget for the value stream, product names, business capability names, and the budgets requested for each.

She then divides the leaders into three groups, each one packed with stakeholders from related products. For instance, one group might handle everything from WMS and Supply Chain Analytics to Transportation Management and Inventory Management—all crucial components of the Supply Chain product group served by Development Value Stream 1.

In each group, leaders and business capability owners mingle, ready to dive deep and provide any additional insights needed.

This is an illustrative view of the budget requested before participatory budgeting:

Input Data Gathered for Product Funding that will Leverage Participatory budgeting process Approach

Input Data for Participatory budget process					Total Budget Provided for DVS 3	12000 K USD	
Sr. No.	Product Name	Business Capabilities/Epics	MVP Budget	Full Scope Budget	Total Budget	Product Wise Budget	DVS number
1	WMS	Integrated Order Processing	200	500	700		
2	WMS	Intelligence Order Routing	250	750	1000	3580	
3	WMS	Shipping Management	180	600	780		
4	WMS	Replenishment	300	800	1100		
5	Transportation Management	Automated Scheduling & Routing	320	700	1020		
6	Transportation Management	Carriers Maintenance Management	150	670	820	2890	
7	Transportation Management	Returns Management	300	750	1050		Development Value Stream (DVS) 3
8	Supply Chain Analytics	SC End to End Analytics	220	910	1130		
9	Supply Chain Analytics	Cost to Serve Analytics	190	700	890	4150	
10	Supply Chain Analytics	Integrated Demand Forecasting	250	680	930		
11	Supply Chain Analytics	Supply & Carrier Connectivity	300	900	1200		
12	Inventory Management	Real Time Inventory Tracking	240	650	890		
13	Inventory Management	Automated Reordering	190	800	990	3710	
14	Inventory Management	Multi Device Access	300	600	900		
15	Inventory Management	Supplier Management	230	700	930		
				Total Budget Needed		14330	

Note: All budget values are in K USD as unit of measure

As per the above view, the total budget needed for all these products and business capabilities comes to $14,330K, but the allocated budget for this entire development value stream is only $12,000K. So, as part of the participatory budgeting process, we need to figure out how to distribute the funds effectively.

Each team receives the total budget and a list of business capabilities with their requested budgets. They then dive into breakout sessions. Here's where the magic happens: every team evaluates each business capability, discussing its business case, expected outcomes, and more. Together, they decide whether to fully fund, partially fund, or reject each capability. Every decision is documented with a clear rationale.

After the breakout sessions, each team shares their findings with the VMO lead. She consolidates all the data to create a comprehensive view, like the one shown below:

Output of Participatory Budgeting Process

Output from Participatory budget process that needs to be Analyzed

Products and Business Capabilities for Supply Chain product Group			Team 1			Team 2			Team 3			Final Funding Decision
Sr.No.	Product Name	Busienss Capabilities/Epics	MVP Budget	Full Scope Budget	Total Budget	MVP Budget	Full Scope Budget	Total Budget	MVP Budget	Full Scope Budget	Total Budget	
1	WMS	Integrated Order Processing	200	500	700	200	500	700	200	500	700	Full
2	WMS	Intelligence Order Routing	250	**250**	500	250	**600**	850	250	500	750	Partial
3	WMS	Shipping Management	180	600	780	180	**400**	580	180	**400**	580	Partial
4	WMS	Replenishment	300	500	800	300	400	700	300	500	800	Partial
5	Transportation Management	Automated Scheduling & Routing	320	700	1020	320	**600**	920	320	**500**	820	Partial
6	Transportation Management	Carriers Maintenance Management	150	**400**	550	150	**450**	600	150	**600**	750	Partial
7	Transportation Management	Returns Management	0	0	0	150	300	450	300	0	300	Fully Rejected
8	Supply Chain Analytics	SC End to End Analytics	220	**800**	1020	220	**700**	920	220	**600**	820	Partial
9	Supply Chain Analytics	Cost to Serve Analytics	190	700	890	190	700	890	190	700	890	Full
10	Supply Chain Analytics	Integrated Demand Forecasting	250	680	930	250	680	930	250	680	930	Full
11	Supply Chain Analytics	Supply & Carrier Connectivity	300	800	1100	300	**700**	1000	300	**700**	1000	Full
12	Inventory Management	Real Time Inventory Tracking	240	650	890	240	**500**	740	240	**500**	740	Partial
13	Inventory Management	Automated Reordering	190	800	990	190	**700**	890	190	**600**	790	Partial
14	Inventory Management	Multi Device Access	300	600	900	300	600	900	300	900	1200	Full
15	Inventory Management	Supplier Management	230	700	930	230	700	930	230	700	930	Full
Total Budget allocated by Each Team					12000			12000			12000	

Note: All budget in K USD unit of measure and Budget values that are in **bold** are partially funded

Then, as a full group, we will regroup and have a brief discussion on any differences to align. This is what the final "output" view of the approved product fund for one value stream will look like: (next page image)

The VMO will monitor the business outcomes committed versus what's actually delivered by each business capability. This will be reviewed during quarterly meetings. Additionally, every six months, the Lean Portfolio Management (LPM) team will gather to assess whether budget adjustments are needed for any products, either increasing or decreasing the allocated funds based on the actual value delivered compared to the budget provided.

Final Approved Product Funds After Analysis of Data from three Different teams

Final Approved budget After Analysis done By all Three Teams

Products and Business Capabilities for Supply Chain product Group			Final Approved Budget by LPM			Product Wise Budget	Final Funding Decision
Sr.No.	Product Name	Busienss Capabilities/Epics	MVP Budget	Full Scope Budget	Total Budget		
1	WMS	Integrated Order Processing	200	500	700	2780	Full
2	WMS	Intelligence Order Routing	250	**250**	500		Partial
3	WMS	Shipping Management	180	**600**	780		Partial
4	WMS	Replenishment	300	**500**	800		Partial
5	Transportation Management	Automated Scheduling & Routing	320	**700**	1020	1570	Partial
6	Transportation Management	Carriers Maintenance Management	150	**400**	550		Partial
7	Transportation Management	Returns Management	0	0	0		Fully Rejected
8	Supply Chain Analytics	SC End to End Analytics	220	**850**	1070	3990	Partial
9	Supply Chain Analytics	Cost to Serve Analytics	190	700	890		Full
10	Supply Chain Analytics	Integrated Demand Forecasting	250	680	930		Full
11	Supply Chain Analytics	Supply & Carrier Connectivity	300	800	1100		Full
12	Inventory Management	Real Time Inventory Tracking	240	**500**	740	3660	Partial
13	Inventory Management	Automated Reordering	190	**600**	790		Partial
14	Inventory Management	Multi Device Access	300	900	1200		Full
15	Inventory Management	Supplier Management	230	700	930		Full
		Total Budget allocated for DVS 1			12000	12000	

Note: All budget in KUSD unit of measure and Budget values that are in **bold** are partially funded

9.2.2.6 Create Product Roadmap

A week later, the LPM team met to review and prioritize the epics. They evaluated each epic based on its business case, budget, and prioritization score. As a result, we had a list of approved epics added to the product roadmaps for the first year. All epics planned for the first six months received funding. We used the participatory budgeting approach as per SAFe to fund prioritized business capabilities. The remaining epics were added to the roadmap for the second and third years.

I shared an illustrative view of the roadmap for products like WMS, SC Operations Management, and Transportation Management, showing the epics/business capabilities to be developed. (next page)

"If we implement these new business capabilities or modernize the existing ones," I explained, "we'll achieve the OKRs for these products and make progress toward our hybrid business strategy."

Just as we wrapped up the discussion on this approach from creating product strategy to roadmap, an engineering lead raised a point, "It seems like this process could take years. Where's the agility in that?"

The room filled with laughter.

I responded with a smile, "I understand it seems detailed and time-consuming. But let's consider a few questions. If we build one of these business capabilities without OKRs, can we measure its success without proper analysis?"

The room fell silent before someone cautiously replied, "No."

"Can we define these OKRs without current state analysis and future state VSM views?" I continued.

More heads nodded slowly, and a few murmured, "No."

"Again?" I asked, "can we define these OKRs without a clear vision of the product that provides these capabilities?"

The silence and nodding indicated understanding.

I posed another question, "Can we define the vision of a product without understanding what our competitors are doing, or knowing the digital opportunities available in the market? Will that vision be compelling enough to create a competitive advantage?"

The answer from everyone was an immediate, "No."

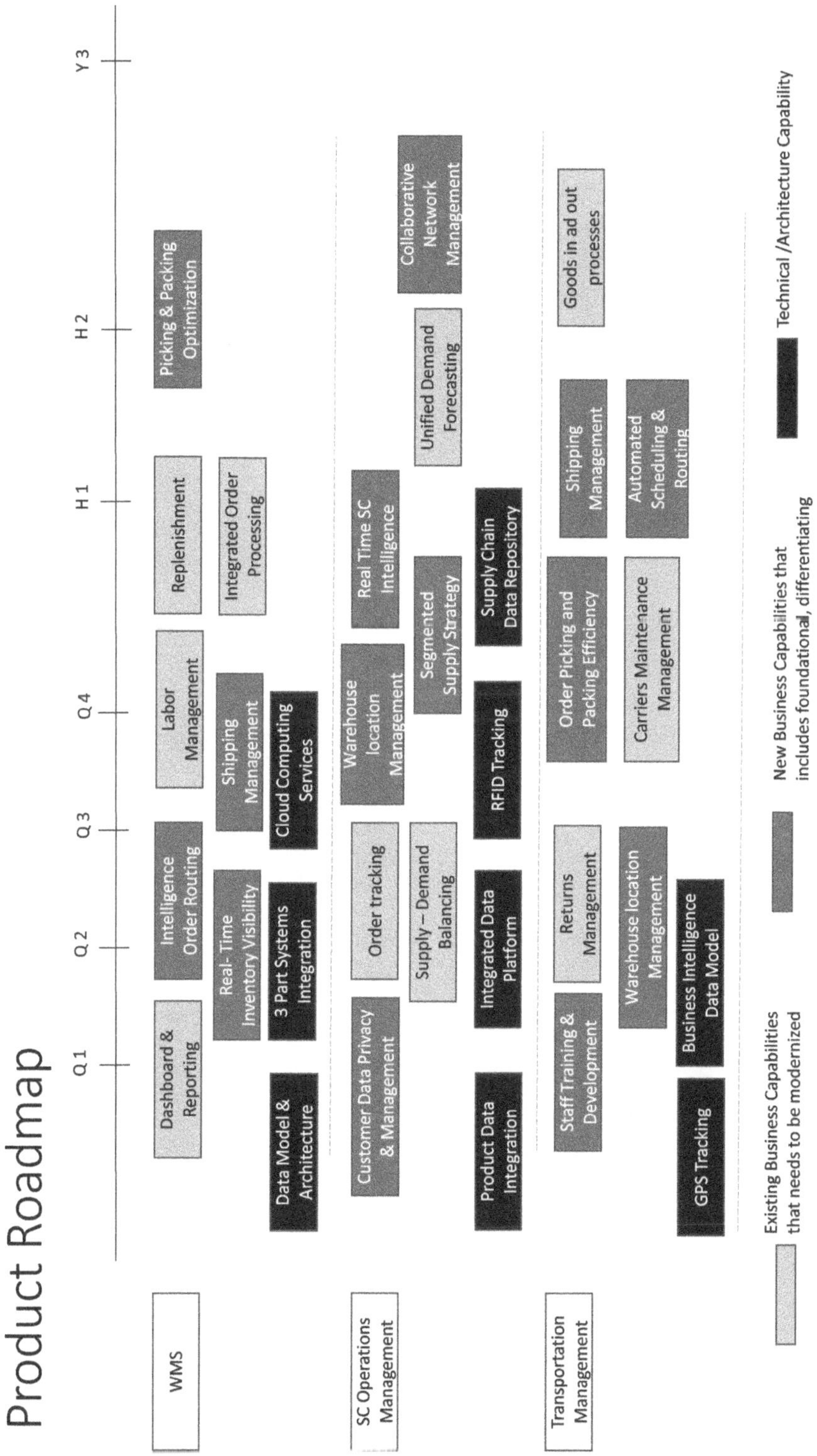

Product Roadmap
Q 1
Q 2
Q 3
Q 4
H 1
H 2
Y 3
WMS
Dashboard & Reporting
Intelligence Order Routing
Labor Management
Replenishment
Picking & Packing Optimization
Real- Time Inventory Visibility
Shipping Management
Integrated Order Processing
Data Model & Architecture
3 Part Systems Integration
Cloud Computing Services
SC Operations Management
Customer Data Privacy & Management
Order tracking
Warehouse location Management
Real Time SC Intelligence
Supply – Demand Balancing
Segmented Supply Strategy
Unified Demand Forecasting
Collaborative Network Management
Product Data Integration
Integrated Data Platform
RFID Tracking
Supply Chain Data Repository
Transportation Management
Staff Training & Development
Returns Management
Order Picking and Packing Efficiency
Shipping Management
Goods in ad out processes
Warehouse location Management
Carriers Maintenance Management
Automated Scheduling & Routing
GPS Tracking
Business Intelligence Data Model
Existing Business Capabilities that needs to be modernized
New Business Capabilities that includes foundational, differentiating
Technical /Architecture Capability

"Can we establish this vision without having the right product strategy that outlines who will use the product and what capabilities are needed?"

Again, the answer was a resounding, "No."

"Finally," I asked, "can we define this product strategy, vision, and OKRs without aligning them with the organization's overall business strategy?"

Everyone responded, "No."

"So, it's critical that we follow all these steps to create the right product that differentiates us from our competitors," I concluded. "As I mentioned earlier, we'll do this periodically in an incremental approach. We'll perform VSM and business case creation every quarter or six months for a set of business capabilities. Product strategy, vision, and OKRs will be done once a year and revisited annually to ensure they remain relevant and competitive."

"To optimize all these preparation activities, we can leverage Gen AI and various tools available in the market," I explained. "For example, there are tools like Tasktop, Kaiburr that automate Value Stream Mapping (VSM). Similarly, we can use Gen AI for secondary market research and competitor analysis. By feeding these inputs into Gen AI, it can help us draft high-level product strategies and OKRs, which we can then refine based on our organization's context."

As I looked around the room, I could see nods of agreement. Everyone seemed aligned with the discussion.

"Thank you all for your tremendous contributions," I said, wrapping up. "Let's continue this exercise offline for other capabilities of the product. Your hard work is paving the way for a successful transformation."

With that, we ended the second workshop on a high note, ready to tackle the next steps with renewed clarity and purpose.

As I walked out of the workshop, I took a moment to mentally recap everything we had covered. We started with the clear objective of creating a product strategy, vision, OKRs, and a roadmap. We discussed how we would achieve this through two workshops and some offline exercises.

First, we reviewed all the inputs from our business strategy and TWOS analysis, which are crucial for shaping our product strategy. Then, we delved into product discovery through thorough market and competitor research. We discussed the market research approach in detail, including how to execute it, and looked at an illustrative sample of the research output.

Next, we began identifying and mapping products and business capabilities—both new and those needing modernization—in line with our business strategy, TWOS analysis, and product discovery 1.

We also recapped the retail store business objectives and strategies that we had defined earlier (as outlined in chapter 5). Then, we talked about how to identify the products and corresponding business capabilities that need to be built or modernized to achieve our various business strategies.

Then we moved on to workshop 2. We started by reviewing the existing list of products and business capabilities that were created as part of chapter 8 (Agenda 1). Next, we reviewed the new list of products and business capabilities that emerged from the first workshop (Agenda 2).

With these inputs in hand, we tackled Agenda 3: creating a portfolio future state view. We discussed the components of this view and how to gather the necessary data to create a future state portfolio canvas.

The next step was to create a product roadmap to achieve this future state portfolio. To do this, we first needed to perform Value Stream Mapping (VSM) and create business cases for each business capability, based on their initial prioritization scores.

We had an in-depth discussion on how to perform current and future state VSMs for business processes, using the example of the "integrated order processing" capability. We broke down the components of the business case template and walked through the process of creating a business case using this example.

Following that, we revisited the prioritization scores of business capabilities based on the VSM and business case outputs. These prioritized business capabilities were then reviewed in the weekly Lean Portfolio Management (LPM) meetings, where they were either approved or rejected.

All approved business capabilities for the next few months were funded using the participatory budgeting approach prescribed in SAFe. Based on whether business capabilities were fully or partially funded, the product roadmap was updated accordingly. This structured and iterative approach ensures that we remain aligned with our strategic goals while continuously adapting to market needs and opportunities.

How to Set Up Product Teams for Each Product Group/Train & Align on Roles

With the success of defining our future state portfolio view, we were ready for the next step. Our team, consisting of the Business Owner, Business Leads, Product Managers, Enterprise Architect, and Engineering Leads, gathered for a crucial workshop. The goal was to select the Product Line, Products, and Agile Release Train (ART)/Program to launch the execution of our product model designed in the previous chapter.

Before this workshop, the internal coach and I had several meetings to prepare. From these sessions, we identified two options, each with its pros and cons:

10.1 Identification of ART/Product Group for First Launch

Option 1: Select an Entire Product Line With All Related Products

Option 2: Select a Couple of Personas (Merchants and Customers) and Their Corresponding Products

I also presented a sample for Option 1 from the Insurance Industry, as detailed below: (next page image)

The moment we shared the slide with our options, the room buzzed with opinions. Tech leads leaned toward Option 1, suggesting it's easier to manage and a small-scale ART would be perfect for testing and learning. Product managers nodded in agreement, emphasizing that selecting at least one product line would allow us to define OKRs clearly and see their impact on the overall Retail Store business line.

On the other hand, business owners and leads were adamant about Option 2. "Focusing on one or two personas to build new business capabilities or modernize existing ones will have a higher impact on our business strategy and OKRs," one of them argued. "We'll achieve our goals faster this way."

I acknowledged their points. "You're all making valid arguments. Let's create a list of parameters to help us decide and review the pros and cons of each option."

Illustrative view of Life Insurance Business Line – Business Operation Value Stream and one Product Line related Product teams

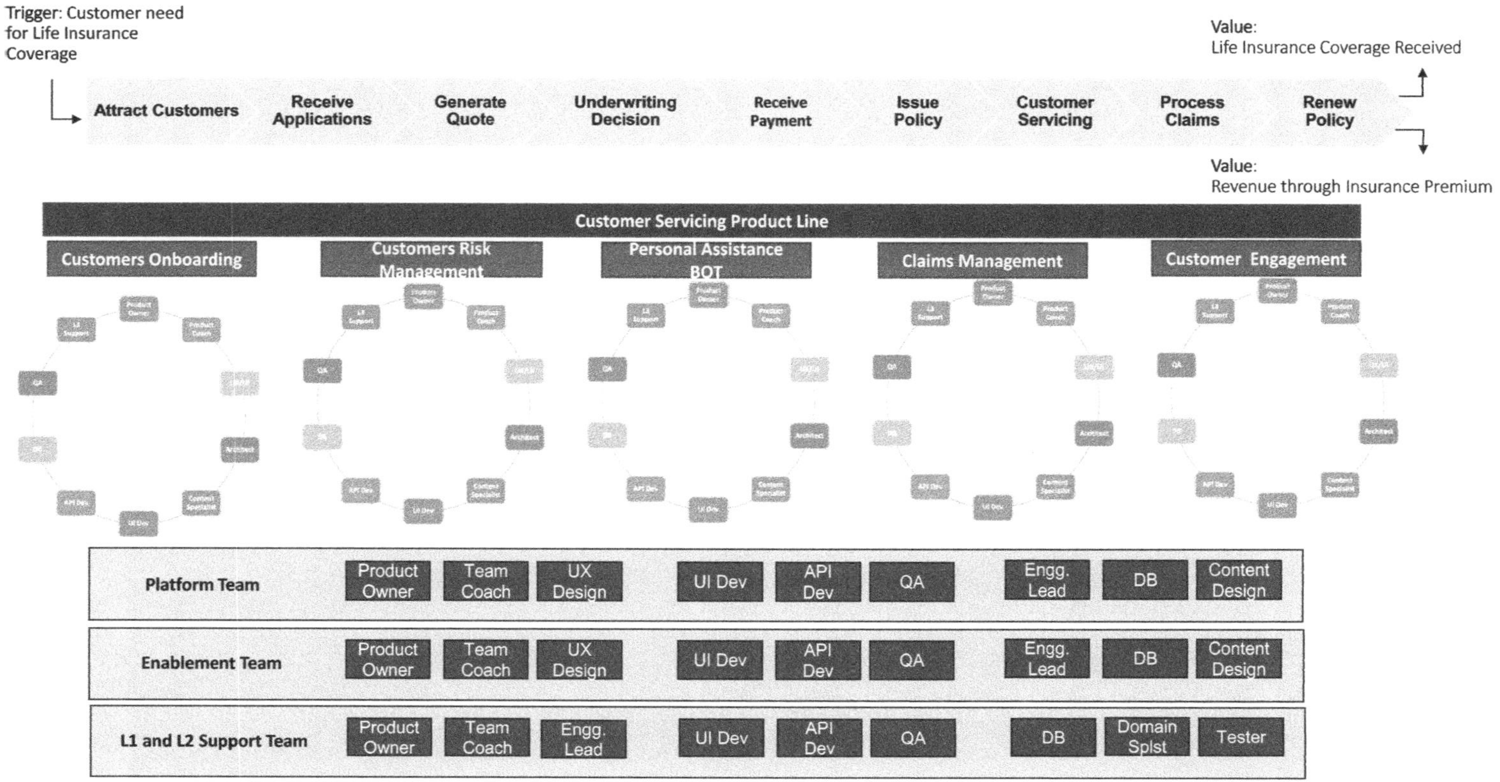

Parameters for Comparing Options

Leadership Support: Do we have strong backing from senior and middle leadership?

Product Definition Maturity: Are the products and business capabilities clearly defined?

Significant Improvement Needs: Which product lines have the most room for improvement?

Team Collaboration: How well do our existing teams collaborate?

New Roles: Are we ready to assign and train new roles?

Team Reorganization: How much change is needed to reorganize teams within the ART?

Architecture Readiness: Is the architecture runway ready for the identified business capabilities?

Volunteering: Do we have any ART or program willing to be an early adopter?

Business Impact: Which product lines will most influence achieving our Business Objectives and OKRs?

We conducted a dot voting session with all stakeholders, calculated the average scores on a scale of 1 to 5, and compiled the results into the following comparison chart:

Evaluation Parameters	Digital Marketing	Merchandizing & Planning	Supply Chain	Store Management	Customer Engagement	Data & Insights
Leadership						
Products definition maturity						
Products that requires significant improvement						
Teams collaboration						
New roles						
Reorganizing teams						
Architecture						
Volunteering						
Business Impact						

After weighing our options, the "Supply Chain" product line seemed like the best choice for launching the ART/program if we went with Option 1. However, as we delved deeper into the parameters, the consensus shifted.

"Given the leadership support, volunteering spirit, and significant business impact, we should go with Option 2," one stakeholder suggested, and the room quickly agreed.

Option 2 had a higher success rate due to strong leadership backing and team enthusiasm. Plus, it promised a significant business outcome as it focuses on two personas related products across entire business operation value stream. If this pilot succeeded, it could spark a transformative wave across the enterprise, setting the stage for extending this transformation to other business lines.

With Option 1, we would simply select an ART for each product line identified in Chapter 8 and launch it. But with Option 2, we're selecting products from almost all product lines that impact both the Merchant and Customer journeys. This means setting up new ARTs specifically for these journeys.

According to option 1, the focus is limited to products from only two groups, which doesn't cover all the products used by a specific persona. Consequently, to enhance this persona's experience, we would have to wait for the launch of all product groups/ARTs, which could take up to a year.

On the other hand, option 2 involves selecting a few critical personas and including all products that influence their journey, followed by launching ART. This approach allows for an improvement in the specific persona's journey from end to end within a few quarters.

"We'll need to set up one ART for the Merchant Journey and another for the Customer Journey," I explained. "To ensure success, we'll mobilize people from the respective product group areas/hire (if needed), bringing together all the necessary skills to form robust product teams."

Given that Option 2 was more demanding in terms of preparation and team setup, and carried a significant risk—where a failure could adversely affect the entire product-centric model transformation—it was essential to approach it with a meticulous strategy.

"Given the complexities and risks associated with Option 2, we've decided to roll it out in three thoughtful phases," I announced, drawing nods from around the room.

Phase 1: Setting the Foundation

"First up, we'll spend two months on ART launch preparations for both the Merchant and Customer Journey ARTs," I detailed. "This phase includes conducting quarterly planning and then moving into the execution phase of these two journeys ARTs, which will last for another three months."

Phase 2: Strengthening the Framework

"In the sixth month, we'll officially launch the two ARTs," I continued. "But the five months leading up to that will be crucial. We'll use this time to strengthen these two ARTs based on nine critical evaluation parameters, such as conducting detailed product and business capability research and completing the incremental architecture etc., for the two ARTs that will be launced for Merchants & Planning, and Supply Chain product lines."

Phase 3: Expanding the Success

"Once we've solidified the foundation, we'll gradually strengthenwith ART launch preparation activities for the other four product lines over the next three months. Our aim is to launch them by the ninth month, ensuring that our product-centric model transformation across the business line gains momentum and effectiveness."

10.2 Setting Up ART/Product Groups for the First Launch

With the phased approach agreed upon, it was time to delve into the details of setting up the ARTs and product groups for the first launch.

"When all six ARTs covering the full range of product lines are launched," I began, "the team members from the merchant and customer journey ARTs will transition to their respective product teams within the product lines. They'll serve as product model champions."

I paused to let the significance of this sink in. "At that point, we won't need journey ARTs anymore. Each product team's business capabilities will naturally enhance the persona journeys they impact."

Everyone nodded in agreement, and we shifted focus.

"Let's discuss the composition of the product teams for these two journey ARTs," I suggested.

After assessing all the identified skills, understanding the nature of the applications beneath those products, and considering the tech stack of those applications, we've decided on the following product teams for each ART decided:

In our discussion about the composition of the Product team, we explored different types such as the streamline/feature team, enablement team, and so on. We talked about certain capabilities that are universally needed across all personas within this business line, and how these can be utilized in other business lines as well. (next and page 130 images)

We decided to create a series of PODs/Product Teams for these shared capabilities and establish them as a distinct Platform ART. Now, the overall ART designs for the entire Retail store business line are as follows: (page 231,232 image)

Illustrative view of ART 1 Set up with Product Teams for "Merchants Journey" of all Products across Product Lines

Product Line/ART Level Roles

| Business Sponsor | Product Managers | Solution Architects | Product Line Coach/RTE |

Customer Spend Analytics Team

Product Owner	Team Coach	UX Design
UI Dev	API Dev	QA
Engg. Lead	DB & L3	Content Design

Product Market Trend Analytics Team

Product Owner	Team Coach	UX Design
UI Dev	API Dev	QA
Engg. Lead	DB & L3	Content Design

Customer Behavior Analytics Team

Product Owner	Team Coach	UX Design
UI Dev	API Dev	QA
Engg. Lead	DB & L3	Content Design

Digital Merchandizing Team

Product Owner	Team Coach	UX Design
UI Dev	API Dev	QA
Engg. Lead	DB & L3	Content Design

Campaign Management Team

Product Owner	Team Coach	UX Design
UI Dev	API Dev	QA
Engg. Lead	DB & L3	Content Design

Store Planning Team

Product Owner	Team Coach	UX Design
UI Dev	API Dev	QA
Engg. Lead	DB & L3	Content Design

Store Inventory Team

Product Owner	Team Coach	UX Design
UI Dev	API Dev	QA
Engg. Lead	DB & L3	Content Design

Partner Management Team

Product Owner	Team Coach	UX Design
UI Dev	API Dev	QA
Engg. Lead	DB & L3	Content Design

Platform Team

| Product Owner | Team Coach | UX Design | UI Dev | API Dev | QA | Engg. Lead | DB | Content Design |

Enablement Team

| Product Owner | Team Coach | UX Design | UI Dev | API Dev | QA | Engg. Lead | DB | Content Design |

L1 and L2 Support Team

| Product Owner | Team Coach | Engg. Lead | UI Dev | API Dev | QA | DB | Domain Splst | Tester |

Illustrative view of ART 2 Set up with Product Teams for "Customer Journey" of all Products across Product Lines

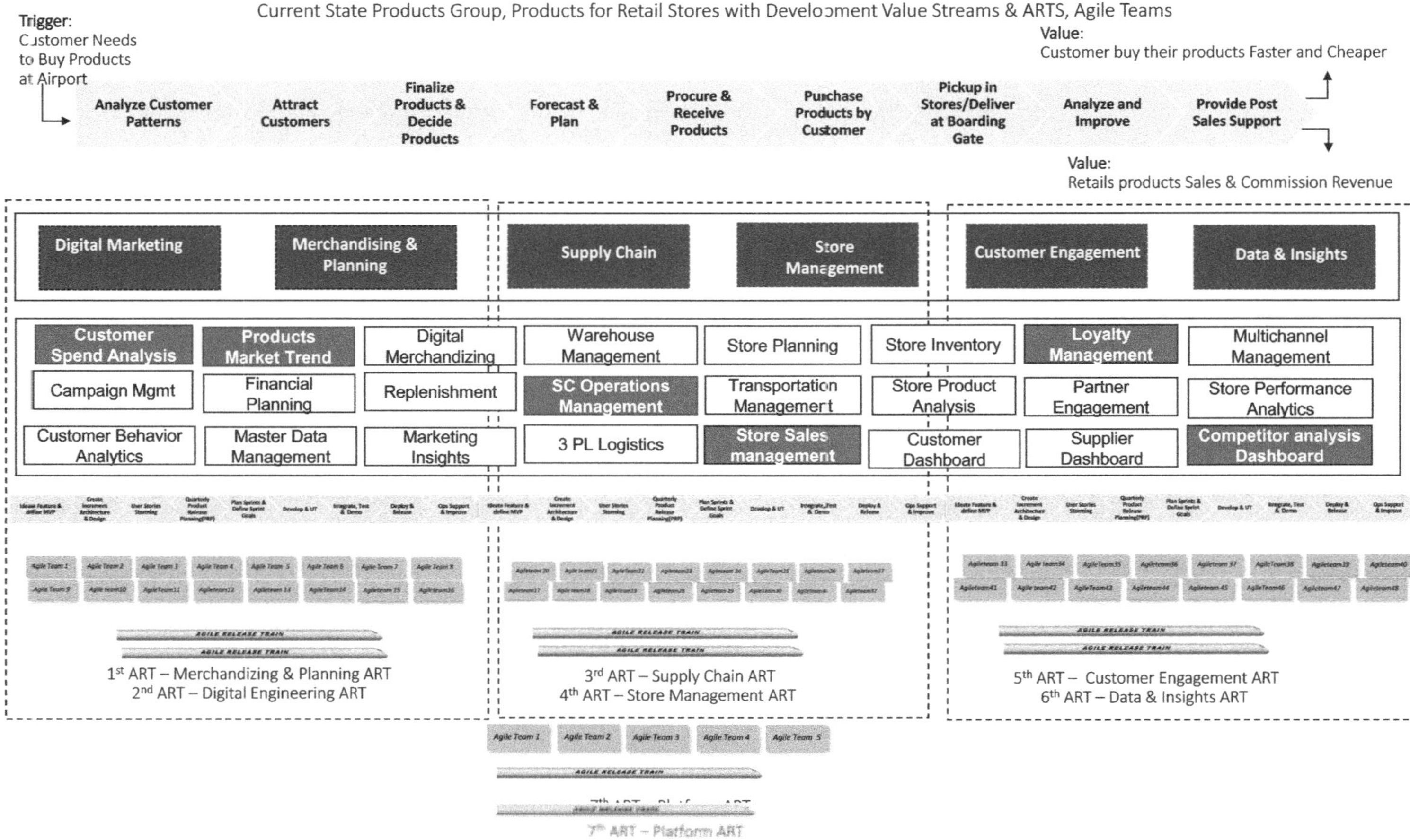

Current State Products Group, Products for Retail Stores with Development Value Streams & ARTS, Agile Teams
Trigger:
Customer Needs to Buy Products at Airport
Value:
Customer buy their products Faster and Cheaper
Analyze Customer Patterns
Attract Customers
Finalize Products & Decide Products
Forecast & Plan
Procure & Receive Products
Purchase Products by Customer
Pickup in Stores/Deliver at Boarding Gate
Analyze and Improve
Provide Post Sales Support
Value:
Retails products Sales & Commission Revenue
Digital Marketing
Merchandising & Planning
Supply Chain
Store Management
Customer Engagement
Data & Insights
Customer Spend Analysis
Products Market Trend
Digital Merchandizing
Warehouse Management
Store Planning
Store Inventory
Loyalty Management
Multichannel Management
Campaign Mgmt
Financial Planning
Replenishment
SC Operations Management
Transportation Management
Store Product Analysis
Partner Engagement
Store Performance Analytics
Customer Behavior Analytics
Master Data Management
Marketing Insights
3 PL Logistics
Store Sales management
Customer Dashboard
Supplier Dashboard
Competitor analysis Dashboard
Ideate Feature & define MVP
Create Increment Architecture & Design
User Stories Storming
Quarterly Product Release Planning(PRP)
Plan Sprints & Define Sprint Goals
Develop & UT
Integrate, Test & Demo
Deploy & Release
Ops Support & Improve
Agile Team 1
Agile Team 2
Agile Team 3
Agile Team 4
Agile Team 5
Agile Team 6
Agile Team 7
Agile Team 8
Agile Team 9
Agile team10
Agile Team11
Agile team12
Agile team13
Agile team14
Agile team15
Agile team16
Agile team17
Agile team18
Agile team19
Agile team20
Agile team21
Agile team22
Agile team23
Agile team24
Agile team25
Agile team26
Agile team27
Agile team28
Agile team29
Agile team30
Agile team31
Agile team32
Agileteam33
Agile team34
Agile Team35
Agile team36
Agile team37
Agile Team38
Agile team39
Agile team40
Agile team41
Agile team42
Agile Team43
Agile team44
Agile team45
Agile Team46
Agile team47
Agile team48
AGILE RELEASE TRAIN
1st ART – Merchandizing & Planning ART
2nd ART – Digital Engineering ART
3rd ART – Supply Chain ART
4th ART – Store Management ART
5th ART – Customer Engagement ART
6th ART – Data & Insights ART
7th ART – Platform ART

Centralized Platforms & Capabilities Portfolio

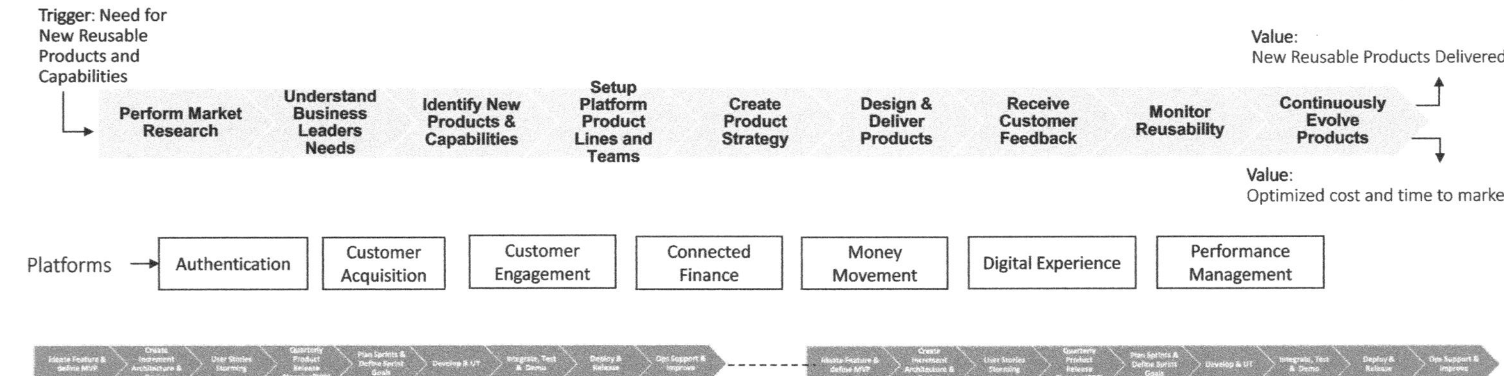

There are 7 DVS. One for each of the platform. To deliver products and capabilities for each Platform, there are multiple product teams. Based on total number of people per platform and total number of product teams needed per platform, number of ARTs are decided

It was agreed to pilot the platform model at the ART level, designating it as the 7th ART for the Retail Store business line. Once successfully implemented, this Platform ART would serve as a blueprint for setting up a centralized "Platforms and Capabilities" portfolio. This centralized portfolio would deliver common products and business capabilities reusable across all business lines in the organization.

"Why are we focusing on a Platform ART?" someone asked.

"Good question," I replied. "Implementing this model successfully will achieve three critical goals: optimizing the development cost and time to market for new products and business capabilities, reducing technology costs through increased reusability, and ensuring a consistent customer experience across all business lines."

Below, I've showcased a view of successful platforms and products implemented as part of a centralized portfolio at a regional bank:

10.3 Developing a Target Operating Model for Two New ARTs/Product Groups

With the decision to pilot the platform model at the ART level, we shifted our focus to the target operating model for the two new ARTs.

"We need a clear operating model to execute phase 1 of our transformation plan," I began, addressing the team. "We've selected 16 products and prioritized the corresponding epics for each journey. These 16 products are categorized into two distinct pathways: Customer Journeys and Merchant Journeys.

I shared the screen displaying the illustrative view of the target operating model for these two product lines.

"As you can see," I continued, "each of these product lines will function like a network of small startups. They'll include both business and technology roles, working together as one cohesive team." (next page image)

With the target operating model in place, we shifted our focus to the people aspect—introducing new roles, repurposing existing ones, and providing the necessary training.

"We need to talk about introducing new roles and redefining some existing ones," I began, addressing the group. "This is crucial for our transition to the product centric model approach."

Target State Governance Model

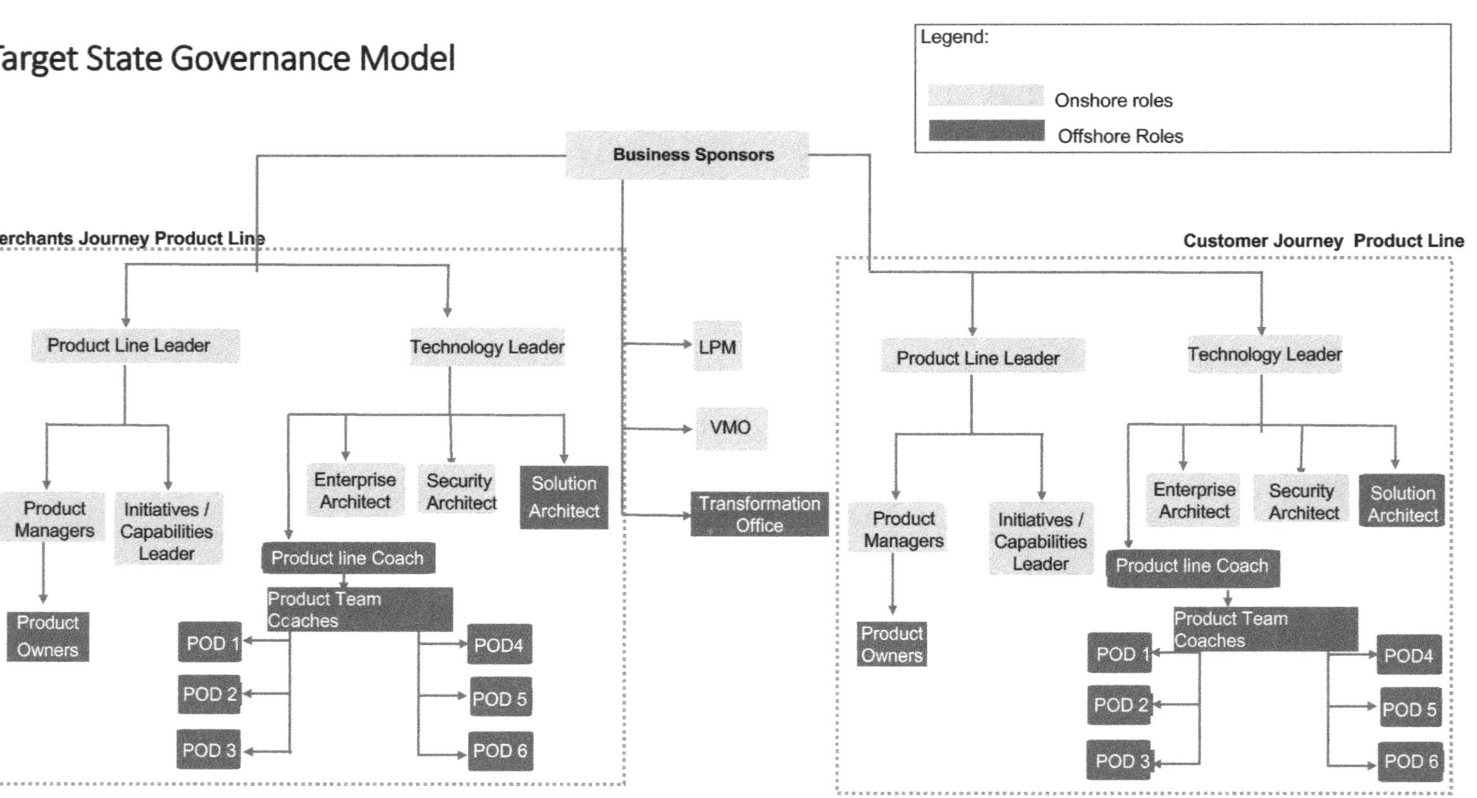

"We'll need to redefine some existing roles with experience/skills and introduce a few new roles, like ART-level Agile Coaches or RTEs," I explained. "Let's start with Product Managers."

One of the business leads jumped in, "How do we find the right people for these roles?"

"We repurposed some of our senior Product Owners," I replied. "Those who have training in SAFe APM, experience in market research, design thinking workshops, defining OKRs, product strategy, vision, and road mapping can transition into Product Manager roles. Additionally, we'll need to hire a few Product Managers from the external market or through internal movement."

"For the RTE role," I continued, "we can repurpose some of our Program Managers. They'll need training on SAFe Practice Consultant and SAFe RTE. We also need to set clear expectations about the difference between a Program Manager and an RTE."

An engineering lead nodded, "And for Scrum Masters/Product Coaches?"

"We'll repurpose some Project Managers who have an agile – lean – product mindset and experience," I responded. "We'll have discussions with them about the differences between their current role and the Product Coach role."

"We should also clearly define the roles and responsibilities for these new positions," another team member suggested.

"Absolutely," I agreed. "It's critical that everyone understands their new responsibilities in line with the SAFe framework."

The workshop was a success, aligning everyone on selecting ART/Programs, setting up product teams/PODs, and defining roles and responsibilities. Afterward, the internal agile coach and I decided to take an evening walk around the office campus.

As we strolled, the coach broke the silence, "I have a point to discuss."

I braced myself, "Come on, don't give me another shocking news."

He chuckled, "Don't worry, I haven't heard any bad news so far."

I raised an eyebrow, "The phrase 'so far' sounds cautious."

He laughed again and continued, "Our RTE/ART coach mentioned she's very excited to be part of this initiative and lead the first ART of our product centric model. She asked if she could meet with you to clarify some points about her roles and responsibilities."

I smiled, genuinely pleased. "That's great to hear! Of course, we can meet with her. Let's also invite the second ART Agile coach to the meeting. We'll brief them on their roles and emphasize how critical their leadership is to the success of these two ARTs. And, of course, assure them of our 100% support."

With renewed enthusiasm, we took a moment to recap the ground we've covered in this workshop:

First, we compared two options for launching ARTs and product lines. After weighing the pros and cons, we decided to launch two ARTs focused on the merchant and customer journeys. The decision was based on key criteria, and everyone agreed it was the best way forward.

Next, we outlined a phased approach for these launches. Phase 1 focuses on the initial launch, followed by extending the ART launches from the two journey ARTs to all six product line ARTs in phases 2 and 3. The plan includes dismantling the journey ARTs and integrating those team members into their respective product teams as champions of the product-centric model, enhancing product line maturity.

We then discussed how to set up these two journey ARTs, including the necessary product teams and support teams like Platform and Enablement teams. We formed the two journey ARTs, identified the required skill sets for each product team, and planned for L1, L2, and L3 production support to be managed by the respective teams and ARTs.

Additionally, we explored the option of a 7th ART as a Platform ART, which can deliver all common reusable products and capabilities for the retail store business line. We also considered extending this Platform ART to become a centralized portfolio of platforms and capabilities that can deliver reusable products across all business lines in the organization. We even looked at an example of a similar centralized portfolio setup in a regional bank.

Finally, we discussed the various roles needed within each product team and at the ART level. We explored options for repurposing some existing roles (like project managers and program managers) into new roles (like Product Coach and ART/Product Line Coach). We also talked about the necessary training for existing people to perform these new roles effectively.

As we wrapped up, we felt a strong sense of accomplishment and alignment, ready to take the next steps in this exciting journey.

Creating a Playbook
to Guide Transformation

Immediately after aligning on the product-centric model and completing the initial SAFe SPC training for the transformation team, we swiftly began crafting a contextualized playbook. This playbook was crafted from SAFe framework inputs.

"To truly say that our organization has transformed from a project to a product-centric model, we need to see a consistent reflection of this change in everyone's behavior," I declared during the workshop. "This starts with training people on new ways of working. Once trained, they'll start executing these new methods. Whenever they need further details or clarifications, our playbook will be their guide."

The playbook is designed to ensure everyone follows the process consistently. This consistency results in successes such as effective product strategy, vision, OKRs, roadmap, quarterly planning preparation, planning, and execution at the product group level, sprint planning and execution, meaningful demos, and productive retrospectives. When these new ways of working are implemented repeatedly and consistently at the team, product group, and portfolio levels, and they demonstrate positive outcomes over a long period, they become the new normal.

"It's crucial that we don't revert to old ways," I emphasized. "The playbook will guide us on this journey, but we also need continuous monitoring, periodic maturity assessments, and feedback surveys to stay on track."

There are three types of personas when it comes to adopting new ways of working.

First, there are those who understand the value of following processes but don't know how to implement them. For these individuals, the playbook will be an invaluable guide.

Next, there are those who don't see the value in following new processes. These folks need coaching to help them understand the benefits. Once they see the value, the playbook can help them get started.

Finally, there are those who know the value and understand how to do it, but they still resist. These individuals need NLP-based coaching to empathize with them, listen to their concerns, and help shift their mindset. This process might take longer, but it's essential to get them on board.

In all three cases, the playbook is crucial for enabling employees to adopt the product-centric model.

"The playbook is our guide," I explained. "It focuses on why we do what we do and how we do it."

Through this playbook, we aim to guide various roles across the portfolio. It will provide day-to-day instructions on what processes to follow, the inputs and outputs for those processes, and the tools needed to implement them successfully.

The objective of our playbook is simple: to be the go-to resource for everyone involved in our product model transformation. It serves several key purposes:

Provides insights into role expectations and necessary processes.

Offers executable guidelines with processes, inputs, outputs, and the tools and templates needed.

Aligns with the SAFe Framework and acts as a contextualized version of SAFe for this industry. It also includes a hyperlink to the SAFe framework for more details as needed.

Covers six elements: Capabilities, Skillset, Competencies, Levels, Guidelines, and Expectations, as shown in the following picture: (next page image)

"This playbook is designed for all roles," I explained. "It's an additional, contextualized guide tailored to our organization's needs, complementing the SAFe training you've already received."

11.1 Playbook Elements: Levels, Capabilities, and Guidelines

We created a comprehensive document that covers three of the six key elements:

Levels: Teams, Product Groups/ARTs, Portfolio, and Enterprise.

Capabilities: Product, Architect & Design, Engineering, Agile.

Guidelines: High-level inputs, processes, outputs, and tools/templates.

Check out what we've got below for a glimpse at the team level: (refer page 240 image)

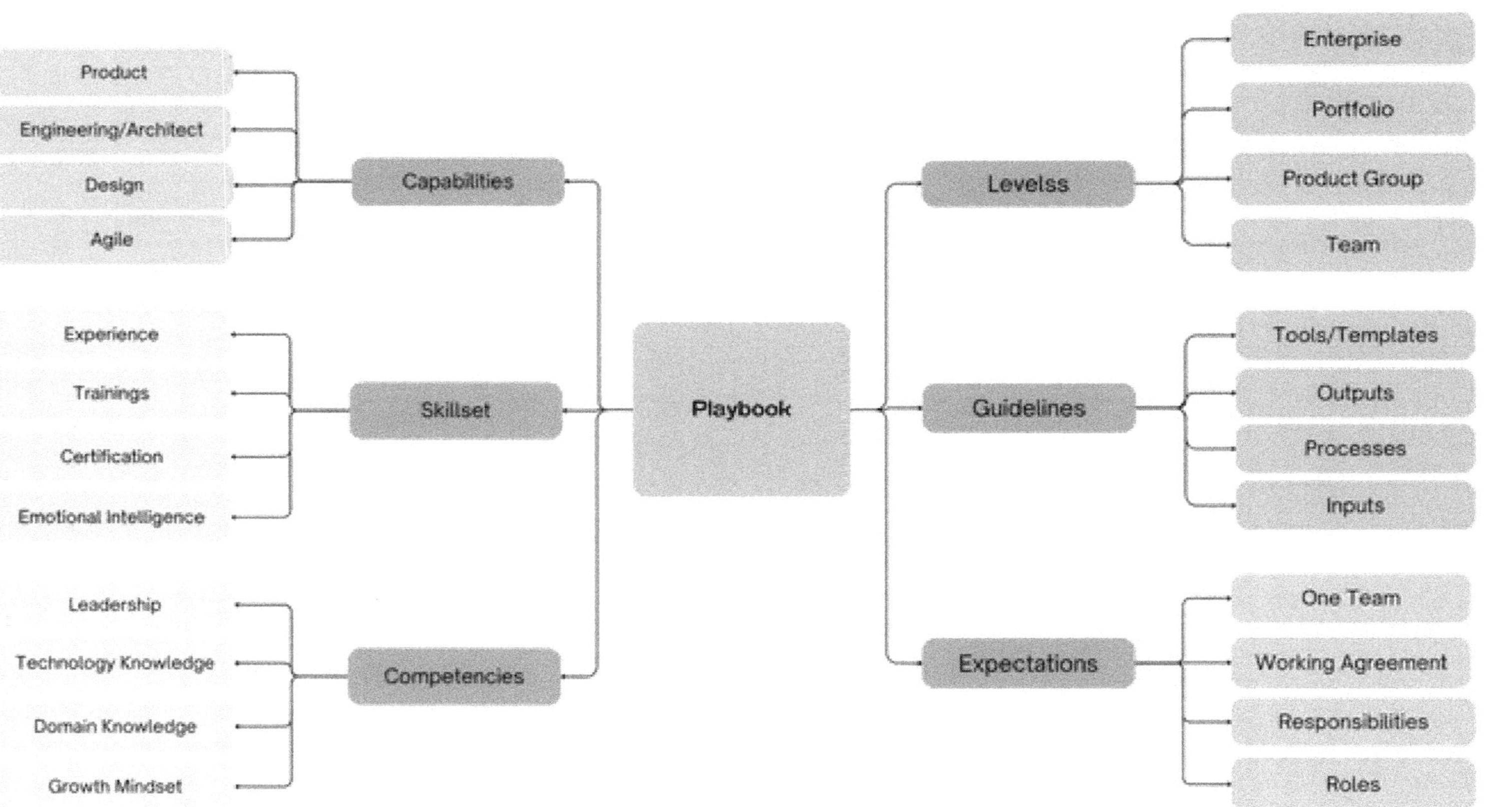
PlayBook Structure and Components
Product
Engineering/Architect
Design
Agile
Capabilities
Experience
Trainings
Certification
Emotional Intelligence
Skillset
Leadership
Technology Knowledge
Domain Knowledge
Growth Mindset
Competencies
Playbook
Levelss
Enterprise
Portfolio
Product Group
Team
Guidelines
Tools/Templates
Outputs
Processes
Inputs
Expectations
One Team
Working Agreement
Responsibilities
Roles

	Team			
	Product Management	**Design**	**Engineering team**	**Agile**
Roles	**Product Owner**	**UX Design Lead**	**Tech Lead**	**Product Coach**
Inputs	- Customer problems & needs - Product Vision, strategy, OKRs, Roadmap - Persona, empathy map, Customer journey map - Prioritized Epics & features	- Product Discovery 1 outputs - Customer problems & needs - Product Vision, strategy, OKRs, Roadmap - Persona, empathy map, Customer journey map - Prioritized epics & features	- User stories Backlog - Dependencies	- All Roles and responsibilities - Teams working Agreement - Various Agile ceremonies inputs, process and outputs
Processes/Activities	- Decompose features into user stories - Backlog refinements - Prioritize user stories - Monitor & address scope related bottle necks - Conduct Sprint demo - Provide Retro inputs - Receive and manage customer feedback - Continuously improve product	- Participate in Discover 2 with Product managers - Analyze empathy & customer journey maps - Create UX design - Create content - Collaborate with engineers to implement design	- Develop code - Collaborate with QA engineers during functional testing - Perform code review & Unit testing - Check in code daily - Demo user stories - Resolve internal defects	- Conduct all team level ceremonies effectively(Backlog refinement, Sprint planning, Daily sync up, Sprint demo, Sprint retrospective) - Coach the team to deliver value at the end of every sprint - Coach the team on conflict management, collaboratin, dependency management, interpersonnel skills - Drive continuous improvement initiatives to become high performing team
Outputs	- User stories backlog - Refined and prioritized user stories - scope related bottle necks/dependecnies addressed - Demo feedback	- UX design - UX content	- Sprint Goal - Code - Unit tet cases & executed - Latest code merged to main branch	- All team level ceremonies outputs - Team coached on various product model ways of working - Team continuously deliver committed values & improve
Guidelines	- Backlog refinement guidelines - Estimation guideline - User stories vertical slicing guidelines - User stories storming guidelines - Product Domain training material - Product Owner Roles & Responsibilities (R & R)	- UX design guidelines - UX design Industry & organization standards - Designers R & R	-Coding standards - Engineering team R & R	- All team level ceremonies guidelines (Backlog refinement, Sprint planning, sprint demo, retrospective) - Team facilitation guide, Coaching guide - Team working agreement - Product Coach R & R
Tools & Templates	- Jira/Devops/Rally - SWOT Templates - Market research	- UX design tools	- Tech stack specific unit testing tools, quality scaning tools	- JIRA/Devops/Rally - Planning poker Fibonacci series - Capacity planning, sprint retrospective templates

We've also designed a similar view for both program and portfolio levels to clearly outline the roles defined and the expectations for each. There will be hyperlinks to each of these inputs, processes, activities, outputs, guidelines, and tools & templates. These links provide detailed descriptions, enabling each role to perform effectively.

11.2 Playbook Element: Expectations

The fourth element of the playbook, "Expectations," is documented separately on the same confluence page where the other elements of the playbook have been documented. It covers roles and responsibilities, teamwork, and working agreements. They are hyperlinked to the team, product group, or portfolio-level documents. For instance, clicking on a role name will take you to the roles and responsibilities document. Similarly, clicking on a working agreement in the guidelines section will take you to the respective document that explains the steps of how each process is to be followed.

11.2.1 Roles and Responsibilities

Each role's R&R has three parts:

Daily Activities: What each role needs to do to ensure team activities and processes are executed consistently and effectively.

Continuous Improvement: Responsibilities that focus on continuously improving daily activities or processes.

Collaboration and Outcomes: Improving team, product line, and portfolio collaboration, inspiring a positive environment, and achieving measurable outcomes.

Here's a look at certain key roles and responsibilities at the team level, featuring the Product Owner, Product Coach, and Engineering Team: (refer 242, 243 images)

Product Owner

- Acts as the customer for developer questions
- **Define, writes features and user stories**
- **Prioritizes user stories** within Sprints to maximize business value taking into account risk, effort, and dependencies with input from the Business Owners
- Maintains Sprint ensuring teams have enough prioritized backlog groomed and shovel ready to keep the pipeline flowing
- Transparency to the sprint plan and backlog
- Works with Product Manager to **plan Program Increments (PI)**
- Brings user stories forward for grooming sessions
- Build **maintain one backlog** by market
- Review & reprioritizes the backlog plan during sprint planning
- **Coordinates and identifies dependencies** with other Product Owners
- Participate in team demo **, validate whether the story meets acceptance criteria** & accept stories as complete
- **Participate in the sprint Retrospective,** where the teams gather to improve their processes
- Drive preparation of the PI system demo, to show the most critical aspects of the solution to the stakeholders

Product Coach

- **Coach Agile team & facilitate team meetings**
- **Effective facilitation of Agile Ceremonies** (sprint planning, daily standup, grooming, sprint backlog, Demo, sprint retrospective)
- Ensure requirements maturity is up to mark for the downstream stakeholders
- Coordinates inter-team cooperation and hand-offs
- **Removes impediments; protects the team from outside influence**
- **Identifies risks & interdependencies** between features and user stories
- Manage external dependencies and raise's risks in **Scrum of Scrum meetings**
- Leads the team efforts in relentless improvement
- Coach team on collaboration, conflict management, building trust etc.
- Guides the team in producing normalized and quality estimates, as well as **how to estimate features & user stories**
- Ensuring estimates account for planning, preparation, grooming, testing, estimation planning, vacation time, etc.
- Assists the team in preparation for ART(Agile Release Train) activities including PI Planning, System Demos etc.

Engineering Team

- **Participate in grooming of user stories & acceptance criteria**
- Develop & commit to Team PI objectives & sprint plans
- **Define** – elaborate & prioritize requirements within a sprint & design their solution elements
- **Build** – write the code & tests that implement their portion of the solution
- **Test** – run unit test cases & validate solution against defined requirements
- Perform development with focus on NFR's, performance, end user experience, and identify risks (if any)
- **Provide build/deploy support** & ensure that code is migrated to all environments
- Regularly call out risks on delivery quality and address timely
- Manage user stories across its lifecycle

Here are some examples of roles and responsibilities at the Product line/ART level:

Business/Market Owner

- **Key stakeholders** on the Agile Release Train
- Ensure that business objectives are understood & agreed to key stakeholders
- Provide input to Epics & features prioritization
- Participate in key activities, including presentation of vision, draft program increment (PI) plan review, assigning business value to team PI objectives & approving final plans
- **Assign business value for features during PI (Program Increment) planning performed quarterly**
- **Help assess actual value versus plan**
- **Approves the Minimum** Viable Products (MVPs)
- Consulted in the Pre- & Post-PI Planning for the release train;
- **Participate & provide feedback for the product Demo**
- Actively address impediments
- Support continuous improvement initiatives with appropriate investments

Product Manager

- **Articulates the business needs, vision, and process**
- Captures and understand the business process
- Establish the voice of the customer and have a clear set of customers in mind when making decisions
- Continuously develop & communicate the vision to the development teams
- **Defines MVP, & prioritizes the Program Backlog**
- Leverage market research & continuous exploration to continually understand customer & market needs.
- Consults with the Business Owners on the prioritization of the user stories and helps inform the roadmap
- **Manages and tracks** features of the capability, along with upcoming milestones
- Collaborates with team to build the required functionality
- Provides oversight to ensure enough features are ready in the backlog at all times
- **Ensure products are deployed to customers & users**
- **Ensure that the products & solutions meet the business goals**
- Ensures business needs/ features and user stories meet quality standards

Solution Architect

- **Provides architectural guidance**
- Identifies opportunities to exploit and integrate data to improve business processes
- **Develop the Architectural runway in support of new business features & capabilities**
- **Establish solution foundation including critical NFRs** & participates in the definition of other features if necessary
- **Accountable for the integration of new work and the Continuous Delivery Pipeline**
- Owns and maintains the updates to overall solution roadmap
- Participate in planning, definition, & high-level design of the solution & exploration of solution alternatives
- Participate in Quarterly Planning , Pre- & Post-PI Planning, epics/capabilities Demos
- **Identifies dependencies at the feature level**
- System envisioning, develop solution, and evolve architectural solution

ART/Product Line Coach

- **Chief coach for the ART/product line**
- **Establish & communicate annual development calendars**
- Leads and guides the scrum masters to ensure coordination of work and delivery
- Facilitate PI Planning readiness through Pre- & Post-PI Planning meetings
- **Facilitate the domain PI planning event**
- Summarize Team PI Objectives into Program PI Objectives & publish
- **Tracks the execution of epics & features against plan**
- Manage & deliver the value of product line/ART and ensure that it enables business objectives
- **Facilitates domain/scrum master daily stand-up**
- **Assist with** facilitating feature & epics estimation during its identification/prioritization
- Coaches Leaders & Scrum Masters in Lean-Agile practices & mindsets
- **Manage domain risks & interdependencies**
- **Provide input to address critical bottlenecks**
- Escalation point to resolve roadblocks and barriers
- Provides transparency to the domain sprint plan and the backlog
- Maintains Release Plan ensuring teams have enough prioritized backlog groomed and shovel ready to keep the pipeline flowing

11.2.2 Working Agreement and One Team

We documented well-defined working agreements for each role. These agreements emphasize everyone's shared responsibility, clearly communicate expectations, improve team efficiency and effectiveness, and empower decentralized decision-making.

Creating and enhancing working agreements involves a two-step process:

Step 1 - Develop a Working Agreement Plan:

Step 2 - Create the Working Agreement:

Here's an illustrative example of a working agreement development plan: (next page image)

Before drafting a working agreement for a specific role, it's crucial to determine all the other roles they'll interact with at the team, product group, and portfolio levels. Take the Product Manager role, for example; they collaborate with the product owner, product team, business sponsor, finance, marketing and sales teams, release manager, and legal and security departments.

Next, the Product Manager should arrange a meeting with all these roles to follow the steps outlined previously, ensuring alignment on the working agreement development plan. This process begins with setting the stage, clarifying the need and purpose of the working agreement, then moving on to actually creating the working agreement and wrapping up with a summary of the next steps.

Once we agreed on working agreement development plan, create the working agreement and communicate all stakeholders and agree to adopt this working agreement. Illustrative view of working agreement shown in step 2.

Step 2: Below is an illustrative example of a working agreement developed for the Product Manager role: (refer 246 image)

We crafted the working agreement through group activities with all stakeholders. This document details the scenarios where the Product Manager will interact with various roles, specifying what the Product Manager needs to do during these interactions. This clarity helps define the collaboration boundaries for the Product Manager, fostering consensus among all roles and shared responsibility for adhering to the processes of the product-centric model. We created similar working agreements for each role at the team, product group, portfolio, and enterprise levels.

Approach to Develop Working Agreement Plan

It's a team exercise, that allows every stakeholders to express their opinions and decide what's considered to be important as explained below:

Provide Context

- Explain the purpose of working Agreement
- Define Ground rules and explain the need for working agreement

Collect Data

- Request every stakeholders to write down the points that they want to consider as part of working agreement

Obtain Consensus

- Logically group the points from all stakeholders
- Obtain consensus on important points that needs to be added to working agreement

Create Agreement

- Create a draft of the full working agreement
- Ensure every stakeholders agrees to it
- Ensure documented version made available for everyone to access

Working Agreement Examples

Respect People

Don't interrupt. Let people finish what they are saying. Its acceptable to disagree with each other. No personal attacks

Respect Timebox

Be on time. End on time. Have agenda and plan for "meet after" to discuss specifics

Be Transparent

No hidden agenda. We provide feedback and we will receive feedback, and we will act on feedback

Make Commitments as team

All if us will be accountable what we commit as a team. Lets support each and deliver our commitments.

Impediments

We will resolve impediments within team. If not possible request product coach support to resolve with dependent team

Team Meeting

Everyone in the team need to participate on sharing inputs, participate in discussion and taking decision

Contribution & Results

Everyone has equal voice, contribution and work towards delivering results

Alignment on Decision

Everyone should align and agree on the decisions as consensus approach. Once decision is taken everyone should adhere

Illustrative Working Agreement Created by one Stakeholder Group – Product Managers(PM)

Each stakeholder group has to create a working agreement that they will follow with each group of stakeholders they interact with. This example provides working agreement that PM will follow with all stakeholder they are interacting with.

Product Team

- Product Managers and Product Owners will meet regularly to discuss priorities, scope changes in the functionalities/ user stores backlog
- Product Coach and Product Manager will meet on regular cadence to discuss impediments

Marketing Team

- Collaborate with marketing team to do market research, gather customer sentiments
- Collaborate with market team and align on new product launch

Finance Team

- PM interacts with Finance team periodically to estimate budget, cost savings
- PM connects with Finance team to measure actual savings and reporting

Architects

- PM coordinates with Architects to assess technical feasibility & prioritize enabler epics

Release Team

- Periodic interaction with release team to coordinate product features release to customers

Business Sponsors

- Periodic cadence with business sponsor to prioritize business capabilities, and share market research and competitor analysis

LPM

- PM interacts with LPM (Lean Portfolio Management) during prioritization of business capabilities/epics and funding approval

Customer Focus Group

- PM customer focus group periodically to understand customer pain, needs etc.
- PM interacts with Customer focus group to get periodic feedback on products

11.3 Playbook's 5th Element: Skillset

Within the roles and responsibilities document, we've clearly defined the skillset requirements for each role. These requirements cover the necessary certifications, overall experience, and specific role-related experience. We also outline the level of soft skills needed, change management experience, and the ability to understand and manage emotions. Additionally, the document specifies the training and learning that each role should complete.

For example, a Product Manager's skillset requirements might include certifications like SAFe Product Owner/Product Manager, SAFe Agile Product Management, experience in market research, proficiency in design thinking workshops, and the ability to define OKRs, product strategy, vision, and road mapping. They should also possess strong soft skills, be adept at change management, and have a high level of emotional intelligence.

Managing emotions is a critical part of improving team dynamics, especially during the transition from old to new ways of working. Some employees will fully grasp the new processes, while others might still be adjusting. This can lead to conflicts.

Take, for example, a Product Owner (PO) who isn't used to attending daily sync meetings. According to the new process, the Product Coach expects the PO to join these meetings. Despite reminders and personal follow-ups, the PO might still not comply. This can create tension.

The Product Coach needs to manage their own emotions and identify which of the three personas the PO fits into. Then, they should have a constructive conversation with the PO, explaining the importance of their presence and the impact of their absence, without escalating the situation.

Conflicts can also arise between developers and QA engineers or between UX designers and developers. It's crucial for the Product Coach to handle these scenarios with emotional intelligence, fostering better team collaboration. This helps maintain high energy levels within the team and ensures consistent value delivery.

11.4 Playbook: 6th Element - Competencies

In the roles and responsibilities documents, we delve into the expected behaviors for each role that showcase a growth mindset. We stress the importance of leadership experience, as well as domain and technology knowledge necessary for each position.

To bring this concept to life, the playbook includes a link to a video simulation demonstrating team interactions. The video contrasts the behaviors of those with a fixed mindset versus those with a growth mindset during agile ceremonies, such as backlog refinement sessions.

For instance, in this backlog refinement scenario, team members with a fixed mindset may hold back, not fully engaging with new ways of working. They might not actively participate, missing opportunities to ask crucial questions about development, testing, or how the work impacts customer needs. Their questions might lack depth concerning how user stories align with product OKRs or the broader business objectives these are meant to advance.

On the flip side, the video shows how individuals with a growth mindset behave differently. They're engaged, asking insightful questions, eager to understand how each piece fits into the bigger picture. They're open to new ideas, ready to take risks, and embrace learning, without fear of failure.

Reflecting on the six elements of our playbook, each covered across three different documents, it becomes clear how they interconnect to guide our new ways of working. All three documents are consolidated on a single confluence page at the product team, product group, and portfolio level.

First, we have the processes view, the foundation that outlines the steps each role needs to follow at various levels, along with the tools they'll use. This document ensures everyone knows what to do and how to do it.

Clicking on a role hyperlink takes you to the second document, detailing the roles and responsibilities, competencies, and expectations for each position. This clarity helps everyone understand their part in the bigger picture.

Next, we have the working agreements, hyperlinked within the guidelines section of the process view. This document outlines the collaborative agreements each role must follow, fostering teamwork and efficiency.

For each sprint-level ceremony, we've defined specific guidelines. Take backlog refinement, for example. We provide clear instructions on how to perform this process, ensuring consistency and thoroughness.

We've also established guidelines for other crucial processes like user story estimation, vertical slicing of user stories, code review, application documentation, and design standards. These detailed guidelines ensure everyone is on the same page, driving towards our common goals with clarity and purpose.

This tool is so integral to our success that I found myself discussing and recapping it with the internal Agile coach over a cup of coffee.

We crafted a comprehensive playbook that serves as a single source of truth for everyone involved—from team members to product group leads, and portfolio managers. This playbook is a living document reflecting best practices from the SAFe framework and industry standards.

Our playbook focuses on six key elements: Capabilities, Skillsets, Competencies, Levels, Guidelines, and Expectations. It's designed to provide clarity and guidance on processes, inputs, outputs, and the tools needed for each role. When someone clicks on a role, they see everything they need: expectations, processes, tools, and required competencies. It's all interconnected.

For instance, if a product manager needs to understand their role better, they can click on their role in the playbook. Instantly, they'll see detailed descriptions of their responsibilities, the skills they need, and the processes they must follow. If they need to understand a specific process, they can click on it to see which roles are involved, what tools are needed, and what mindset is expected.

This playbook is a tool for inspiring a growth mindset. It helps team members understand the behaviors expected of them, promoting a culture of continuous improvement and collaboration. For example, during a backlog refinement session, the playbook will show how a growth mindset can transform a routine meeting into a dynamic, productive discussion.

We emphasized the importance of contextualizing the SAFe framework to our organization's unique needs. This ensures that the playbook is a tailored guide that helps our team navigate the transition smoothly and effectively.

This playbook also provides comprehensive guidelines, processes, tools, inputs, and outputs from each capability perspective—Product, Design, Engineering, and Agile. For instance, if someone in the Product community needs to know which processes and tools to leverage, they can simply click on the relevant hyperlinks. These links will take them to the specific pages in the playbook, making it easy to find what they need.

The playbook is designed to be user-friendly and hyperlinked from various perspectives—people/roles, capabilities, tools, and processes. This way, anyone can reference anything from anywhere within the playbook.

We also delved into the three levels of process guidelines—team, product group, and portfolio. Each level outlines the roles involved in executing those processes, making this playbook a one-stop solution for all process, tool, and people-related guidelines that are tailored for our organization. If someone needs more information than what's available in the playbook, we've included links to the SAFe framework, directing them to the relevant pages on the official SAFe website. (www.scaleagileframework.com)

This approach ensures that everyone, regardless of their role or level, has access to the information they need to perform effectively and contribute to our overall success.

12

Product Release Planning (PRP) Preparation

We gathered for another workshop with Business leads, PMs, Business architects, enterprise and solution architects, and the RTE/ART coaches for the two ARTs we plan to launch. I kicked things off, setting the context and explaining our next steps.

"With our future state portfolio view and the epics/business capabilities roadmap already laid out," I began, "we're going to talk about how to bring that future state to life through three major elements."

I pointed to the picture on the screen. "First, we need to prepare for our first PI/Quarterly Product Release Planning (PRP). We'll dive into that in this chapter, and it typically takes 2 to 3 months. Next, we'll conduct the quarterly PRP/PI event, which we'll cover in Chapter 13. This step takes 2 to 3 days. Finally, we'll execute the PI/PRP, detailed in Chapter 14. This phase spans 3 months."

I paused to let the team absorb the information. "So, over the next 6 months, we'll move through these three elements: 3 months of preparation, a few days of planning, and 3 months of executing our first quarterly plan. This cycle will repeat every quarter, allowing us to deliver value incrementally."

I could see the gears turning in their minds as they considered the roadmap ahead. It was crucial to ensure everyone was on the same page and ready for the journey.

Below is an illustration of how those three elements will be implemented over the next six months: (next page image)

"As part of this workshop," I continued, "we need to align on the activities we must complete in the next three months. This aligns with the first element on the left side of the figure."

I reminded everyone, "We've already defined the OKRs for our business line. We know which products need modernization with new business capabilities to achieve these OKRs, and we've laid out the product roadmap in Chapters 5 and 9. We chose products impacting two personas' journeys, Merchants and Customers,

Illustrative view of Quarterly PRP/PI Preparation, Planning & Execution

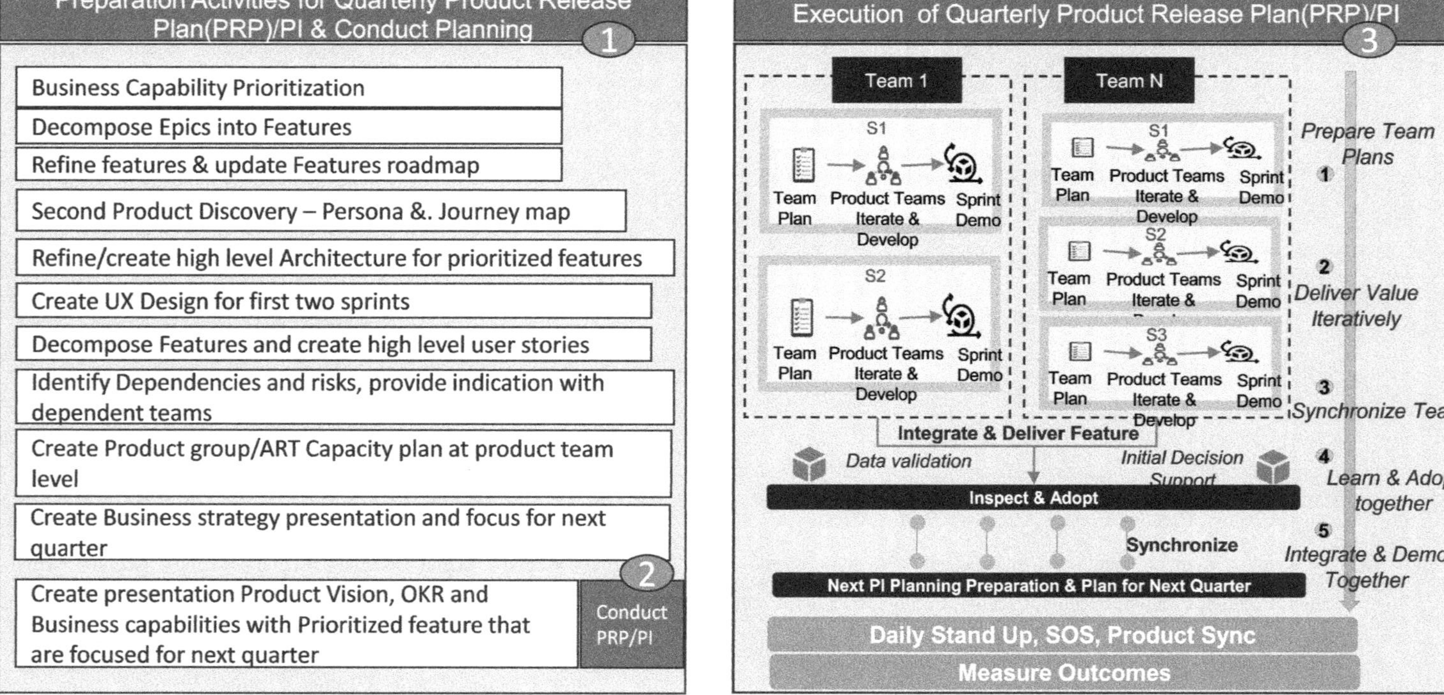

and set up two ARTs with product teams to deliver these new capabilities. We've also prioritized the business capabilities for the first quarter."

Now, it was time to dive into the preparation activities for Quarterly Product Release Planning (PRP) or PI.

"Here's what we need to focus on over the next three months," I continued.

Review Product Roadmap: Look at the roadmap of epics, product vision, Product OKRs, and the Minimum Viable Product (MVP) at the product level. Ensure these align with business outcomes (lagging indicators) and KPIs (leading indicators) to be achieved by each epic, as discussed in the epic-level business case.

Architectural Decisions: Decide on the technology stack and identify any necessary changes to the existing architecture. Conduct feasibility analyses and start creating or updating the architecture to implement the MVP scope epics.

Decompose Business Capabilities: Break down the business capabilities / epics into functionalities/ features.

Design Thinking: Use design thinking tools to identify personas, empathize with them, and create customer journeys. This product discovery phase 2 helps us understand "how" customers use the product and "why" they use it.

Refine Product Epics Roadmap: Update based on Product Discovery 2 outcomes. Add any new epics or features to the portfolio epic Kanban or the product group/ ART backlog, and prioritize them for the current or next quarter.

Competitor Analysis: Review competitor product features and digital/Gen AI opportunities in the market.

Review Future State Business Processes: Update these processes based on new features or insights from Product Discovery 2.

Prioritize Top Features: Define these as MVPs for each epic and create a feature-level roadmap for the next 3 quarters.

Decompose Features into User Stories: The Product owners and UX team will work on this, while the UX team creates UI designs and content.

Identify Dependencies and Risks: Inform dependent teams of upcoming needs for the next quarter.

"By the end of the third month, we should have identified customer problems and needs, defined the minimum set of features required to address these, established hypotheses to test at the end of each epic-level MVP, and developed high-level architecture and UX design along with high-level user stories."

12.2 Diving Deep into Workshop Activities

After I finished explaining the plan, everyone started sharing their thoughts. One of the PMs spoke up, "I like the idea of MVPs at two levels. It helps align on the necessary business capabilities for delivering a product and then pinpoints the essential functionalities within each capability."

"Exactly," I responded. "And there's even another level of MVP—what we call MMF, or minimum marketable features. This identifies the minimum set of user stories needed to deliver a functionality."

Another PM chimed in, "That makes sense. It's what we learned during the SAFe APM & POPM training, and now we see how it fits into the overall context."

"Precisely," I said, pulling up a diagram. "We discussed this in Chapter 4 using the 'Digital Customer Onboarding' product as an example."

Product -> MVP List of Epics -> MVP of Features for Each Epic -> MMF Stories for Each Feature

The architect then jumped in, "For modernizing existing products in the latest microservices-oriented architectures, changes to implement MVP epics might be quicker. But if we're talking about legacy tech stacks or developing new products, creating the first increment architecture might take longer than three months."

I nodded, "That's a good point. We need to prioritize agility in our decisions, align with enterprise architecture guidelines and standards, and mobilize people early. These actions are crucial to build the first increment of architecture within three months, develop the MVP in the next three months, and launch the first version of the product within six months. After that, we can roll out enhancements bi-weekly, monthly, or quarterly, depending on the market dynamics."

The UX Design lead spoke up, "We need to start UX design activities based on the initial decomposition of epics into features, its prioritization and refine additional features at the end of discovery 2. This should be based on persona journey maps and empathy maps."

"Absolutely," I agreed. "As the UX Design lead, you should work closely with the PM and Architect to create UX designs for at least the first two sprints.

This way, product teams can start their development work as soon as the quarterly planning is completed."

One of the ART coaches then chimed in, "It's our responsibility to drive these activities in collaboration with Business, PM, Architects, UX leads, and POs over the next three months."

"Exactly!" I emphasized. "It's critical that you drive and ensure the 'right' products and values are defined and ready for quarterly planning. To maintain close collaboration and progress faster, I suggest having weekly sync-ups among all these stakeholders."

One of the Product Owners (PO) raised a concern, "Our involvement usually starts only after the features are prioritized for the upcoming quarter. Isn't our role mainly about execution?"

I smiled and shook my head. "Not really. You can support your respective Product Managers (PMs) during the discovery phase, market analysis, vision setting, OKR definition, and roadmap creation. If you can't support during these activities, make sure to collect all the details from the PM. This will help you connect better with customer problems and needs, and then you can communicate those insights to your POD/product teams to develop features aligned with customer needs."

A PM then spoke up, "To complete all these activities in three months, performing research and competitor analysis needs to be done within one month. That seems like a lot of effort and time. How can we manage it?"

"Good point," I acknowledged. "You're right about the logical timeline. When we start from scratch, defining personas and so on, it does take more time. We need to plan our first quarterly preparation timeline accordingly. We can leverage initial inputs gathered during Discovery 1 and perform secondary research for personas and empathy exercises to optimize the time needed for Discovery 2."

After a lively discussion and several clarifications, I walked them through an example from the insurance industry where we had performed similar preparation activities. This example provided a concrete illustration of how to efficiently manage the process and achieve the desired outcomes within the timeline.

Example of **current** state Auto Insurance Industry Business Operation Value Stream , Products, Business capabilities and Functionalities

1. Define Business Operation Value stream

Value:
Vehicle Insurance Coverage Received

Trigger: Customer need for Auto Insurance Coverage →

Attract Customers	Receive Applications	Generate Quote	Underwriting Decision	Receive Payment	Issue Policy	Customer Servicing	Process Claims	Renew Policy

Value:
Revenue through Insurance Premium

2. Define Business Operation Value stream

Digital Marketing	Customers Onboarding	Customers Risk Management	Personal Assistance BOT	Under Writing & Pricing	Policy Administration	Customer Servicing	Claims Management	Data Insights

3. Identifying the Business Capabilities

Lead Management	Communication Management	Payment Management	Service Request Management	Automated Underwriting	Dynamic Pricing	Community Forums	Automated Claims Workflow	Premium Vs Claims Analytics
Multi-Channel Accessibility	Driver Behavior Analytics	Insurance Product Catalog	Policy Management	AI Driven FAQs	Policy Records Mgmt	Fraud Prevention & Mgmt	Claims team Capacity Mgmt	Customer Segmentation Analytics

4. Identifying the Functionalities and Applications that offers those Functionalities

Lead Qualification & Allocation	Profile Creation	Payment Options	Driver behavior capture	Personalized Engagement	Risk Assessment	Identify At-Risk Policyholders	Claims Reporting	Vehicle Driving data capture
Consolidate Communications Received	Personalized View of Policies	Safe Driving Incentives	Customer Communication	Fraud Detection	Notifications	Trend Identification	Claims Verification	Customer Demographics

Application 1	Application 2	Application 3	Application 4	Application 5	Application 6	Application 7	Application 8	Application 9

5. Identifying the Platform Capabilities

Data Driven Insights	Risk Evaluation & Prediction	Data Analytics & Reporting	Authentication	Login & Identity Proofing	Appointment Scheduling	IOT & Telematics

Note: its an illustrative view of digital products and business capabilities. Based on organization size and complexity, number of products and its business capabilities may vary. Platform capabilities are built and managed centrally that can be reused by all business lines

12.3 Quarterly Planning: Preparation Activities Explained with Insurance Industry Examples

This is a visual blueprint outlining the current state of business operations, including value streams, products, business capabilities, and functionalities.

Business Objectives: Increase total customer foot print by 20%; Increase market share by 25%; Improve customer NPS to 80. (previous page image)

I'll be focusing on "Claims Management" from the list of products mentioned (Digital marketing, Customer onboarding, Claims management, Data insights, etc.). We will dive into all the quarterly planning preparation activities using this product as an example. Let's take a closer look at the business capabilities and functionalities already established, as outlined in the future state portfolio vision in Chapter 9.

Let's explore the future state of product and business capabilities in the roadmap shown below, focusing on the functionalities envisioned for our portfolio, as outlined in Chapter 9. (next page image)

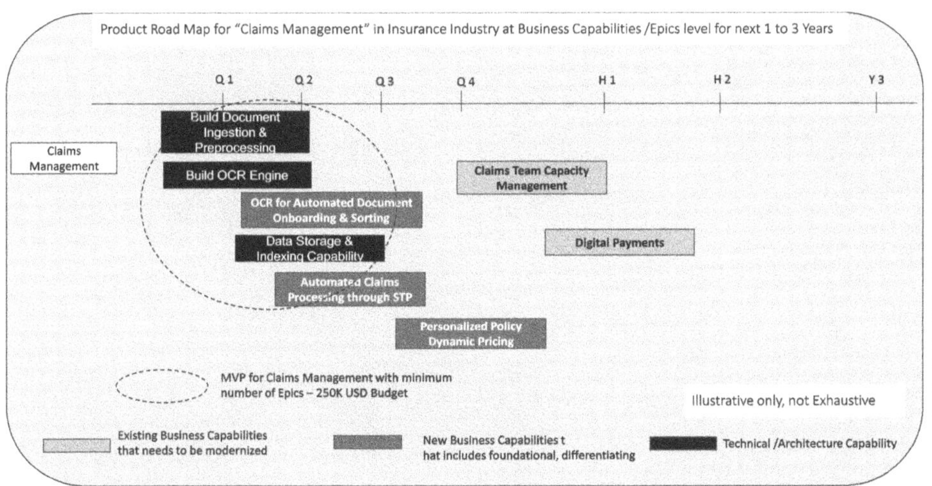

With the above inputs, we began creating the deliverables for our quarterly planning preparation:

Our first deliverable was the product vision. For the Claims Management product, we crafted a vision statement meant to inspire everyone involved in its design, development, and support. Here's an illustrative example:

Illustrative example of "**Claims Management**" Product **Current** state View with Business Capabilities and its functionalities

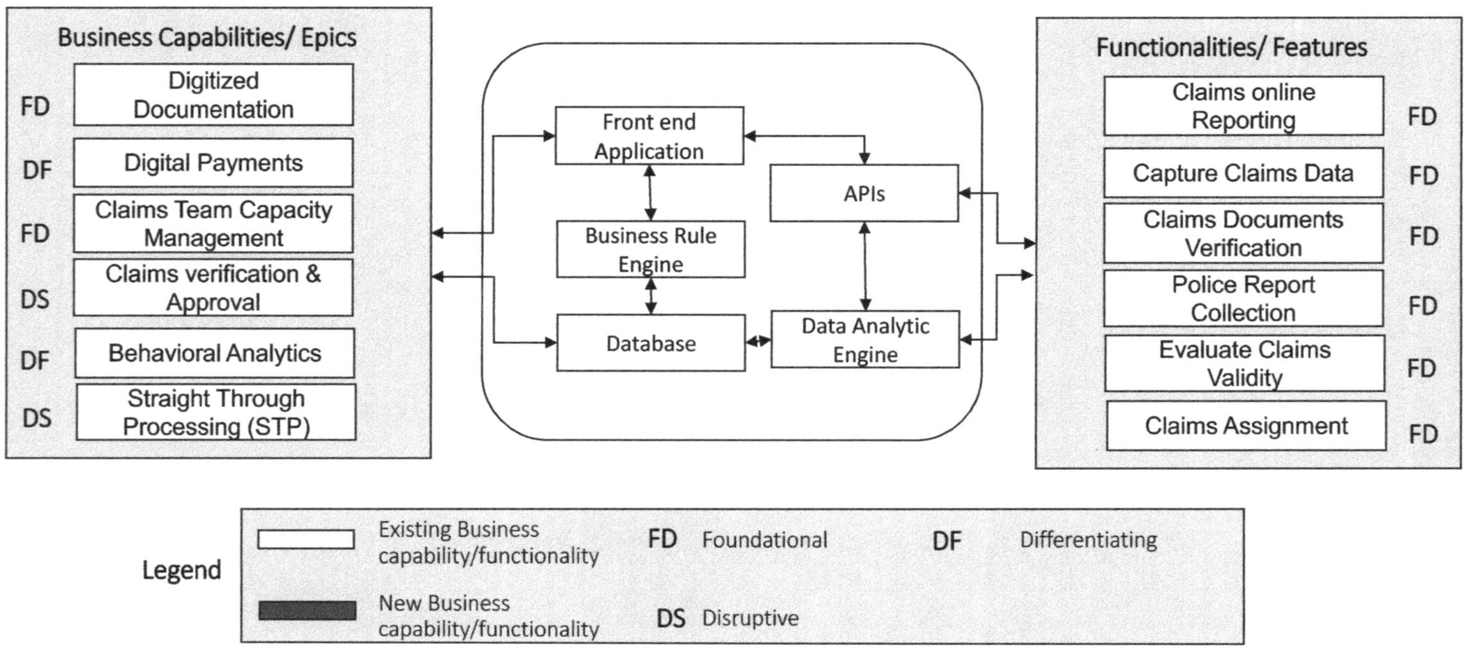

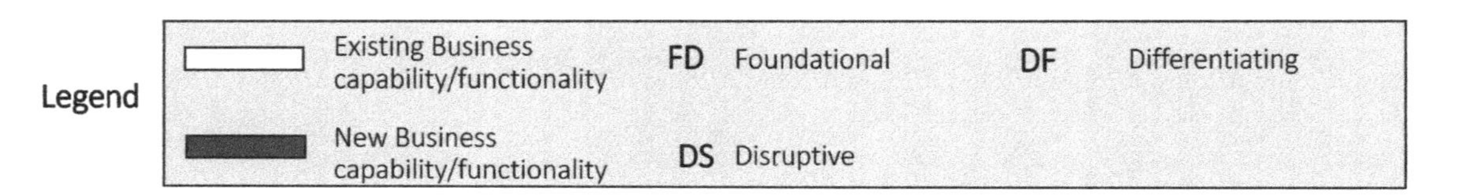

Note:: This illustrative view of Business capabilities and Functionalities does not include all. There are many more business capabilities and functionalities that are not shown here as it's an illustrative purpose

Vision: Empowering Trust and Resilience

At the heart of our mission lies a commitment to our policyholders: to be there when they need us most. Our "Claims Management" digital product is more than just a system—it's a bridge between empathy and efficiency, a testament to our promise of protection

As an policy holder, I am able to submit claims seamlessly with no paper work, get real-time updates on claims status, claims processed in hours than weeks, and receive claims payments faster

As an claim processing team, we are able to verify and validate through automation, automated risk assessment and future risk, process more claims per day with very few minutes of manual effort

This product has achieved many business outcomes that includes achieving increased operation efficiency, improved customer experience ad increased accuracy of claims approval

Next, we tackled the Product OKRs. To measure our progress towards achieving the vision through our defined business capabilities, we established the following OKRs for the Claims Management product:

Illustrative Product OKRs for "Claims Management" Product of an Insurance Industry

Sr. No.	Business Objective	OKRs
1	Achieve a **Net Promoter Score (NPS)** of **75 or higher**	• Increase positive customer feedback by **20%** on review platforms. • Resolve **95%** of customer inquiries within **24 hours**.
2	Improve risk assessment methodologies for more accurate underwriting	• Develop and implement **two new risk models** that reduce underwriting errors by **15%**. • Train underwriters on updated risk assessment techniques, achieving **100% participation**
3	Streamline internal processes to reduce operational costs.	• Implement an **OCR (Optical Character Recognition)** system for automated document onboarding and sorting. • Reduce claims processing time by **20%**through automation. • Achieve 100% accuracy in Claims data extraction using OCR technology

Our third deliverable in the preparation phase was conducting a second product discovery to understand how customers use this Claims Management product and why they use it. During this discovery, we identified personas who use the product, like the Tech-Savvy Insurance Buyer. With this understanding, we delved into the details of defining and empathizing with these personas.

For the insurance industry example, we defined personas based on initial secondary research. We started by identifying persona segments such as customer and agent. Then, for each segment, we defined various personas based on demographic parameters like age, profession, region, and sex. Here is an example of a tech-savvy agent persona we defined based on our secondary research: (next page image)

Design Digital Product from Persona perspective

Persona: Tech Savvy Insurance Buyer

Note: This persona represents. Tech Savvy community who wants to buy auto insurance to secure their vehicle with insurance coverage

Name: Steve

Age: 30

Occupation: Software Engineer

Lifestyle: Urban, fast-paced

"Steve loves gadgets, stays updated on the latest tech trends, and appreciates cutting-edge features. He values convenience and efficiency in all aspects of life"

Key Pain Points

- Generic policies don't address his tech-related concerns (e.g., coverage for expensive gadgets, electronic car components)

- Outdated processes (paperwork, phone calls) frustrate him. He wants to manage policies online, receive digital notifications, and access services via apps

- Lengthy claim processes or lack of digital claims submission options frustrate him

Goal and Motivation

- Steve wants auto insurance coverage that aligns with his specific requirements.

- Steve seeks seamless integration between his insurance and digital life

- Steve values safety features in both his car and insurance policy.

- Steve expects quick and efficient claims handling

- Steve's goal is to find an auto insurance policy that covers not only the basics but also tech-related risks (e.g., stolen gadgets, cyber threats).

Design Considerations

- Use targeted online ads, social media, and tech blogs to reach Steve

- Consider tech-friendly features (e.g., app-based claims, digital policy management).

- Design Personalized communication to Steve's preferences (email, app notifications).

- Create blog posts or videos explaining tech-related insurance aspects (e.g., coverage for electric cars, cybersecurity)

Our fourth deliverable was to empathize with these personas by identifying real people who fit the persona category. This involved a mix of secondary research and primary research, where we interacted with real individuals to truly understand their perspectives. We conducted surveys covering various parameters, including what they do, feel, say, and think. Here's an empathy map created from that exercise:

As I wrapped up this part, one of the PMs asked, "Why can't persona definition and empathy mapping be done together?" It was a great question.

I responded, "They actually need to be done in two stages. First, we define personas—fictional characters expected to behave similarly while using the product—through secondary research. Then, as a second step, we empathize with these types of personas by engaging with real people who fit those personas. Both activities serve distinct purposes and have different approaches."

I continued, "The third step is to create a journey map for each persona. This step can be combined with the empathy mapping stage. For each persona, we empathize with them first and then capture their experiences throughout their journey."

Our fifth deliverable for quarterly planning preparation was creating a journey map for the persona. In this case, we mapped the journey of a tech-savvy agent from the initial search for the right insurance company to continuous engagement with the company from whom they bought the insurance policy. Here's an illustrative view: (refer 262, 263 images)

"We need to keep our persona, empathy map, and journey map up-to-date as we deliver new product features and as customer needs evolve," I explained. "While implementing these features, we must continually interact with our personas to gather interim feedback."

Our sixth and final deliverable for quarterly planning preparation was to update the existing list of functionalities, reflecting the product's future state business capabilities and functionalities. We added new functionalities identified through our design thinking tools like persona, empathy map, and customer journey map. These features address both the problems customers face and the needs they express. Here's an illustrative view of the functionalities/features roadmap which includes prioritized features of that other products delivered by a certain ART/ Product group:

Tech Savvy Auto Insurance Buyer Journey Map that drives Product vision and Functionalities

Tech Savvy Persona's Journey Map captured with integration touch points and journey experiences and improvement opportunities				
1 Research & Discovery	**2** Pre-Purchase	**3** Quote & Customization	**4** Policy Purchase	**5** Post Purchase Interaction
"I begin by researching auto insurance options online. I read reviews, compares coverage, and explores different insurers' websites"	"I visit insurance company websites, exploring policy details, pricing, and coverage options"	"I enter vehicle details, driving habits, and preferences into online quote calculators"	"I complete the purchase online, customizing his policy to include coverage for gadgets and electronic components"	"I download the insurer's mobile app to manage his policy"
Find Best Auto insurance option • Uses search engines, • Review sites, and social media platforms • Gather information about insurers and their offerings.	Gather details about Insurer • He looks for transparency, clear communication, and user-friendly interfaces. Trust is crucial for him	Receive Quote • He enters his vehicle details, driving habits, and preferences into online quote calculators	Purchase Insurance Policy • He receives an instant confirmation email or notification	Set up Policy page to manage • He uses the app to view policy documents, pay premiums, and track claims
I FEEL CONFUSED	DECISSIVE	COFUSED	ANXIOUS	SATISFIED
I NEEED GUIDE	GUIDE	MENTOR	ADVISOR	MENTOR
Not able to find reviews very concise and not enabling right decisions making	Not able to utilize personalized pricing options, and various insurance products benefits	Take long time to receive quotes Accuracy of quote is not reliable	Policy document not providing information in quick read ways	Post policy purchase and managing it is not very user frienndly

Tech Savvy Auto Insurance Buyer Journey Map that drives Product vision and Functionalities

Tech Savvy Persona's Journey Map captured with integration touch points and journey experiences and improvement opportunities

6 Claims Process	7 Customer Support	8 Renewal & Maintenance	9 Feedback & Accuracy	10 Continuous Engagement
"If I had an accident, he uses the app to submit a claim. He uploads photos of the damage and provides relevant details"	"I prefer digital channels for inquiries. He interacts with chatbots or live agents through the app"	"I receive reminders to renew his policy via email or app notifications"	"I share my experience by leaving reviews and ratings on review sites or social media"	"I receive personalized offers based on his driving behavior and preferences"
Submit Claims & Documents ⇒	Get Assistance from support team ⇒	Manage policy and Renew ⇒	Provide Feedback ⇒	Obtain Additional Coverage
▪ Steve receives notifications about the claim status, adjuster visits, and repair progress	▪ He appreciates timely and accurate answers to his questions	▪ The app provides maintenance reminders and safety tips for his tech-equipped car	▪ If satisfied, he recommends the insurer to friends and family	▪ The insurer rewards his loyalty with discounts or additional coverage
I FEEL CONFUSED	DECISSIVE	COFUSED	ANXIOUS	SATISFIED
I NEEED GUIDE	GUIDE	MENTOR	ADVISOR	MENTOR
Claims submission process requires lot of documents Claim process takes longer time to approve	24 / 7 customer support available is not effective. They are unable to solve problem/it takes longer time.	Renewal reminders not sent via all channels Renewal process is complex ad takes longer time	Multi-Channels to provide feedback are not available	Additional coverage related information is not transparent

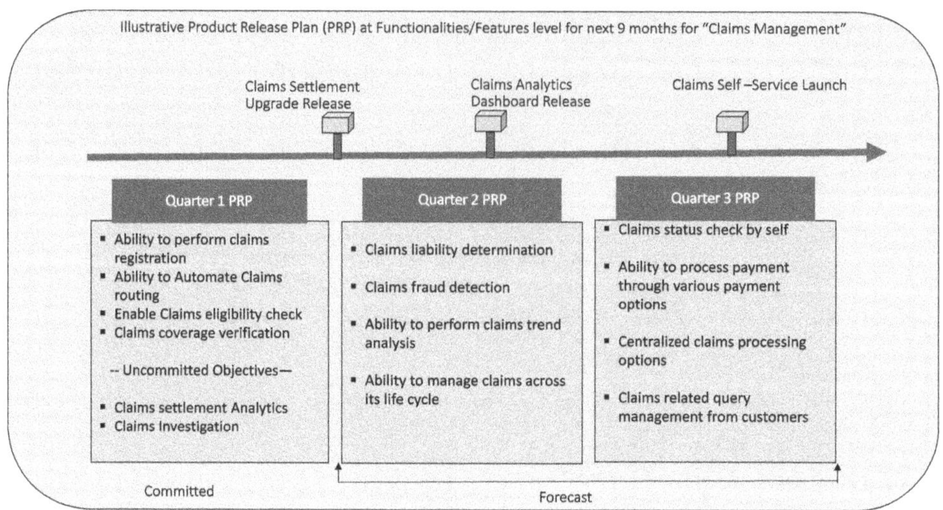

All these deliverables were created through a series of workshops, brainstorming sessions, Gemba walks with customers, and customer focus interviews. With these six deliverables in hand, the Claims Management product team decomposed the first quarter's prioritized features into high-level user stories, while the UX design team simultaneously created designs for the first two sprints' user stories. The product team also identified dependencies and risks, and began coordinating with dependent teams in preparation for the Quarterly Product Release Planning (PRP)/PI.

Both ART leaders and leads from each product team listened intently. They could visualize the extensive work required in the next two to three months. Each role understood clearly, thanks to the illustrative examples that brought to life the conceptual discussions we had in sections 12.1 and 12.2 of this chapter.

12.4 Planning the Next Steps: Quarterly Preparation for Two ARTs

With the examples fresh in everyone's minds, we agreed to conduct a series of workshops to create all these outputs for the two personas-related products of Retail store business products. The ART coach stepped up, ready to lead and drive these sessions, while we agreed to have interim touchpoints and provide support as needed from the transformation team.

"Collaboration among Product, Design, Engineering, and Agile roles is crucial," I emphasized, showing the picture illustrating this point. "Developing and delivering activities will be performed incrementally during quarterly plan execution in bi-weekly sprints, with bi-weekly or weekly releases, receiving feedback, refining the next sprint plan, monthly governance, quarterly full product releases, and retrospects."

The ART Agile coach nodded. "I'll ensure this collaboration happens and address any impediments like SME availability, bandwidth challenges, conflicting priorities, or infrastructure issues."

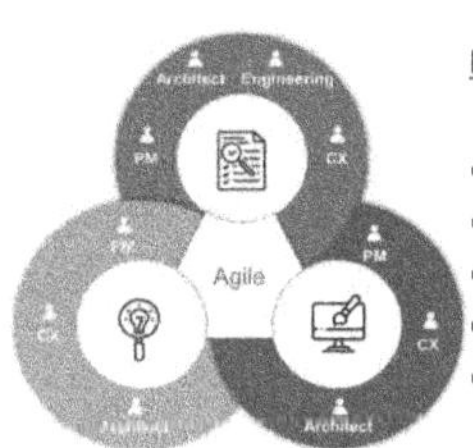

Within the next month, our team successfully completed the research and exercises. Using personas, empathy maps, and customer journey inputs, we identified new epics and features needed to modernize the MVP business capabilities of 16 digital products that influence two key personas: Merchants and Customers. We created a features backlog, prioritized the features, and assigned them to the respective product teams within the ARTs/Product Group.

During our session, one of the PMs raised a question, "Is it mandatory for a single team to deliver the entire feature?"

"Not necessarily," I responded. "Ideally, a team should own end-to-end features related to all the business capabilities of a product. That is how these product teams are ideally constructed to ensure work on all related user stories and delivery without dependencies on other teams within the ART. However, that's not always feasible due to teams' knowledge, experience, or dependent applications. In those cases, multiple teams might work on a single feature. One team's PO should own the feature and collaborate with other POs within the ART to prioritize and plan related user stories."

Once we assigned the features to teams, the respective Product Owners (POs) began decomposing them into high-level user stories. They used user story mapping templates for workflow-type features and other user story splitting techniques from the book "Extreme Programming Explained" by Cynthia Andres and Kent Beck.

"Alright," I said, "let's make sure we conduct backlog refinement sessions with the teams to walk through all the features and high-level user stories before the PI/Quarterly Product Release planning. This way, everyone has a clear understanding of the upcoming quarter's work and can contribute effectively during the planning."

Here's a summary of the preparation activities for the two ARTs in our Retail stores: (next page image)

The final step of the preparation phase is to hold a pre-PI planning/quarterly planning meeting for three to four hours. In this session, key leaders such as Product Managers, Business Owners/Leads, Architects, ART Coaches, POs, and Scrum Masters from both ARTs of one DVS will align on priorities, dependencies, and release timelines. Based on these alignments, each ART will conduct its respective quarterly planning.

As I wrapped up the walkthrough, I felt it was important to recap the stages of preparation to underscore their value and importance.

"In summary," I began, "we covered the inputs from previous chapters, which are crucial for performing the preparation activities before quarterly planning. We discussed the outputs we've created through these activities."

I continued, "We listed the quarterly planning preparation activities that need to be completed before the Quarterly Product Release Planning (PRP)/PI Planning. Then, we delved into each activity, outlining how they should be done and which roles at the product group and team levels need to be involved."

"We also explored each preparation activity with examples from the insurance industry," I added, "showing who needs to perform these activities and the role of the ART coach. These examples provided visual clarity to the conceptual discussions."

I emphasized the six key deliverables from the preparation activities, also known as the second product discovery: product vision, product OKRs, persona, empathy map, customer journey map, and features roadmap.

Illustrative View of ART 1 "Merchant Journey" Quarterly planning preparation Outcomes

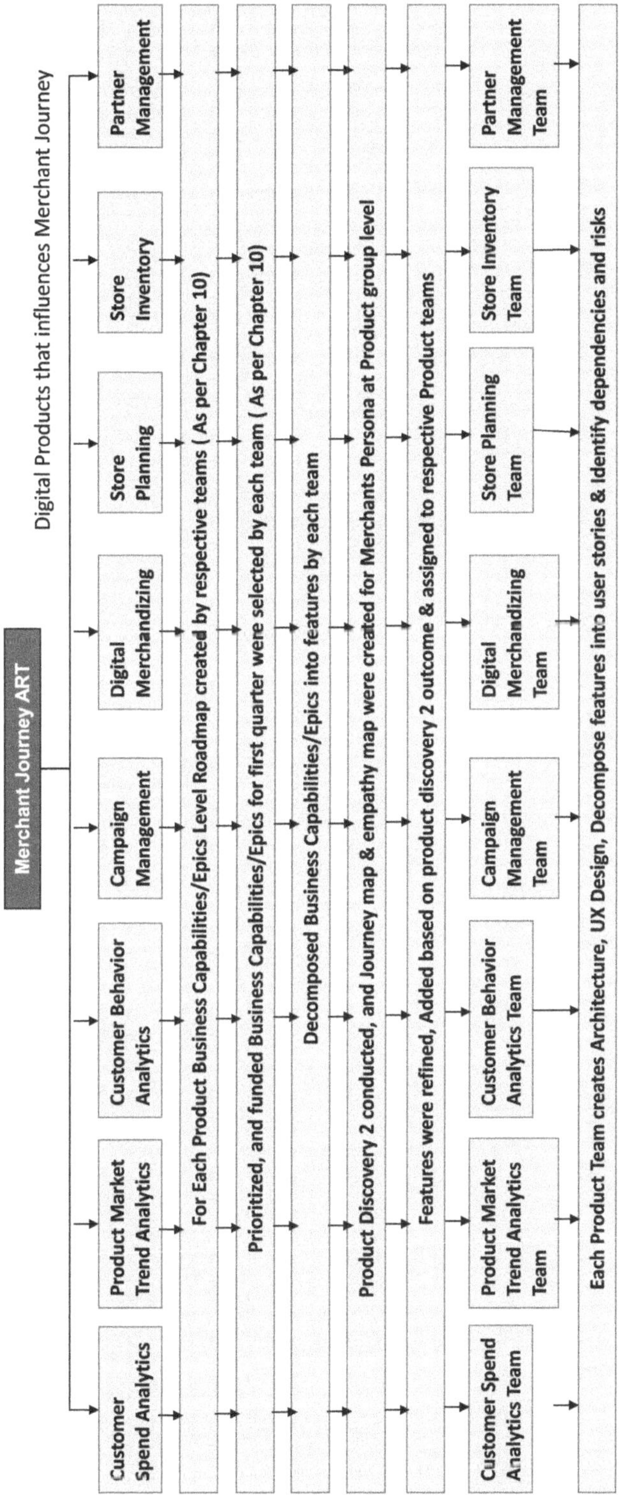

"We also laid out the next steps and plans for the two ARTs product teams for the next 2 to 3 months," I said, "based on our detailed discussions and examples. We summarized all the preparation activities into a single slide view for easy reference."

"We addressed some potential challenges stakeholders might face," I noted, "and discussed the collaboration model we need to implement to successfully execute the preparation activities."

With this recap, I wanted to ensure everyone understood the importance and sequence of our preparation stages, setting a clear path forward.

Product Release Planning

We've reached an exciting milestone in our product model transformation. Today marks the start of our first short-term win: Day 1 of the PI/ Quarterly Product Release Planning. Since this is a virtual event, we've spread it over three days. We have two parallel sessions for both Journey ARTs. Let's dive into the planning journey for ART 1, the "Customer Journey ART."

After selecting 16 products for the two newly formed Journey-based ARTs and aligning on their backlogs, we conducted detailed preparation sessions to identify the top features for each product. POs decomposed these features into high-level user stories, which were then shared with their respective teams. All team members have been trained on SAFe for Teams, and we conducted a role play dry run with all roles, including business leaders, PMs, Architects, POs, and ART coaches. This ensures a synchronized common cadence for both ARTs as they launch their quarterly planning.

Our ART coach kicked off Day 1 by walking us through the agenda for the next three days, as proposed by SAFe. "We're all set to witness a critical event that will be a turning point for our organization," the coach said. "This is where we start gaining business growth momentum."

Since this is the first planning session, the internal coach and I agreed to provide support to ensure these three days go smoothly and we achieve all the event's outputs.

Now, let's dive into the event and witness the major activities.

The ART coach greeted everyone with a lively "Good morning, everyone!" The response was muted, so he repeated, "Good morning, everyone!" The response improved. He tried once more, and this time, almost everyone joined in with a resounding "Good morning!" He beamed, "Fantastic! This is the energy we need for the next three days."

He kicked things off with a quick welcome note and explained the purpose of the planning event. "Our goal is to align on what value and PI objectives we aim to deliver in the next three months, considering the ART's capacity. We'll identify the business outcomes these PI objectives will achieve and address any dependencies and risks. By the end, as product teams and the ART, we'll commit to our plan with a 'fist of five' confidence vote."

Next, he presented the agenda, highlighting each step we would cover over the three days. Then, he turned to the Business Owner and said, "Could you please set the stage with the business context and our differentiating business objectives?"

Here is a glimpse into the 3-day agenda that we adopted from SAFe:

The Business Owner began with a story: (page 271, 272, 273 images)

"I was at the airport, waiting to board my flight from New York to Singapore. While observing people picking up their packages purchased from one of our retail stores at the boarding gate, I noticed there was still one package left unclaimed. As the boarding continued for the next hour, my curiosity grew about who would pick up that last package.

Finally, it was the final call for boarding, and I had to get on the plane. Just as they were about to close the gate, a woman hurried onto the flight, carrying the last package. She placed all her bags, including our package, in the overhead bin and coincidentally sat right next to me.

I gave her a moment to catch her breath and settle in. After about ten minutes, I introduced myself and said, 'Hello, hope you had a good trip despite the last-minute rush to board the flight.'

She smiled and introduced herself as Maya, the CTO of a leading company in North America. She replied, 'Hi, no, this trip has been exhausting. It was a whirlwind of executive-level presentations, last-minute preparations, schedule changes, and content revisions. I didn't even have time to shop for a gift for my son's birthday tomorrow. But thanks to Thiran Retail, I was able to get it delivered to the gate without spending a minute shopping. That was the only good part of this trip,' she laughed.

We continued to chat for a while longer, but I didn't mention that I am one of the co-founders of Thiran Retail."

He continued, "To achieve this, every one of us plays a part:

Our frontline staff, the face of our warmth and hospitality.

The digital team, who weave our heart into the online experience.

Distributed Teams - Day One Agenda

Time Zone 1	Time Zone 2	Subject	Description and Presenter
08:00 – 8:30 am	08:30 – 09:00 pm	Opening	Introduction, agenda, objectives, and working agreements (Facilitator) Planning context and deliverables (Facilitator) ART and PI Planning context as needed (Facilitator) Review of release cadence - Iterations and PIs (Facilitator)
08:30 – 09:00 am	09:00 – 09:30 pm	Business Context	State of the business (Executive) Upcoming objectives (Executive)
09:00 – 10:30 am	09:30 – 11:00 pm	Product/Solution Vision	Vision of Solution, products/services, and prioritized Features (Product Management)
10:30 – 10:45 am	11:00 – 11:15 pm	Break	
10:45 – 11:15 am	11:15 – 11:45 pm	Architecture Vision	Vision for architecture, new architecture Epics, common frameworks, and ART-level NFRs (Technology Office, System Architect)
11:15 – 11:45 am	11:45 – 12:15 am	Development practices	Updates on Agile tooling, improvements in engineering practices, etc. (Development Management)
11:45 – 12:15 pm	12:15 – 12:45 am	Planning requirements	Specific planning process, draft plan acceptance criteria, etc. (Facilitator)
12:15 – 01:00 pm		Meal break	
01:00 – 04:00 pm		Team breakouts (1 of 2) Hourly Coach Sync checkpoint	Features broken into Stories (each team) PI plan and Objectives drafted (each team) Risks and impediments identified (each team) Hourly Coach Sync checkpoint to discuss planning status, ART impediments, and dependencies (Scrum Masters/Team Coaches) ART planning board continuously updated (Scrum Masters/Team Coaches) Architects and Product Managers circulate

Distributed Teams - Day Two Agenda

Time Zone 1	Time Zone 2	Subject	Description and Presenter
	05:30 – 08:30 pm	Team breakouts (1 of 2) / Hourly Coach Sync checkpoint	Features broken into Stories (each team) / PI plan and Objectives drafted (each team) / Risks and impediments identified (each team) / Hourly Coach Sync checkpoint to discuss planning status, ART impediments, and dependencies (Scrum Masters/Team Coaches) / ART planning board continuously updated (Scrum Masters/Team Coaches) / Architects and Product Managers circulate
08:00 – 09:00 am	08:30 – 09:30 pm	Team synchronization	Distributed teams collaborate with Product Management and System Architect to synchronize
09:00 – 10:00 am	09:30 – 10:30 pm	Draft plan review	Capacity and Load / Overview of plan flow / Draft PI Objectives / ART PI Risks, impediments, and ART planning board dependencies
10:00 – 10:15 am	10:30 – 10:45 pm	Break	
10:15 – 11:15 am	10:45 – 11:45 pm	Management review and problem solving	Discussion of scope, challenges to plan, risks, and impediments (Line Management, Product Management, Architects, and Team Representatives) / Adjustments of scope and resources as necessary (same as above)
11:15 – 11:45 am	11:45 – 12:15 am	Planning adjustments	Management review and problem solving meeting readout – adjustments to plan, scope, resources, etc. (Managers)
11:45 – 12:30 pm	12:15 am – finish	Meal	
12:30 – 03:00 pm		Team breakouts (2 of 2) / Hourly Coach Sync checkpoint	PI plan and Objectives finalized / Risks and impediments finalized / Hourly Coach Sync checkpoint to discuss planning status, ART impediments, and dependencies (Scrum Masters/Team Coaches) / ART planning board continuously updated (Scrum Masters/Team Coaches) / Architects and Product Managers circulate / Business Owners review objectives and assign business value

Distributed Teams - Day Three Agenda

Time Zone 1	Time Zone 2	Subject	Description and Presenter
	08:00 – 08:30 pm	Team breakouts (2 of 2)	(see previous slide)
08:00 – 09:00 am	08:30 – 09:30 pm	Team synchronization and finalized objectives	Distributed teams collaborate with Product Management and System Architect to synchronize Business Owners review objectives and finalize business value
09:00 – 11:00 am	09:30 – 11:30 am	Final plan review	Changes to capacity and load Final PI Objectives with business value ART PI Risks, impediments, and ART planning board dependencies
11:00 – 11:15 am	11:30 – 11:45 pm	Break	
11:15 – 12:15 pm	11:45 – 12:45 am	ART PI Risks	Remaining ART PI Risks are discussed and ROAMed – resolved, owned, accepted, or mitigated (Facilitator, with Management at the front of the room)
12:15 – 01:00 pm	12:45 – 01:30 am	**Meal Break**	
01:00 – 01:15 pm	01:30 – 01:45 am	PI confidence vote	Facilitator asks each team for a fist of five 'confidence vote' and PI commitment Facilitator asks all teams for a fist of five 'confidence vote' for the ART as a whole
01:15 pm – ?	01:45 am – ???	Plan rework if necessary	If high confidence is not achieved, adjust scope and continue planning until commitment is achieved
When commitment is achieved		Planning retrospective	Retrospective for the PI Planning meeting – what went well, what didn't, and what can we do better next time (Facilitator) Record for continuous improvement backlog (Release Train Engineer)
		Final instructions	Process for capturing plans, risks, ART planning board, and improvement backlog items in tooling (Facilitator) Final instructions and closing remarks (Facilitator)

The logistics crew, the silent heroes ensuring our shelves are never empty.

The customer service stars, who listen and solve with empathy and grace."

He paused, letting those roles sink in before explaining the impact.

"If we succeed," he said, "we become more than a store. We become a haven, a place where memories are made, where travelers find solace. Our sales will reflect the love we give, and our brand will be synonymous with the joy of travel."

Mr. Business Owner concluded, "Like Maya, every traveler has a story. Our mission is to be a part of that story, to be a home away from home. Let's make every journey unforgettable, together."

"As you all heard me mention, our retail store revenue has been declining by 3 to 5% quarter on quarter. Our market share has dropped from 45% to 32%. The reasons are many: changing customer spending patterns, new shopping behaviors, and shifting interests. It's crucial that we turn this around and start growing again. To achieve a 6 to 9% growth in the next two quarters, we need to improve both customer and merchant experiences. We've prioritized digital initiatives to be delivered through 16 digital products. Delivering MVPs of these products is essential for enhancing the experience.

We also plan to expand beyond airports and introduce options for buying online with pickup or delivery at boarding counters across all airports. This will require all of us working together to achieve.

One team member raised their hand and asked, 'Thank you for sharing your inspiring experience and our business goals. You mentioned focusing on sixteen technology solutions. Will that alone help us get back on track and grow? Shouldn't we also focus on the products we sell and their pricing?'

The Business Owner smiled and replied, 'Great question. Our business has two key parts: "One key part is 'what' we sell and 'how' we sell it. The products we offer must meet the needs of travelers, and they should be able to buy them efficiently and enjoyably. We need to predict what products customers want, what brands they prefer, the prices they're willing to pay, the channels they use (online or in-store), their preferred payment methods, and how they want to pick up their purchases or have them delivered. To understand and serve customers from these perspectives, digital solutions with Gen AI capabilities are crucial." These 16 products enable it. As part of the subsequent launch of ARTs/product groups, we will cover the entire product landscape.

Another team member chimed in, "We've identified two personas and corresponding digital products to enhance the experience and efficiency of their journeys. Do we have a strategy for incorporating other internal/external personas, such as inventory managers and store sales teams, etc.?"

The Business Owner responded positively, "That's another excellent question. Indeed, we will identify all other personas and enhance their journeys by modernizing related products in the next phase. However, the modernization of products related to those personas or the development of new business capabilities will be handled by the respective product teams. This will occur within the product group or ART, as by that time, we will have launched all product groups within the retail business line."

13.2 Product Management Session

After that, the ART coach turned to the product managers and said, "It's your turn now."

They began discussing their product vision, OKRs, the overall roadmap, and the MVP epics and features for the next quarter (as detailed in Chapter 12). Here's a summary of the eight digital products, their prioritized business capabilities/epics, and features: (next page image)

All these functionalities aim to enhance customer experience at every touchpoint, from product search to collecting their items at the boarding gate. Each product team will focus on their respective set of features listed above.

Suddenly, one of the PMs presenting asked, "How many of us have faced a situation where our card doesn't support international currency or we don't have cash in the local currency?" Almost 30 to 40% of the ART participants raised their hands.

She continued, "As customers, wouldn't we want that problem solved?" A chorus of "Yes!" filled the room.

The PM explained, "There's a feature called 'Payment Online' in the next quarter's plan, to be delivered by the Customer Shop & Pay product team. This feature will allow customers to choose to pay in their home currency at Thiran stores in the arrival airport. This means, even if you don't have an international card or local currency, you can still buy products without hassle. When the product team breaks down this feature into user stories, they'll see which story addresses which part of the payment problem. As they write each line of code, they'll know

8 Digital Products, Business Capabilities and its Functionalities That influences "Customer Journey"

Customer Shop & Pay	Customer Self-Service	Store Product Analytics	Loyalty Management	Replenishment	Customer Dashboard	Customer Interaction BOT	In-Store Management
Browse & Shop online	Account Management	Sales & Transaction Tracking	Offers Management	Demand Forecasting	Customer data integration & Visualization	Personalize Recommendation	Realtime Inventory Tracking
Payment online	Customer Profile	Customer Segmentation	Comprehensive Customer View	Supplier Order Management	Personalization & Segmentation	Realtime Customer support	Order Processing instore and online
Order Fulfillment	Order Management	Price Optimization	Loyalty Performance Management	Real-time Inventory Visibility	Customer Performance Metrics Tracking	Order Tracking and Updates	Staff Scheduling and Task Allocation
Real-time Inventory Update	Omni Channel Communication	Promotion and Campaigns	Customer Data Privacy Management	Dynamic reorder and Safety Stock	Feedback & Surveys	Product Search Optimization	Pricing & Promotions
Search products	Customer Self-account creation	Realtime Sales Monitoring	Campaign Execution and tracking	Automated replenishment Triggers	Realtime customer journey mapping	Natural Language Understanding	Mobile point of Sale to reduce Checkout Queue
Payment options	Add more contact information	Product Affinity Analysis	Track Campaign effectiveness	Calculate Lead time for Products refill	Forecast individual customer preferences	Chatbot identify user intentions	Digital screen product Display
Shopping cart Update	Create Profile	Predict Future sales of products	Earn and Redeem in store , online	Modify Replenishment parameters	Recommend products before traveler search	Route queries to relevant department	Click-and- collect Integration
Place order	Order Submission	Customer Life Time Value calculation	Real-time point accrual and redemption	Predictive out of stock Alerts	Display Loyalty Points and Rewards status	Suggest relevant product as per history	Customer notifications on order readiness
Order confirmation Notification	Order Status Monitoring	Visualize Customer movements in Store	Redeem points at customer checkout	Evaluate Vendor Performance	Suggest Redeem Options	Suggest Redeem Options	AI – driven recommendation for product placement
Personalized product Recommendations	Order Modification	Customer journey Analysis	Behavior Segmentation	Ability to monitor invent flow, reduce storage ti	Trigger promotion based on airport zones	Handle order inquiries	RFID Tags
Choose Delivery Options	Communication through email	Automated Replenishment Alerts	Forecast customer churn Risk	ML to optimize replenishment decision	Social media sharing & Engagement	Handles order cancel & modifications	Realtime Alerts for Suspicious Activity
Order Status Notification	Notifications & Alerts	Product wise price Analysis	Recommend Personalized Offers	Emergency replenishment	Personalized view of Dashboard	Realtime update on order status	Analyze store Layout
Customer Feedback	Chatbot	Display Personalized Promotions	Location based promotions	Monitor replenishment performance	Send Notification of sales or flight delays	Chatbot log complaints	Digital map to guide customer to products
New product Arrivals Updates	Manager Profile	Notify product Recommendations	Reward Referrals	Benchmark Vendor Performance	Benchmark Vendor Performance	Informs ongoing promotions	Price adjustments and Displays

exactly which customer problem that line solves. This is the product mindset we all need to embrace—solving customer problems through user stories."

She concluded, "Every feature listed here is designed to solve customer problems or meet their needs. In turn, this helps us achieve our business objectives."

Here's an illustrative example of a Product Vision, OKR, and Roadmap that was presented to ART participants:

"Customer Shop & Pay" Product Vision:

Illustrative Product Vision for "Customer Shop & Pay" Product of a Retail Industry

Vision: Revolutionizing travel retail with speed and convenience

Our customer-centric shop and pay digital platform transforms airport retail stores into hubs of efficiency. Designed for the modern traveler, our solution enabled quick swift online shopping, hassle-free in-store pickup, and prompt delivery right to the boarding gate.

Our Customer Shop & Buy product has accelerated the shopping process and simplifying payments, providing a plethora of options to cater to every traveler's need. Our product has redefined airport retail, making every transaction fast, easy, and enjoyable, ensuring our customers have more time to relax and less to worry about before they fly

As frequent travel, I am able to shop while I am in flight, get real-time updates on order status, Products packaging status, and waiting at the boarding gate for me to pickup. I don't even spent in airport to shop things. I am able to manage time efficiently and relax at airport.

This product has achieved many business outcomes that includes achieving improved customer experience, Faster and seamless payment and one click purchase with accurate personalized recommendations of products

"Customer Shop & Pay" Product OKR:

Illustrative Product OKRs for "Customer Shop & Pay" Product of a Retail Industry

Sr. No.	Business Objective	OKRs
1	Create a seamless and efficient shopping experience for airport travelers that maximizes convenience and minimizes time spent on transactions	• **Reduce the average transaction time** by 40% for online purchases and in-store pickups. • **Launch the boarding gate delivery service** at 20 major airports within the next quarter. • **Increase the usage of digital payment options** by 50%, ensuring all popular payment methods are supported. • **Achieve a customer satisfaction rate of 90%** for the shopping and payment experience. • **Grow the number of active users** by 30% month-over-month through targeted marketing and partnerships with airlines

"Customer Shop & Pay" Product Roadmap:

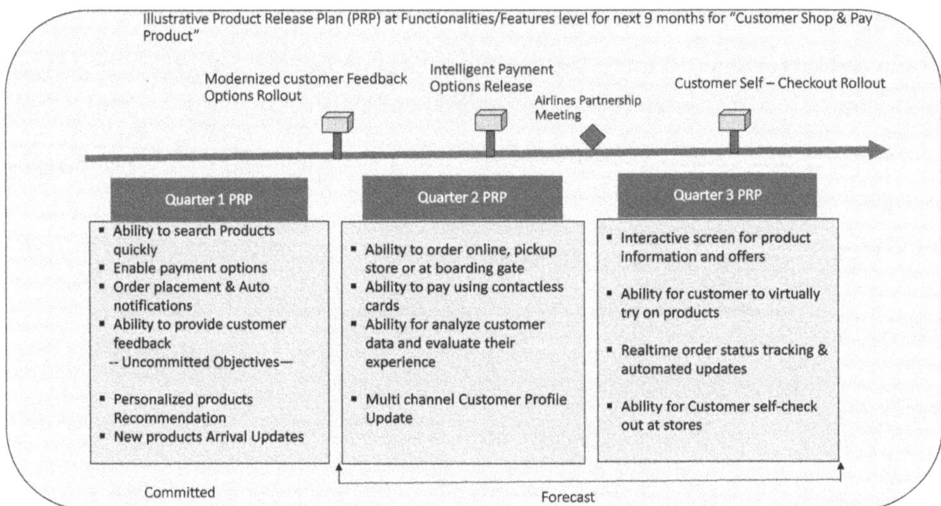

As soon as the PM finished her presentation, a tech lead raised a question, "According to your roadmap, it looks like the product OKRs will be achieved by the end of the third quarter when we deliver all features related to the product MVP. How can these products start enabling business growth by the end of the second quarter?"

The PM responded, "That's a fantastic question. You're absolutely right. That's why we're exploring options to accommodate all these features in the next quarter itself. We'll decide on that after reviewing the outcomes and lessons learned from our first quarter."

Another developer chimed in, "The PO walked us through the personas, empathy, and journey maps. We have a good understanding of how the user stories we're going to develop will address customer problems and needs. Are we planning for an early release and feedback from those customers? It will help us validate our approach and course-correct if needed."

The PM replied, "That's exactly the plan. If you look at the roadmap, there are external milestones to release products at the end of every month. Even before the formal release, we'll connect with a focus group of customers and get their feedback on the MVP features. This way, we can ensure we're on the right track and make necessary adjustments early on."

13.3 Architect and UX Design Session:

Following the PM team's successful presentation, the ART coach invited the Architect and UX Design leads to present their plans.

The Architect began by explaining the high-level architecture designed to support the prioritized features. He outlined the architectural changes planned for the next quarter, ensuring the architecture runway would be ready for the second quarter planning, as detailed in the three-quarter PI roadmap. He also shared their plans to enhance the DevOps pipeline, focusing on automation for merge requests, continuous builds, and increased automation percentages.

Next, the UX Design lead presented the completed UX and UI designs, highlighting the features ready for development as soon as planning concluded.

A QA team member raised a question, "You mentioned increasing functional testing automation. Does that mean we won't have in-sprint automation for next quarter's execution?"

The Architect responded, "Yes, you're correct."

The QA person replied, "In that case, we'll have a lot of manual activities, which might prevent us from meeting all DOD requirements within the sprint timeline, leading to sprint spillover and reduced sprint predictability, as we discussed during SAFe for Teams training."

"You're spot on," the Architect acknowledged. "We expect slower value delivery during this quarter's execution. The current plan is to gather interim feedback from customers and release value every month. But from the next quarter, we aim to significantly improve our delivery speed, aiming for bi-weekly releases. Within two to three quarters, our goal is to achieve multiple releases a week, as required by the business."

At the end of the presentation, we had a 15-minute break. I chatted with a couple of leaders, and they were thrilled to see the team leads and members already embracing a product mindset and demonstrating behaviors focused on faster value delivery. It was clear that everyone in the ART, from the business owner to the team members, was aligned. The internal agile coach and I were delighted to witness these changes during the planning sessions and hear such positive feedback from the leads.

13.4 Breakout Session Number 1:

After the break, the ART coach set the expectations for the first breakout session, explaining what each product team needed to accomplish. Before diving in, the ART coach shared a few illustrative examples:

"Here's a prioritized list of features for quarterly planning. from a real-time example. Remember, this is just for illustrative purposes, so the content may not be entirely accurate." (next page image)

Illustrative view of ART/Product line capacity: (page 282 image)

The ART coach then set the expectations:

Prioritize and refine user stories with the team.

Estimate user stories.

Identify dependencies and align with dependent teams on dates.

Assign user stories to capacity allocated for each slice (business, enabler, and defect).

Start creating PI objectives for each team.

Identify any team and ART-level risks.

She emphasized, "We'll meet every hour for Scrum of Scrums (SoS) to review progress and ensure we're on track to achieve the draft plan. Product coaches of each product team will join these breakouts to provide any clarification or additional input needed."

With this context, each team moved into their virtual breakouts. Those in one location gathered in a room, while others joined virtually via Teams. The internal agile coach, ART coach, and I jumped between breakouts to clarify questions and involve the right SMEs when necessary.

13.4.1 Breakout Session Number 1 Execution:

Each team presented their sprint-wise capacity in story points and showed the capacity split for business, enabler, and defect work, all in line with the capacity allocation policy.

The Product Owner (PO) began presenting user stories in priority order. Team members asked questions from both development and QA perspectives, refining their understanding. They discussed revisiting the estimations of user stories, adjusting them based on the team's feedback. For those without prior

Products	Epics	Feature	# stores	Teams	Release	Story Points for Features based on History	Story Points for Feature
	Browse & Shop online	Ability to. Search products	20	Avengers	21.06	80	57
Customer Shop & Pay	Payment online	Ability to process payments through Payment options	18	Avengers	21.06	40	50
	Order Fulfillment	Ability to Shopping cart Update	22	Avengers	21.06	40	51
	Order Fulfillment	Ability to Place order	12	Avengers	21.06	40	36
	Account Management	Ability to create Customer Self-account	19	Kings	21.06	20	22
Customer Self Service	Account Management	Add more contact information	16	Kings	21.06	60	53
	Customer Profile	Create Profile	15	Kings	21.06	20	36
	Order Management	Ability for Order Submission	22	Kings	21.06	60	42
	Sales & Transaction Tracking	Realtime Sales Monitoring	15	Super Stars	21.06	60	44
Store Product Analytics	Customer Segmentation	Product Affinity Analysis	5	Super Stars	21.06	20	14
	Price Optimization	Predict Future sales of products	25	Super Stars	21.06	60	53
	Customer Segmentation	Customer Life Time Value calculation	12	Super Stars	21.04	20	27
	Offers Management	Campaign Execution and tracking	22	Lion	21.04	40	35
	Offers Management	Track Campaign effectiveness	9	Lion	21.04	20	19
Loyalty Management	Loyalty Performance Management	Earn and Redeem in store , online	8	Lion	21.04	40	19
	Loyalty Performance Management	Real-time point accrual and redemption	12	Lion	21.04	20	21
	Demand Forecasting	Automated replenishment Triggers	11	Mars	21.06	40	28
Replenishment	Demand Forecasting	Calculate Lead time for Products refill	18	Mars	21.06	20	32
	Supplier Order Management	Modify Replenishment parameters	21	Mars	21.06	20	28
	Supplier Order Management	Predictive out of stock Alerts	21	Mars	21.06	40	40
	Customer data integration & Visualization	Realtime customer journey mapping	19	Spiders	21.06	60	58
Customer Dashboard	Personalization & Segmentation	Forecast individual customer preferences	13	Spiders	21.06	40	30
	Personalization & Segmentation	Recommend products before traveler search	17	Spiders	21.06	20	27
	Personalization & Segmentation	Display Loyalty Points and Rewards status	21	Spiders	21.06	60	52

Teams	Sprint 1	Sprint 2	Sprint 3	Sprint 4	Sprint 5	Sprint 6 (IP)	
Date	(1/26/21 - 2/8/21)	(2/9/21 - 2/22/21)	(2/23/21 - 3/8/21)	(3/9/21 - 3/22/21)	(3/23/21 - 4/5/21)	(4/6/21 - 4/19/21)	
Avengers	40	50	46	54	42	0	
Kings	43	50	46	54	40	0	
Super Stars	47	45	48	45	42	0	
Lion	37	49	44	41	49	0	
Spider	40	46	49	46	48	0	1141

Team Avengers	Sprint 1	Sprint 2	Sprint 3	Sprint 4	Sprint 5	Sprint 6 (IP)	
	(1/26/21 - 2/8/21)	(2/9/21 - 2/22/21)	(2/23/21 - 3/8/21)	(3/9/21 - 3/22/21)	(3/23/21 - 4/5/21)	(4/6/21 - 4/19/21)	
Stories	31	37	37	37	31	0	224
Defects	1	2	1	1	3	0	
Enablers	8	11	8	16	8	0	

Team Kings	Sprint 1	Sprint 2	Sprint 3	Sprint 4	Sprint 5	Sprint 6 (IP)	
	(1/26/21 - 2/8/21)	(2/9/21 - 2/22/21)	(2/23/21 - 3/8/21)	(3/9/21 - 3/22/21)	(3/23/21 - 4/5/21)	(4/6/21 - 4/19/21)	
Stories	27	33	33	33	27	0	208
Defects	5	5	5	5	5	0	
Enablers	11	12	8	16	8	0	

Team Super Stars	Sprint 1	Sprint 2	Sprint 3	Sprint 4	Sprint 5	Sprint 6 (IP)	
	(1/26/21 - 2/8/21)	(2/9/21 - 2/22/21)	(2/23/21 - 3/8/21)	(3/9/21 - 3/22/21)	(3/23/21 - 4/5/21)	(4/6/21 - 4/19/21)	
Stories	29	35	35	35	29	0	217
Defects	2	2	2	2	2	0	
Enablers	16	8	11	8	11	0	
Release Support	0	0	0	0	0	0	

Team Lion	Sprint 1	Sprint 2	Sprint 3	Sprint 4	Sprint 5	Sprint 6 (IP)	
	(1/26/21 - 2/8/21)	(2/9/21 - 2/22/21)	(2/23/21 - 3/8/21)	(3/9/21 - 3/22/21)	(3/23/21 - 4/5/21)	(4/6/21 - 4/19/21)	
Stories	27	33	28	28	28	0	195
Defects	5	5	5	5	5	0	
Enablers	5	11	11	8	16	0	

Team Spider	Sprint 1	Sprint 2	Sprint 3	Sprint 4	Sprint 5	Sprint 6 (IP)	
	(1/26/21 - 2/8/21)	(2/9/21 - 2/22/21)	(2/23/21 - 3/8/21)	(3/9/21 - 3/22/21)	(3/23/21 - 4/5/21)	(4/6/21 - 4/19/21)	
Stories	31	37	37	37	31	0	224
Defects	1	1	1	1	1	0	

estimations, the team worked together to provide accurate estimates. They also identified dependencies on the UX team and other teams both within and outside the ART.

The product team coaches guided the teams through refining user stories, identifying dependencies, and estimating tasks. They communicated with the dependent teams' product coaches to align on delivery dates for those dependent user stories. This breakout process was followed by all eight product teams simultaneously. For illustration, we focused on the "Customer Shop & Pay" product team.

13.4.2 Breakout Session 1: SOS

At the end of the first hour, we had our first Scrum of Scrums (SOS). While the teams continued their breakout activities, the ART coach gathered all the product team coaches for a progress review.

"Alright, let's check in," the ART coach began. "How's everyone doing? Any major roadblocks?"

Using a structured checkpoint list, the ART coach asked each product coach for a quick update.

"Customer Shop & Pay - AVENGERS, how's it going?" the ART coach asked.

"We're on track," their coach responded. "We've prioritized our user stories and identified dependencies."

"Great. What about the others?" The ART coach systematically reviewed each team's progress, noting any issues.

After gathering the updates, the ART coach concluded, "Keep pushing forward, everyone. If you need help, reach out."

By the end of the first hour, five teams had completed their plans for the first sprint, having done high-level refinement during the preparation phase.

Three teams, however, were behind schedule and hadn't finished planning for the first sprint. Meanwhile, one of the five teams had even completed 50% of their second sprint plan.

13.4.3 Breakout Session 1: Continuation

The ART coach then focused on the three teams that were behind schedule. Analyzing the delays, she provided targeted support to speed up their sessions.

"Rider team, I heard there's a dependency issue with Warriors team?" the ART coach asked.

"Yes, they're not prioritizing our request," the Rider coach explained.

"Let's get leadership involved to resolve this within the next 30 minutes," the ART coach decided.

Another challenge was the availability of the UX team. A new user story added to the first sprint required early UX input, but the UX team lacked sufficient capacity.

"Let's talk to the UX lead," the ART coach suggested. "We might need to reprioritize some of their work or borrow capacity from another team."

One team had a dependency issue with another ART. The coach decided to join the dependent team's breakout session to discuss and align on a timeline.

Another challenge involved a supplier dependency. The ART coach suggested setting up a call for the next day, inviting the supplier to the second breakout session to discuss and resolve the issue.

13.4.4 Breakout Session 1: SOS 2 and Continuation

The ART coach held a second SOS, offering additional support where needed. The teams continued their planning, assigning user stories to their capacity slices.

Each team planned their sprints with a margin for flexibility. They allocated 80% of their capacity for their three work item slices, leaving 20% for agile team and ART-level ceremonies. Out of the 80% capacity, 15-20% was reserved for uncommitted user stories—those with more unknowns, risks, or unresolved dependencies. These uncommitted stories would be worked on within the team's capacity but weren't guaranteed for delivery unless the issues were resolved during the sprint.

Here's how the scope margin works: if your team's total capacity is 100%, 20% is set aside for agile ceremonies. With the remaining 80%, if your team can deliver 50 story points (SP), then you'll commit to 40 SP worth of work. The remaining 10 SP is uncommitted due to risks or unknowns.

Teams can choose to use either capacity margin or scope margin when planning their sprint work.

On the second day, during India hours, the India team took over from the US team. They continued with story decomposition, sprint planning, and identifying dependencies. Any issues requiring US leadership support were flagged for discussion when the US team rejoined.

Before day 2's planning event, an onshore-offshore sync-up was held to align on the draft plans. The India team then continued with breakout session 1 for a few more hours with the US team.

13.5 Draft Plan Presentation

At the end of the first breakout session, all teams reconvened in the main virtual room with stakeholders present. Each team took turns presenting their progress, focusing on the user stories planned so far and highlighting any risks and dependencies.

Here's a look at the draft plan for the "Customer Shop & Pay - Avengers" team:

Dependencies identified for the "Customer Shop & Pay" team include:

S. No	Dependent User Stories	Dependencies Description	Dependent Team "From"	Dependent Team "To"	Committed Sprint
1	**As a Traveler**, I want to **search for specific products** so that I can quickly find what I need during my layover or before my flight	The **Customer Shop and Pay** team relies on the **Loyalty Management** team to integrate loyalty features into the shopping experience.	Loyalty Management Team	Not applicable	Sprint 3
2	**As a Group Traveler**, I want to **leave collective feedback** for shared experiences (e.g., airport lounges, dining areas).	Customer feedback data provided are ingested, stored and displayed by Customer Feedback team	Not applicable	Customer Feedback Team	Sprint 2

An illustrative look at Team-level PI objectives:

S. No	PI Objectives	Business Value (BV)	Actual Business Value (AV)
1	Implement ability of search products and required details with Improved efficiency and accuracy to optimize **Search Response Time**: Reduce average search response time to **less than 500 milliseconds**	9	
2	Streamline the cart summary and checkout process for frequent travelers **and** Reduce cart abandonment rate by **15%** within the next six months.	6	
3	Enhance the budget-conscious customer's experience by integrating discounts and loyalty points to Increase usage of discount codes and loyalty points by **20%**within the next quarter	8	
4	Implement ability to facilitate group shopping experiences for travelers and Enable successful cart sharing and bill splitting for at least **80%** of group travelers	5	
5	Improve customer satisfaction by providing flexible delivery options. Achieve a **10% increase** in positive customer feedback related to delivery choices within the next quarter	10	

Customer Search & Shop Team Sprint wise planning

Sprint 1	Sprint 2	Sprint 3
As a Traveler, I want to **search for specific products** so that I can quickly find what I need during my layover or before my flight.	As a **Budget-Conscious Customer**, I want to **apply discount codes or loyalty points** during checkout.	As an **In-Store Shopper**, I want to **scan product barcodes** using my mobile app to add items to my cart.
As a **Frequent Traveler**, I want to **save my payment details securely** for future purchases.	As a **Group Traveler**, I want to **split the receipt** with my fellow travelers (e.g., for shared expenses).	As a **Group Traveler**, I want to **receive group recommendations** for shared experiences (e.g., travel guides, family games).
As a **Budget-Conscious Customer**, I want to **apply discount codes or loyalty points** during checkout.	As a **Trendy Shopper**, I want to **discover new products** by browsing popular or trending items.	As a **Frequent Flyer**, I want to **split my bill** with my travel companions.
As a **Last-Minute Traveler**, I want to **save my cart for later** if I need to leave the website.	As a **Price-Conscious Traveler**, I want to **search for discounted products** or items on sale.	As an **Online Shopper**, I want to **pay using my preferred method** so that I can complete my purchase seamlessly.
As an **In-Store Shopper**, I want to **scan product barcodes** using my mobile app to add items to my cart.	As a **Frequent Flyer**, I want to **filter search results** based on specific criteria to narrow down my choices.	As a **Last-Minute Shopper**, I want to **receive real-time notifications** if there are any issues with my order (e.g., out of stock, payment declined).
As a **Shopper**, I want to **sort search results** by relevance, price (low to high or high to low), and customer ratings.		As an **In-Store Shopper**, I want to **pay conveniently** without carrying cash.
As a **Tech-Savvy Traveler**, I want to **scan a QR code** on my receipt to verify the purchase and track my loyalty points.		As a **Last-Minute Traveler**, I want to **save my cart for later** if I need to leave the website.
Setup Notification Infrastructure that includes provision of servers or cloud resources	As a **Last-Minute Traveler**, I want to **split my bill** with my travel companions.	
Create architecture for handling notifications services	As a **Foreign Traveler**, I want to **pay in my home currency** to avoid exchange rate surprises.	

Customer Search & Shop Team Sprint wise planning

Sprint 1	Sprint 2	Sprint 3
As an Online Shopper, I want to select my preferred delivery method during checkout so that I can receive my order conveniently.	As a Tech-Savvy Traveler, I want to scan a QR code on my receipt to access a feedback form.	As a Traveler, I want to search for specific products so that I can quickly find what I need during my layover or before my flight.
As a Frequent Traveler, I want to specify a delivery address different from my billing address.	As a Group Traveler, I want to leave collective feedback for shared experiences (e.g., airport lounges, dining areas).	As a Last-Minute Shopper, I want to receive urgent recommendations for items that are in stock and available for immediate purchase.
		As an In-Store Shopper, I want to receive personalized recommendations from store associates.
As a Traveler, I want to search for specific products so that I can quickly find what I need during my layover or before my flight.	As an Online Shopper, I want to provide feedback on my shopping experience after completing a purchase.	
As a Traveler, I want to search for specific products so that I can quickly find what I need during my layover or before my flight.	As a Frequent Traveler, I want to report any issues or bugs encountered while using the online store.	As a Last-Minute Shopper, I want to suggest improvements for the website's navigation or checkout process.
		As an In-Store Shopper, I want to rate my in-store experience using a feedback kiosk or mobile app.
As a Last-Minute Shopper, I want to pick up my order at the airport store before my flight.	As a Traveler, I want to search for specific products so that I can quickly find what I need during my layover or before my flight.	
As a Budget-Conscious Customer, I want to see estimated delivery costs before finalising my purchase.	As a Traveler, I want to search for specific products so that I can quickly find what I need during my layover or before my flight.	As a Traveler, I want to search for specific products so that I can quickly find what I need during my layover or before my flight.

After all teams finished their presentations, the ART coach thanked everyone for their hard work. "Great job, team. Let's sync up with onshore leads before day 3. For now, all team members can log off. I'd like the BO, Business Leads, PM, Architects, UX leads, Product Team coaches, and ART coaches to stay back for a management review and problem-solving session."

The room quieted down as the broader team logged off, leaving the key stakeholders. The ART coach pulled up a list of challenges and issues that had been highlighted during the presentations.

13. 6 Management Review and Problem-Solving Meeting

"Let's tackle these one by one," the ART coach began. "First, Avengers are facing a capacity challenge with completing all UX stories on time. What can we do here?"

One of the Business Leads suggested, "Can we reallocate some resources or perhaps adjust the timeline for some of the less critical UX stories?"

"Good idea," the ART coach agreed. "We'll look into resource reallocation and timeline adjustments."

Next up were the Warriors, who had dependencies with suppliers and other ARTs that still needed alignment. "What's our action plan for these dependencies?" the ART coach asked.

"We need to set up urgent meetings with the suppliers and the other ARTs," said the PM. "We can prioritize these discussions to ensure alignment."

"Let's make that happen," the ART coach confirmed. "Now, about the Riders team—many of them have planned leaves. How do we manage this?"

An Architect suggested, "We could prioritize the most critical features and perhaps bring in temporary support if needed."

"Agreed," the ART coach nodded. "We'll prioritize critical tasks and explore temporary support options."

During the "Management Review and Problem Solving Meeting," we tackled various challenges from all product teams, received input on priorities and scope changes from business owners, and agreed on the following changes, illustrated below for one of the teams:

S. No	Nature of change	Management Change Description	Impacted product Teams
1	Scope Change	One of the Business owners requested for additional feature of integrating with social media platforms.	Customer Shop & Pay
2	Team Capacity	Customer shop & Pay team have some capacity additional capacity during sprint 3 and sprint 4 .	Customer Shop & Pay
3	Change in Priority	One of the Business owners requesting Payment processing feature implementation over customer feedback feature. To accommodate this, user stories related to these features needs to be reordered across sprints	Customer Shop & Pay

With these actions agreed upon for all the teams, the ART coach wrapped up the session. "Thanks, everyone, for your input and dedication. We're making great progress. Let's keep up the momentum."

13.7 Planning Adjustment Communication

It's Day 3, and the ART coach kicked off the session with the "Planning Adjustments" agenda. She presented the changes needed in the draft plan, which were agreed upon the previous day with the management team.

"Good morning, everyone," the ART coach began. "Today, we'll go through the planning adjustments. These changes need to be made by the respective product teams."

She paused, looking around the room. "If anyone has questions or needs clarifications on these changes, now is the time to ask."

A few hands went up. Some teams had questions about the scope and dependencies, which the PMs quickly clarified. Other teams had technical and design-related queries, which were addressed by the business, architect, and UX leads.

"Alright, with those clarifications out of the way," the ART coach continued, "I need the impacted teams to make these changes. Then, continue your breakout sessions with additional user stories planning and start writing your PI objectives."

A team member raised a hand. "Why do we need to define PI objectives? Can't we just align on the features to be delivered and the related user stories?"

The ART coach smiled. "Great question. The purpose of this planning exercise is to commit to what PI objectives (these are KPIs to respective Business capability OKRs) will be delivered by your teams. These objectives are written in business terms and outcomes, which is what the Business Owner needs. These PI objectives are defined based on the features and user stories that are in scope for each product team, as illustrated in the figure in the next section of this chapter. This gives us clarity and alignment."

13.8 Breakout Session 2

After the initial adjustments, teams were asked to head into Breakout Session 2. The India team and US teams continued their work.

In this session, they followed the same process as Breakout 1, planning the remaining user stories for the sprints. Additionally, they defined PI objectives based on the user stories and features planned, using a bottom-up approach.

The Business Owner provided a Business Value (BV) score for each PI objective on a scale from 1 to 10, with 1 being the lowest importance and 10 being the highest from delivery perspective. For enabler-related PI objectives, the Business Owner requested more details to provide an accurate BV score, which the architect and engineering leads supplied.

Each product team presented their refined final plans, showing their team-wise capacity versus load, PI objectives, risks, and dependencies to the entire ART.

13.9 Final Plan Presentation by Each Team

Here's an illustrative view of the "Customer Shop & Pay" product team's deliverables at the end of both Breakout Sessions 1 and 2:

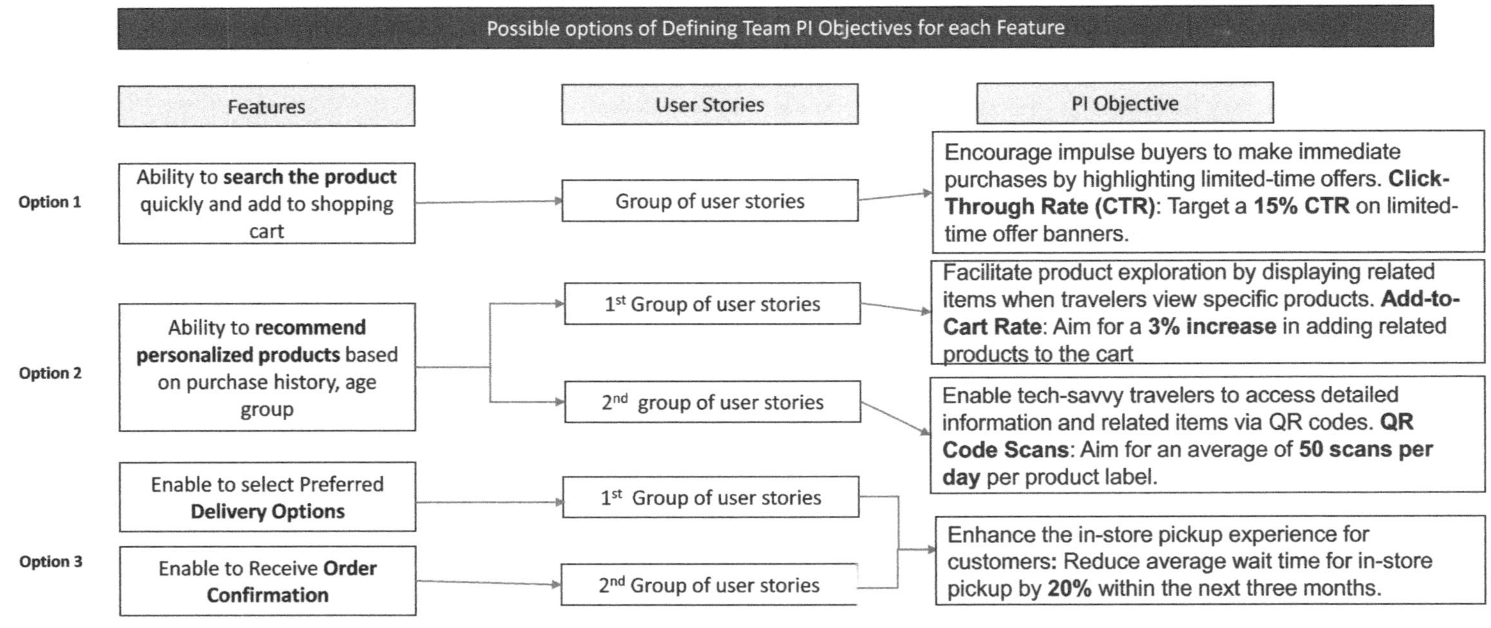

Possible options of Defining Team PI Objectives for each Feature

Features
User Stories
PI Objective

Option 1
Ability to search the product quickly and add to shopping cart
Group of user stories
Encourage impulse buyers to make immediate purchases by highlighting limited-time offers. Click-Through Rate (CTR): Target a 15% CTR on limited-time offer banners.

Option 2
Ability to recommend personalized products based on purchase history, age group
1st Group of user stories
Facilitate product exploration by displaying related items when travelers view specific products. Add-to-Cart Rate: Aim for a 3% increase in adding related products to the cart

2nd group of user stories
Enable tech-savvy travelers to access detailed information and related items via QR codes. QR Code Scans: Aim for an average of 50 scans per day per product label.

Option 3
Enable to select Preferred Delivery Options
1st Group of user stories

Enable to Receive Order Confirmation
2nd Group of user stories
Enhance the in-store pickup experience for customers: Reduce average wait time for in-store pickup by 20% within the next three months.

Customer Search & Shop Team Sprint wise planning

Sprint 1	Sprint 2	Sprint 3	Sprint 4	Sprint 5
As a Traveler, I want to **search for specific products** so that I can quickly find what I need during my layover or before my flight (5)	As a Budget-Conscious Customer, I want to **apply discount codes or loyalty points** during checkout. (3)	As an In-Store Shopper, I want to **scan product barcodes** using my mobile app to add items to my cart. (3)	As a Gift Buyer, I want to **search for gift items** by occasion (e.g., birthday, anniversary) or recipient (e.g., for kids, for him, for her). (3)	As an Online Shopper, I want to **receive an order confirmation email** immediately after placing an order. (1)
As a Frequent Traveler, I want to **save my payment details securely** for future purchases. (2)	As a Group Traveler, I want to **split the receipt** with my fellow travelers (e.g., for shared expenses). (2)	As a Group Traveler, I want to **receive group recommendations** for shared experiences (e.g., travel guides, family games). (3)	As an In-Store Shopper, I want to **receive an instant receipt** after making a purchase at the airport store. (1)	As a Frequent Traveler, I want to **view my order summary on the website** after completing the checkout process. (3)
As a Budget-Conscious Customer, I want to **apply discount codes or loyalty points** during checkout. (3)	As a Trendy Shopper, I want to **discover new products** by browsing popular or trending items. (3)	As a Frequent Flyer, I want to **split my bill** with my travel companions. (2)	As a Budget-Conscious Customer, I want to **apply discount codes or loyalty points** during checkout. (3)	As a Foreign Traveler, I want to **pay in my home currency** to avoid exchange rate surprises. (2)
As a Last-Minute Traveler, I want to **save my cart for later** if I need to leave the website. (1)	As a Price-Conscious Traveler, I want to **search for discounted products** or items on sale. (5)	As an Online Shopper, I want to **pay using my preferred method** so that I can complete my purchase seamlessly. (3)	As an Online Shopper, I want to **add products to my cart** so that I can review and purchase them later. (2)	As an Online Shopper, I want to **add products to my cart** so that I can review and purchase them later. (2)
As an In-Store Shopper, I want to **scan product barcodes** using my mobile app to add items to my cart. (3)	As a Frequent Flyer, I want to **filter search results** based on specific criteria to narrow down my choices. (3)	As a Last-Minute Shopper, I want to **receive real-time notifications** if there are any issues with my order (e.g., out of stock, payment declined). (3)	As a Frequent Traveler, I want to **view my cart summary** before checkout. (1)	As a Frequent Traveler, I want to **view my cart summary** before checkout. (3)
As a Shopper, I want to **sort search results** by relevance, price (low to high or high to low), and customer ratings. (3)	A payment gateway acts as a bridge between the customer and the merchant's bank account. It facilitates the acceptance of financial credentials (credit/debit cards, mobile wallets) during checkout (5)	As an In-Store Shopper, I want to **pay conveniently** without carrying cash. (2)	Create architecture for handling notifications services (3)	As a Last-Minute Traveler, I want to **split my bill** with my travel companions. (3)
As a Tech-Savvy Traveler, I want to **scan a QR code** on my receipt to verify the purchase and track my loyalty points. (3)	**Setup Notification infrastructure that includes provision of servers or cloud resources** (5)	As a Last-Minute Traveler, I want to **save my cart for later** if I need to leave the website. (3)		

Customer Shop & Pay Product Team. Its Features and User Stories

Search products **F1**	Payment options **F2**	Shopping cart **F3**	Place order **F4**	Order confirmation Notification **F5**
As a Traveler, I want to **search for specific products** so that I can quickly find what I need during my layover or before my flight.	**As an Online Shopper**, I want to **pay using my preferred method** so that I can complete my purchase seamlessly.	**As an Online Shopper**, I want to **add products to my cart** so that I can review and purchase them later.	**As an Online Shopper**, I want to **add products to my cart** so that I can review and purchase them later.	**As an Online Shopper**, I want to **receive an order confirmation email** immediately after placing an order.
As a Frequent Flyer, I want to **filter search results** based on specific criteria to narrow down my choices.	**As a Frequent Traveler**, I want to **save my payment details securely** for future purchases.	**As a Frequent Traveler**, I want to **view my cart summary** before checkout.	**As a Frequent Traveler**, I want to **view my cart summary** before checkout.	**As a Frequent Traveler**, I want to **view my order summary on the website** after completing the checkout process.
As a Shopper, I want to **sort search results** by relevance, price (low to high or high to low), and customer ratings.	**As a Budget-Conscious Customer**, I want to **apply discount codes or loyalty points** during checkout.	**As a Budget-Conscious Customer**, I want to **apply discount codes or loyalty points** during checkout.	**As a Budget-Conscious Customer**, I want to **apply discount codes or loyalty points** during checkout.	**As a Last-Minute Shopper**, I want to **receive real-time notifications** if there are any issues with my order (e.g., out of stock, payment declined).
As a Gift Buyer, I want to **search for gift items** by occasion (e.g., birthday, anniversary) or recipient (e.g., for kids, for him, for her).	**As an In-Store Shopper**, I want to **pay conveniently** without carrying cash.	**As a Last-Minute Traveler**, I want to **save my cart for later** if I need to leave the website.	**As a Last-Minute Traveler**, I want to **save my cart for later** if I need to leave the website.	**As an In-Store Shopper**, I want to **receive an instant receipt** after making a purchase at the airport store.
As a Trendy Shopper, I want to **discover new products** by browsing popular or trending items.	**As a Last-Minute Traveler**, I want to **split my bill** with my travel companions.	**As an In-Store Shopper**, I want to **scan product barcodes** using my mobile app to add items to my cart.	**As an In-Store Shopper**, I want to **scan product barcodes** using my mobile app to add items to my cart.	**As a Tech-Savvy Traveler**, I want to **scan a QR code** on my receipt to verify the purchase and track my loyalty points.
As a Price-Conscious Traveler, I want to **search for discounted products** or items on sale.	**As a Foreign Traveler**, I want to **pay in my home currency** to avoid exchange rate surprises.	**As a Group Traveler**, I want to **receive group recommendations** for shared experiences (e.g., travel guides, family games).	**As a Frequent Flyer**, I want to **split my bill** with my travel companions.	**As a Group Traveler**, I want to **split the receipt** with my fellow travelers (e.g., for shared expenses).

Product Team Name: Customer Shop & Pay			
S. No	PI Objectives	Business Value (BV)	Actual Business Value (AV)
1	Implement ability of search products and required details with Improved efficiency and accuracy to optimize **Search Response Time**: Reduce average search response time to **less than 500 milliseconds**	9	
2	Streamline the cart summary and checkout process for frequent travelers **and** Reduce cart abandonment rate by **15%** within the next six months.	6	
3	Enhance the budget-conscious customer's experience by integrating discounts and loyalty points to Increase usage of discount codes and loyalty points by **20%**within the next quarter	8	
4	Implement ability to facilitate group shopping experiences for travelers and Enable successful cart sharing and bill splitting for at least **80%** of group travelers	5	
5	Improve customer satisfaction by providing flexible delivery options. Achieve a **10% increase** in positive customer feedback related to delivery choices within the next quarter	10	
6	Enhance the in-store pickup experience for customers and Reduce average wait time for in-store pickup by **20%** within the next six months.	8	
7	Enhance customer trust by promptly confirming online orders with **Confirmation Email Delivery Rate**: Target a **95% delivery rate** for order confirmation emails.	9	
8	Provide immediate confirmation to in-store shoppers. **Receipt Delivery Time**: Ensure that receipts are provided **within 1 minute** of purchase.	9	
9	Improve conversion rates by providing relevant product suggestions to online shoppers: **Click-Through Rate (CTR)**: Target a **10% increase** in CTR for personalized recommendations.	10	
10	Enable tech-savvy travelers to access detailed information and related items via QR codes: **QR Code Scans**: Aim for an average of **50 scans per day** per product label.	5	
11	Build Prototype to receive international wire transfer complying to regulatory requirements for pay option feature with goal o**f receive wire transfer confirmation with in 1 minute**	6	
12	Create architecture for data ingestion, storage and display for personalized product functionality with **improved efficiency of providing inputs in 500 milliseconds with more than 90% accuracy.**	7	

Dependencies for Customer Shop & Pay Product Team

S. No	Dependent User Stories	Dependencies Description	Dependent Team "From"	Dependent Team "To"	Committed Sprint
1	**As a Traveler**, I want to **search for specific products** so that I can quickly find what I need during my layover or before my flight	The **Customer Shop and Pay** team relies on the **Loyalty Management** team to integrate loyalty features into the shopping experience.	Loyalty Management Team	Not applicable	Sprint 3
2	**As a Group Traveler**, I want to **leave collective feedback** for shared experiences (e.g., airport lounges, dining areas).	Customer feedback data provided are ingested, stored and displayed by Customer Feedback team	Not applicable	Customer Feedback Team	Sprint 2
3	**As an Online Shopper**, I want to **receive personalized product suggestions** based on my browsing history and preferences.	The **Customer Self-Service** team maintains the search functionality. The **Customer Shop and Pay** team relies on their search capabilit es to help customers find products efficiently	Customer Self – Service team	Not applicable	Sprint 2
4	**As a Tech-Savvy Traveler**, I want to **receive real-time notifications** when my in-store order is ready.	The **Customer Self-Service**team provides real-time order status updates. The **Customer Shop and Pay** team displays this information to customers.	Customer Self – Service team	Not applicable	Sprint 4
5	**As a Trendy Shopper**, I want to **discover new products** by browsing popular or trending items.	The **Customer Shop and Pay** team depends on the **Replenishment** team to manage inventory levels and restock products pf trendy products	Replenishment	Not applicable	Sprint 1

During the final plan presentation, the entire ART/product line teams moved on to the next item on the agenda, which involved discussing the risk ROAM. This discussion covered risks at both the team and ART levels. Each risk was thoroughly discussed and addressed through the ROAM process. Below is an example of the risks identified by the "Customer Shop & Pay" product team:

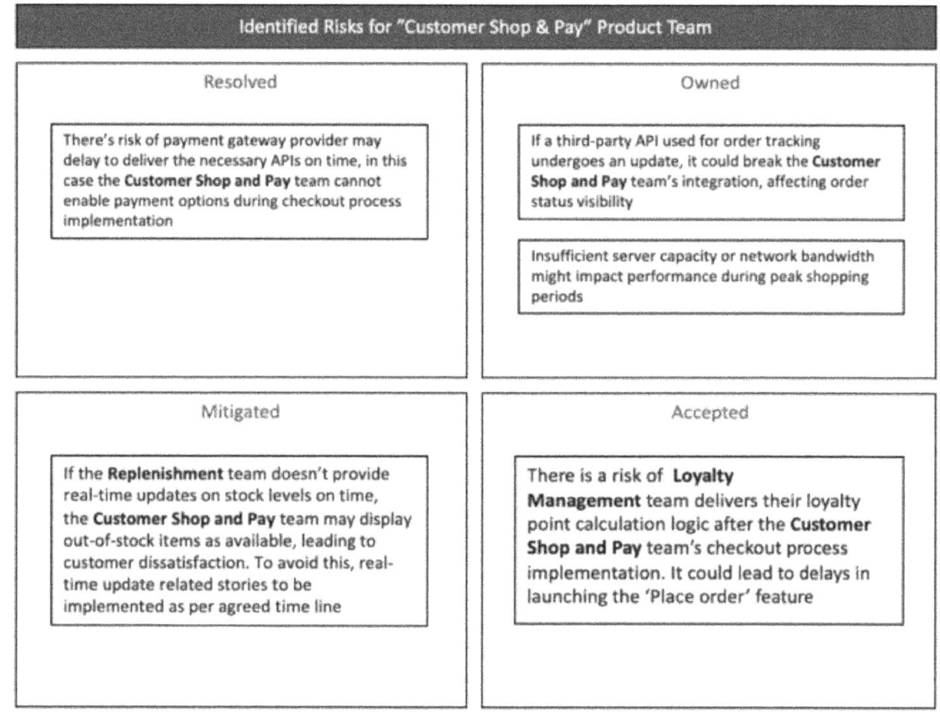

As we wrapped up the team breakout sessions, we systematically addressed the risks we'd identified earlier. Here's how each was handled:

Firstly, we faced a risk related to a supplier's capability to deliver an external API. This supplier was experiencing capacity issues, which put our timeline in jeopardy. During the breakouts, the ART coach took the initiative to liaise with our procurement team. They agreed to take charge of this issue, leading to the risk being categorized as "Owned."

Next, we resolved an earlier identified risk concerning internal dependencies. By Day 2, the dependent team had successfully addressed this issue, allowing us to mark this risk as "Resolved."

Another risk emerged when two team members planned a week-long leave during the critical sprint 3. Given that all other product teams were operating at full capacity and unable to absorb additional user stories, we decided to accept this risk as "Accepted."

Lastly, there was concern about the Replenishment team potentially delaying real-time updates. After a productive discussion, they committed to a mitigation plan to ensure timely delivery, allowing us to update this risk's status to "Mitigated." This is how all the identified risks were ROAMed and completed the risk of ROAMing agenda.

13.10 ART/Product Group level Risks ROAMing:

Following the team level risk management, we also scrutinized ART level risks using the same ROAM framework. This comprehensive approach ensures that both team and ART level risks are managed effectively, keeping our ART/Product group on track and responsive to any challenges that arise against delivering committed PI objectives.

S#	Risks/Dependencies	Resolved	Owned	Accepted	Mitigated
1	EMME Engagement - Template Setup & Integration for eSignature Feature (Snipers) - (Sprint 3)		Owned (Discussion required)		
2	OEDB Dependencies for Trailblazers	Resolved			
3	OEDB Dependencies for Warriors			Accepted	
4	Snipers Dependencies for Riders				Mitigated
5	Riders Interdependencies (MedSupp Save & Submit functionality) for Explorer & Snipers				Mitigated
6	D2C Engagement - Design & Integration Test for eSignature Feature . (Sprint 4)		Owned		

13.11 Fist of Five Confidence Voting

Next on the agenda was confidence voting. Each team was asked to gauge their confidence in delivering the plan on a scale of 1 to 5. One finger signified very low confidence, while five fingers indicated very high confidence.

"Alright everyone, cameras on," the ART coach instructed. "On the count of three, show your confidence levels. Ready? Three, two, one!"

Everyone held up their hands, fingers extended in varying numbers. We tallied the votes, averaging the confidence scores for each team.

For example, one team had 10 members voting, joined by 8 ART stakeholders. All 18 votes were summed and averaged. If the average score was 3 or above, it was deemed acceptable. Scores below 3 indicated the need for a rework of the plan.

Two teams scored 2.6 and 2.8. When we asked for feedback, they cited unresolved risks, unknowns, and dependencies. We agreed to revisit these issues after the quarterly planning, address the concerns, and redo the confidence voting.

An illustrative perspective on the "Fist of Five" confidence voting score, calculated for the "Customer Shop & Pay" team:

	Fist of Score for "Customer Shop & Pay" Product Team				
Voting scale from 1 to 5	1	2	3	4	5
Number of Product team members Voted	0	0	4	4	1
Number of Product Group members Voted	0	1	5	3	2
Vote Sum	0	2	27	28	13
Vote Average	= 70/20= **3.5**				

Note: Based on vote from both team level and at ART/product group level, Overall confidence level of executing committed plan is 3.5 in the scale of 1 to 5. its considered as very good situation sign off this plan

Throughout the three days, each team diligently updated their plans in Jira. This made it easy for the ART coach and PMs to consolidate everything. The ART coach and PMs then presented the consolidated final ART quarterly plan, which included ART-level PI objectives derived from rolling up the various team-level PI objectives. This comprehensive plan was shared with the Business Owners (BOs) and the entire product line, all updated in Jira.

"Alright, team, let's get feedback from the BOs," the ART coach said. "BOs, do you accept the plan or reject it?"

The BOs reviewed the final plan and, with a caveat to rework the plans of the two teams that had fist-of-five scores below 3.

"Plan approved!" the ART coach announced.

13.12 Consolidated Final Plan for the Entire ART/Product Group

Here's an illustrative view of the ART/product line plan for the next quarter that was approved by business owner: (next page image)

Team Names	Sprint 1	Sprint 2	Sprint 3	Sprint 4	Innovation & Planning Sprint
Customer Shop & Pay - Avengers	Feature 5	Feature 2, Feature 3	Feature 7, Feature 4, Feature 8	Feature 5, Feature 6, Feature 9, Feature 10	
Customer Self Service- Kings	Feature 1, Feature 10	Feature 5, Feature 3	Feature 4, Feature 6, Feature 8	Feature 7, Feature 6, Feature 9	
Store Product Analytics – Super Stars	Feature 2, Feature 9	Feature 1, Feature 3, Feature 8	Feature 7, Feature 4	Feature 5, Feature 6, Feature 10	
Loyalty Management - Lion	Feature 4	Feature 2, Feature 3, Feature 9	Feature 7, Feature 4, Feature 5	Feature 5, Feature 6, Feature 10	
Replenishment - Mars	Feature 1, Feature 8	Feature 2, Feature 3	Feature 7, Feature 4, Feature 6	Feature 5, Feature 9, Feature 10	
Customer Dashboard - Spiders	Feature 6	Feature 2, Feature 3	Feature 7, Feature 4, Feature 8	Feature 5, Feature 6, Feature 9, Feature 10	
Customer Interaction BOT - Riders	Feature 7	Feature 2, Feature 3, Feature 10	Feature 7, Feature 4, Feature 8	Feature 5, Feature 6, Feature 9	
In-Store Management - Warriors	Feature 5	Feature 1, Feature 3	Feature 7, Feature 4, Feature 8	Feature 2, Feature 6, Feature 9, Feature 10	

All Product Teams – PI/ ART/Product Group level overall PI Objectives			
S. No	**PI /ART/Product Group Objectives**	**Business Value (BV)**	**Actual Business Value (AV)**
1	Implement ability of search products and required details with Improved efficiency and accuracy: ■ **Search Response Time**: Reduce average search response time to **less than 500 milliseconds**. ■ **User Engagement**: Increase the click-through rate on search results by **15%**.	8	
2	Implement Ability to add products faster and Enhance Shopping cart experience: ■ **Cart Abandonment Rate**: Decrease cart abandonment rate to **less than 20%**. ■ **Conversion Rate**: Increase the conversion rate from cart to checkout by **10%**. ■ **Cart Load Time**: Ensure the shopping cart page loads within **2 seconds**.	8	
3	Implement different cards and modes of payment types that Provides seamless payment methods: ■ **Payment Success Rate**: Achieve a **95% or higher** successful payment transaction rate. ■ **Payment Gateway Integration**: Integrate **at least three** additional payment gateways. ■ **Fraud Detection**: Implement fraud detection mechanisms to reduce fraudulent transactions by **30%**	5	
4	Enable Ability to streamline the order placement processes and improve efficiency: ■ **Order Completion Time**: Reduce the time taken to place an order to **under 3 minutes**. ■ **Error Rate**: Ensure that order placement errors occur in **less than 1%** of transactions. ■ **Guest Checkout Adoption**: Increase guest checkout adoption by **20%**.	7	
5	Ability to implement Enhance post-order communication with customers: ■ **Confirmation Email Open Rate**: Achieve an email open rate of **at least 50%** for order confirmations. ■ **SMS Notifications**: Implement SMS notifications for order status updates with a **90% delivery rate**. ■ **Customer Satisfaction**: Maintain a post-order satisfaction score of **4.5 out of 5**.	6	
6	Implement personalized product recommendation functionality to Improve product discovery and recommend right choice of products: ■ **Click-Through Rate on Recommendations**: Increase the click-through rate on personalized recommendations by **25%**. ■ **Recommendation Algorithm Accuracy**: Maintain an accuracy rate of **80%** for personalized recommendations.	9	
7	Inform customers about new arrivals: ■ **Email Open Rate**: Achieve an email open rate of **at least 40%** for new product announcements. ■ **Push Notification Engagement**: Increase push notification engagement for new arrivals by **15%**.	10	
8	Increase the Net Promoter Score (NPS) by 10 points by the end of the quarter through customer feedback related features that includes Implement a real-time feedback mechanism at checkout counters: ■ **Reduce average wait time** for customers by 20%. ■ Resolve 90% of customer complaints within 24 hours.	6	

Take a look at how we crafted our ART/product line PI objectives: Starting from the ground up, we gathered all the team-level PI objectives and wove them together to achieve our overarching ART/product group goals: (previous page)

13.13 PRP/PI Retrospective

We then moved to the final agenda: the retrospective for our three-day quarterly planning. We had a virtual whiteboard where everyone could add sticky notes under four categories: what went well, what could have gone better, what needs improvement, and appreciations. Each team member had five minutes to add their thoughts.

This whiteboard was available from day one, so team members had been adding their notes throughout the event. During the last five minutes, they added any missing points, and the ART coach consolidated and merged similar or duplicate notes. (next page image)

We discussed each sticky note in detail and identified improvement actions where needed. Here's an illustrative view of our Quarterly Planning Retrospective:

The ART coach then thanked everyone for their great contributions and officially ended the quarterly planning session.

The next day, the two teams with lower confidence scores met with ART stakeholders and the ART coach to address risks, dependencies, and unknowns. After two hours of detailed discussion, which included input from other ART stakeholders and suppliers, the teams completed their rework. They then held another confidence vote, and this time, the scores were much better: 3.4 and 3.8.

With these improved scores, everyone felt confident and ready to move forward. The planning session was a success, and we left with clear plans and renewed energy for the quarter ahead.

With the closing of our intensive planning sessions, we took a moment to reflect, gathering around with a collective sense of accomplishment and a shared anticipation for the future. Here's a snapshot of how our days unfolded:

From the outset, our ART coach outlined the roadmap for the three days, setting clear expectations for each product team and what we aimed to achieve together. Her guidance was precise, paving the way for effective planning.

The Business Owner stepped up first, painting a vivid picture of our current standings. He outlined our urgent need for growth and the consequences of

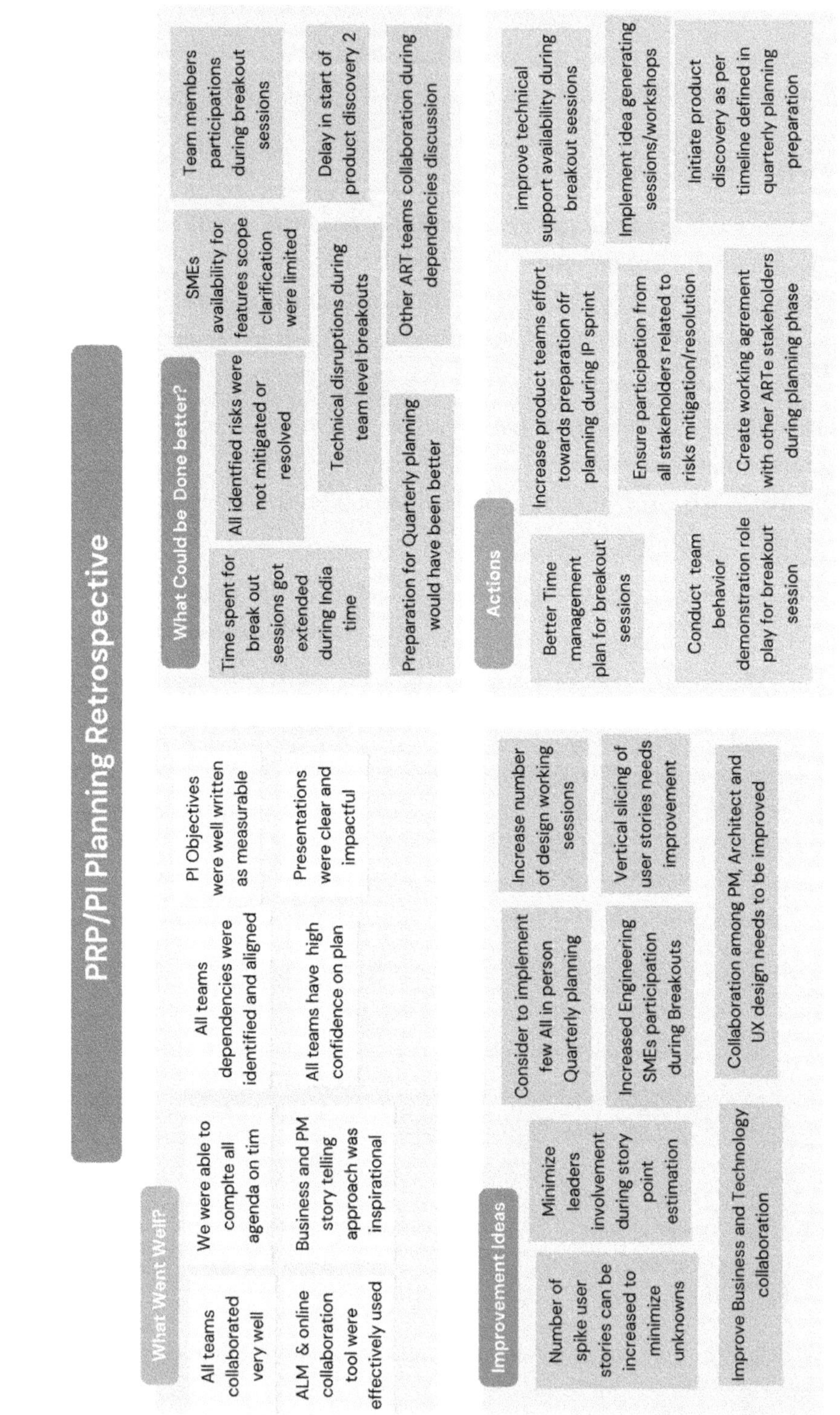

PRP/PI Planning Retrospective

What Went Well?

- All teams collaborated very well
- We were able to complte all agenda on tim
- All teams dependencies were identified and aligned
- PI Objectives were well written as measurable
- ALM & online collaboration tool were effectively used
- Business and PM story telling approach was inspirational
- All teams have high confidence on plan
- Presentations were clear and impactful

What Could be Done better?

- Time spent for break out sessions got extended during India time
- All identfied risks were not mitigated or resolved
- SMEs availability for features scope clarification were limited
- Team members participations during breakout sessions
- Technical disruptions during team level breakouts
- Delay in start of product discovery 2
- Preparation for Quarterly planning would have been better
- Other ART teams collaboration during dependencies discussion

Improvement Ideas

- Number of spike user stories can be increased to minimize unknowns
- Minimize leaders involvement during story point estimation
- Consider to implement few All in person Quarterly planning
- Increase number of design working sessions
- Increased Engineering SMEs participation during Breakouts
- Vertical slicing of user stories needs improvement
- Improve Business and Technology collaboration
- Collaboration among PM, Architect and UX design needs to be improved

Actions

- Better Time management plan for breakout sessions
- Increase product teams effort towards preparation ofr planning during IP sprint
- improve technical support availability during breakout sessions
- Conduct team behavior demonstration role play for breakout session
- Ensure participation from all stakeholders related to risks mitigation/resolution
- Implement idea generating sessions/workshops
- Create working agrement with other ARTe stakeholders during planning phase
- Initiate product discovery as per timeline defined in quarterly planning preparation

stagnancy, sharing our overarching business strategy and focusing on the critical next three to six months. His talk was a clarion call to all of us: to step up, to align, and to drive our strategy home.

Following this, our Product Management teams took the stage, each presenting their product vision and OKRs, along with a roadmap for their respective areas. They highlighted the key features prioritized for this quarter—each chosen for its potential to enhance customer experience dramatically.

Then, our Architects and UX Design leaders showcased the incremental architecture and the UX designs prepped for the initial sprints. Their presentations connected the dots between the strategic visions laid out and the tangible, customer-focused actions we planned to implement.

The ART coach initially set the expectations for the teams from the perspective of the first breakout, leading to the teams dividing into their respective breakout sessions. During these sessions, each team worked on creating a draft plan. This marked the end of day 1 for the India teams, while the US teams continued their efforts. The following day started with a quick handover from the US team to the Indian team, allowing them to continue with their breakout sessions.

On the second day, we conducted walkthroughs where each team presented their draft plan. These presentations included the refined user stories, estimates, sprint planning, dependencies, and draft PI objectives.

Following these presentations, the management held a review and problem-solving meeting attended only by the team leads. During this meeting, they discussed and agreed upon the necessary changes to each team's draft plans. They decided to communicate these agreed changes to all teams on day 3.

On the third day, the ART coach outlined necessary planning adjustments for each team. Following these guidelines, teams proceeded to refine their plans during the second draft breakout session, incorporating feedback from the management review and problem-solving meeting.

Subsequently, each team finalized their draft plans for the next five sprints, taking into account the available capacity. They also established PI objectives for their respective teams, agreed on dependencies and timelines with each other, and identified and documented potential risks.

The ART coach then facilitated a "fist of five" confidence voting event, where each team and ART stakeholders expressed their confidence in the collective plans developed over the last three days. The voting was on a scale of 1 to 5, with 1 indicating low confidence and 5 indicating high confidence. Plans from teams that received an overall score of less than 3 were slated for reevaluation and adjustments.

All the teams presented their final plans to the entire ART. All stakeholders consented to the proposed plan. Subsequently, the ART coach and Product Managers collaborated to develop a consolidated view of the Planning board in JIRA, which was then officially approved by the Business Owner. Following this, the ART coach spearheaded an ART-level risk ROAMing exercise, which was then followed by the quarterly planning session.

Each session built on the last, building together a narrative of preparation, strategic intent, and future-focused action. It was a reaffirmation of our commitment to our goals and to each other.

Implement and Coach PRP Execution

Welcome to a crucial step in our journey towards a product-centric model. This is where we take our PRP/PI plan and turn it into real, tangible value, delivered incrementally through sprints, months, and quarters.

In this chapter, we'll dive into point 11 of our 12-point process for transforming to a product and platform-centric model. This is where all our planning starts to pay off, as we bring our strategies to life.

To illustrate this, let's look at an example from the Education industry. This case study will guide us from the initial concept all the way to measurable outcomes, showing the full journey of product transformation:

Steps 1 to 3: These steps involve creating the product and breaking it down into business capabilities. We covered these phases in Chapter 9, where we visualized the future state portfolio.

Steps 4 to 8: Here, we focus on feature discovery and grooming. We prepared for these steps in Chapter 12 during our PRP/PI planning.

Steps 9 and 10: These were put into action during the detailed planning sessions in Chapter 13.

Steps 11 and 12: Now, we execute the plans outlined in Chapter 14 and measure our outcomes in Chapter 15.

Illustrative Product Centric Model to Improve Outcomes (1/4)

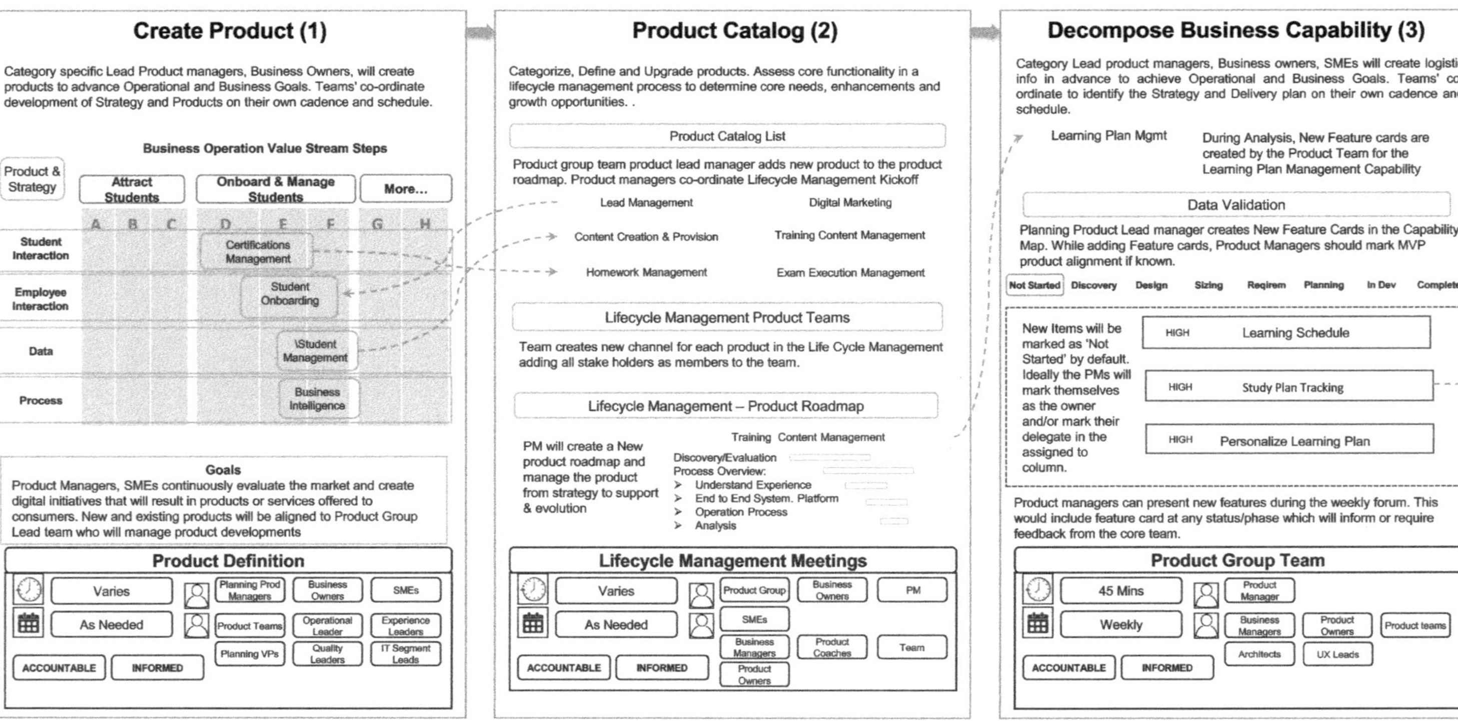

Illustrative Product Centric Model to Improve Outcomes (2/4)

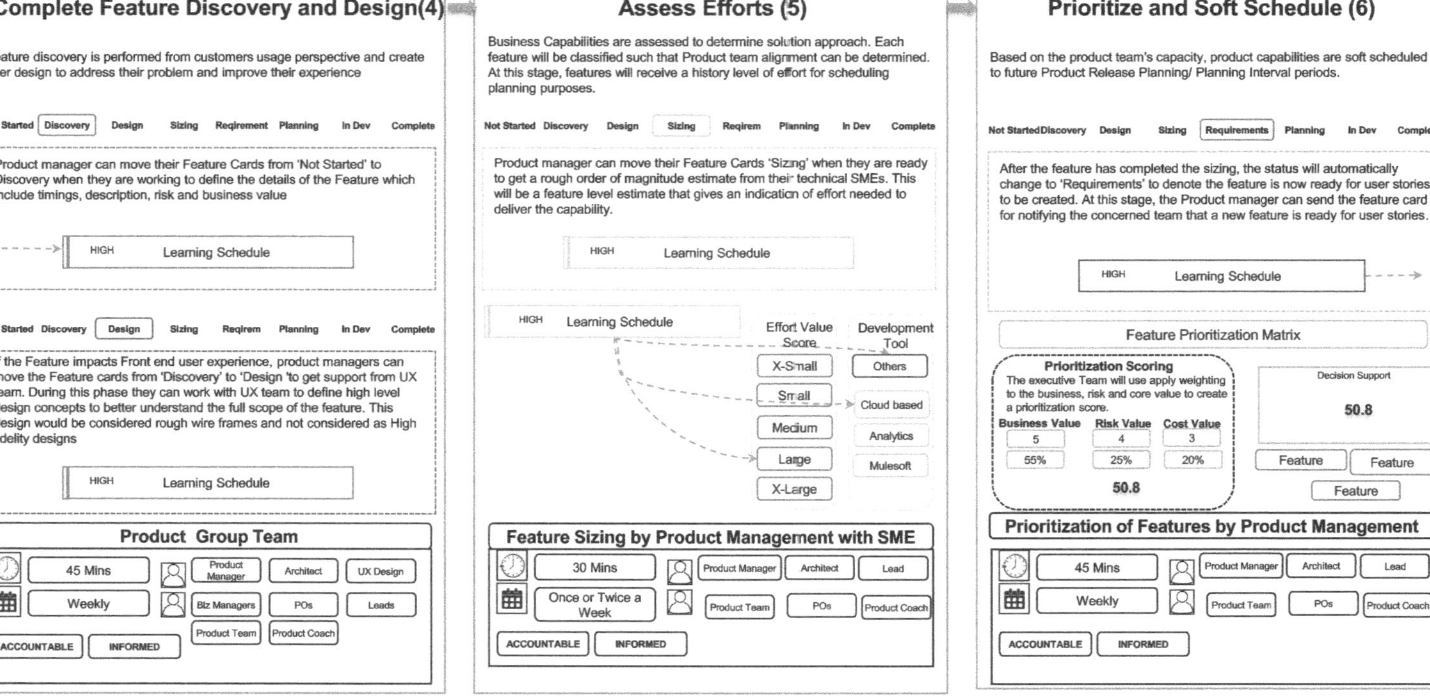

Illustrative Product Centric Model to Improve Outcomes (3/4)

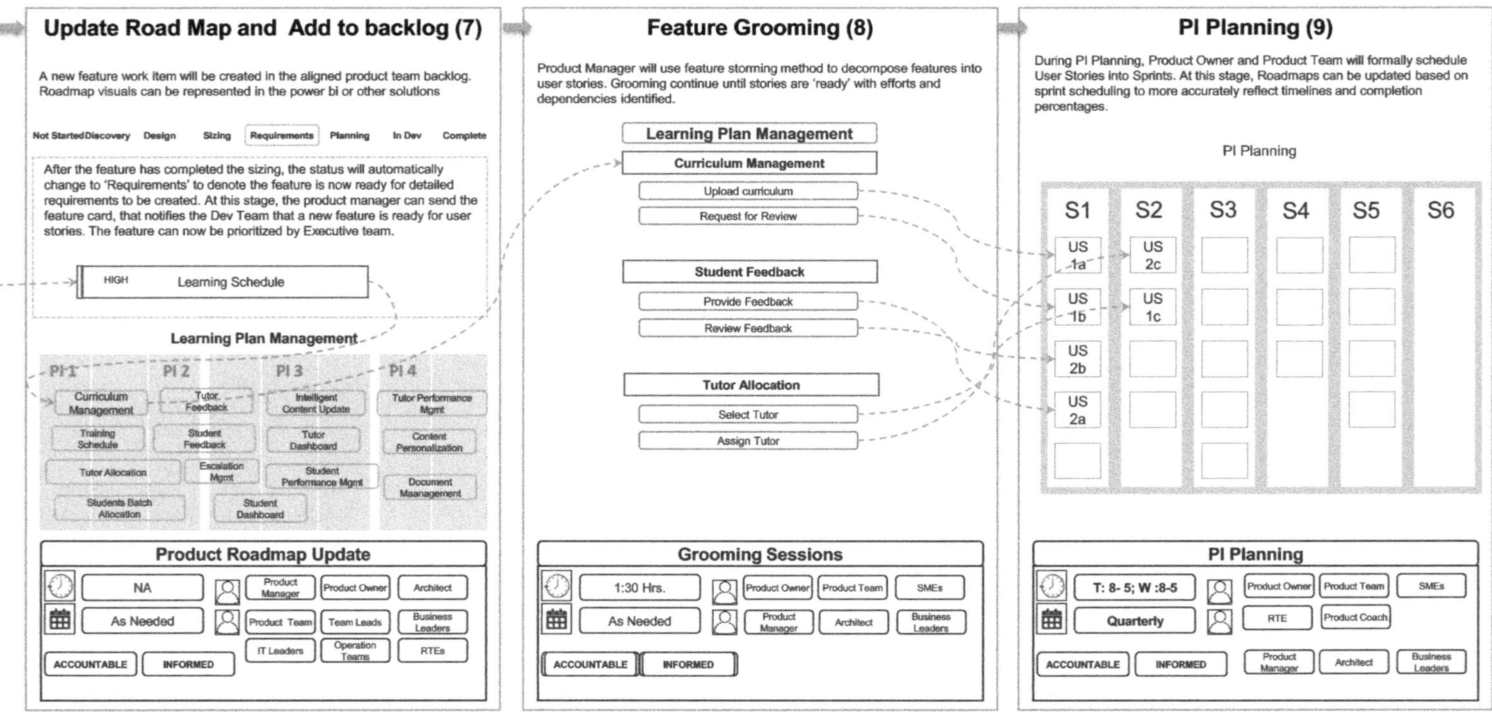

Illustrative Product Centric Model to Improve Outcomes (4/4)

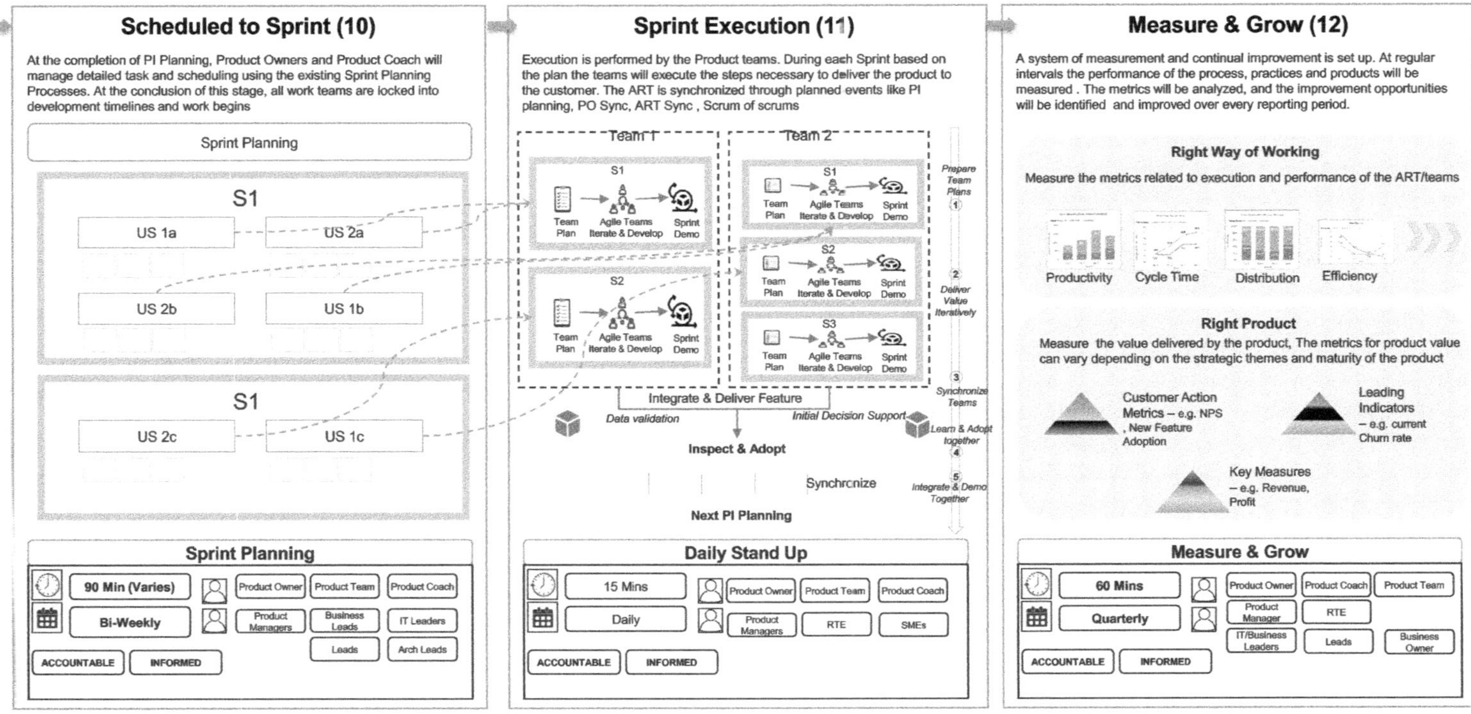

In this chapter, let's dive into points 10 and 11 of our transformation journey.

14.1 Begin PRP/PI Plan Execution

After wrapping up our first quarterly planning session on Friday, the product coaches made sure all sprint plans were updated in Jira. This included dependencies and risks.

On the following Tuesday, the teams gathered for the first sprint planning session. They quickly reviewed the sprint 1 scope and priorities. Stories were sized (If not correctly sized or missed during the quarterly planning event, and for stories that are newly added) at 1, 2, or 3, with a maximum of 5 points. The team ensured that all stories met the Definition of Ready (DOR) criteria, adhering to the INVEST approach for user stories. Each team member was encouraged to pick up user stories.

All functional stories were vertically sliced to include UI, API, and QA scopes. While some team members picked up stories easily, others needed help. The PO and Product Coach guided them through the process, recognizing that Agile was still new to many.

The Product Coach ensured the team's workload matched their capacity, considering business, enabler, and defect slices. They defined sprint goals using the SMART template, aligning them with the Team PI Objectives. After a round of fist-of-five voting, the team committed to their sprint goals.

Illustrative view of sprint 1 sprint goals in line with user stories committed for the sprint and overall team PI objectives: (nexxt page image)

From the next day, the product team jumped into action, tackling larger stories to ensure the QA team had ample time for testing. As developers built functionalities, QA members created test cases, prepared test data, and ensured the test environment was ready, all with a shift-left focus. Meeting sprint goals each week meant the team was steadily progressing towards their PI objectives set during the quarterly planning.

Every day, the Product Coach led a sync-up meeting using the team Kanban board in Jira. This board detailed who was working on what, highlighted dependencies, and flagged potential blockers.

Each team member shared their progress from the previous day and their plans for the current day. Things were running smoothly. By the third day of

Illustrative Sprint Goals for 1st Sprint

Goal No.	Sprint Goal	Metric	Set of User Stories Addressed
1	Implement an advanced product search feature.	Increase search accuracy by 80%.	Traveler's product search, Shopper's sorting preferences.
2	Develop a secure payment system with loyalty program integration.	Achieve a 90% success rate in payment detail encryption.	Frequent Traveler's payment details, Budget-Conscious Customer's discount and loyalty points.
3	Update the mobile app for barcode and QR code scanning.	Ensure a 95% accuracy rate in scanning.	In-Store Shopper's barcode scanning, Tech-Savvy Traveler's QR code verification.
4	Set up a notification infrastructure with cloud resources.	Support the delivery of 5,000 notifications per hour with 99% uptime.	Notification infrastructure setup, architecture for handling notifications.
5	Enable selection of delivery preferences and display estimated costs.	Implement three delivery options and provide cost estimates with 98% accuracy.	Online Shopper's delivery

Note: Achieving these sprint goals will enable team to progress toward team level PI objectives that in turn will help to achieve epics & Product OKRs. It will lead to achieving Business Objectives

the sprint, the Warriors team delivered their first user story, which was promptly demoed to the PO. The PO verified that it met the acceptance criteria written in the Given-When-Then format.

14.2 Overcoming Challenges During Execution

The next day, during the daily sync, the Product Coach asked, "Why didn't the story move to QA as planned yesterday?"

A team member responded, "Code review and unit testing couldn't be completed because I had to take a half-day leave."

The coach asked, "Why didn't someone else pick it up to complete it?"

The team member looked around and said, "I guess we didn't think of it. I'm back today, so I'll finish it."

The coach nodded. "Remember, it's the team's collective responsibility to ensure the work is delivered quickly. It's not just on one individual."

Another team member spoke up, "I can take over if needed. I didn't realize you were back today."

"Great initiative," the coach said, "but since she's here, she'll complete it. In the future, if someone has to take unplanned leave, let's ensure someone else steps up to minimize Work In Progress (WIP). More WIP means longer cycle times for user stories."

Every day, the Product Coach presented the burndown chart during the sync-up meeting to keep the team focused on completing user stories regularly.

"We need to avoid completing all stories on day seven or eight," the coach emphasized, "as this leaves the QA team with little time to finish functional testing within the sprint."

In one of the daily sync-ups, a team member pointed out, "We have a dependency from Team Spider that wasn't completed as agreed yesterday."

The Product Coach nodded. "I'll escalate this to the Spider team's Product Coach. If it's not resolved soon, I'll bring it up during the Scrum of Scrums (SoS) later today."

Over the next couple of days, more stories were delivered as planned. During the first sprint, all Product Owners (POs) of the ART/product line met to

Current Sprint Status Distribution

Issue Type — Total Issues: 46

Issue Type	
Business Story	36
Defect	4
Design	3
Enabler Story	3

Current Sprint Distribution by Assignee

Assignee — Total Issues: 46

Assignee	
Emily	8
Harry	5
Jane	5
Jenn	8
John	5
Matt	3
Rob	6
Tim	6

Alpha_EC-003 Epic Status

Key	Summary	Status	Epic Status	Target Date	ΣProgress
ECS-014	Search products	TESTING	In Progress	29/Jul/24	2
ECS-015	Unable to see Product details	IN PROGRESS	In Progress	30/Jul/24	3
ECS-016	List items for selling	DONE	In Progress	26/Jul/24	3
ECS-017	View product details	TO DO	In Progress	31/Jul/24	2
ECS-018	Product Catalogue creation	DONE	In Progress	24/Jul/24	5
ECS-019	Understand technical difficulties for Produc	TESTING	In Progress	29/Jul/24	1

Alpha_EC-001 Epic Progress

Status	Count	Percentage	
Accepted	5		83.3%
Rejected	1		16.7%
Total	6		

Alpha_EC-003 Epic Issue Types

Issue Type	Count	Percentage	
Business Story	5		71.4%
Defect	1		14.3%
Enabler Story	1		14.3%
Total	7		

Current Sprint Team Statistics

Assignee	TO DO	IN PROGRESS	TESTING	DONE	Total
Emily	3	1	2	2	8
Harry	1	0	3	1	5
Jane	2	0	0	3	5
Jenn	1	1	4	2	8
John	3	1	1	0	5
Matt	1	1	1	0	3
Rob	1	1	2	2	6
Tim	2	0	2	2	6
Total Unique Issues	14	5	15	12	46

Agile Wallboard

To Do	IN PROGRESS	TESTING	PO REVIEW	PO ACCEPTED	DONE

Retail Sales and Service (Alpha)

Illustrative Metrics that are Analyzed during Execution of Every Sprint

Sr. No.	Metrics	How the Metrics Calculated/Benefits	Possible Root Causes	Possible Actions
1	Sprint Burn Down Chart	This Dashboard shows what's total story points committed for a sprint Vs how many story point is completed so far	▪ Team may not burn down regularly through out the sprint due to story size huge, dependencies, high complexity, not updating story status on time etc.	▪ Decompose user story as small as possible ▪ Once team member started to work on user story, complete it, instead of leaving it in WIP and work on other story
2	Average time spent in Development/Work in Progress/on hold	This dashboard shows the trend of what's an average time spent by every user story in "in development", "on hold", "ready for release"	▪ Longer development time due to increased complexity, dependencies not resolved, longer time for integration/dependent story not available for integration	▪ Improve accuracy of complexity estimation, resolve dependencies on time ▪ Implement Continuous integration & Continuous Testing practices
3	Overall Sprint Progress	This dashboard shows how much time elapsed in current sprint, what % of work completed, what % of work scope changed, % of work yet to be started, % work in progress (At User Stories level)	▪ Lot of WIP- teams started the work and moved to other user story ▪ Dependencies are not resolved	▪ Once team starts any user story, they need to complete it and start next user story. If requires, other member of the team can also support to complete started work
4	Dependencies TO other Teams	Dashboard shows the "open" dependencies that product team need to resolve for other teams	▪ Dependent team has time to resolve it before committed date ▪ Dependent team working on it	▪ Responsible dependent team need to do everything possible to resolve on time as per commitment (follow working agreement) & improve predictability
5	Dependencies FROM other teams	Dashboard shows the "open" dependencies that other product teams need to resolve for this team	▪ Dependent team has time to resolve it before committed date ▪ Dependent team working on it	▪ Responsible dependent team need to do everything possible to resolve on time as per commitment (follow working agreement) & improve predictability
6	Number of WIP (Work In Progress) User stories – Flow Load	This dashboard shows what's total number of WIP user stories at any given point with spilt of current stages like (in Development, on hold, ready for release etc.,)	▪ High complexity than estimated ▪ Each team member focusing on their respective stories/instead of support others to push the work to next stage	▪ Focus as team to deliver work than as individual (support each other to complete stories)
7	Open Impediments (At User Stories level)	Create dashboard that shows open impediments that needs to be addressed to progress an user story	▪ Dependent team priorities changed/not collaborating ▪ Infrastructure issues/dependent team capacity issues	▪ Dependent teams to adhere to the commitment made to other teams ▪ Leadership team provide support on priorities realignment

discuss any changes in scope, priorities, or dependencies that required leadership attention.

Illustrative view of team sprint execution metrics: (page 313,314 images)

Then, two stories hit blocker status due to a design rework. The business proposed a design change, causing some rework. These two stories were likely to spill over into the next sprint.

The team discussed this with the business, and it was deemed necessary. The PO, Product Coach, and team agreed to rework the code to accommodate the design changes. However, they had to reprioritize one of the stories and move it to the next sprint to make room for the change.

The business and PM agreed with this plan.

The next day brought another challenge: the QA environment was down, halting testing for a full day. Despite this, the team managed to write functional test automation scripts and complete test automation for all finished user stories. This step was crucial for regression testing.

On the last day of the sprint, the team prepared for a demo with the PO for the final set of stories. They ensured that only stories meeting the Definition of Done (DoD) were closed. The sprint concluded, and any spillover stories were moved to the next sprint.

The team then held a retrospective meeting. The Product Coach, well-prepared, presented the team's performance flow metrics, which included sprint velocity (45 SP), sprint disruption (15%), sprint predictability (65%), cycle time (9 days), average WIP (5 user stories), and sprint distribution (60% business stories, 25% enabler stories, 15% defects). All these metrics needed improvement.

Illustrative view of Team level performance flow metrics that are measured at the end of every sprint, possible root causes and actions to improve these metrics: (page 316, 317 images)

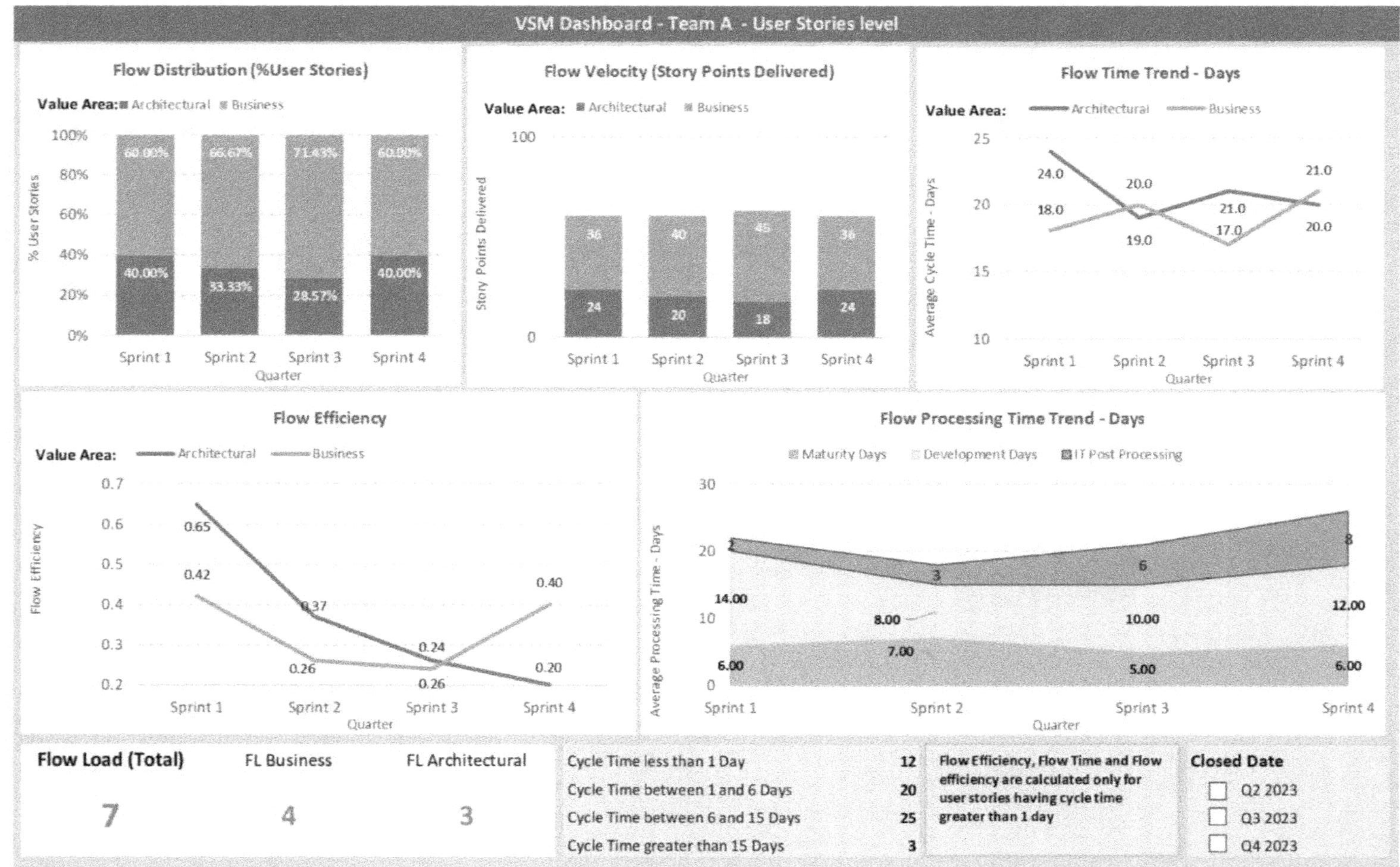

VSM Dashboard - Team A - User Stories level
Flow Distribution (%User Stories)
Value Area: Architectural Business
100%
80%
60%
40%
20%
0%
% User Stories
60.00% 66.67% 71.43% 60.00%
40.00% 33.33% 28.57% 40.00%
Sprint 1 Sprint 2 Sprint 3 Sprint 4
Quarter
Flow Velocity (Story Points Delivered)
Value Area: Architectural Business
100
0
Story Points Delivered
36 40 45 36
24 20 18 24
Sprint 1 Sprint 2 Sprint 3 Sprint 4
Quarter
Flow Time Trend - Days
Value Area: Architectural Business
25
20
15
10
Average Cycle Time - Days
24.0 20.0 21.0 21.0
18.0 19.0 17.0 20.0
Sprint 1 Sprint 2 Sprint 3 Sprint 4
Quarter
Flow Efficiency
Value Area: Architectural Business
0.7
0.6
0.5
0.4
0.3
0.2
Flow Efficiency
0.65 0.37 0.24 0.40
0.42 0.26 0.26 0.20
Sprint 1 Sprint 2 Sprint 3 Sprint 4
Quarter
Flow Processing Time Trend - Days
Maturity Days Development Days IT Post Processing
30
20
10
0
Average Processing Time - Days
2 3 6 8
14.00 8.00 10.00 12.00
6.00 7.00 5.00 6.00
Sprint 1 Sprint 2 Sprint 3 Sprint 4
Quarter
Flow Load (Total)   FL Business   FL Architectural
7   4   3
Cycle Time less than 1 Day   12
Cycle Time between 1 and 6 Days   20
Cycle Time between 6 and 15 Days   25
Cycle Time greater than 15 Days   3
Flow Efficiency, Flow Time and Flow efficiency are calculated only for user stories having cycle time greater than 1 day
Closed Date
Q2 2023
Q3 2023
Q4 2023

Illustrative Metrics that are Analyzed at the end of Every Sprint

Sr. No.	Metrics	How the Metrics Calculated/Benefits	Possible Root Causes	Possible Actions
1	Deployment Frequency & Failed Deployments Trends	This metrics calculated based number of successful deployments in production environment for specific period. This helps to understand the rate at which value is delivered for end users	• Delay in completing user stories as per DOD requirements • Lower and higher environments availability issues	• Value stream mapping(VSM) from user story active to deployment and identify bottle necks in the flow • Continuous monitoring of environment, create virtual environments on the go / service virtualization
2	Mean time to Restore	This metrics calculates the duration it takes to bring the application functionalities up & running. It shows the team ability to bring normalcy when production incidents occurred	• Complex/monolithic architecture • Time not allocating adequate capacity to fix production issues	• Improve architecture with micro services to increase the speed of fixing incidents • Implement capacity planning policy for every type of work that's done by team
3	Automation coverage trend	Its calculated based on testing effort that's automated Vs total testing effort	• Lack of team capacity to allocate testing automation effort • Lack of early test planning/creation	• Allocate some capacity for test automation purpose, leverage test automation tools, and create plan for automation across environments
4	Code coverage trend	Its calculated based on number of lines of code tested Vs total number of lines of code	• Insufficient testing due to lack of capacity • Test cases do not cover all scenarios	• Allocate more capacity for testing, implement continuous integration • Ensure tests cover wide range of inputs and paths
5	Defects Trend	Number of defects injected Vs closed in every sprint	• Design & Coding standards/guidelines not followed • User stories have not been adequately written with well defined acceptance criteria	• Define, communicate, train team on standards and guidelines with focus on "first time right'/prevention • Improve detection control with approaches like TDD
6	Backlog Health	It calculated based on total Story Points equalent user stories ready for development in comparison to available product team capacity per sprint. Objective is to have N+2 sprints backlog ready	• Product teams not spending sufficient time for backlog refinement • Features are not clearly defined and feature storming not conducted periodically	• Ensure product discovery – 2 conducted, features are added/refined and stormed to identify high level user stories periodically • Increase frequency of backlog refinement sessions as needed
7	Sprint Throughput (Kanban)	Average number of user stories/story points delivered per sprint. It helps to forecast how long a team take to work through backlog	• Bottlenecks across user story life cycle due to which team not able to meet their commitments	• Value stream mapping(VSM) from user story active to deployment and identify bottle necks

"Alright team," the Product Coach began, "let's discuss the reasons behind our performance. What do you think impacted our metrics?"

"I think the unexpected QA environment downtime really threw us off. We lost a whole day."

"And the design rework on those two stories caused a lot of disruptions."

The Product Coach nodded, "Great points. Any suggestions on how we can handle such disruptions better next time?"

"We should have a backup environment ready for QA."

"And maybe a better way to handle design changes."

The team agreed, and the Product Coach noted these down as actions to improve.

Moving to the second part of the retrospective, the Product Coach asked, "Now, let's share what went well, what could have been done better, what needs improvement, and any appreciations."

"I think we did a great job with our first user story demo. The acceptance criteria were clear, and it passed with flying colors," the PO shared his inputs and continued, "But we could improve our communication when someone has to take an unplanned leave."

"Absolutely," said the Product Coach. "Let's prioritize these points and discuss how we can address them."

Every team member contributed by placing sticky notes on the virtual board, sharing their insights from four different perspectives.

The team concluded that most of the sprint goals were met, and they reviewed their influence on the overall team level PI objectives. Sprint goals related to the spillover stories that weren't completed in the current sprint would be met in the next sprint.

"We've met most of our sprint goals," one team member noted. "The spillover stories will be tackled next sprint."

"Great," the Product Coach responded. "Any risks in meeting all team level PI objectives by the end of the quarter?"

"No risks," another member replied confidently. "We should meet all objectives on time."

"Perfect," said the Product Coach. "Let's add the outcomes of this sprint retrospective to our continuous improvement backlog. We'll prioritize the top three improvement actions to implement during the next sprint."

The team agreed and prioritized their top three improvement actions.

Product group coaches leveraged the playbook extensively to guide and coach team members. "If you have any questions about expectations from your role, or about process inputs and outputs," the Product Coach reminded, "refer to the playbook."

One team member asked, "What about scenarios like team collaboration and conflict management?"

The Product Coach responded, "We'll focus on improving openness, building trust, and respecting each other's views." These are critical for improved collaboration and minimal personal conflicts.

Product group/ ART coaches acted as change agents, driving the transformation at the ART/product group level towards new product-centric model ways of working. They used playbook content specific to roles at ART/ product group levels, including business owners, product managers, architects, engineering leads, and UX design leads. This ensured alignment and effective collaboration across all roles.

Overall, product coaches acted as change agents at the product team level, focusing on three main areas:

Effective execution of sprint ceremonies.

Coaching, mentoring, and training team members on processes and interpersonal skills like collaboration and emotional intelligence.

Continuously improving processes and product outputs delivered in each sprint.

14.3 Conducting Product Coach/SOS Syncs, PO Syncs, PM Syncs, and Architect Syncs

Weekly sync meetings were a vital part of our routine. The ART/product group coach held regular sessions with product coaches and POs.

In the Product Coach/SOS (Scrum of Scrum) meetings, all product team coaches participated. "Let's ensure dependencies and bottlenecks are managed well to achieve higher predictability in delivering value each sprint," the coach emphasized. If any dependencies required leadership support, they were discussed and escalated promptly.

Similarly, the PO sync meetings included all POs from the product group. "Our goal is to manage scope priorities effectively and eliminate scope-related dependencies to meet our sprint commitments," the coach reminded.

During the current quarterly plan execution, we also held PMs and Architects sync meetings in parallel. "Most organizations focus only on governing execution activities," the coach noted. "But governing preparation activities is equally important." The purpose of these meetings was to ensure the preparation for the next quarterly planning was on track, following the plan, timeline, and responsibilities laid out in Chapter 12.

In our discussions during sync meetings, if we hit a snag—say in product discovery phase 2, or while creating incremental architectures or UX designs for the upcoming quarter's first two sprints—these aren't just minor hiccups. When someone from the team pipes up about these delays or capacity issues, it's crucial. We take it to the leadership team to hash out solutions right away.

"Why does it matter so much?" someone might ask. Well, preparing for next quarter's planning is as crucial as the execution itself. Only with thorough preparation can we ensure robust planning that leads to seamless execution. That's why we emphasize having "well-defined capacity" for these preparatory activities.

Imagine not spending enough time on these. What happens? Our quarterly plans might look good on paper but end up being poorly executed. Poor execution means not just failing to deliver as planned but also failing to deliver the right value through our business capabilities and functionalities. That's why we focus so much attention on making sure our planning preparation activities are spot-on, ensuring that every aspect of our products' business capabilities and functionalities is well-defined and ready to roll.

14.4 Continuing Execution from Sprint 2 Onwards

As we moved into the second sprint, all teams picked up where they left off, implementing some of the improvements identified during the first sprint retrospective. These included ensuring test data and environment refreshes were completed as per SLA, making sure team members picked up user stories they were interested in, and emphasizing better collaboration to complete user stories faster—working as a team, not as individuals.

I scheduled a sync-up meeting with the Product Group/ART product coaches, the Product Managers, coaches, and all POs to gauge the team's sentiment in these new ways of working.

During the meeting, there were mixed responses. Some noted that the structured approach, from sprint planning to retrospective, was really helping them see the Plan-Do-Check-Adjust cycle at each sprint level. They felt the focus on value delivery from the customer's perspective was becoming clearer. However, a few others felt that while it seemed like a streamlined approach, they still didn't see it in full effect.

"It's great to hear everyone's honest views," I said. "It's our collective responsibility to keep gathering these challenges and address them. If a challenge is specific to one team, we'll handle it at that level. But if it's a sentiment felt across many teams, we need to act on it at the Product Line/Group level."

We wrapped up the meeting with the agreement to reconvene at the end of the second sprint to reassess and adjust as needed.

Let's take a look at some of the challenges:

Id	Possible Challenges List	Type	Recommendations Mapping	Process Level
1	Programs are not structured as product line/set of products that delivers business value	Process	R1, R81, R82	Intake
2	The capabilities/epics are not aligned to business objective/strategic themes that leads to reprioritization at downstream	Process	R3,R5,R6,R7	Intake
3	Problem statement & benefit hypothesis not properly captured during intake	Process	R2,R3	Intake
4	There is no standard prioritization process / framework and not done using WSJF(industry best practice) that leads to incorrect prioritization of epics/features and less value delivery	Process	R5	Ideation
5	Prioritization process not followed across all levels (Capabilities/Epics/Features/ User Stories)	Process	R6	Ideation
6	Multiple re-prioritization happens downstream	Process	R5,R7	Ideation
7	Yearly roadmap with quarterly split is not defined comprehensively in line with business objectives	Process	R11	Intake
8	Technical feasibility not evaluated at an earlier stage	Process	R15	Design
9	There is a significant difference between the initial and final estimation of epics/features/user stories	Process	R9	Feature planning
10	Expected business value vs delivered is not reviewed regularly at epics and features level	Process	R33	Feature planning
11	Architectural design/infrastructure related features/user stories are not implemented at n-1/n-2 levels to improve feature/user stories cycle time	Process	R18	Feature planning
12	The MVP is not established before feature/PI /quarterly planning	Process	R13	Feature planning

Here is a glimpse into the recommendations:

ID	Recommendations	Type	Priority	Metrics	Process level
R1	Define product line/program aligned operating model to improve value delivery speed	Process	1	CT,LT	Intake
R2	Define and implement a standard Intake process	Process	1	CT,LT,P	Intake
R3	Perform initial impact analysis during intake and a detailed impact analysis after ideation	Process	2	DF,P	Intake
R4	Implement traceability matrix approach from capabilities/initiatives, epics to feature to user stories	Process	2	CT,LT,DF,P	Intake
R5	Define and implement a standard prioritization process also implement WSJF(Weighted Shortest Job First) to improve accuracy of prioritization	Process	1	CT,LT	Intake
R6	Follow the prioritization guidelines across all level (capabilities , Epics, Features, User Story)	Process	2	CT,LT,P	Intake
R7	Involve both Business & IT stakeholders in Prioritization	People	3	DF	Intake
R8	Decompose applications using API /visible architecture strategy to improve change speed	Tech	1	CT,LT,DF,P	Ideation
R9	Define a standard estimation techniques like planning poker/story point estimation. Size the features and Userstories to fit within the release/sprint	Process	1	CT,LT,DF,P	Feature planning
R10	The estimations should be arrived collaboratively using industry best practices	People	2	CT,P	Feature planning
R11	Establish a robust yearly calendar with quarterly split	Process	1	CT,LT,P	Intake
R12	Perform Capacity planning at program/product line level and sprint level	People	2	DF	Feature planning
R13	Define MVP before Quarterly/PI/feature planning	Process	2	DF	Feature planning
R14	Define and Implement quarterly/PI/feature Planning process including all stakeholders; Feature planning should happen at least one sprint in advance	Process	1	CT,LT,DF,P	Feature planning

CT – Cycle Time ,LT – Lead Time ,DF – Deployment Frequency ,P - Productivity

During our sync-up, a couple of product coaches raised a concern: their team leads were advocating for monitoring user stories at the individual team member level, aiming to optimize individual utilization. I quickly addressed this, "Focusing on individual performance is an agile anti-pattern. We're here to build a cohesive team, not isolated performers. Monitoring individuals can lead to silos within the team, where everyone is just trying to finish their tasks without seeing the bigger picture of our collective sprint goals. Let's meet with those leads one-on-one and help them understand the 'why' behind our approach."

14.5 Mid-Quarter PRP/PI Plan Change Proposal:

As we were deep into executing the second sprint, a new need emerged from the business side—there was a sudden necessity to introduce two critical new features for planning procurement items and supplier management. Just as we were wrapping up the second sprint, it became clear we needed to adapt our current quarter's plan to include these features.

We quickly convened a meeting with all leaders at the ART/product group level, along with POs and product coaches. A lively discussion unfolded, debating why these features were suddenly critical, questioning why they hadn't been identified during last month's feature prioritization, and figuring out how such an oversight had happened. Ultimately, we reached a consensus to include these two new features in the current quarter's scope with a couple of agreements:

We would adjust the scope by excluding some of the current features to fit the new demands within our capacity limits.

We committed to refining our feature prioritization process (specifically our WSJF – Weighted Shortest Job First approach) to avoid similar issues in the future.

Additionally, it was decided that the new features would be integrated starting from sprint 4. The third sprint was about to commence the next day, and all necessary refinement and prioritization for it had already been completed.

As we charged through the third sprint, a collaborative decision unfolded among the PM, POs, and UX design team. They agreed to break down the newly approved features into user stories and kick off the UX work, setting the stage for these stories to be tackled in sprint 4. Given the high volume of business stories anticipated for sprints 4 and 5, all teams concurred to ramp up their capacity allocation for business stories, planning to handle some defect fixes during the Innovation and Planning (IP) sprint.

Wrapping up sprint 2, I gathered with the product line coaches, product coaches, POs, and engineering leads for an overall execution review. A common thread in our discussion was the recurring sprint spillovers, predominantly caused by QA automation and integration tasks. We brainstormed various solutions and settled on a strategic shift: QA automation tasks would now fall under the purview of the Enablement product team—dedicated to providing technological support to other teams—while integration tasks would be managed by the Platform product team, which handles essential services like APIs tracking customer purchase patterns.

This strategic realignment was designed to reduce sprint spillovers, enhance sprint predictability, and optimize cycle times. With automation tasks shifted away from the product teams, we refined the Definition of Done (DoD) to reflect this change.

To keep a pulse on our quarterly goals, we established a feature-level dashboard. This tool tracks our progress, displaying the percentage of features progressed, the number of features completed, open risks and dependencies, and the alignment of feature delivery with planned release dates. (refer page 324, 325 images)

Quarterly Product Release Planning (PRP)/ PI Planning Execution Monitoring

Sr. No.	Issue Description	Status	Planned Quarter	Target Start	Target End	Jan 2023	Feb 2023	Mar 2023
1	Feature 1	In progress	2023 Q1	12/Jan/2023		15%	85%	
	- User Story 1	Done		S 02 Feb 2023	S 02 Feb 2023			
	- User Story 2	In Progress		S 14 Feb 2023	S 28 Feb 2023			
	- User Story N	To Do		S 28 Feb 2023	S 10 Mar 2023			
2	Feature 2		2023 Q1					
	- User Story 1	In progress		S 14 Feb 2023	S 28 Feb 2023		100%	
	- User Story 2	In Progress		S 14 Feb 2023	S 28 Feb 2023			
	- User Story N	To Do		S 28 Feb 2023	S 10 Mar 2023			

% Completed   % In Progress   % To Do

Illustrative view of possible root causes and actions that we need to implement to improve PRP/PI level execution progress:

Illustrative Metrics that are Analyzed during Execution of Every PRP/PI Plan			
Sr. No.	Metrics	How the Metrics Calculated/Benefits	Possible Root Causes	Possible Actions
1	PRP/PI Burn Down Chart	This Dashboard shows what's total story points committed for a Quarter Vs how many story point is completed so far	▪ Team may not burn down regularly through out the quarter due to story size huge, dependencies, high complexity, not updating story status on time etc.	▪ Decompose user story as small as possible ▪ Once team member started to work on user story, complete it, instead of leaving it in WIP and work on other story
2	Feature Average time spent in Development/Work in Progress/on hold	This dashboard shows the trend of what's an average time spent by every user story in "in development", "on hold", "ready for release"	▪ Longer development time due to increased complexity, dependencies not resolved, longer time for integration/dependent story not available for integration	▪ Improve accuracy of complexity estimation, resolve dependencies on time ▪ Implement Continuous integration & Continuous Testing practices
3	Overall PRP/PI Progress	This dashboard shows how much time elapsed in current PI, what % of work completed, what % of work scope changed, % of work yet to be started, % work in progress (at Features level)	▪ Lot of WIP- teams started the work and moved to other user story ▪ Dependencies are not resolved	▪ Once team starts any user story, they need to complete it and start next user story. If requires, other member of the team can also support to complete started work
4	Number of Features WIP (Work In Progress) User stories – Flow Load	This dashboard shows what's total number of WIP user stories at any given point with spilt of current stages like (in Development, on hold, ready for release etc.,)	▪ High complexity than estimated ▪ Each team member focusing on their respective stories/instead of support others to push the work to next stage	▪ Focus as team to deliver work than as individual (support each other to complete stories)
5	Open Impediments (At Feature level)	Create dashboard that shows open impediments that needs to be addressed to progress Feature	▪ Dependent team priorities changed/not collaborating ▪ Infrastructure issues/dependent team capacity issues	▪ Dependent teams to adhere to the commitment made to other teams ▪ Leadership team provide support on priorities realignment

On the 45th day since our first quarterly plan execution began, features from each team across both ARTs/product lines were released to their targeted customers. These features were seamlessly integrated by the platform teams with each product line and demoed as they progressed. Product-level metrics were gathered and analyzed through telemetry, aligned with the leading indicators we had set for these features.

Let's examine one of these features - the Search Products feature with improved personalized recommendations aimed at enhancing online shopping experiences. The goal was simple yet ambitious: enhance conversion rates by offering shoppers personalized product suggestions. Here's what we were aiming for:

A 10% increase in the Click-Through Rate (CTR) from customers clicking on personalized recommendations.

A 10 to 15% uptick in sales from these personalized suggestions.

The rollout of this feature in the APAC region was like watching a plan flawlessly unfold. Telemetry insights showed that a whopping 80% of customers engaged with this new feature. But the real test was the customer feedback—how did the feature resonate with them in their shopping experience? PMs met with store managers to gauge the initial reactions, and they didn't stop there. They also sifted through online feedback directly from the customers.

The adoption rate was through the roof. It turned out that these personalized recommendations were hitting the mark, aligning perfectly with what customers were looking to buy, tailored to their lifestyles and behaviors. Every feature we released went under the microscope, continuously monitored to ensure they lived up to our expectations and, more importantly, our customers' expectations. It was about making real impacts in the shopping experiences of our users.

The platform team, which supports the entire ART/product group, faced some integration challenges at the end of every sprint. Even though they received all the functionally tested user stories from the respective teams, completing the integration within a couple of days post-sprint was a struggle. The main culprits? Integration environment availability and test data availability—issues that had plagued us in the past as well.

We held a meeting with the platform team, the Business Owner, PMs, and QA leads to tackle this head-on. We agreed to automate test data and implement test data on demand best practices. To make this happen, we decided to add an enable epic to the portfolio backlog. Just like the product team level best practices, we created a list of challenges and recommendations for the ART/Product line level too. These insights were shared across both ARTs/product lines to enhance their product centric model adoption. Each ART/Product group set up flow metrics to monitor quarterly performance. This included metrics like feature-level flow distribution, average cycle time, productivity at the product line level, flow efficiency, and flow load/WIP. These metrics were crucial in keeping us on track and ensuring continuous improvement.

14.6 Continuing PRP/PI Plan Execution:

Starting from sprint 4, we seamlessly integrated the new features added mid-quarter. The process was straightforward: sprint planning, sprint execution, measuring and improving sprint-level performance, releasing features to customers, gathering feedback, and evaluating performance using flow metrics and product metrics, both leading and lagging indicators. This cycle repeated across five sprints. Each sprint brought valuable lessons at both the team and ART level. These lessons were meticulously logged, analyzed, and turned into actionable improvements.

Illustrative view of metrics, possible root causes and action that needs to be implemented at the end of every PRP/PI execution: (refer 328, 329 images)

14.7 Governance Guardrails:

During the quarterly PRP/PI execution, we held three types of governance meetings. The first was the monthly governance meeting, where we reviewed execution progress, identified any blockers needing leadership support, addressed changes in epic or feature priorities, and analyzed metrics from completed sprints. We also assessed the progress of teams' product-centric model maturity, discussed risks and issues, and tracked the preparation for the next quarter's planning.

This portfolio-level meeting included all product group leads and portfolio leads (LPM). Each product group presented their progress, sparking discussions that led to actionable plans to keep everything on track.

Secondly, the Quarterly Business Review, held every three months and always one month before our big PRP/PI planning session. Picture this: all the portfolio leads gathered around, reviewing the strides every product group has made toward our grand portfolio future state. They scrutinize the outcomes of business capabilities and epics, and mull over any adjustments needed in budgets

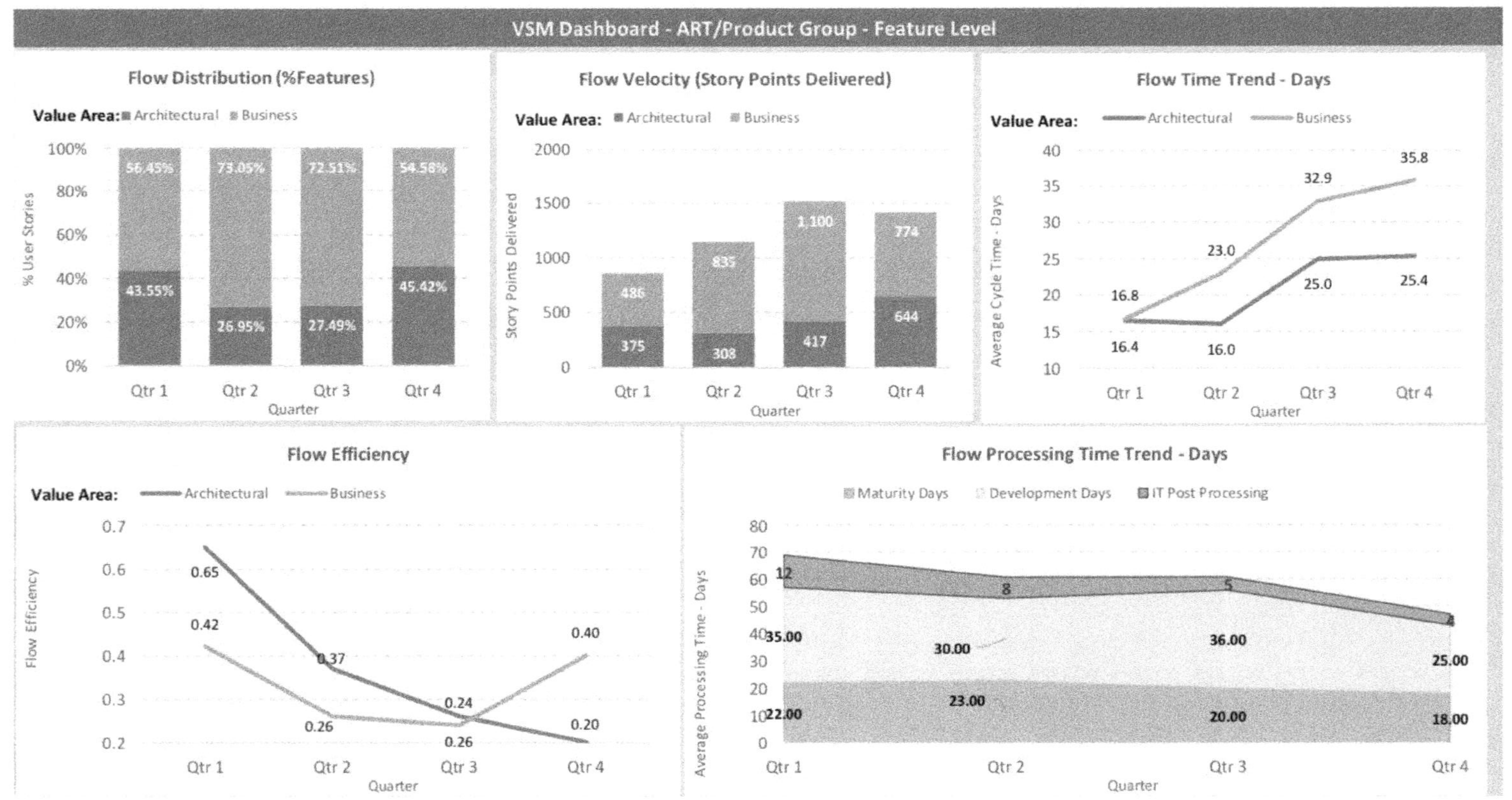

VSM Dashboard - ART/Product Group - Feature Level
Flow Distribution (%Features)
Value Area: Architectural Business
% User Stories
100%
80%
60%
40%
20%
0%
56.45%
43.55%
73.05%
26.95%
72.51%
27.49%
54.58%
45.42%
Qtr 1
Qtr 2
Qtr 3
Qtr 4
Quarter
Flow Velocity (Story Points Delivered)
Value Area: Architectural Business
Story Points Delivered
2000
1500
1000
500
0
486
375
835
308
1,100
417
774
644
Qtr 1
Qtr 2
Qtr 3
Qtr 4
Quarter
Flow Time Trend - Days
Value Area: Architectural Business
Average Cycle Time - Days
40
35
30
25
20
15
10
16.8
16.4
23.0
16.0
32.9
25.0
35.8
25.4
Qtr 1
Qtr 2
Qtr 3
Qtr 4
Quarter
Flow Efficiency
Value Area: Architectural Business
Flow Efficiency
0.7
0.6
0.5
0.4
0.3
0.2
0.65
0.42
0.37
0.26
0.24
0.26
0.40
0.20
Qtr 1
Qtr 2
Qtr 3
Qtr 4
Quarter
Flow Processing Time Trend - Days
Maturity Days Development Days IT Post Processing
Average Processing Time - Days
80
70
60
50
40
30
20
10
0
12
35.00
22.00
8
30.00
23.00
5
36.00
20.00
4
25.00
18.00
Qtr 1
Qtr 2
Qtr 3
Qtr 4
Quarter

Illustrative Metrics that are Analyzed at the end of Every PRP/PI Plan Execution

Sr. No.	Metrics	How the Metrics Calculated/Benefits	Possible Root Causes	Possible Actions
1	Product Group/ART Velocity	This metric is calculated based on total story points work delivered by all product teams with in a product group	• Sprint spill over from various product teams due to overcommitment • Poor cross team dependencies management	• Commit SP work based on available capacity – follow scope/capacity margin • Improve Scrum of Scrum (SOS) process effectiveness
2	Product Group Predictability	This metric is calculated based on Planned Business Value (BV) and Actual BV	• All user stories related to PI objectives/Features were not completed • Completed Features were not meeting Definition of Done criteria	• Improve cross team collaboration, dependency management process • Improve design, coding standards compliance • Improve code review, Unit test coverages
3	Flow Load	This metric is calculated based on number of Work In Progress (WIP) features at any point in time	• Start to work on one feature, then switch to another feature • Poor cross team dependencies management	• Focus more team performance than individual performance • Improve effectiveness of dependencies management process
4	Flow Time	This metric is calculated based on Feature start date to completion date in terms of number of days or weeks	• Increased WIP (work in progress) items • Start to work on one feature, then switch to another feature • Value stream bottlenecks	• Limit WIP and avoid start and switch/ stop practices • Improve prioritization and dependency management • Perform development value stream mapping to identify and remove bottlenecks
5	Flow Efficiency	This metric is calculated based on Average value add time from start to complete Vs total number of days/weeks (Flow time)	• Lot of manual activities like Merge request, code review, deployment etc. • Lot of wait time between value-add activities	• Conduct value stream mapping exercise to quantify time spent in manual activities and explore options to automate • Minimize wait time by managing demand Vs capacity, automation of some review and approval processes

at the product level or across development value streams. The decisions made here don't just echo; they shape our next quarterly planning, influencing what gets prioritized or adjusted.

Then, every six months, we dive into the Participatory Budget Meeting. Here's where the rubber meets the road. We evaluate what each product and group has achieved against the budget they've burned through. If a product group's output is lighting up our portfolio's future like a beacon, they might just earn themselves a bigger slice of the budget pie for the next semester. Conversely, if another group's efforts aren't hitting the mark, they might find their funds trimmed.

And for all these crucial discussions, our VMO team is the unsung hero. They gather all the necessary data, metrics, and progress reports in collaboration with product group and ART leads, ensuring every decision is informed and every stakeholder is equipped to steer their ship effectively in the seas of business strategy.

14. 8 Last Sprint of PRP/PI Plan Execution: IP Sprint

As we wrapped up our last sprint of the PRP/PI plan, the teams across both ARTs embarked on the Innovation & Planning (IP) sprint. This was our time to tidy up—the teams buckled down to polish off any spill-over work, zap bugs, absorb some learning, and tidy up our documentation. Meanwhile, the POs were neck-deep in refining the backlog based on the features set for the next quarter's assault. You're right; it's a non-stop world here. While teams cranked on the current quarter's goals, the big guns—BOs, PMs, Architects, UX design leads, and Product line coaches—were already in the thick of sculpting the next phase: discovery, hammering out OKRs, prioritizing epics and features, and sketching out the incremental architecture and designs, just as we unpacked back in chapter 13.

Then came the demo time—a showcase at the product line level of all those features that hadn't quite made the cut during our regular sprint integrations. The BOs, with eyes like hawks, gauged the actual Business Value (AV) of each feature related PI objectives, ensuring nothing slipped through without merit.

We also took a deep dive into our quarterly retrospective. It's a two-parter: the first is all numbers—predictability scores from the product line coach, comparing the planned Business Value (BV) with the AV from the demos, alongside a slew of flow metrics at both the team and product line levels. We pored over these, pinpointing where we nailed it and where we could dial up our game.

The second part got personal. Everyone chimed in with their thoughts on what soared, what stumbled, and where we could smooth out the bumps. It was a moment for candid chat and genuine appreciation, as each voice contributed to painting a full picture of our journey through the quarter.

At our ART, we dove into a problem-solving workshop that felt more like a brainstorming bonanza. We asked every team member to jot down the biggest hurdles they'd faced—a sea of issues appeared on our virtual whiteboard, each on its own sticky note. Then came the dot voting; everyone got three dots to place on the problems they felt were most critical, the ones screaming for a swift resolution.

From this democratic process, three major issues rose to the top, drawing the most dots and concern. We then called for volunteers—people who felt a personal pull or believed they had the chops to crack these cases. It was heartening to see hands go up, ready to tackle the challenges head-on.

We split into three squads, each armed with the 6-step problem-solving method from SAFe, and set the clock: one hour to dig deep. What came next was a blend of intense discussion, rapid-fire brainstorming, and bursts of insight. At the hour's mark, each group presented their findings complete with visuals and proposed solutions, ready to be slotted into our continuous improvement backlog.

Here's a snapshot of what one team tackled:

11. **Problem Statement:** Low predictability in our Merchandize Planning product ART—only 60% of committed PI objectives hit their mark in the first PI Q4 2022. This shortfall led to palpable business dissatisfaction, with a Net Promoter Score (NPS) dropping to 50 and a dreaded 20% increase in time to market. (next page images)

Illustrative Route Cause Analysis, Why-Why Analysis & Dot Voting

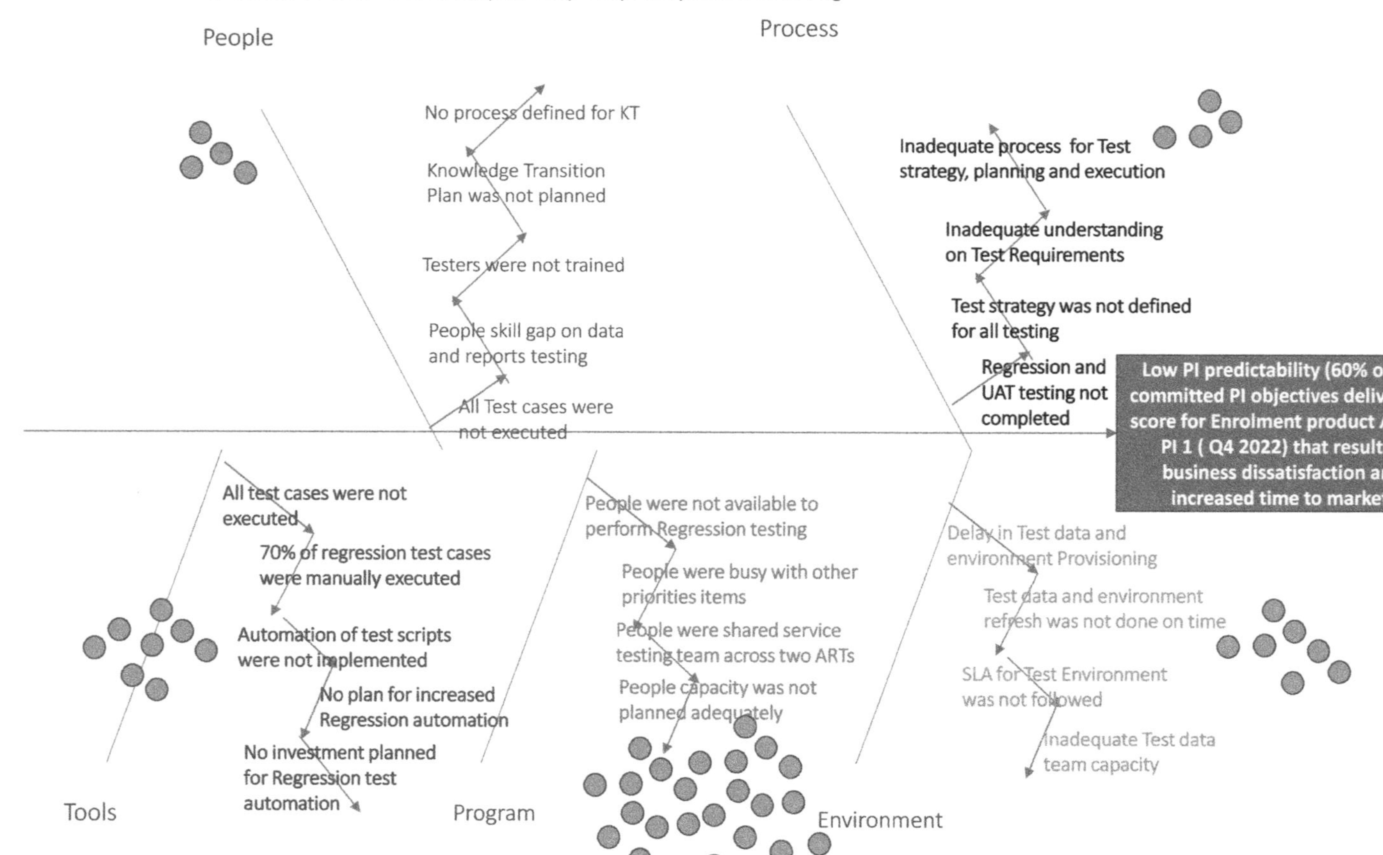

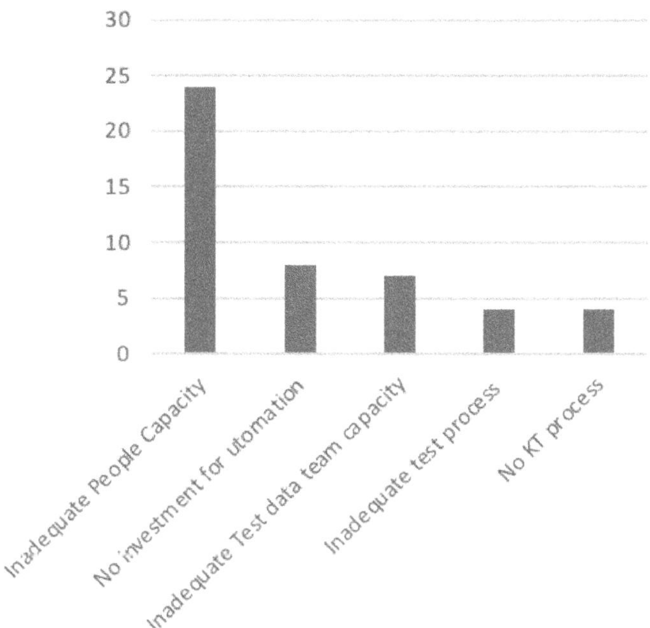

Suggested Solutions:

Scrutinize and recalibrate the capacity needed specifically for regression testing.

Establish a dedicated agile team focused solely on regression and integration testing.

Boost our commitment to developing regression automation scripts, ensuring this capacity is baked into our planning from the get-go.

As we wrapped up the IP sprint, we plunged into quarterly planning for the next round of ARTs/product lines. This was for all ARTs and product lines of our Retail stores business. We meticulously prepared, planned, and executed, learning from each cycle and continuously improving our processes.

Let's take a moment to reflect on this journey.

We kicked off by diving into the first sprint after a successful quarterly PI/PRP event. Each product team reviewed their first sprint plan, making any necessary adjustments. Team members eagerly picked up user stories and got to work.

Throughout the sprint, we emphasized the importance of monitoring and guiding each team in these new ways of working. We directed them to the playbook whenever needed to ensure they adopted new processes seamlessly.

Regular sync-ups with the leads allowed us to gather insights on the challenges team members faced. We proposed recommendations based on past experiences and the unique context of our organization, ensuring everyone felt supported and empowered.

As we progressed through our ART/Product Group's transformation journey, our ART Coach led a series of critical sync-up meetings. These meetings were essential checkpoints on our path to success. Picture the command center where we monitored the pulse of our PRP/PI plan. Daily SOS and PO syncs ensured smooth execution of our commitments, while strategic PM and Architect syncs meticulously prepared for the upcoming quarterly planning event.

Our teams were engaged in a continuous loop of feedback and foresight. We evaluated sprint-level efforts through two perspectives. First, we gauged the live action of ongoing tasks, ready to steer back on course at a moment's notice. Then, we stepped back post-sprint to analyze outcomes through a robust set of metrics. This dual perspective extended to the grand canvas of our quarterly performance, ensuring each piece fit perfectly into the larger picture.

Our discussions highlighted how product coaches transformed daily scrum rituals into powerful moments of learning and adaptation. These were not mere meetings but workshops where the art of agile was honed. The philosophy of our new product-centric model was taught and embedded into our way of working.

Mid-quarter adjustments often sprang up like challenges, testing our preparedness and agility. Together, we navigated these changes, understanding their origins, strategizing responses, and integrating these lessons to prevent future occurrences.

As we concluded the quarter with the IP sprint, it was both a reflective pause and a planning powerhouse. We merged quantitative rigor and qualitative reflections of our journey. We evaluated predictability, celebrated successes, and delved into a problem-solving workshop that tackled significant challenges head-on.

This narrative reflects our team's journey towards mastering a dynamic, product-centric world.

Meet the Management Team

Standing in the same room where, nine months ago, we faced a sea of challenges with the CXOs, I couldn't help but reflect on the journey. The room was buzzing with a different energy now, a stark contrast to the thick air of debates and discussions that once filled it. Turning to the internal agile coach beside me, I asked, "How do you feel about all this?"

With a slight chuckle, he confessed, "Scary, to be honest. Remember all those heated debates? Sometimes, it feels surreal—like, is this real or am I dreaming? The turnaround we've achieved... it's nothing short of magic."

I nodded, understanding his mix of awe and disbelief. "It's been quite the ride, hasn't it? Even though I've seen similar transformations elsewhere, the critical nature of our situation back then adds a whole different layer of amazement."

Just then, the room began to fill with the familiar faces of our leadership team—the CIO, CPO, CDO, business sponsors, and CTO. The apprehension once evident in their expressions had transformed into a shared anticipation and enthusiasm.

We exchanged warm greetings, marking the start of our meeting with a collective sense of accomplishment and readiness to tackle the agenda:

A look back at what we've accomplished.

A summary of the outcomes we've delivered.

Discussing the ongoing support we need from senior leadership.

Outlining the next steps forward.

15.1 Overview of what we have done so far:

I began the meeting by casting our minds back to the ambitious start of our journey nine months ago. "Back in Q3 2022, we set out with a clear goal—to launch two Journey ARTs," I explained. The room was filled with the key players who had seen this vision come to life. "Thanks to your unwavering leadership and the hard-earned buy-in from teams at every level, we tackled the usual teething problems of change management. It wasn't easy, but your support was pivotal."

I continued, "We executed diligently. After rounds of preparation, we rolled into our first sprint in October, turning over a new leaf in our approach to product development."

Looking around, I saw nods of agreement and smiles of accomplishment. "That week at the end of September was a milestone, marking a significant shift towards a product-centric model with launch of first PRP/PI planning."

I made sure to express my gratitude, "I can't thank you enough for helping us steer through this transformation. It's your support that has anchored this change.

Here's a visual overview of our product lines' quarterly plans, including what we've launched, what's currently in progress, and what's planned for the upcoming quarters: (next page image)

Let's take a moment to explore one of our product line launch activities and the outcomes achieved at various times: (refer page 338, 339 images)

15.2 Summary View of Outcomes Delivered

Over the past two quarters, both Journey ARTs have made significant strides, delivering numerous business capabilities that have greatly enhanced customer and merchant experiences. Each of the 16 products formed under these ARTs has consistently prepared, planned, and executed their quarterly goals.

"All our product teams, comprising roles from business, design, engineering, and more, are now functioning as a cohesive unit," I said, highlighting the team's synergy. "They've shown incredible energy and teamwork, delivering user stories every sprint with impressive consistency. When challenges arose, they didn't shy away but worked together to find and address root causes."

These 16 teams have consistently delivered value through business capabilities, each achieving its target outcomes and KPIs, thus contributing to the overall product-level OKRs. Their commitment is evident, with each team delivering their promised user story points in every sprint, maintaining an average predictability of 70 to 80%. There's been a noticeable improvement in both lead time and cycle time for delivering new features and user stories.

Here is a vivid snapshot of results from one of our standout products, "Customer Shop & Pay," a key highlight in the Customer Journey ART. (refer 340)

Retail Store Business line Product Centric Model Adoption / Scaling Product Centric Model Adoption

Product Groups	Product Group	Q4 2022	Q1 2023	Q2 2023	Q3 2023	Year 2 - 2024	Year – 2025
Customer Journey	Temp Product Group				X		
Merchant Journey	Temp Product Group				X		
Merchandizing & Planning	PG 1						
Supply Chain	PG 2						
Store Management	PG 3						
Customer Management	PG 4						
Digital Marketing	PG 5						
Data & Insights	PG 6						

Online Retail Business Line (Year 2 - 2024)

Wholesale Retail Business Line (Year – 2025)

Legend:

- First Quarterly Product Release Plan Execution
- Second Quarterly Product Release Plan Execution
- Third Quarterly Product Release Plan Execution
- All 6 product Groups of Retail Store business line will continue to develop/modernize products

From Q3 2023, both Journey ART/Product Groups were dismantled as all of those products are developed/modernized through 6 Product Groups ARTs

Timeline	Transformation Key Milestones	Expected / Actual Outcomes
2n week of May 2022	Define Enterprise Goal	Increase revenue by 3X in 3 years
1st week of June 2022	Define Retail Stores Business Line Objectives	▪ Increase revenue by 15 % YoY ▪ Improve NPS by 40% ▪ Increase operational efficiency by 30% in next 2 years ▪ Increase product Mix by 30%
2nd week of June 2022	Product Discovery – 1: Market and competitor analysis to decide what digital products to be built or refined	▪ Global airport retailing is expected to grow with 90 billion USD by 2033 ▪ Mu;tiple key players – Dufry, Gebr Heinemann, Dubai duty free, china duty free group etc. ▪ Custmer spend pattern increases 2X ▪ Customer focuses on brands that offers unique experiences ▪ Customers looking for a seamless shopping experience with minimal transaction time
3rd week of June 2022	Product Groups and products are defined	▪ Merchandize & Planning, Supply chain etc. Total 8 product Lines were defined ▪ Two Journey ARTs/product Groups were selected to launch product centric model transformation
Last week of June 2022	Define Product Vision and OKR	▪ **Reduce the average transaction time** by 40% for online purchases and in-store pickups. ▪ **Launch the boarding gate delivery service** at 20 major airports within the next quarter. ▪ **Achieve a customer satisfaction rate of 90%** for the shopping and payment experience.
3rd week of July 2022	Prioritization of Digtial Products	▪ Pilot products were selected based on prioritization WSJF score (Value Vs Effort) from Two Journey ARTs
1st week of August 2022	▪ Architecture and UX Design Decisions ▪ Start create incremental Architecture	▪ Select & Rationalize Technology products (Build or buy or Rationalize) ▪ Refine/Define Incremental Architecture & UX Design
3rd week of August 2022	Product Discovery 2 - Define Persona, Create empathy Map, journey map	▪ Customer problems captured. Current experience and efficiency baselined ▪ Captured current process and envisioned future state of process for Customer and Merchants in the context of current digital products are being used
1st week of September 2022	Define MVP – Prioritize Business Capabilities of two journey's digital products	▪ Illustrative of 8 products prioritized business capabilities are shown in Chapter 13. ▪ For example – Customer shop and Pay product : Browse & Shop online, Payment Online, order fulfillment, and real-time inventory updates are prioritized business capabilities

Timeline	Transformation Key Milestones	Expected / Actual Outcomes
From 3rd week of September 2022	Create UX Design – Analysis & Design	Example – Create UX Design for selecting payment options; Create UX design for view and select personalized products list
1st week of October to last week of December 2022	Build & Demo MVP	▪ Demo of search products, payment options, real-time sales monitoring etc. ▪ MVP evaluated against benefit hypothesis – Desirability, Viability and predictability
1st week of January 2023	Build Whole product	Continue to build additional features of Browse & shop online, Payment online related features and Initiate next set of features from new Business capabilities
2nd week of January 2023	Measure business outcome – Leading Indicator	▪ Merchandize & Planning, Supply chain etc. Total 8 product Lines were defined ▪ Two Journey ARTs/product Groups were selected to launch product centric model transformation
2nd week of April 2023	Measure business outcome – Lagging indicator	▪ **Reduce the average transaction time** by 40% for online purchases and in-store pickups. ▪ **Launch the boarding gate delivery service** at 20 major airports within the next quarter. ▪ **Achieve a customer satisfaction rate of 90%** for the shopping and payment experience.

Customer Journey ART/Product Group – Customer Shop & Pay Product			
Metrics Category	**Metrics Planned**	**Type of Metrics**	**Metrics Actuals**
Ways of working Maturity	Product team product model adoption maturity score	Leading	3.2 (in the scale of 1 to 5)
Product Outcomes	**Launch the boarding gate delivery service** at 20 major airports within the next quarter in APAC.	Leading	▪ 10 Airports
	Increase the usage of digital payment options by 50%, ensuring all popular payment methods are supported.		▪ 30% increase in customers uses digital pay options
	Achieve a customer satisfaction rate of 90% for the shopping and payment experience.	Lagging	▪ Customer Satisfaction Score 80%
Faster Delivery	▪ Lead Time to release new Feature	Leading	▪ 21 weeks
	▪ Average Cycle time for new feature		▪ 18 Weeks
	▪ Average Velocity per Quarter	Lagging	▪ 270 SPs
	▪ Average Delivery Predictability		▪ 69%
Business Outcomes	**Reduce the average transaction time** by 40% for online purchases and in-store pickups	Leading	▪ Average transaction time reduced by 15 %
	Grow the number of active users by 30% month-over-month through targeted marketing and partnerships with airlines	Lagging	▪ Number of Active customers growing by 5%

"We've compiled similar performance views for all 16 products across the two Journey ARTs," I explained to the leadership team, presenting the data. This sparked a deep discussion on data sources, calculation formulas, and strategies for further improvement.

We agreed on several action points, including continuing with Product Discovery 1 with a stronger focus on competitor analysis and integrating Gen AI to enhance outcomes. Additionally, we decided to incorporate features for telemetric data collection to automate some of the currently manual metrics measurements.

As I wrapped up the second agenda item, the room's door swung open. To my utter surprise, the CPO stepped back in, trailed by the CEO and other senior leaders, right as a roller table bearing a cake glided through the doorway. My jaw dropped—seeing the CEO was completely unexpected, and from the look on the internal coach's face, I wasn't alone in my astonishment. Applause filled the room.

The CPO beamed as he unveiled the cake, its icing proudly proclaiming, "Product Centric Model Success!!" The moment was nothing short of electric.

After the ceremonial cake cutting, it was time for feedback—a moment we all awaited with bated breath.

The CEO was the first to speak up, his voice filled with pride: "The Product Centric model we've dreamt of for the last two years is finally operational. A massive congratulations to the entire retail store business line for their unwavering dedication."

The CIO chimed in, nodding in agreement. "It's working! I've seen our technology teams function as a unit and synergize closely with other functions/ capability groups such product management."

The CDO added, "Our digital transformation initiatives are nearing their successful completion, achieving well-defined outcomes."

Then the CPO shared a particularly touching insight. "There's a noticeable shift in mindset. Just the other day, I spoke to an API developer who detailed how her work integrates with the UI developers and QA testers to ensure functionality. That's a true product mindset at play."

Business sponsors rounded off the testimonials. "My trust in our technology teams has solidified. They're delivering the business capabilities we commit to and ensuring these are driving the expected business outcomes—and they keep evolving."

15.3 Challenges and Leadership Support Needed

We conducted a retrospective with the CXO leaders to gather their insights. Next-level leaders were also involved to share their views on the transformation journey. We structured the session around four key questions: "What went well?", "What could have been better?", "What are the improvement ideas?", and "What is the action plan?"

The one-hour session was divided as follows:

First 15 minutes: Discussing and capturing "What went well" inputs.

Next 15 minutes: Identifying "What could have been better."

Following 15 minutes: Collecting improvement ideas from each leader.

Last 15 minutes: Reviewing all inputs and forming action plans.

Here's a snapshot of the outcomes from our retrospective. The action plan is especially critical as it captures all the support needed from leadership—ranging from necessary investments to their involvement in product funding decisions and their consistent engagement during product outcomes presentations. (next page)

15.4 Next Steps

Looking ahead, we laid out our next steps with clarity and determination. We decided on a monthly 15-minute governance call, strictly to monitor the progress of these actions and ensure the necessary support for their implementation.

Moreover, buoyed by our success, we agreed to extend the product-centric model to the Online Retail business line starting Q1 2024. We've already brought stakeholders from this line into the fold, involving them in vital events from PRP/PI planning to demos and outcome presentations. Their enthusiasm is palpable—they're geared up and ready to embark on their own product-centric journey. This step marks a progression and a promising expansion of our transformative efforts.

As we gear up to roll out the product-centric model to the Online business line, we're looking at a dynamic structure that bridges distinct needs across multiple sectors. Imagine two main arteries pumping vitality into our business: one that caters exclusively to specific business lines—think of a product team crafting tailored business capabilities that are specific to a business line—and another, a common technology portfolio that builds digital products designed to support multiple lines with essential services like merchandising, planning, and supply chain management that can be leveraged by multiple business lines including retail

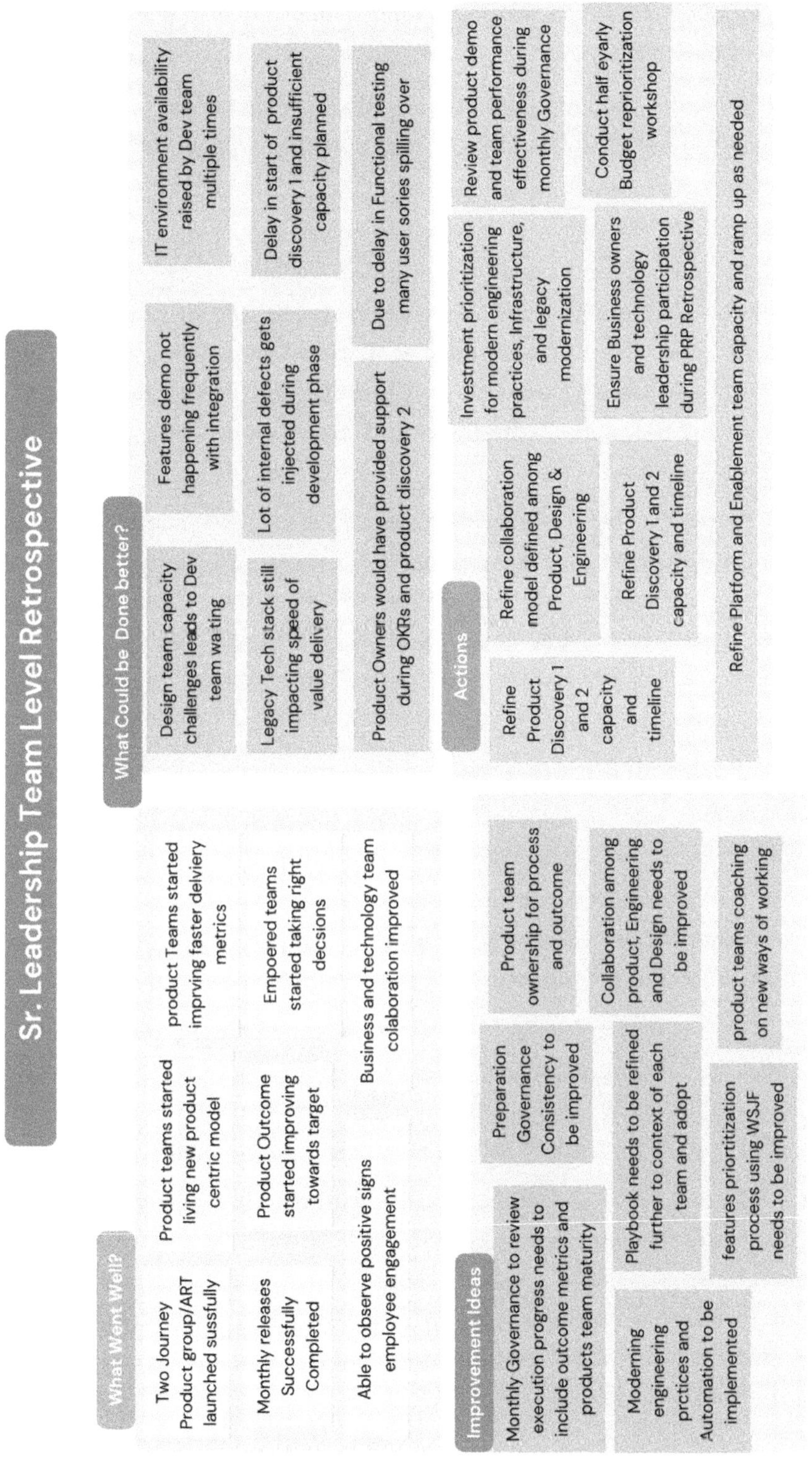

Sr. Leadership Team Level Retrospective

What Went Well?

Two Journey Product group/ART launched sussfully

Product teams started living new product centric model

product Teams started imprving faster delviery metrics

Monthly releases Successfully Completed

Product Outcome started improving towards target

Empoered teams started taking right decsions

Able to observe positive signs employee engagement

Business and technology team colaboration improved

What Could be Done better?

Design team capacity challenges leads to Dev team wa ting

Features demo not happening frequently with integration

IT environment availability raised by Dev team multiple times

Legacy Tech stack still impacting speed of value delivery

Lot of internal defects gets injected during development phase

Delay in start of product discovery 1 and insufficient capacity planned

Product Owners would have provided support during OKRs and product discovery 2

Due to delay in Functional testing many user sories spilling over

Improvement Ideas

Monthly Governance to review execution progress needs to include outcome metrics and products team maturity

Preparation Governance Consistency to be improved

Product team ownership for process and outcome

Moderning engineering prctices and Automation to be implemented

Playbook needs to be refined further to context of each team and adopt

Collaboration among product, Engineering and Design needs to be improved

features priortitization process using WSJF needs to be improved

product teams coaching on new ways of working

Actions

Refine Product Discovery 1 and 2 capacity and timeline

Refine collaboration model defined among Product, Design & Engineering

Investment prioritization for modern engineering practices, Infrastructure, and legacy modernization

Review product demo and team performance effectiveness during monthly Governance

Refine Product Discovery 1 and 2 capacity and timeline

Ensure Business owners and technology leadership participation during PRP Retrospective

Conduct half eyarly Budget reprioritization workshop

Refine Platform and Enablement team capacity and ramp up as needed

stores, online retail, and wholesale retail. These portfolios are called Centralized Digital Organizations.

We're not just stopping there. Picture us also carving out a robust platform for products and capabilities that all segments can tap into. This includes everything from login and authentication systems to KYC and omnichannel services—tools that streamline and unify our customer experiences across the board.

The strategy is to inspire innovation while ensuring efficiency, and to do this, we're planning to bring together the heads of our Online and Wholesale segments. We'll lay out a compelling business case for a shared 'Platform & Product Capabilities' portfolio. This meeting is a crucial step towards knitting together a cohesive, powerful framework that leverages common strengths while celebrating unique needs.

Before our big meeting, the Internal Agile Coach and I took a moment to catch our breath and lay the groundwork for our discussion. It was a chance to reflect on our journey and prepare for the discussions ahead. We structured our recap around four pivotal areas: what we've achieved, the outcomes so far, the challenges faced, and the support we need from leadership. Finally, we outlined our forward steps in transforming towards a product-centric model.

We started with a rundown on the progress: the ARTs and product groups we've launched across the retail store business line, and our plans to introduce this model to the online retail sphere next.

Then, we delved into the fruits of our labor—the tangible outcomes. This was about the maturity we've gained in our product-centric approaches, the acceleration in delivering value, and the positive shifts in our business results.

The leadership-level retrospective was especially revealing. We discussed the hurdles we've encountered and the kind of leadership backing essential for tackling future challenges. We listened as senior leaders shared their candid feedback: what's worked, what hasn't, and what adjustments could propel us forward.

To cap it off, we outlined our forward march: deploying this model to the online retail line and discussing how we'll deliver vital products and capabilities through two clusters of product groups/ARTs. Plus, we introduced an ambitious plan to create a new portfolio for platforms and capabilities—a third cluster designed to forge reusable products and tools.

Measuring Outcomes: What We Delivered

Exactly nine months have passed since our product-centric transformation journey began with that vital meeting with the CIO. It's been a roller coaster, full of highs and lows. Back then, convincing the leadership team that we had a problem and that the 12 PM product-centric model was the best solution was a major hurdle. We've faced numerous challenges at various stages of transformation, from different levels of the organization.

Despite these obstacles, we've celebrated milestones along the way. We've created a blueprint of our current state, envisioned our future state, defined a set of Product Lines/ARTs, and kicked off our first quarterly planning for two journey ARTs with a clear set of products. We've successfully executed the PRP/PI plan. Now, we stand at the threshold of measuring the outcomes achieved at the end of this first quarterly plan.

Our progress and success can be seen from four key perspectives:

Right Ways of Working: We've adopted the product model ways of working at both the product team level and the product line/ART level.

Faster Delivery: Our product teams and product lines have proven their ability to deliver value more rapidly.

Right Products: We've hit our product OKRs, demonstrating that we're delivering the right outcomes.

Right Business Strategy: By achieving these product OKRs, we've also met our broader business objectives.

16.1 Embracing the New Ways of Working

It's essential that everyone on the team and across product lines fully adopts our new product-centric model. Moving away from the old ways and consistently embracing the new methods is critical for the transformation's success. For us to deliver product business capabilities faster and achieve our product OKRs, every member—from the Business Owner to each team member—must implement these new practices consistently.

Over the past six months, both Journey ARTs and their 16 related product teams have implemented practices from product strategy and road mapping to delivering MVP features. Now, it's time to measure how well these new ways of working have been adopted, establish a baseline for maturity, and identify areas for improvement.

To do this, we leveraged the Measure and Grow assessment framework from SAFe, customizing some questions to fit our organization's context, product lines, and practices.

I scheduled a meeting with the individual product line stakeholders. The internal coach and I prepared thoroughly, setting the expectation that the product line coach would lead the discussion. All product line leads and product team leads were invited.

The product line coach opened the meeting with a clear purpose. "Today's goal is to understand and embrace the self-assessment process, a critical step towards enhancing our approach to product development," she began, outlining the steps we'd be taking together.

First, she explained, we'd walk through the expectations for the self-assessment, which we were covering in this very meeting. Next, each lead would conduct their assessments independently, reflecting on their team's behaviors, data from ALM tools, and the quality of their deliverables.

"Once you've completed your assessments offline, we'll gather and consolidate your insights," she continued. This would lead to a follow-up meeting where all leads would present their findings and together, brainstorm improvement actions to update our transformation backlog.

16.1.1 Understanding Self-Assessment Expectations

During this meeting, the product line coach walked everyone through the SAFe framework toolkit questions, explaining how to respond based on observations of team behaviors, data from ALM tools, and reviews of team and ART/product line deliverables.

"We want you to look at these questions through the lens of your daily experiences," she explained. "Consider how your teams behave, the data you see, and the deliverables you produce."

The leads were expected to review these assessment questions offline and provide their responses. This included:

Product Team Leads: PO, UX Lead, Engineering Lead, and Product Coach.

Product Line/ART Leads: Lead Product Manager, UX Lead, Engineering, and Product Line Coach.

Once the responses were collected, a maturity score for each core competency as per SAFe, and an overall maturity score for the team and product line, would be calculated.

The coach emphasized the following points when responding to each question:

What does this statement mean in our context?

Do we understand why this is a desired state?

Is it part of our current transformation plan?

Whose responsibility is it?

What changes to our existing processes would be needed to bring this about?

"Think about these questions critically," she urged. "This is not just a box-ticking exercise. Your insights will help us understand where we stand and what we need to improve."

After completing the responses, each lead shared their assessment sheets with the ART and product team coaches, who would then create consolidated views for both the product line and product team levels. The product team coach was assigned to lead the consolidation and analysis efforts. The meeting lasted two hours and ended smoothly.

"What if there are conflicting responses from the leads?" someone asked.

"We'll discuss those differences during our analysis meeting and align on the responses through consensus," the ART coach replied. "For example, if the product manager says yes and the engineering lead says no, we'll hear the reasons from both sides and come to an agreement."

Everyone agreed to submit their responses within a week.

16.1.2 Offline Self-Assessment by Product and Product Line Leads

Each lead then conducted their offline assessment, going through the SAFe framework questions individually. They marked their responses as YES (process fully adopted), NO (process not adopted at all), PARTIAL (process partially adopted), or NOT APPLICABLE, based on their observations of team behavior, data from ALM tools, and other relevant metrics.

After completing their assessments, the product team leads sent their responses to the product coach, while the product group/ART leads sent theirs to the ART/product group coach.

Gathering and Consolidating Self-Assessment Inputs

A week later, each product team coach and product group coach received the responses and created a consolidated view. This involved compiling all the inputs to form a comprehensive picture of the current state.

"Let's review the consolidated assessments," the product team coach said, "and identify any discrepancies we need to address."

What we're looking at is a snapshot view for one product team, based on a sample set of questions: (next page)

Here's a look at one Product Group level, using a set of sample questions to guide us:

16.1.4 Deliberating on Self-Assessment Outcomes

A week after collecting everyone's assessments, the product group and team coaches sat down to hash out the details. This wasn't just any meeting; it was a deep dive into how each team and product line saw themselves in the mirror of their day-to-day operations. The room was divided into separate clusters for product lines and teams, each camp setting out on a two-hour journey to sift through their competencies assessments.

"Why are we seeing different answers to the same questions?" one lead asked as discrepancies popped up.

Through discussions, the leaders unpacked the reasons behind each divergent viewpoint, working tirelessly to reach a mutual understanding and consensus. By the end of these intense sessions, they had agreed on definitive answers: YES, NO, PARTIAL, or NOT APPLICABLE, aligning their perspectives into a unified front.

Stage	Outcome	Capability	Description	Acceptance Criteria	Product Team
Start	Team Formed & Multiskilled	Clear Team Purpose	Team has clearly defined goals with an aligned set of expectations enabling autonomy. They understand how their work ties into the larger whole.	Team members are able to articulate the value their team is chartered to provide Team members understand the customer-focused vision their work helps the larger organization realize Team members understand, can articulate, and played a part in the creation of their Team's mission to help realize the larger vision The Team understands the factors that make up their success	YES
		Stakeholders Identified	The team should know who has a stake in the outcome of the products they are building and who sets the direction.	The Team understands who the their Stakeholders are The Team understands the difference between those who are "Interested" and those who are "Invested" Team Members understand and are empowered to redirect Stakeholders to the appropriate roles, e.g., Product Owner or Scrum Master	NO
		Roles Fulfilled	Team roles and responsibilities are clearly defined, assigned, and understood by all.	Team members understand the roles Team members understand the responsibilities of each role Team members understand their new role, or how their existing role has changed Team members understand the roles other members of their team have in their new way of working Each role has someone who is fulfilling that role	PARTIAL
		Working Agreements	Setting expectations around the way members of a team prefer to work together creates a foundation of openness and accountability from the start. These should be regularly revisited.	The Team has working agreements published for how they will work and collaborate The Teams' values are defined and agreed upon (courage, listening, edification, etc.) The Team agrees on the process and events it will follow The Team agrees on the criteria for a backlog item to be considered Done The Team has a clear definition for what criteria must be met to be ready to start work on a backlog item	YES

Stage	Outcome	Capability	Description	Acceptance Criteria	Product Group
Start	Teams Aligned to Value	Value Streams Identified	The ways in which value is delivered and how it flows is understood.	All places where work originates have been identified Incoming work is characterized to identify major types, groupings, percentages, etc. All steps to complete that work have been identified All places where work is delivered have been identified	NO
		Teams Aligned to Value Streams	Cross-functional teams have been created for the value streams with minimal dependencies and handoffs.	Skills and people needed to complete different types of work has been determined Cross-functional teams have been created Teams have been grouped appropriately to deliver value in targeted value stream Team grouping minimizes dependencies and handoffs outside of the value stream Consensus achieved on new org model aligned around value	YES
		Clear Value Proposition	The needs of the market and/or stakeholders define the teams purpose and guide value delivery.	Key stakeholder or market success drivers are known Team members can articulate their team's value proposition Measures of success are defined	YES

At last, we achieved a unified perspective of our product line, as illustrated below:

Product Group

88%	Teams Aligned to Value	Detail & Notes	65%	Ability to Measure	Detail & Notes	17%	Ability to Forecast	Detail & Notes	55%	Faster Time to Value	Detail & Notes	60%	Product Funding	Detail & Notes
86%	Product Stratgey Defined	Detail & Notes	81%	Cross-Team Coordination	Detail & Notes	65%	Product Discovery	Detail & Notes	71%	Product Outcomes Measured	Detail & Notes	62%	product Group level Governance	Detail & Notes
90%	Product OKRs and Roadmap Defined	Detail & Notes	75%	Teams are Long Lived & Empowered	Detail & Notes	33%	Multi-Team Predictability	Detail & Notes	65%	Modern Engineering Practices	Detail & Notes	71%	Product centric Model Extended	Detail & Notes

Each product team should have its own maturity assessment:

Product Team

76%	Teams are formed & Multiskilled	Detail & Notes	86%	Product Defined	Detail & Notes	85%	Predictable Delivery	Detail & Notes	65%	Faster Delivery	Detail & Notes	73%	Product Continuously Evolved	Detail & Notes
75%	Team Collaboration	Detail & Notes	75%	Product Ownership	Detail & Notes	67%	Quality Feedback Locp Shortened	Detail & Notes	25%	Release Continuously	Detail & Notes	85%	Customer Centered	Detail & Notes

16.1.5 Brainstorming Improvement Actions and Updating the Transformation Backlog

With a consensus in place, the team didn't skip a beat, planning another meet-up just a few days later. This brief interlude gave the lead coaches just enough time to dig into the root causes of the less-than-satisfactory responses and to brainstorm potential improvements.

Armed with their findings, they reconvened for a focused brainstorming session. One by one, they tackled each problematic area, laying out the underlying issues and proposed actions.

"Let's dissect these PARTIAL responses—what's really going on here?" a lead coach proposed, initiating a robust discussion that went beyond surface-level fixes.

Together, they debated and refined their strategies, ensuring every suggestion was robust enough to tackle the core issues.

Following the deep dive in our analysis meeting, we've pinpointed key root causes and mapped out improvement actions across three critical phases: preparing for quarterly planning, the planning process itself, and its execution. (next page)

We decided to tackle our improvement actions with a sharp eye on their value versus the effort they required, using the SAFe WSJF method to prioritize them. This method helps us see which actions will give us the biggest bang for our buck. We all agreed to keep a close watch on how these actions progress during our regular governance meetings at both the product line and product team levels.

16.2 Faster Delivery

In a crucial meeting that included the internal coach, product line coach, product team coaches, and myself, we dived into the flow metrics dashboard reflecting the performance of our first quarterly plan. The meeting, which lasted two hours, revolved around the team-level and product line-level dashboards (as discussed in Chapter 14).

We laid everything on the table—the good, the bad, and the metrics in between. "One major issue causing longer cycle times," noted one coach, "is the number of manual activities from code check-in to production deployment. This includes manual pull request processes, environment unavailability, and manual testing."

Illustrative Examples: Quarterly Planning Preparation Phase Observations & Improvements

Sr. No.	Observations	Root Causes	Improvement Actions
1	Consistency in defining discovery related objectives in every quarter to prioritize Features for N+1 quarter	Product leads spent their most of the capacity to current quarter execution	Define product leads capacity needed for for current quarter execution and next quarter preparation
2	Improve Feature definitions & sizing and to fit in one quarter	Product group following in consistent guideline to estimate feature based on historical data	Redefine feature sizing guideline based on historical data.
3	Consistency in adoption of WSJF for all Products feature prioritization to be improved	Product group's understanding on prioritization process needs improvement. Contextualization of WSJF also not very suitable to product group	Refine WSJF guideline in context to the product group. Train Product groups on refined WSJF Guideline
4	Optimize timeline for features prioritization and refinement and complete design at least one sprint	Timeline defined for quarterly planning preparation activities were not followed	Product group leads needs to be coached and mentored on need for following timeline
5	Consistency in Product 2 discovery and getting feedback from customer on released features needs to be improved	Product discovery 2 effectiveness needs to be improved. Considerable effort is not planned to receive customer feedback	Product discovery capacity needs to be increased based on past quarter effort to improve effectiveness and plan sufficient time for customer interaction & feedback

Illustrative examples: Quarterly Planning Phase Observations & Improvements

Sr. No.	Observations	Root Causes	Improvement Actions
1	Consistency in planning features release dates needs improvement based on market and internal milestones	Features release dates were not decided taking into consideration of external and internal milestones/expectations	Define features release dates in collaboration with internal and external stakeholders
2	Improve risks and dependencies alignment	Risks and dependencies were not identified with broader perspectives considerations	Risks and dependencies needs to be identified taking into consideration of impacted systems (upstream & downstream) and based on discovery inputs
3	Refinement of user stories meeting DOR criteria for at least N+2 Sprints needs to be improved	Product teams did not spend enough time for backlog refinement during IP sprint. Backlog processes effectiveness needs to be improved	Product coaches ensure that allocated effort for quarterly preparation fully utilized by the teams. Product teams needs to be coached on the backlog refinement process
4	Consistency in Features definition and meeting DOR criteria needs to be improved	Feature template was not adopted consistently	Product group leads and Product manager need to be trained and guideline to update feature as per template needs to be prepared
5	Quarterly PRP/PI plan scope changes during planning event needs to be minimized	Enough discovery work to finalize features and its prioritization was not done	Product group leads needs to be coached on the feature definition and prioritization, it impact of changes during planning event

Illustrative Examples: Product Teams Level Observations & Improvements

Sr. No.	Observations	Root Causes	Improvement Actions
1	Number of incomplete user stories that gets moved to next sprint that needs to be minimized/eliminated	▪ User stories size 8 SP or above ▪ Focusing on individual team members utilization rather than team velocity ▪ Most of the user stories development gets completed on day 7th onwards ▪ Leads pursuing estimation instead of team estimating user stories ▪ IT environment unavailability ▪ Unplanned leaves from team members	▪ Implement User stories Splitting techniques. It should be sized 1 to 3 or 5 SP. ▪ Adopt industry best practice of measuring team performance as team velocity, not individual velocity ▪ Estimate story size in the range of 1 to 3 or max 5 SP, to start deliver user stories from day 2 or onwards during sprint execution ▪ Forecast 7 plan leaves ahead and explore possibility of having flex associates at product group level ▪ Improve environment availability through automation/service virtualization
2	Sprint retrospectives are conducted. Tracking improvements actions for its closure and reviewing it during next sprint retrospective needs to be improved	▪ No defined approach for tracking the improvement actions implementation and its outcome ▪ Not all team members are actively participating to share feedback and implementation ▪ Lack of consistency in adopting tracking and reviewing implementation effectiveness	▪ Standardize retrospective tracking approach with improvement backlog, add and track user stories in JIRA ▪ Add an agenda of reviewing previous sprint improvement actions progress status in every sprint ▪ Measure effectiveness/outcome of improvement actions implemented ▪ Product team members needs to be coached on retrospective process and need for their active participation with role play examples

There were several such issues leading to longer cycle times. We agreed to perform a detailed development value stream mapping exercise, covering everything from feature ideation to deployment. This would help identify bottlenecks, wait times, and non-value-added activities. We also decided to conduct SAFe DevOps training for all leads across teams and the product line.

For each flow metric, we discussed the challenges and aligned on possible improvement actions.

An illustrative overview of flow metrics at both the team and product line levels:

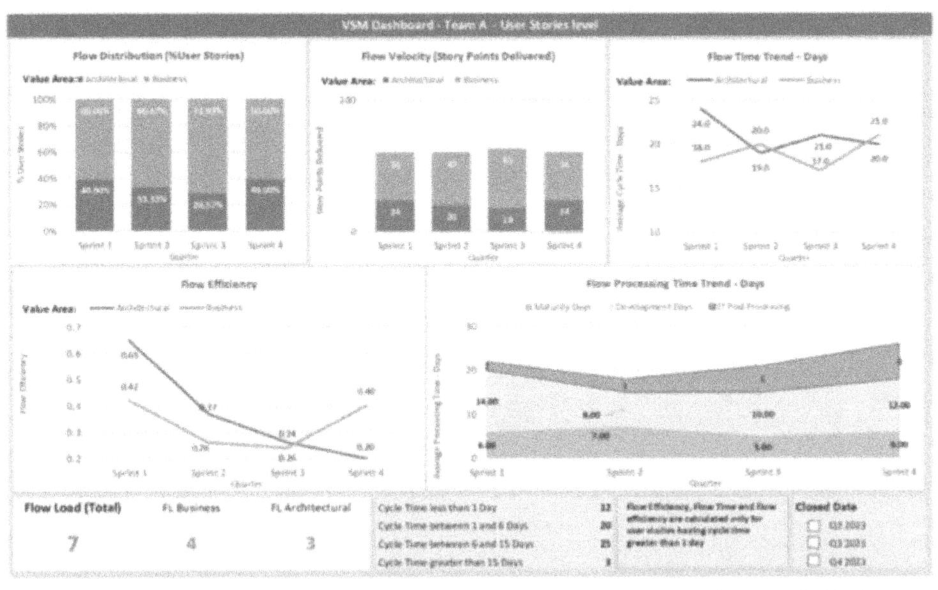

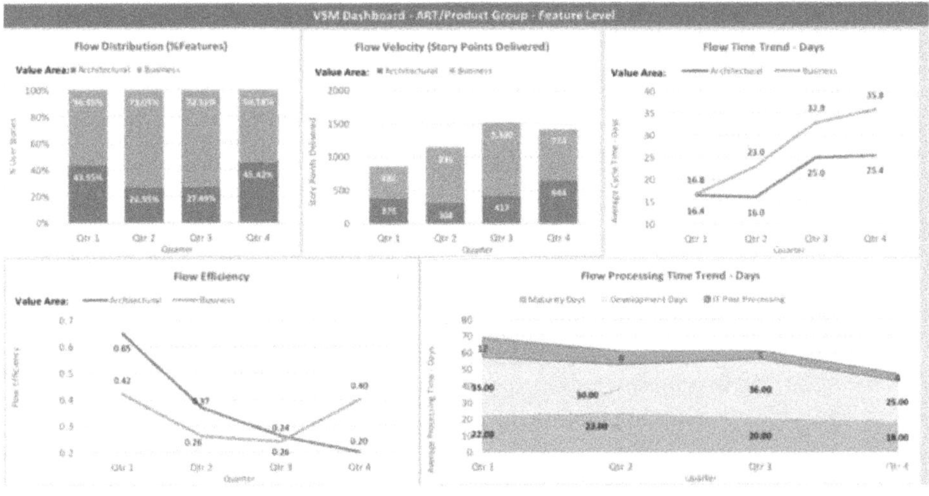

The following actions were pinpointed to enhance flow metrics:

Possible Challenges List	Type	Recommendations Mapping	Impacting Processes
Absence of Test Management Process	Process	R19	Development & testing
Features remain in feature planning stage for a longer duration	Process	R6,R33	Feature planning
SIT is not completed in the same sprint; And UAT is not completed within n+1 sprint	Process	R45, R84, R85	Development & testing
UAT is completed against the entire flow vs incrementally delivered pieces	Process	R46	Development & testing
Internal process delays movement from UAT sign off to Production release	Process	R35, R98	Product delivery
Security Scans are time consuming	Process	R35	Product delivery
Implementation Innovation and Planning (IP) sprint is not practiced	Process	R48	Product delivery
There is no collaboration between the Business , IT and other stakeholders in the identification and prioritization of epics/features	People	R7	Ideation
Technical feasibility is not arrived collaboratively	People	R16	Design
High level estimates are not arrived collaboratively and does not consider all impacted systems and unknowns (if any)	People	R10	Ideation
Capacity planning and funding is not carried out at Program/product line level to measure value delivery	People	R12	Feature planning
Less collaboration between teams resulting in rework and waiting time to deliver user stories and features	People	R27,R30,R28,R37	Development & testing
The team members are not multi-skilled such as design,dev,test (SIT & UAT) etc. to deliver features/user stories independently	People	R36	Development & testing
Feature/PI/quarterly planning does not include all relevant stakeholders that leads to reprioritization/rework/increased cycle time	People	R14	Feature planning
All agile practices such as planning, daily standup, backlog refinement, demo and retrospectives are not followed effectively	People	R39	Development & testing
Coordination between developers and testers is less	People	R22,R28,R37	Development & testing
Lack of process knowledge in the team	People	R36,R37	Development & testing
The size of the release/number of user stories is higher than what the team can handle /team's velocity	People	R11,R12	Feature planning
Identification of higher defects during UAT phase/ Post Production	People	R23,R19	Development & testing
Role clarity at program and team level can be improved	People	R37	Product delivery
Applications are not decomposed as products/service to improve cycle time for change implementation	Tech	R8	Ideation
There is no end to end traceability of the intake request that leads to lack of alignment from epics to user stories	Tech	R2,R4	Intake

ID	Recommendations	Type	Priority	Metrics	Process level
R21	Define a Dev/Test Data Management process	Process	2	CT,LT,P	Development & testing
R22	Implement CA - TDM for seamless test data management	Tech	3	DF	Development & testing
R23	Groom the user stories at least one sprint before development ; Document user stories using industry best practices such as 3Cs, INVEST	Process	1	CT,LT,DF,P	Development & testing
R24	Involve all related stakeholders in the User story grooming session	People	1	CT,LT,P	Development & testing
R25	Document the capabilities/Epics/Features/ user stories adequately by adopting best parctices and minimize changes at later stages	Process	2	CT,LT	Feature planning
R25	Implement RMS Azure , Jira Align etc. For better requirement tracking Utilize ideation in JIRA align to enter and prioritize intake of work	Tech	3	CT,LT,P	Intake
R27	Establish dependency between teams at User story level	Process	2	DF	Feature planning
R28	Establish Process/ Guidelines for multiple teams to work together	People	1	CT,LT,DF,P	Product delivery
R29	Identify risks and have a mitigation plan for each quarterly/PI/feature planning	Process	3	CT	Feature planning
R30	Establish quarterly/PI/feature objectives and create program board	Process	1	CT,LT,P	
R31	Implement PCF/GCP/Azure cloud strategies for environment management	Tech	3	DF	Development & testing
R32	Increase Test Automation across testing (Unit, SIT , UAT) . Extend automation to enabler features as well	Tech	3	CT,LT,DF,P	Development & testing
R33	Conduct periodic reviews to analyze the business value delivered at all levels as applicable (user story/feature/epic)	Process	2	CT,LT,P	Product delivery
R34	Implement Devops (Release and Build Automation)	Tech	2	CT,LT,P	Development & testing
R35	Automate Change Management process using GLAPI	Tech	3	CT,LT	Product delivery
R36	Impart trainings , Upskill and Cross Skill the team	People	2	CT,LT,P	Product delivery
R37	Clearly define and implement roles and responsibilities at program and teams level	People	1	DF,P	Product delivery
R38	Define and track metrics like velocity/burn up/predictability/feature and user story cycle time etc. to improve performance	Process	2	CT,LT,DF,P	Product delivery
R39	Follow all agile practices such as planning, daily standup, backlog refinement, demo and retrospectives effectively	Process	1	P	Product delivery
R40	Enter intake in Jira Align only after gaining commitment from business	Process	1	P	Intake
R41	Coach/Improve teams understanding on the various stages from intake to product delivery	People	2	P	Product delivery
R42	Define and implement standard ideation process	Process	1	CT,LT,P	Ideation
R43	Restructure team to be cross functional	People	3	CT,LT,P	Product delivery

As a coaching team, we set our priorities, agreed on the implementation timeline, and decided to review progress during product line and product team governance meetings.

I shared examples of how we monitor flow metrics trends every quarter at both team and product line levels. "Here's an example of our development value stream mapping (VSM) exercise," I said, pointing to the visuals depicted below. "

And this is our future state of the development value stream.

I continued, "By addressing all bottlenecks and leveraging the automations from our SAFe DevOps course, this is what our future state will look like." The above chart I presented outlined the seamless journey from feature ideation right through to release, illustrating a streamlined development value stream energized by our proposed improvements.

Another example of VSM implementation to optimize user story cycle time is illustrated below:

We achieved the future state of our Value Stream Mapping (VSM) by smartly integrating Generative AI and other automation tools within our DevOps pipeline. This comprehensive approach spans from code generation all the way to customer release and includes several innovative steps. We use Generative AI, specifically Large Language Models (LLM), to create code that meets the specific needs outlined in user stories and acceptance criteria. To ensure quality, we automate the creation and execution of unit test cases using Continuous Integration (CI) tools. The code review process is streamlined through automated static code analysis tools, and the merge request (MR) process is automated, triggering only after successful code reviews and unit tests. Once merged, we set up automated builds and integration. Quality assurance isn't left behind; we incorporate automated functional QA within the CI/CD pipeline, ensuring that every aspect of the software is tested. The deployment process is also automated, smoothly transitioning the software into staging and production environments. Finally, we automate the release process to customers, incorporating a feature toggle option to manage the deployment of new features smoothly. This holistic approach ensures a seamless transition from code generation to customer release, enhancing efficiency and reducing the time to market.

Future State – Process Flow

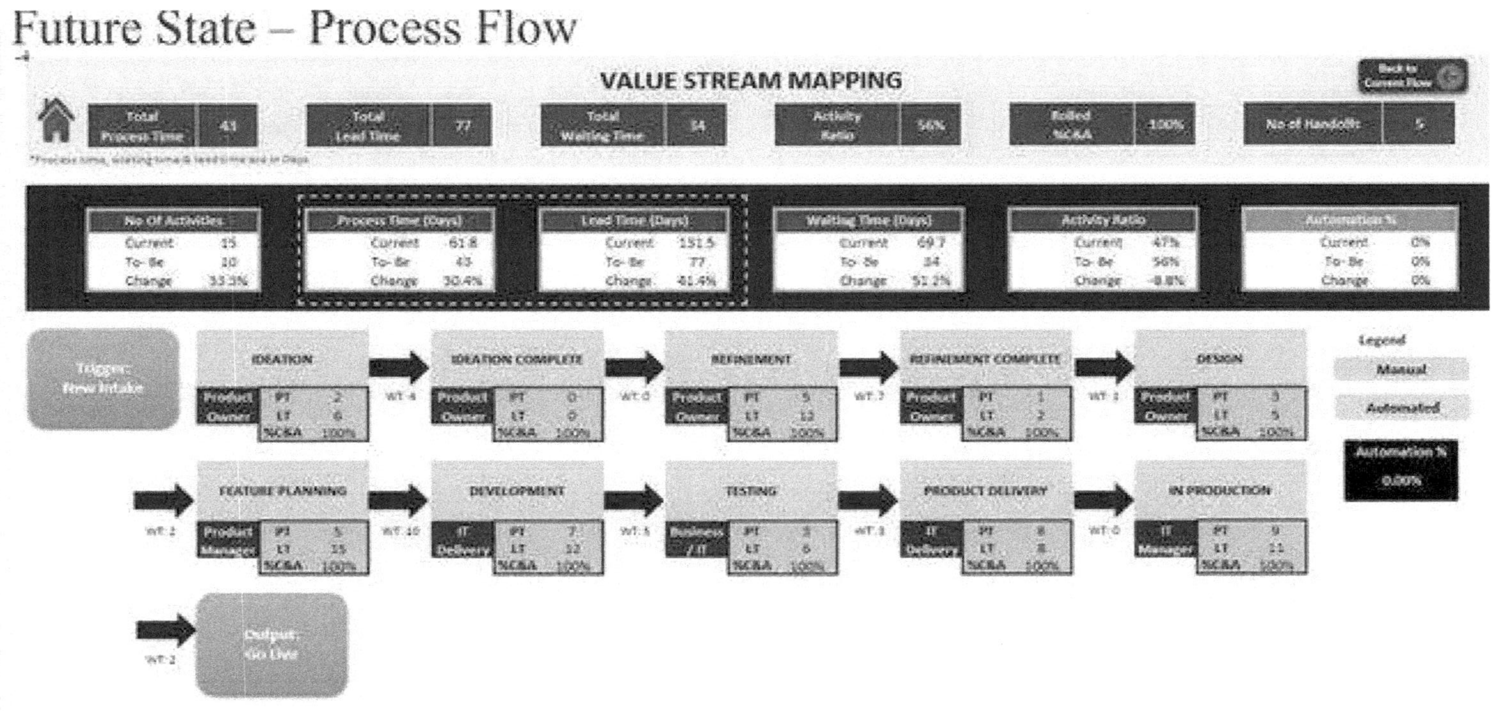

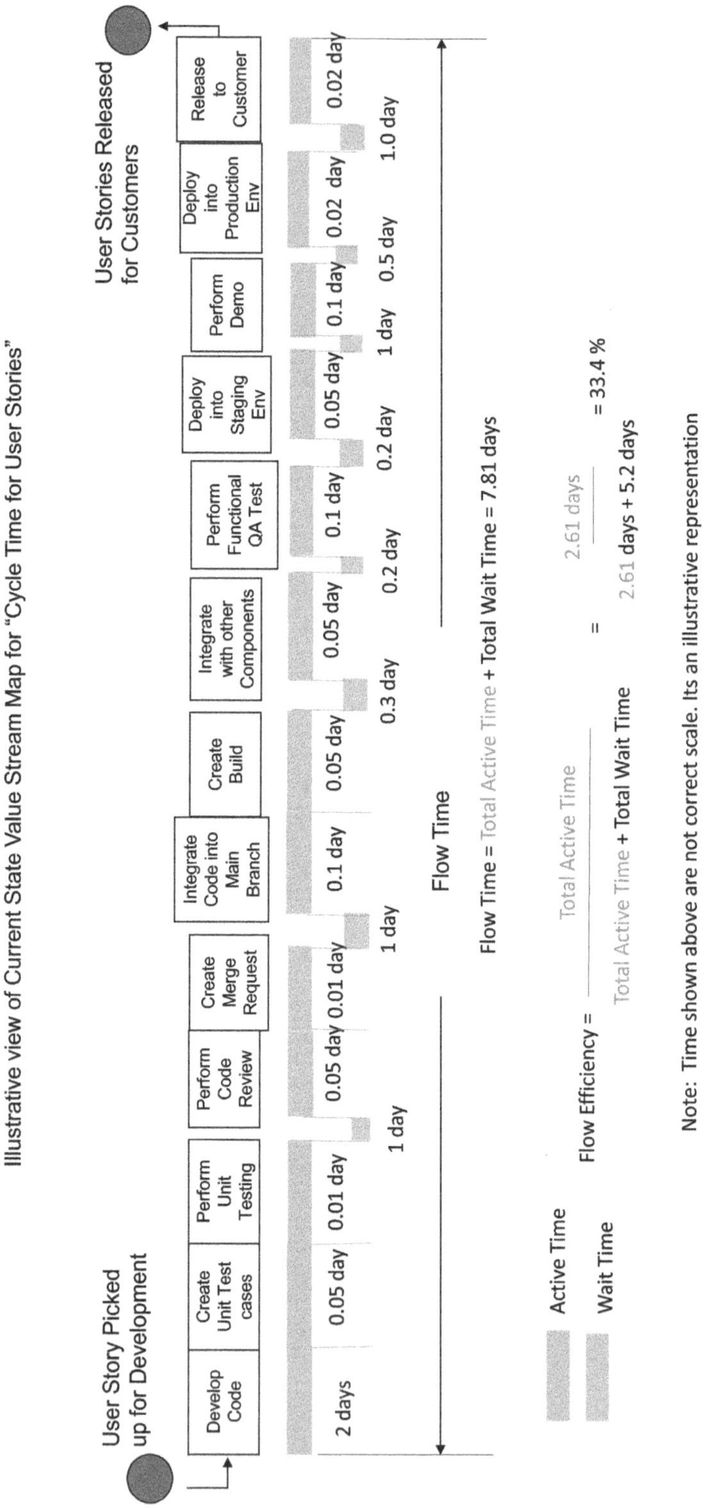

Illustrative view of Current State Value Stream Map for "Cycle Time for User Stories"

Illustrative view of Future State Value Stream Map for "Cycle Time for User Stories"

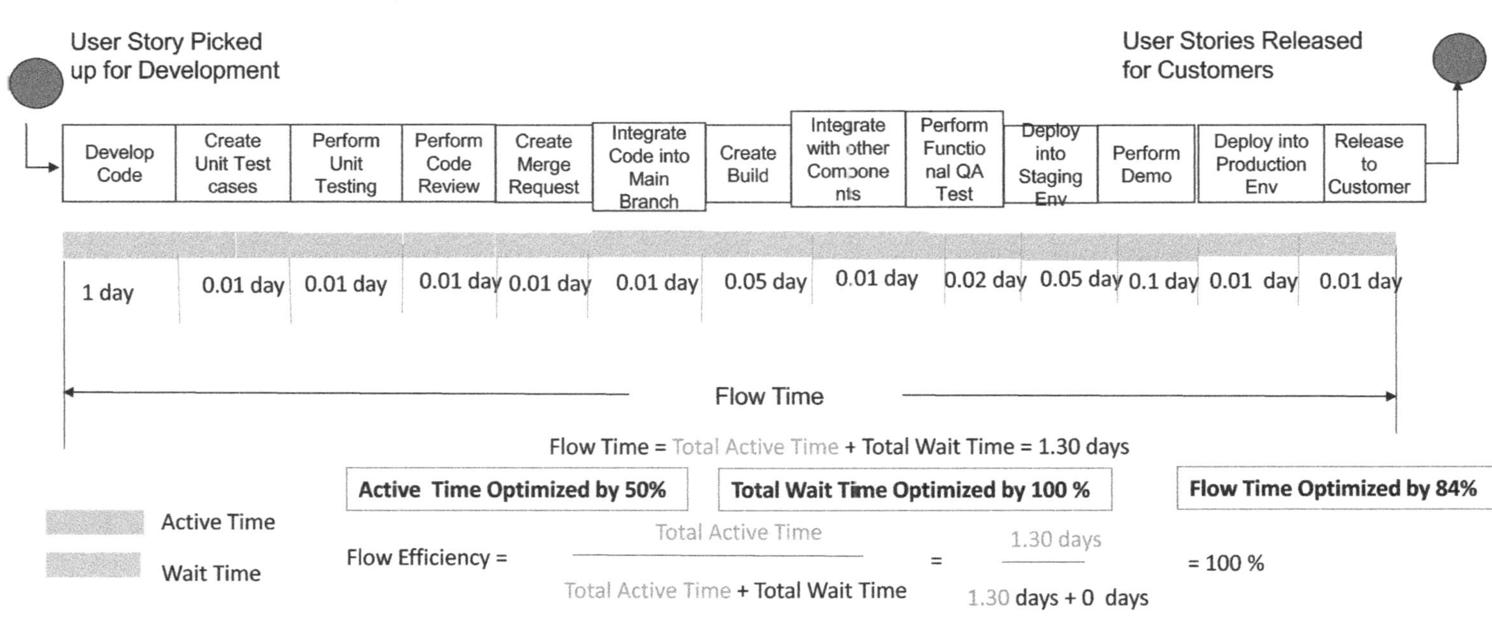

$$\text{Flow Efficiency} = \frac{\text{Total Active Time}}{\text{Total Active Time} + \text{Total Wait Time}} = \frac{1.30 \text{ days}}{1.30 \text{ days} + 0 \text{ days}} = 100\,\%$$

Note: Time shown above are not correct scale. Its an illustrative representation

Together, the coaching team and the leads affirmed the need to monitor flow metrics at various levels rigorously. We discussed the methodologies to measure these metrics effectively, the tools we would employ like VSM to pinpoint improvement opportunities, and the strategies to accelerate the speed of value delivery.

16.3 Product OKRs

The entire coaching ensemble—encompassing product team coaches, product group coaches, product management, product owners, and business owners—gathered for a pivotal product OKRs and outcomes review meeting. Before this, the product teams and coaching staff had delved deep in offline sessions to dissect the OKRs: what we aimed for versus what we achieved, and the reasons for any deviations. These findings set the stage for today's dynamic discussion.

Here's a snapshot of what we unpacked in those preparatory meetings: We sifted through product metrics tracking both outcomes (lagging indicators) and KPIs (leading indicators).

For leading indicators, we looked at:

Usage of new functionalities by merchants hit 70%, while 60% of store managers leveraged them.

A striking 75% of customers interacted with personalized product recommendations. These metrics, captured through telematic data, were showcased on our dashboards.

We also pinpointed areas needing a boost, such as enhancing communication about the launch of new business capabilities and augmenting training with more intuitive video and screen navigation guides.

As for the impact on operational times (lagging indicators):

Merchants saw end-to-end processing times slashed from 6 minutes to a brisk 2 minutes per order.

Customers enjoyed a streamlined shopping experience, with personalized recommendations cutting down their browsing time from 10 minutes to just 3.

Store managers benefited significantly, with daily inventory management time reduced from 30 minutes to 5.

We delved into the revamped business process flows, especially post-implementation of new epics and business capabilities in Replenishment and 3rd Party Logistics (3PL) products. For instance, with the roll-out of "smart inventory management" and "smart order creation," we charted a much-improved business process flow and journey map from the merchants' perspective, marking substantial strides in efficiency and user experience.

Without these two capabilities, the current merchant journey, as depicted below, faced numerous barriers and was time-consuming, from order creation to managing order delivery confirmation: (refer next page image)

Before Implementation:

Average Time Per Purchase Order: 6 minutes

Issues: Multiple barriers, time-consuming processes from order creation to delivery confirmation.

After implementing these two business capabilities, the merchant journey experienced significant improvements, as detailed below. This saved effort and enhanced their overall experience.

After Implementation:

Average Time Per Purchase Order: Optimized to 2 minutes

Telemetry: These capabilities were integrated with telemetry, allowing us to capture and display this reduced time on our dashboards.

Efficiency Gain: A significant 150% increase in efficiency for the merchant journey.

We didn't stop there. We measured similar efficiency gains across other merchant journeys and different personas, such as customers and store managers. The improvements were averaged to calculate an overall efficiency gain for the Retail Store business line, which came out to an impressive 9%.

Implementing just a few digital capabilities for these two products led to a 9% efficiency gain. Imagine the potential if we modernized all business capabilities across every product in our end-to-end business operational value stream. Such enhancements would optimize overall operational costs and significantly improve profit margins.

Current Merchant Journey Map

	LOGIN	ANALYZE PRODUCTS	VIEW PRODUCTS & BRANDS	VIEW CONTRACTING INFORMATION	CREATE, REVIEW & SUBMIT PURCHASE ORDER	RECIEVE EMAIL FROM SUPPLIER	EMAIL RECEIVED FRM 3PL	PRODUCTS RECEIVED BY 3PL	MERCHANTS RECEIVES CONFIRMATION	MERCHNATS REVIEW STORE FORECAST	MERCHNAT ISSUE ORDER TO 3PL	PRODUCTS RECEIVED BY STORES	MERCHANTS RECEIVES CONFIRMATION
OBJECTIVES	To securely access the merchant portal	To understand customer preferences and product performance	To gauge market trends and brand popularity	To review terms and conditions of supplier agreements	To procure products efficiently	To get updates on products delivery	To get updates on logistics and delivery	To accept delivery of goods	To confirm receipt of goods	To predict future sales and stock needs	To initiate delivery to stores	To ensure stores receive their orders	To finalize the delivery process
NEEDS	Easy and secure login process	Detailed analytics tools and reports	Market research data and comparison tools	Easy access to current and past contracts	Streamlined purchase order process	Clear communication from supplier	Clear communication from third-party logistics	Timely and accurate delivery	Simple confirmation process	Accurate forecasting tools	Efficient order system to 3PL	Confirmation of delivery and stock integrity	Acknowledgment of successful delivery
FEELINGS	Expectation of a hassle-free entry	Curiosity about trends and customer behavior	Desire to stay competitive and informed	Vigilance in maintaining favorable terms	Responsibility to ensure accuracy and best terms	Hassle free update supplier that products are ready to send	Anticipation of timely updates.	Relief upon receiving expected shipments.	Satisfaction of completing a transaction	Concern for future business planning	Urgency to keep stores stocked	Assurance that stores are ready for customers	Contentment with the completed process
BARRIERS	Complex login procedures, forgotten passwords	Lack of comprehensive data, poor analytics interface	Inaccessible market data, overwhelming information	Disorganized contract management, outdated information	Cumbersome PO creation, approval delays	Delay in communication or updates	Miscommunication, email delays or spam filters	Delivery errors, damaged goods	Inefficient confirmation systems	Unreliable forecasting, unpredictable market conditions	Inefficient ordering process, 3PL delays	Inventory discrepancies, store receiving issues	Delayed or missing delivery confirmations.

	LOGIN	ANALYZE PRODUCTS	VIEW PRODUCTS & BRANDS	VIEW CONTRACTING INFORMATION	CREATE, REVIEW & SUBMIT PURCHASE ORDER	RECIEVE EMAIL FROM SUPPLIER	EMAIL RECEIVED FRM 3PL	PRODUCTS RECEIVED BY 3PL	MERCHANTS RECEIVES CONFIRMATION	MERCHNATS REVIEW STORE FORECAST	MERCHNAT ISSUE ORDER TO 3PL	PRODUCTS RECEIVED BY STORES	MERCHANTS RECEIVES CONFIRMATION
OBJECTIVES	To securely access the merchant portal	To understand customer preferences and product performance	To gauge market trends and brand popularity	To review terms and conditions of supplier agreements	To procure products efficiently	To get updates on products delivery	To get updates on logistics and delivery	To accept delivery of goods	To confirm receipt of goods	To predict future sales and stock needs	To initiate delivery to stores	To ensure stores receive their orders	To finalize the delivery process
NEEDS	Easy and secure login process	Detailed analytics tools and reports	Market research data and comparison tools	Easy access to current and past contracts	Streamlined purchase order process	Clear communication from supplier	Clear communication from third-party logistics	Timely and accurate delivery	Simple confirmation process	Accurate forecasting tools	Efficient order system to 3PL	Confirmation of delivery and stock integrity	Acknowledgment of successful delivery
FEELINGS	Biometric authentication (fingerprint or facial recognition) to eliminate password dependency	AI-driven analytics dashboard that automatically compiles and presents customer data trends	Real-time market data integration within the portal, providing instant brand consumption patterns	Cloud-based contract management system with smart notifications for renewals and changes	Automated PO generation based on inventory levels, with one-click approval and digital signatures	Direct integration of 3PL systems into the merchant portal for real-time updates and alerts	Direct integration of 3PL systems into the merchant portal for real-time updates and alerts	Relief upon receiving expected shipments.	Satisfaction of completing a transaction	Predictive analytics tools that use historical data and AI to forecast future sales and stock requirements	Automated order system that schedules deliveries based on predictive analytics and store requests	Automated inventory management systems that confirm and restock products upon reception	Automated confirmation alerts to merchants once stores confirm product reception

16.4 Right Business Strategy

In the context of achieving our business objectives, we closely monitored both leading and lagging indicators. However, truly understanding the impact of our new business capabilities meant playing the waiting game—observing the tangible results unfolded over months, not just at the quarterly finish line.

Leading Indicators:

With the implementation of the smart order creation capability, we saw significant improvements in our leading indicators:

Forecast Accuracy: We achieved a 95% accuracy rate between planned product purchases and actual sales at our stores.

Customer Footprints: The availability of new products and brands, based on customer spending patterns, increased the number of customer visits.

These metrics were measurable soon after a few features were released mid-quarterly plan execution.

Lagging Indicators:

We also observed positive changes in our lagging indicators:

Sales Increase: There was a 2% overall sales increase in our North American retail stores.

Merchant Satisfaction: The smart order capability, which considered customer spending patterns by product and brand, ensured that all purchased products were sold. This boosted merchant satisfaction, as reflected in an improved NPS score from 65 to 75.

It's essential to note that the full influence of new features on business objectives can only be measured over time. For example, an increase in sales of new products and brands can be consistently measured over 3 to 4 months following the rollout of the smart order feature. Only then can we identify patterns of repeated sales of specific products and understand their impact on overall sales and revenue.

So with just a few new business capabilities across two products, we saw remarkable improvements. Persona-level journeys became more efficient, overall operations saw a boost, revenue from sales increased, and both merchants and store managers reported higher satisfaction scores.

Thanks to inbuilt telemetry, we eliminated manual effort in measuring these metrics, enhancing both their accuracy and reliability. This means we can confidently rely on these metrics to make well-informed decisions.

On Presentation Day, we showcased the outcomes achieved in these four key areas over a 45-minute session. Here's a summary of the metrics we hit by the end of the quarterly plan execution:

Right Ways of Working Summary Metrics: Showcasing metrics at the Product Group level and Product Teams level.

Illustrative View: Right Ways of Working Product Teams Maturity Overall Summary: Customer Journey Teams				
S.no.	Category	Metrics	Parameters	Metrics value
1	Right ways of working – Product Level	Customer Journey ART/Products maturity score	Product line 1 (8 Digital Products that influences Customer journey)	65%
		Merchant Journey ART/Products maturity score	Product line 2 (8 Digital Products that influences Merchant journey)	68%

Illustrative View: Right Ways of Working Product Teams Maturity Summary Team level: Customer Journey Teams									
Sr. No.	Parameters	Product Team 1	Team 2	Team 3	Team 4	Team 5	Team 6	Team 7	Team 8	Overall Average
1	Teams are formed & Multiskilled	76%	45%	28%	56%	86%	65%	70%	45%	58%
2	Team Collaboration	75%	82%	65%	80%	45%	70%	68%	56%	67%
3	Product Defined	86%	65%	75%	82%	45%	50%	67%	82%	69%
4	Product Ownership	75%	43%	56%	72%	45%	50%	82%	25%	56%
5	Predictable Delivery	85%	54%	67%	67%	25%	45%	48%	58%	56%
6	Quality Feedback Loop Shortened	67%	75%	70%	67%	83%	76%	63%	58%	69%
7	Faster Delivery	65%	87%	57%	65%	66%	82%	54%	75%	68%
8	Release Continuously	25%	75%	58%	45%	65%	74%	80%	65%	60%
9	Product Continuously Evolved	73%	57%	67%	73%	54%	81%	73%	86%	70%
10	Customer Centered	85%	82%	60%	85%	78%	54%	84%	68%	74%
	Overall Average	71%	66%	60%	69%	59%	64%	64%	61%	65%

1 to 25% - Red	26 to 84% - Amber	85 to 100% - Green

Illustrative View of One of the 16 Products: Highlighting Right Ways of Working, Faster Delivery, Product OKRs, and Business Metrics. (next page)

We created similar views for all 16 products that were modernized through the two ARTs/Product Groups.

At the end of each section—like Right Ways of Working or Delivery Speed Metrics—I paused and asked if there were any questions. But there were none. The room was silent, everyone just observing. I couldn't help but wonder: Did I present everything correctly? Was the improvement not as impressive as I thought? My mind buzzed with uncertainty.

After my presentation wrapped up, the room erupted into applause. It wasn't just any applause—it lasted a full minute, rich with enthusiasm and pride. The

Customer Journey ART/Product Group – Customer Shop & Pay Product			
Metrics Category	**Metrics Planned**	**Type of Metrics**	**Metrics Actuals**
Ways of working Maturity	Product team product model adoption maturity score	Leading	71%
Product Outcomes	**Launch the boarding gate delivery service** at 20 major airports within the next quarter in APAC.	Leading	10 Airports
	Increase the usage of digital payment options by 50%, ensuring all popular payment methods are supported.		30% increase in customers uses digital pay options
	Achieve a customer satisfaction rate of 90% for the shopping and payment experience.	Lagging	Customer Satisfaction Score 80%
Faster Delivery	Lead Time to release new Feature		14 weeks
	Average Cycle time for new feature	Leading	12 Weeks
	Average Velocity per Quarter		270 SPs
	Average Delivery Predictability	Lagging	69%
Business Outcomes	**Reduce the average transaction time** by 40% for online purchases and in-store pickups	Leading	Average transaction time reduced by 15 %
	Grow the number of active users by 10% Quarter over Quarter through targeted marketing and partnerships with airlines	Lagging	Number of Active customers growing by 5%

business sponsors, product managers, and other key leaders were visibly moved by the tangible results we'd just shared. It was more than metrics on a screen; it was proof of our collective hard work becoming real, impactful change.

From the beginning, setting the right strategy, choosing the right products, and defining the best ways of working were steeped in challenges. Yet, here we were, having tackled these challenges head-on and seen through them to this point of celebration.

The excitement was palpable as they recognized the advancements in adopting the product centric model, though everyone acknowledged that there was still much room for improvement. The journey was ongoing, and the commitment to continuous enhancement was clear. They noted the accelerated value delivery, evidenced by improved flow metrics and the fruitful outcomes of our development value stream mapping, which pinpointed and addressed critical bottlenecks.

The influence of refined product OKRs was undeniable, enhancing the efficiency of end-to-end persona journeys and business processes. This improvement was not just procedural but profoundly financial and cultural. We saw a positive surge in overall revenue and sales growth and significant boosts in merchant and store manager NPS scores.

The leaders of both Journey ARTs and product lines were buzzing with excitement over the achievements of the past nine months and eager for what the upcoming quarters would bring. This was a defining moment for the retail store business line. The two newly formed Journey ARTs, pioneers in this transformation, were now shining examples for the entire organization. Their success marked a major milestone in our transformation journey, setting a high standard and a path forward for everyone involved.

The illustrative view below shows the maturity of one product's outcomes and how it has improved over the course of one year. This improvement was achieved through the incremental implementation of new business capabilities, functionalities, or modernization: (next page)

Reflecting on this moment felt fitting—it was a time to celebrate and truly grasp the transformation we had achieved. The objective of this chapter was to measure and communicate the outcomes of our product-centric model implementation from different perspectives. We focused on four key perspectives, each revealing a layer of our success.

Customer Journey ART/Product Group – Customer Shop & Pay Product			Metrics Actuals			
Metrics Category	Metrics Planned	Type of Metrics	Q1	Q2	Q3	Q4
Ways of working Maturity	Product team product model adoption maturity score	Leading	71%	75%	80%	88%
Product Outcomes	**Launch the boarding gate delivery service** at 20 major airports within the next quarter in APAC.	Leading	10	15	25	50
	Increase the usage of digital payment options by 50%, ensuring all popular payment methods are supported.		30%	35%	45%	65%
	Achieve a customer satisfaction rate of 90% for the shopping and payment experience.	Lagging	80%	80%	90%	95%
Faster Delivery	Lead Time to release new Feature (in weeks)	Leading	14	14	13	12
	Average Cycle time for new feature (in weeks)		12	11	11	9
	Average Velocity per Quarter	Lagging	270 SPs	300 SPs	280 SPs	350 SPs
	Average Delivery Predictability		69%	75%	83%	88%
Business Outcomes	**Reduce the average transaction time** by 40% for online purchases and in-store pickups	Leading	Reduced by 15 %	Reduced by 20 %	Reduced by 35 %	Reduced by 45 %
	Grow the number of active users by 10% Quarter over Quarter through targeted marketing and partnerships with airlines	Lagging	5%	10%	28%	40%

We delved into the various processes adopted at both the product team and product group levels. This wasn't just about following procedures; it was about embracing a new way of thinking and operating. We measured the adoption levels—whether they were fully adopted (YES), partially adopted (PARTIAL), not adopted at all (NO), or not applicable. Each team's and group's process adoption was assessed, and maturity scores were calculated. This gave us a clear picture of where we stood and where we needed to improve. Together, we identified and agreed on improvement actions to elevate our maturity in adopting the product-centric model processes.

We celebrated the speed at which our teams delivered value. We examined flow metrics, capturing and measuring data at both the team and group levels. These metrics highlighted our strengths and revealed areas needing attention, such as increased cycle times for user stories. We didn't shy away from discussing these challenges. Instead, we brainstormed and outlined possible improvement actions to enhance our delivery speed.

We dove into how our product OKRs had significantly improved, especially from an efficiency standpoint. We took a closer look at the Smart Order product, designed to enhance the merchant journey. By implementing a couple of business capabilities, this product demonstrated remarkable efficiency and effectiveness gains. We explored the merchant journey before and after these implementations, showcasing the tangible improvements and the positive impact on their experience.

We examined how our business objectives were achieved by delivering the right products and meeting their OKRs. Using a set of leading and lagging indicators, we measured outcomes like increased sales and improved Merchant and Store Manager NPS scores. These metrics highlighted our success in aligning product delivery with our strategic goals.

We wrapped up this chapter with a resounding acknowledgment from all leaders and team members. The product-centric model had empowered our retail store business line to adopt, define, and deliver the right products more efficiently, ultimately achieving our business objectives. This holistic success was not just an internal triumph but was recognized and celebrated by everyone across the retail store business line. The journey had its challenges, but the results spoke volumes about our collective effort and dedication.

Way Forward

After a game-changing meeting with management, where we celebrated our achievements and set a bold agenda for the next 12 months, it's time to dive into the dynamic shifts planned for our retail store business line. We're not just riding the wave of success—we're pushing the boundaries further.

17.1 Launch PRP/PI for all Product lines

Building on the solid foundation laid in previous chapters, we're rolling out quarterly product release planning and execution across all product lines. Remember the excitement when we launched the initial two journey-related products? We're replicating that success across the board. By the end of the ninth month, we had already set in motion two additional ARTs for Merchandise & Planning and Supply Chain in the first quarter of 2023. Leaders and teams from these lines underwent intensive SAFe training and jumped head-first into a three-day quarterly planning marathon.

With the dawn of Q2 2023, we embarked on an ambitious expansion by launching four more ARTs/Product groups: Digital Marketing, Store Management, Customer Management, and Data & Insights. These groups underwent comprehensive SAFe training, touching on every role to ensure a solid foundation for their upcoming challenges.

During a packed three-day quarterly planning session, the leaders and teams from these new groups were more than just participants—they were keen observers, learning the ropes. They absorbed everything from how to prepare and present, to understanding the crucial outputs needed by the close of the third day. While they geared up for their inaugural planning session, our first two product lines weren't resting on their laurels; they were deep into the preparations for their second quarterly sprint.

The image below captures the essence of our approach: all six product lines marching in lockstep, synchronizing their efforts as they prepared for the quarterly showdown. (next page image)

Current State Products Group, Products for Retail Stores with Development Value Streams & ARTS, Agile Teams
Trigger:
Customer Needs
to Buy Products
at Airport
Value:
Customer buy their products Faster and Cheaper
Analyze Customer Patterns
Attract Customers
Finalize Products & Decide Products
Forecast & Plan
Procure & Receive Products
Purchase Products by Customer
Pickup in Stores/Deliver at Boarding Gate
Analyze and Improve
Provide Post Sales Support
Value:
Retails products Sales & Commission Revenue
Digital Marketing
Merchandising & Planning
Supply Chain
Store Management
Customer Engagement
Data & Insights
Customer Spend Analysis
Products Market Trend
Digital Merchandizing
Warehouse Management
Store Planning
Store Inventory
Loyalty Management
Multichannel Management
Campaign Mgmt
Financial Planning
Replenishment
SC Operations Management
Transportation Management
Store Product Analysis
Partner Engagement
Store Performance Analytics
Customer Behavior Analytics
Master Data Management
Marketing Insights
3 PL Logistics
Store Sales management
Customer Dashboard
Supplier Dashboard
Competitor analysis Dashboard
AGILE RELEASE TRAIN
AGILE RELEASE TRAIN
1st ART – Merchandizing & Planning ART
2nd ART – Digital Engineering ART
3rd ART – Supply Chain ART
4th ART – Store Management ART
5th ART – Customer Engagement ART
6th ART – Data & Insights ART
Agile Team 1
Agile Team 2
Agile Team 3
Agile Team 4
Agile Team 5
AGILE RELEASE TRAIN
7th ART – Platform ART

Here's a snapshot of the groundwork laid by each team:

Conducted thorough market analysis and SWOT assessments tailored to their respective products.

Pinpointed new business capabilities and epics ripe for modernization.

Crafted a dynamic epics Kanban view to streamline management across the retail business line.

Developed crisp product visions and OKRs.

Mapped out epic-level roadmaps for each product.

Business capability leaders put forth compelling business cases which, after rigorous review by our Portfolio Leadership Team (LPM), received the green light.

Updated epic-level product roadmaps following approvals or necessary rejections.

Kicked off incremental architecture efforts for top-priority epics.

Began decomposing approved epics into features, with UX design teams starting their magic in the Discovery 2 phase.

After our teams completed the rigorous preparation phase, the leaders of each logical cluster—three in total—convened for a critical pre-quarterly planning sync-up. They dissected priorities, analyzed impacts, and untangled dependencies, setting the stage for what was to come.

With this groundwork laid, we launched into action: initiating four new product lines/ARTs with their first quarterly planning session, while concurrently managing the second quarterly planning for the first two established product lines.

As the landscape of our product groups evolved, the original journey ART product teams were either seamlessly integrated into existing product teams or transformed into new ones within their respective product groups. This reorganization was driven by the strategic alignment of team skills and product needs, ensuring a smooth transition and enhanced focus on delivery.

The structuring of our product groups and ARTs followed three strategic options:

Option 1: Specific product teams dedicated to our retail stores business line were grouped into one cluster, forming one or more ARTs based on the complexity and number of products involved. This configuration aimed at concentrated efforts on specific retail-related functionalities.

Option 2: A more unified approach was adopted for products and business capabilities utilized across all business lines, forming a comprehensive technology portfolio/ Centralized Digital Organization. This included the six product groups ranging from Digital Marketing to Data & Insights. Within this setup, ARTs were either organized by business lines to balance priorities effectively or by business capabilities, where multi-skilled teams were responsible for delivering features to all business lines, managing a scalable product log within each team.

Option 3: Representing a centralized strategy, the 7th ART, known as the Platform ART, was designated as a distinct portfolio. This team was tasked with designing, developing, delivering, and maintaining reusable platforms, products, and capabilities.

For Option 1 and Option 3 products, the funding will come directly from the retail business line. This means the retail store business line will provide the necessary funds. As we scale Option 3 from a single platform ART to a centralized portfolio (which we'll discuss in section 17.4 of this chapter), the funding will shift to come from a common organizational fund shared by all business lines.

For Option 2, the portfolio will request an annual budget from all business lines based on the planned digital initiatives, products and capabilities. Additionally, if specific products or capabilities are needed for a particular business line, that business line will provide separate funding.

The view of delivering digital products across these three options unfolds like this: (next page image)

Here's how the product teams are organized:

Option 1: Product teams are grouped as product groups, funded, and owned by their respective business lines.

Option 2: Product teams are grouped into a centralized portfolio to deliver digital products for all business lines.

Option 3: Product teams are grouped into platforms/product groups and form a centralized portfolio to deliver common reusable products and capabilities.

All business lines need digital products from these three options. However, it's up to the organization to decide how to build and deliver these digital products. They can follow one of these operating models:

Operating Model 1: A combination of decentralized (Option 1) and centralized (Option 2 and Option 3). In this model, some digital products are

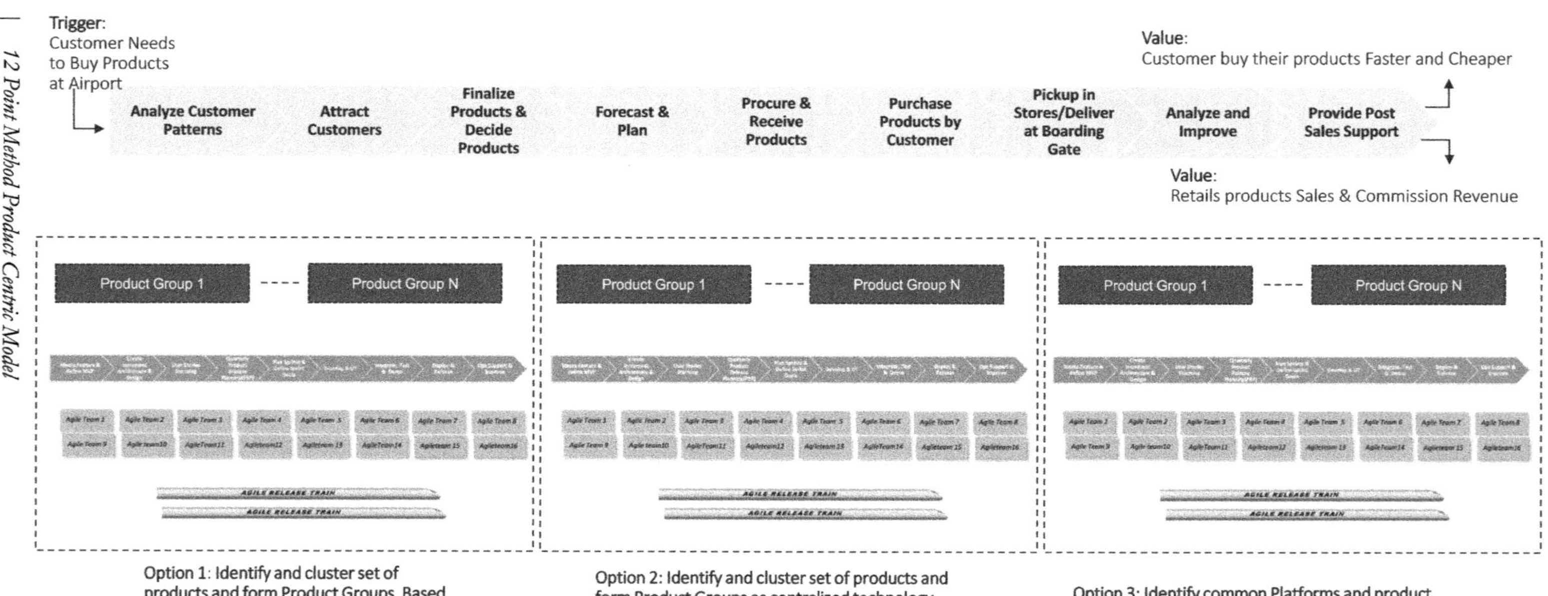

Option 1: Identify and cluster set of products and form Product Groups. Based on number of product groups and its complexity, number of ARTs will be decided

Option 2: Identify and cluster set of products and form Product Groups as centralized technology Portfolio. Based on number of product groups and its complexity, number of ARTs will be decided. This centralized portfolio will deliver digital products to all business lines

Option 3: Identify common Platforms and product that can be reused by all Business lines. Set up as a centralized Portfolio that will deliver only reusable platforms, products and capabilities

Note: Each business line needs digital products from all three options to get all required digital products to manage end to end business operations at optimal cost with faster time to market built internally by the business lines, while others are provided by two centralized portfolios/ digital organization.

Operating Model 2: Fully decentralized, where all digital products from the three options are built by the respective business lines themselves. This is how we began our product-centric digital transformation journey for the retail stores business line.

Operating Model 3: Fully centralized, where all digital products from the three options are provided through centralized portfolios only.

Based on what I've observed across various industries, many organizations gravitate towards Operating Model 1. This choice stems from its ability to boost market speed, cut costs and redundancies, and ensure a consistent customer experience.

For Operating Model 1 and 3, leadership under the Chief Digital Officer (CDO), supported by CPOs and CIOs, steers the ship. In contrast, under Option 2, CPOs have a direct line to the business leadership team, embedding themselves more deeply with the strategic direction of their respective lines.

No matter the operating model a company opts for, the structure of product teams and groups remains consistent, as we dissected in chapter 10.3. Imagine each product group as a nimble startup within a vast network, all rolling up into a broader portfolio. The size and scope of these portfolios adjust based on the number of product groups each model supports.

Setting up Options 1 and 2 involves aligning product groups, DVS, and ARTs in a manner similar to what we've seen earlier in this chapter. However, Option 3 shifts the paradigm slightly. It introduces a centralized Platform ART designed to support a singular business line. This centralized hub aims to pinpoint and deploy common products and business capabilities that all product lines can utilize, ensuring efficiency and coherence across the board. This strategic alignment not only cuts down redundancy but also scales up reusability and cost efficiency, all while enhancing the customer experience and speeding up the introduction of new products and capabilities.

Here's a snapshot of the platform view: (next page image)

Once the platform ART model shows its mettle within the "retail store business," the next move for Option 3 is grander. We're planning a centralized portfolio that crafts and dispenses common products and capabilities, serving

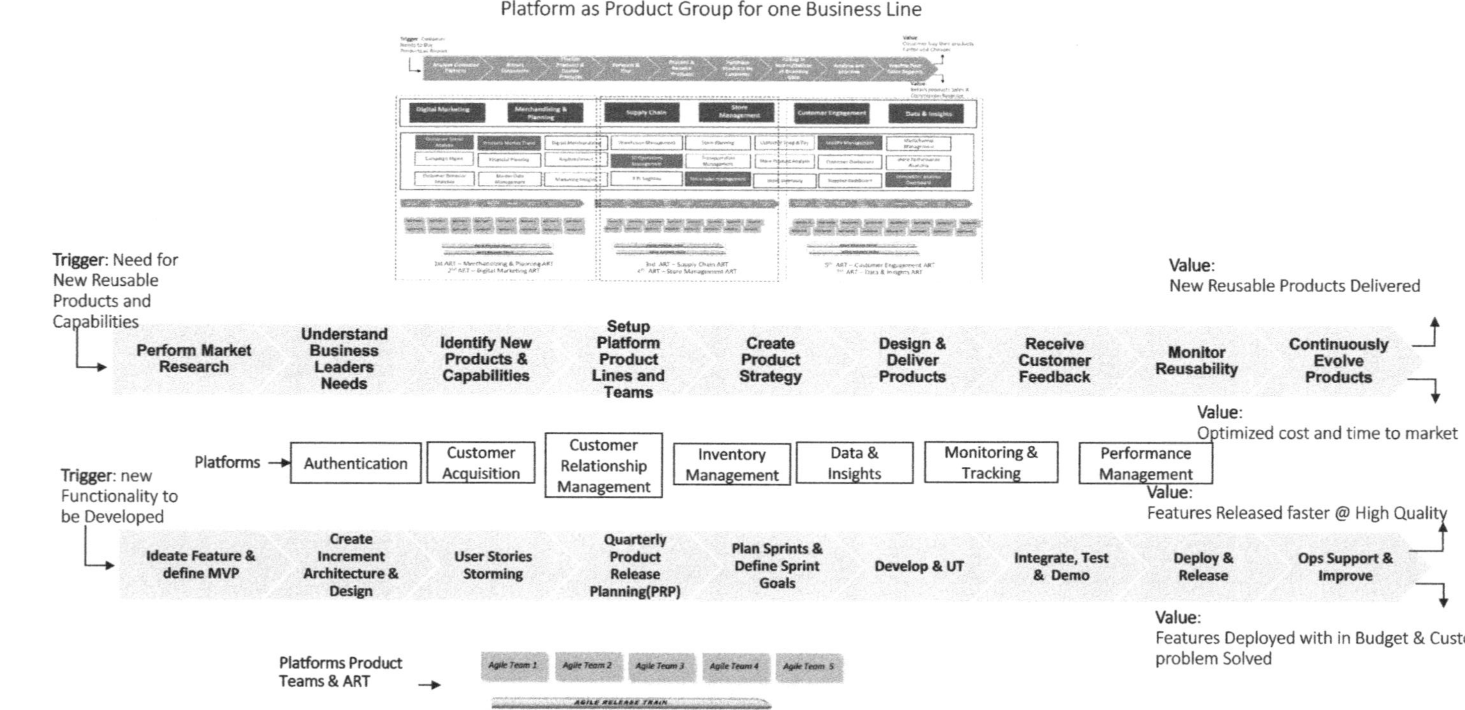

Platform as Product Group for one Business Line
Trigger: Need for New Reusable Products and Capabilities
Perform Market Research
Understand Business Leaders Needs
Identify New Products & Capabilities
Setup Platform Product Lines and Teams
Create Product Strategy
Design & Deliver Products
Receive Customer Feedback
Monitor Reusability
Continuously Evolve Products
Value: New Reusable Products Delivered
Value: Optimized cost and time to market
Platforms
Authentication
Customer Acquisition
Customer Relationship Management
Inventory Management
Data & Insights
Monitoring & Tracking
Performance Management
Value: Features Released faster @ High Quality
Trigger: new Functionality to be Developed
Ideate Feature & define MVP
Create Increment Architecture & Design
User Stories Storming
Quarterly Product Release Planning(PRP)
Plan Sprints & Define Sprint Goals
Develop & UT
Integrate, Test & Demo
Deploy & Release
Ops Support & Improve
Value: Features Deployed with in Budget & Customer problem Solved
Platforms Product Teams & ART
Agile Team 1
Agile Team 2
Agile Team 3
Agile Team 4
Agile Team 5
AGILE RELEASE TRAIN
Digital Marketing
Merchandising & Planning
Supply Chain
Store Management
Customer Engagement
Data & Insights
1st ART – Merchandising & Planning ART
2nd ART – Digital Marketing ART
3rd ART – Supply Chain ART
4th ART – Store Management ART
5th ART – Customer Engagement ART
6th ART – Data & Insights ART

them up as reusable assets for the whole organization across all business lines. This expansive strategy is laid out in more detail in section 17.4 of this chapter.

17.2 Launching a Sub Business Line Within Retail Stores:

In the world of retail, a fresh business opportunity has emerged, tapping into a new customer behavior—shopping with zero upfront payment. Recent market analysis reveals a shift from saving to spending, especially noticeable during peak shopping periods like festivals and year-end sales. It turns out, a whopping 45% of customers whip out their credit cards for these purchases.

Seeing this trend, retail store leaders are springing into action. They're setting up a brand new sub-business line focused solely on this burgeoning opportunity. This isn't just a minor addition; it's like launching a mini business within the larger retail framework. It will have its own funding, its own profit and loss accounts, and its own dedicated team.

The goal is to lure in that 45% of shoppers with enticing "retail loans" offered through strategic partnerships with multiple banks.

To boost sales and revenue by drawing in customers looking to purchase products without needing cash upfront, retail stores might consider delving into the following business opportunities:

Retail Loans Business Opportunities Exists in the market

Business Opportunity	Opportunity Description
Partnership with Financial Institutions	Collaborate with banks and non-banking financial companies (NBFCs) that offer zero-interest EMI options. This can be a significant draw for customers who prefer to spread their payments over time without additional costs
Digital Payment Solutions	Implement digital payment platforms that support EMI transactions. Ensuring seamless integration with popular payment gateways can enhance the customer experience
Marketing Campaigns	Run targeted marketing campaigns highlighting the availability of zero-interest EMI options. This can be done through social media, email marketing, and in-store promotions.
Loyalty Programs	Introduce loyalty programs that reward customers for using the EMI option, which can encourage repeat business

Business Objectives for Retail Loans Sub business line

Business Objective	Target
Rollout "ZERO Cost EMI"	50+ Airports in 1st year; 200+ Airports in 2nd year; 1000+ Airports in 3rd year
Revenue Target	100 mn USD in 1st year; 300 mn USD in 2nd Year and 500 mn USD in 3rd year

Digital initiatives for Retail stores entering the zero-interest EMI loan market include

Digital Initiatives	Opportunity Description
E-commerce Integration	Develop an online shopping platform that supports EMI transactions.
Mobile App Development	Create a mobile app that allows customers to manage their EMI plans and payments.
Data Analytics	Use data analytics to understand customer purchasing patterns and tailor EMI options accordingly.
Customer Relationship	Implement CRM systems to track customer interactions and preferences related to

Let's explore what the business operation value stream will look like:

We're on a mission to transform shopping with an innovative financial model that makes zero-payment options a reality for customers who want to buy now and pay later. This approach isn't just about easing payment processes; it's about creating a seamless integration of financial solutions in both physical and digital retail spaces.

Here's how it unfolds: We need to draw in a diverse crowd—financial institutions that can offer attractive terms, customers looking for hassle-free financing, and franchisees and store managers who will advocate for these options directly to the shoppers. Imagine a customer walking into a store or browsing online, finding something they love but not worrying about the price tag because our retail loan system is in place to handle the heavy lifting.

During checkout, whether in-store or online, customers can choose their preferred loan options, select their bank, and complete the purchase—all within a few clicks or taps. The payment goes directly from the bank to the retail store, and customers manage their repayments through automated setups that are as simple as setting a calendar reminder.

To make this all happen, we need to leverage every tool at our disposal to build/modernize or reuse digital products. Following options were implemented:

Utilize existing products and business capabilities, like those from Salesforce CRM.

Tap into the reservoir of platform products and capabilities already developed by our Platform ART/ product lines.

Develop fresh products and business capabilities tailored to support this new financial service sub business line.

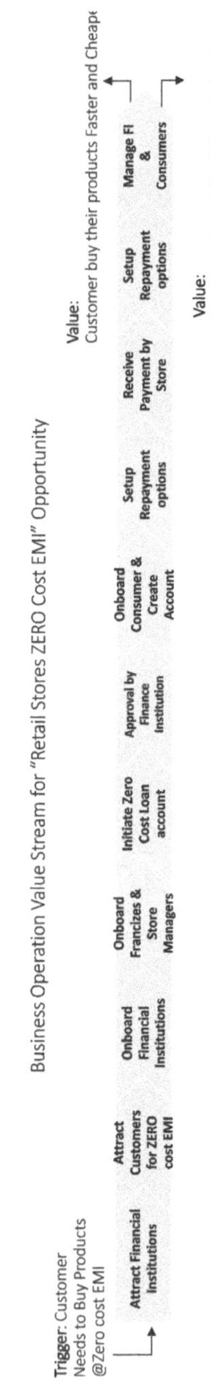

And modernize our existing products and out of box business capabilities that were already implemented by business lines as needed.

We set up a dedicated product management team and several product teams. The product management team dove into market research, shaping the product strategy, vision, OKRs, and roadmap. The product teams focused on creating incremental architecture and delivering top-notch experiences for customers and store managers.

The new product teams took charge of creating and modernizing products, as outlined in points 3 and 4. Meanwhile, business sponsors and leads collaborated with other product lines and platform teams to request new or enhanced business capabilities needed as per points 1 and 2 explained above.

A look at the value stream of business operations and its products, outlining the business capabilities that need to be developed as a Minimum Viable Product (MVP) to kickstart this new sub-business line:

Here's a visual representation of one of the product's OKRs, business capabilities, and KPIs:

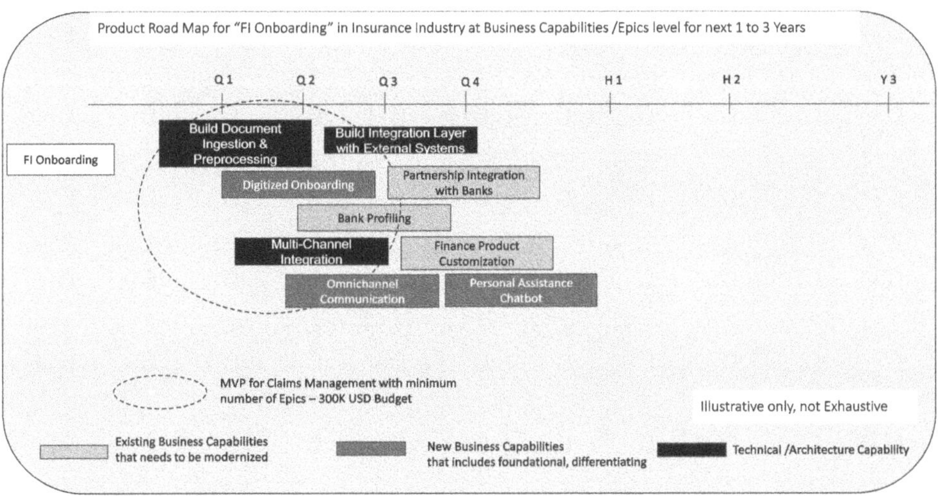

Example of **Future** state Retail Industry Business Operation Value Stream , Products, Business capabilities and Functionalities from attract customers and provide services

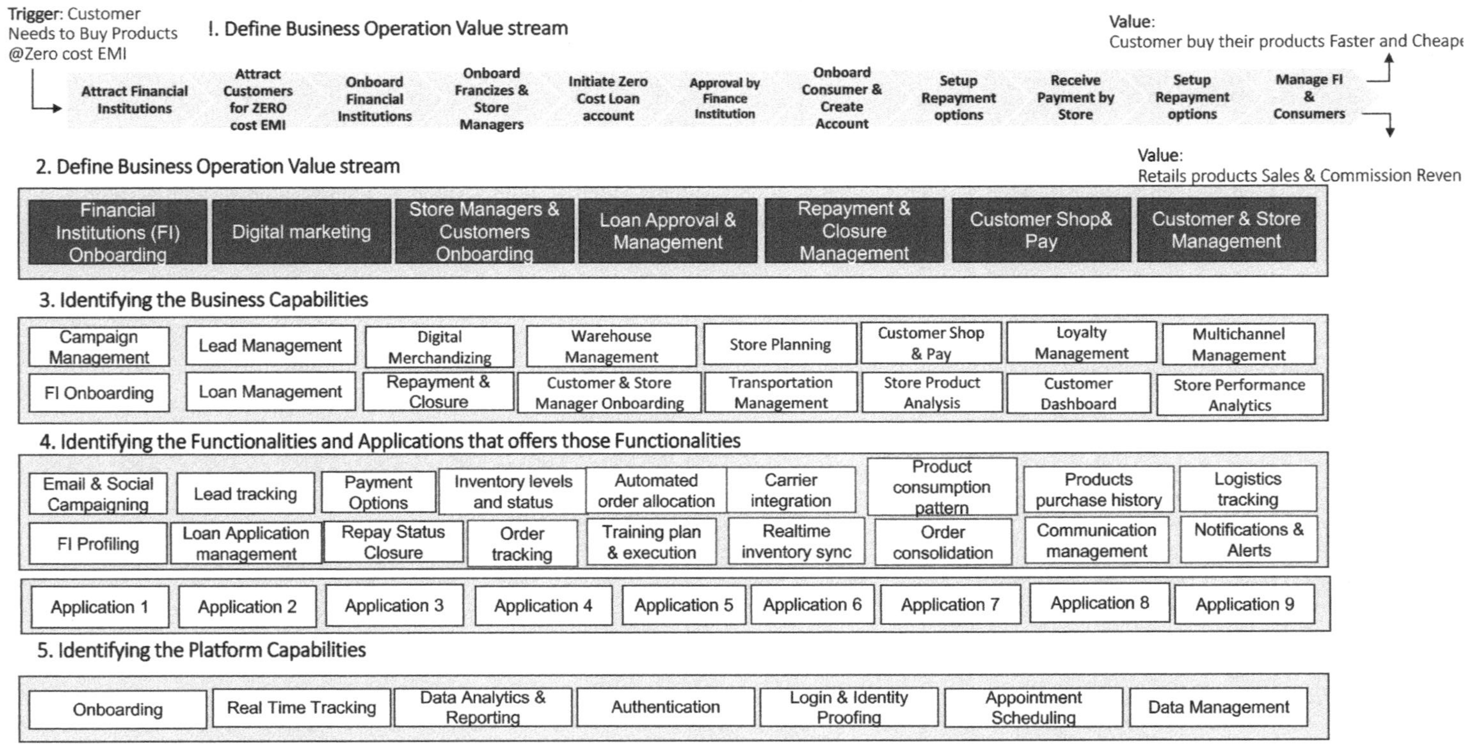

Trigger: Customer Needs to Buy Products @Zero cost EMI

Value: Customer buy their products Faster and Cheape

1. Define Business Operation Value stream

Attract Financial Institutions	Attract Customers for ZERO cost EMI	Onboard Financial Institutions	Onboard Francizes & Store Managers	Initiate Zero Cost Loan account	Approval by Finance Institution	Onboard Consumer & Create Account	Setup Repayment options	Receive Payment by Store	Setup Repayment options	Manage FI & Consumers

Value: Retails products Sales & Commission Reven

2. Define Business Operation Value stream

Financial Institutions (FI) Onboarding	Digital marketing	Store Managers & Customers Onboarding	Loan Approval & Management	Repayment & Closure Management	Customer Shop& Pay	Customer & Store Management

3. Identifying the Business Capabilities

Campaign Management	Lead Management	Digital Merchandizing	Warehouse Management	Store Planning	Customer Shop & Pay	Loyalty Management	Multichannel Management
FI Onboarding	Loan Management	Repayment & Closure	Customer & Store Manager Onboarding	Transportation Management	Store Product Analysis	Customer Dashboard	Store Performance Analytics

4. Identifying the Functionalities and Applications that offers those Functionalities

Email & Social Campaigning	Lead tracking	Payment Options	Inventory levels and status	Automated order allocation	Carrier integration	Product consumption pattern	Products purchase history	Logistics tracking
FI Profiling	Loan Application management	Repay Status Closure	Order tracking	Training plan & execution	Realtime inventory sync	Order consolidation	Communication management	Notifications & Alerts

Application 1	Application 2	Application 3	Application 4	Application 5	Application 6	Application 7	Application 8	Application 9

5. Identifying the Platform Capabilities

Onboarding	Real Time Tracking	Data Analytics & Reporting	Authentication	Login & Identity Proofing	Appointment Scheduling	Data Management

Note: its an illustrative view of digital products and business capabilities. Based on organization size and complexity, number of products and its business capabilities may vary. Platform capabilities are built and managed centrally that can be consumed by all business lines

Illustrative example of "**Financial Institution(FI) Onboarding**" Product **Future** state View with Business Capabilities and its functionalities from Retail Industry

Product OKRs: Optimize **FI Onboarding** time by 30% through automation ; Optimize **FI Verification processing time by 50%.**

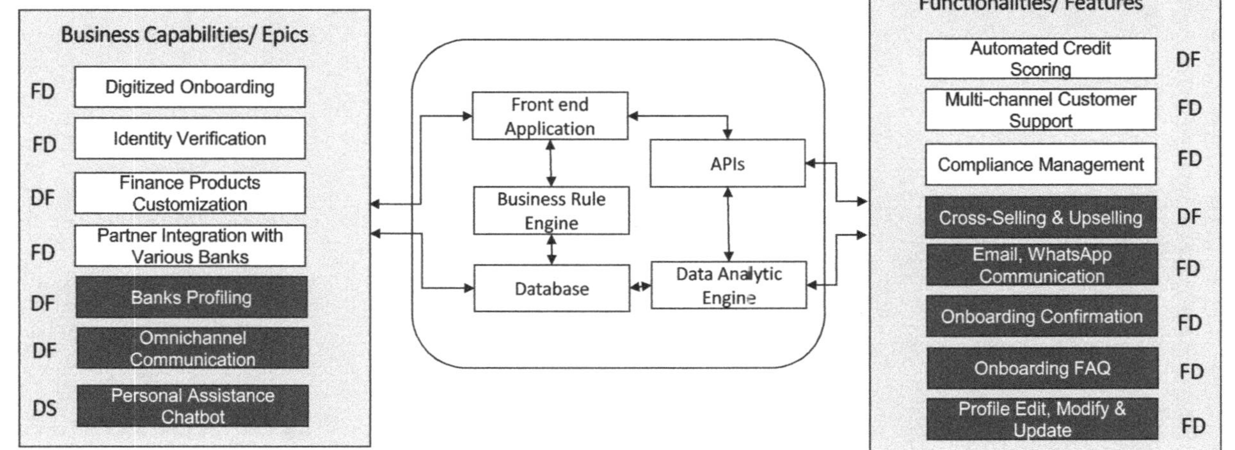

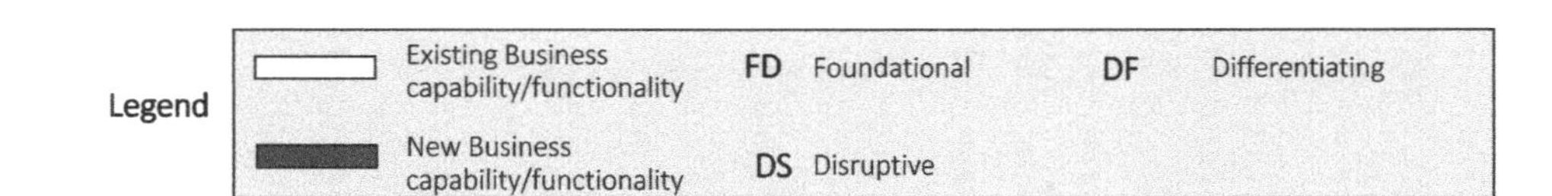

Note:: This illustrative view of Business capabilities and Functionalities does not include all that are needed for this kind of digital product. There are many more business capabilities and functionalities that are not shown here as it's an illustrative purpose

An illustrated overview of the product's quarterly roadmap:

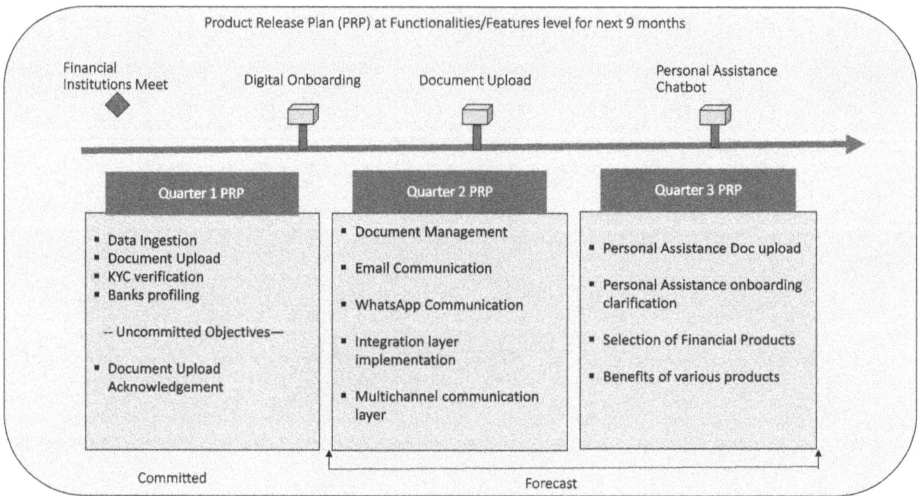

This provides a detailed look at the operating model of a sub-business line, showcasing the related value stream along with the corresponding product lines, Product Group/ART roles, and the product teams developing & managing these products:

Within eight months, the new sub-business line was operational with MVP products and business capabilities. Business sponsors and product teams set clear business objectives and product-level OKRs for the upcoming year. They mapped out what new products and capabilities needed to be built or modernized, specifying which would come from other business lines, Centralized Digital Organizations (options 2 and 3) and which they would develop or modernize themselves (option 1). (next page image)

17.3 Implementing Product Model Across Business Lines: Online Retail, Wholesale, and Beyond

It's been a whirlwind 18 months since we began our product centric model transformation journey. The retail business line has shown remarkable agility and success. For instance, they launched a new sub-business line in just eight months and turned around their revenue trends impressively, posting gains of 5% and 10% in the last two quarters. The product lines and teams, riding high on their ability to seamlessly adopt the new ways of working, played a pivotal role in boosting the organization's revenue. They're committed to continuing this transformation, adapting swiftly to market shifts and evolving customer needs and behaviors.

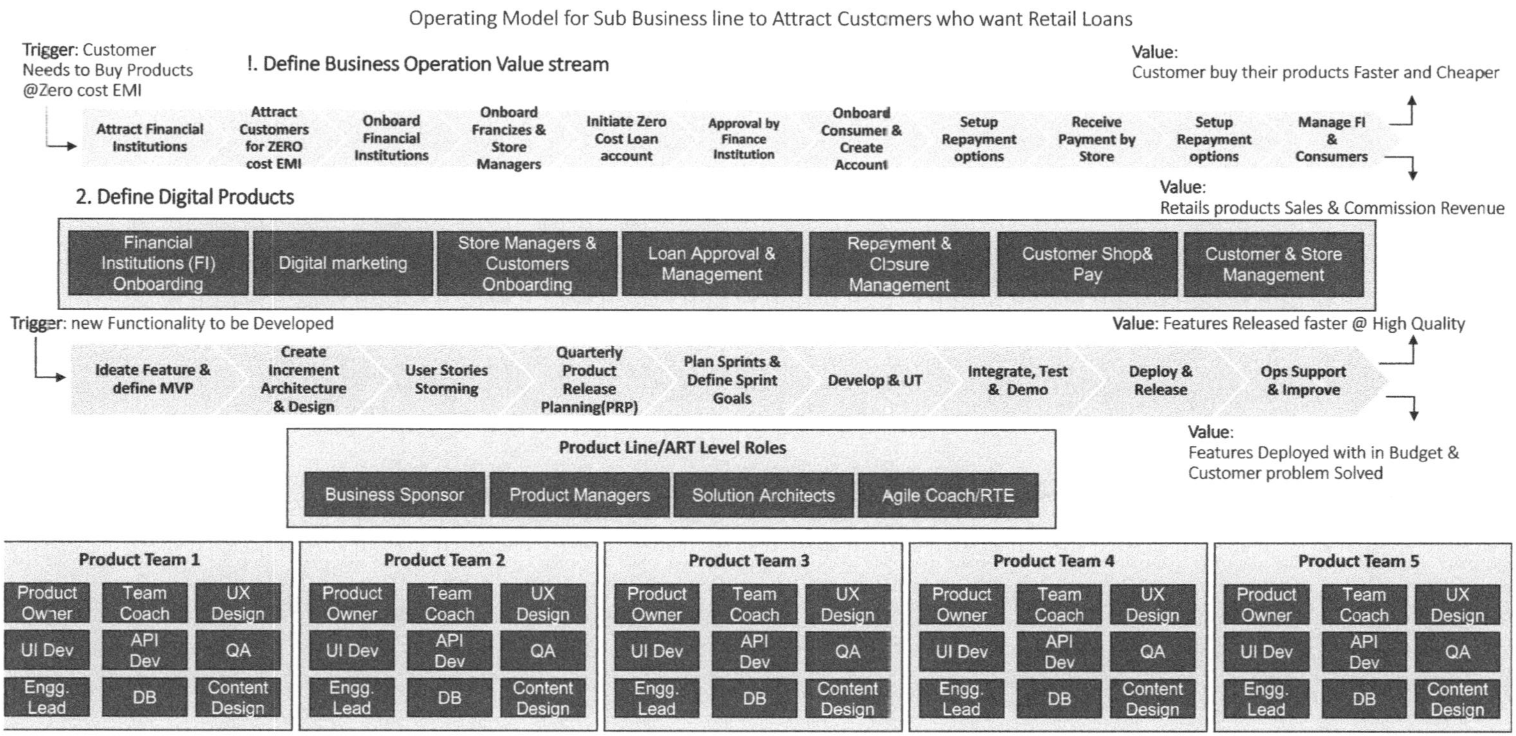

Operating Model for Sub Business line to Attract Customers who want Retail Loans

Trigger: Customer Needs to Buy Products @Zero cost EMI

1. Define Business Operation Value stream

Value: Customer buy their products Faster and Cheaper

2. Define Digital Products

Value: Retails products Sales & Commission Revenue

Trigger: new Functionality to be Developed

Value: Features Released faster @ High Quality

Value: Features Deployed with in Budget & Customer problem Solved

Product Line/ART Level Roles

Product Team 1

Product Team 2

Product Team 3

Product Team 4

Product Team 5

Note:
1. These 5 Products of sub business line will act as network teams to build new products like FI onboarding, Store manager onboarding etc.
2. These product teams will customize and reuse Platform products & Capabilities and other existing products and capabilities such as Digital Marketing, Customer Relationship Management.

During a meeting with the CXOs, the excitement was palpable. The CEO began, "We've seen fantastic results with the retail business line. The agility and growth are commendable."

The CIO added, "The new sub-business line was operationalized in record time. The increase in revenue speaks for itself."

Buoyed by this success, the CXOs decided it was time to expand this product-centric transformation to other business lines, including online retail and wholesale. They turned to me and said, "We want you to lead this effort across these new frontiers, with the support of our internal agile coaches."

I nodded, feeling a sense of pride and responsibility. "We've navigated the full spectrum of change—from igniting the initial urgency and aligning on core issues to solving them and driving revenue growth. Our transformation office is well-equipped to lead this charge."

However, the CXOs suggested, "We're on the right track, but we need your expertise a bit longer to solidify our foundation. Can you stay on for another 6 to 9 months to help launch the first quarterly product release plan across all business lines?" they asked. I nodded, "Of course, I'm committed to seeing this through with you all."

Over the next six months, as an enterprise transformation coach, we repeated all transformation activities from chapters 2 to 16 for the online retail business line. Here's what we covered:

Align on the Problem to Solve (Chapter 3): We identified the core issues and confirmed that the product centric model was the right solution (Chapter 4).

Role-Based Training: We trained all roles across levels, from leadership to teams, with various SAFe role-based trainings.

Create Business Strategy (Chapter 5): We created a business strategy for each business line and aligned with the next level of leadership and across levels down to features and user stories (Chapter 6).

Set Up Transformation Office & Lean Portfolio Management: We established the Transformation Office and a Hub and Spoke model for Lean Portfolio Management as one of the options suggested by SAFe to drive organization wide transformation.

Prepare for a Two-Day Workshop (Chapter 7): We prepared to create the current state blueprint of products, business capabilities, functionalities, and applications.

Create Current State Blueprint (Chapter 8): During the two-day workshop, we created the current state blueprint.

Conduct Project vs. Product Model Workshops: We held workshops to discuss and align on the transition from project to product models.

Create Future State of Each Business Portfolio (Chapter 9): We envisioned the future state for each business portfolio.

Set Up Multiple Product Lines/ARTs (Chapter 10): We organized multiple Agile Release Trains (ARTs) and product lines.

Select Pilot Product Line (Chapter 11): We selected a pilot product line for the first quarterly product release/PI planning and began preparation (Chapter 12).

Conduct First Quarterly Plan (Chapter 13): We executed the first quarterly planning session.

Execute the Quarterly Plan (Chapter 14): We ensured the execution of the quarterly plan.

Monthly and Quarterly Portfolio Sync-Up and Strategic Reviews: We held regular sync-ups and reviews to monitor progress and make necessary adjustments.

Measure Outcomes (Chapter 16): We measured the outcomes to ensure we were meeting our objectives.

Extended Launch of First Quarterly Product Release Planning for Other Product Lines (Chapter 17): We expanded the quarterly planning process to other product lines within each business line.

Additionally, we set up a centralized portfolio to deliver common products and business capabilities.

17.4 Setting Up and Launching a New Portfolio of Platforms and Products for Use Across All Business Lines within the Organization

After witnessing the success of a single platform product line in the Retail Stores business (as discussed in section 17.2), the CXOs decided to establish a centralized portfolio comprising multiple platforms. Each platform would have several product lines, and each product line would consist of one or more Agile Release Trains (ARTs) or teams of product teams.

Here's a peek at what the centralized platform portfolio looks like:

"Let's centralize our efforts to maximize efficiency and reusability," one of the CXOs suggested. (next page image)

We agreed and set up various platforms like Authentication, Customer Acquisition, CRM, and Inventory Management. For each platform, we identified existing product lines. For example, under Authentication, we had Login & KYC and Lead Management product lines. Each product line had multiple products, such as Identity Management, Login Web, Login Mobile, and KYC Validation.

For each product line, we organized clusters of product teams responsible for owning and delivering products and business capabilities.

As we began setting up and operationalizing the platform and products portfolio, we followed a series of strategic and tactical steps to ensure our platforms were robust and fully integrated across different business lines. Here's how we made it happen:

Identifying Common Ground: First, we pinpointed the common products and business capabilities utilized by multiple business lines. This step was crucial for streamlining our efforts moving forward.

Setting Our Goals: We then defined our business objectives, focusing on eliminating redundancy, boosting reusability, cutting costs, optimizing time to market, and ensuring a consistent, seamless customer experience.

Blueprinting the Current State: Next, we created a current state blueprint of product and business capabilities and mapped these to specific platforms, laying out a clear structure for our tech landscape.

Market Research: With the blueprint in place, we dived into market research to pinpoint necessary modernizations for our existing products and business capabilities, keeping an eye on digital opportunities and competitive positioning.

Alignment Workshop: We convened a workshop with all business lines to align on the proposed modernizations for our platform portfolio.

Gemba Walks: Our team conducted Gemba walks across various business lines to deeply understand their needs and the problems they face from a reusable product and capability perspective.

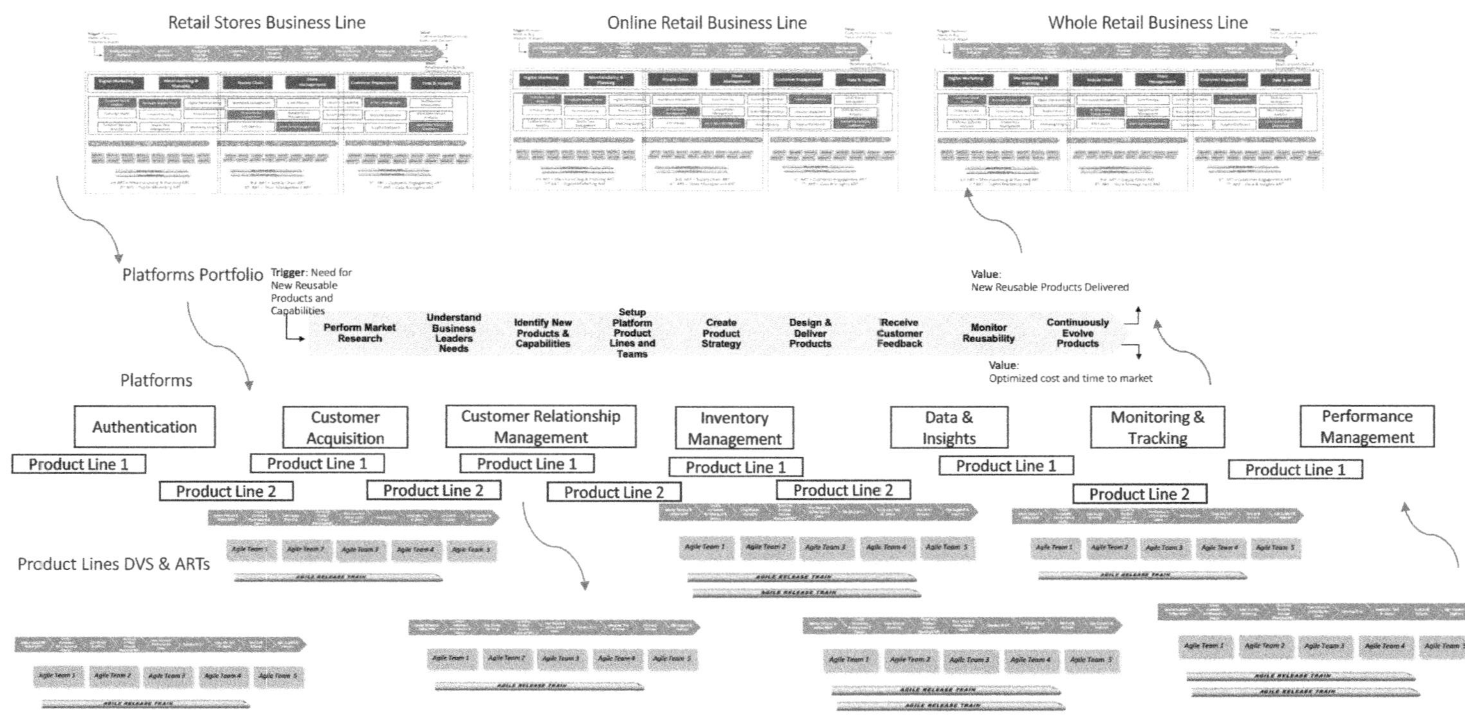

Platforms as Portfolio with multiple Product Groups that Deliver Reusable Products for all Business Lines
Retail Stores Business Line
Online Retail Business Line
Whole Retail Business Line
Platforms Portfolio
Trigger: Need for New Reusable Products and Capabilities
Value: New Reusable Products Delivered
Perform Market Research
Understand Business Leaders Needs
Identify New Products & Capabilities
Setup Platform Product Lines and Teams
Create Product Strategy
Design & Deliver Products
Receive Customer Feedback
Monitor Reusability
Continuously Evolve Products
Value: Optimized cost and time to market
Platforms
Authentication
Customer Acquisition
Customer Relationship Management
Inventory Management
Data & Insights
Monitoring & Tracking
Performance Management
Product Line 1
Product Line 2
Product Lines DVS & ARTs
Agile Team 1
Agile Team 2
Agile Team 3
Agile Team 4
Agile Team 5
AGILE RELEASE TRAIN

Defining Platform Objectives: For each platform, we crafted business objectives and developed a product strategy, vision, and roadmap.

Structuring Product Lines: Based on the complexity and number of products, we structured product lines under each platform.

Launching the First Wave: We selected which platform and product lines to launch with our first quarterly product release planning and began preparations.

Executing and Measuring: With the planning in place, we executed our quarterly plans and measured outcomes to gauge our success and areas for improvement.

Management Engagement: Regular meetings with management ensured we had the support needed to push our initiatives forward.

Scaling the Model: Finally, we scaled the adoption of the product centric model across other platforms, ensuring that our transformation touched every corner of the organization.

At this crucial juncture, filled with tangible progress and dynamic action, the Internal Agile Coach and I reconvened. With a mutual nod and a smile reflecting our satisfaction with the strides we'd made, we took a moment to strategize the next phases of our journey. It was more than a meeting—it was a checkpoint on a transformative path we had embarked on together.

As part of this chapter, we discussed four possible next steps for scaling product-centric model adoption across the organization: launching all product groups/ARTs within the business line, launching a sub-business line within the retail store business line to capitalize on the "Zero cost EMI" opportunity, implementing product centric model for product groups/ARTs in other business lines like online retail and wholesale, and setting up platforms and products as a centralized portfolio to build and deliver common reusable capabilities.

We then moved to a deep dive into each of these next steps. For the first one, we discussed how we selected two more product groups/ARTs and launched their first quarterly planning. We also discussed the launch of four additional product groups/ARTs within the retail store business line and all the necessary steps and activities required for these launches.

We explored the three options of product groups/products needed for a retail store to develop and deliver digital products. Additionally, we reviewed the three operating models for setting up product groups/ ARTs that will develop digital products and delivering them effectively.

As part of our first step, we delved into how one platform ART/group setup would fit within the broader context of the other six product groups/ARTs. We outlined all the activities needed to establish this platform ART, ensuring it integrates seamlessly with the existing structure.

Next, we tackled the second step: launching a sub-business line within the retail store to tap into a new revenue stream. We discussed the activities required to launch this new sub-business line, including defining its business objectives and operational value stream, and identifying three options for digital products. Options 2 and 3 were already available within the retail store business line and could be utilized, but Option 1—digital products specific to this sub-business line like financial institution onboarding and loan management—needed to be built. For this, we set up new product teams and operated as a separate product group/ART.

We then moved to the third step, which was scaling the product-centric model adoption to other business lines within the retail organization, including online retail and wholesale. We discussed all the necessary activities, from defining the business strategy to preparing for the first quarterly planning, executing the quarterly planning, and its subsequent execution. Essentially, we would be repeating the steps outlined from chapters 2 to 16.

Finally, we addressed the last step: converting a single platform product group/ART into a centralized platforms and products portfolio. We discussed the sequence of steps involved in setting up this centralized portfolio. This transition would allow us to build reusable products and capabilities at a larger scale across multiple product groups/ARTs. Previously, these reusable products were consumed by only one business line. With this change, all business lines within the organization would benefit from these products and capabilities.

By the end of our discussion, it was clear that each step was a critical piece of our overarching transformation strategy. We were shaping the future, ensuring every detail was accounted for and every potential was realized.

18

Operationalization Guide for Success

When Thiran—a retail store—nails its digital transformation using a product-centric approach in line with SAFe principles, it begs the question: why do 92% of organizations across various domains struggle to fully embrace and operationalize this model? And what about those industries still transitioning from project-based to product-focused frameworks? Can they not achieve similar success?

As a transformation coach, along with my talented team, we've steered Thiran through its journey, proving that effective guidance and strategic execution can make a monumental difference. If we could do it, why not the broader community of digital transformation coaches and practitioners around the globe?

This book isn't just an account of one retail store's successful transformation. It's a manual for every level of an organization striving to adopt a product-centric model. From senior leaders steering the ship to product teams on the ground— this guide is crafted to help you understand and implement the practices that can lead your company toward significant digital advancement.

And let me tell you, it is entirely within our reach! As an organization, as a collective of digital transformation coaches, and as a committed group of practitioners, we have the blueprint to replicate the success we've seen with the product-centric model. This operationalization guide, coupled with SAFe training and certifications, isn't just a manual—it's your playbook for revolution.

To truly harness the power of this guide, every coach and practitioner needs to complete their role-specific SAFe certifications. From chapters 2 through 16, we've laid out the 12 PM product-centric model using real-life examples from various industries. This entails sparking a revolution in how organizations approach digital transformation.

The approach of Platforms developments for internal customers (As discussed in chapter 17.4) are being extended to external customers/end users as well. For example Microsoft building platforms which are made available for customers to consume. This approach of building platform requires solution mind set, it requires rethinking of how each function within organization need to work differently including sales, marketing etc.

We're talking about 10 critical success factors here that can dramatically shift the effectiveness of this transformation. This is about enhancing customer experiences, boosting business efficiency, and, ultimately, contributing to global economic growth.

Let's embrace a product-centric model as our roadmap to digital transformation success, revolutionizing customer experience, turbocharging business efficiency and effectiveness, and fueling global economic growth!

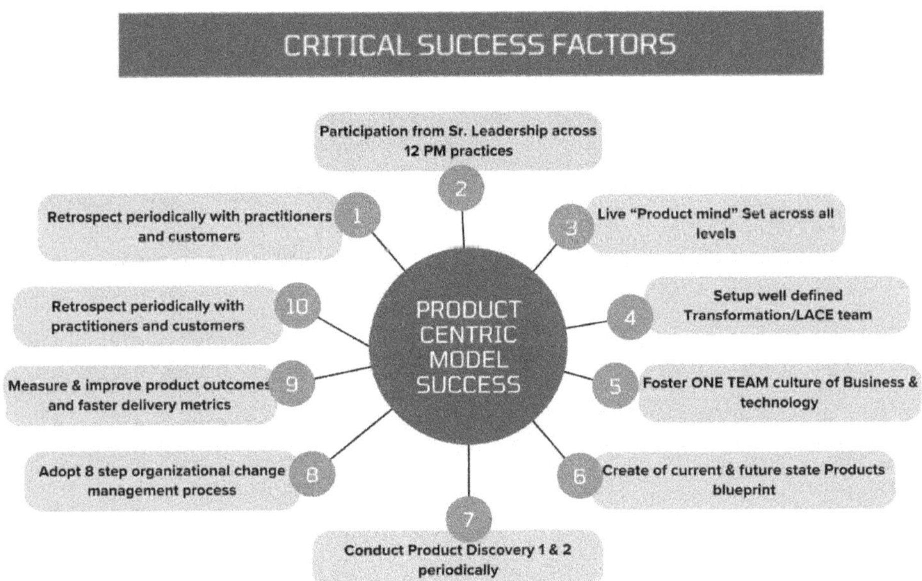